Studies in Economic Ethics and Philosophy

Peter Koslowski
Editor

The Discovery of Historicity in German Idealism and Historism

With 3 Figures

Springer

Professor Dr. Dr. h.c. Peter Koslowski
Department of Philosophy
Vrije Universiteit Amsterdam / Free University Amsterdam
De Boelelaan 1105
1081 HV Amsterdam, The Netherlands
E-mail: p.koslowski@ph.vu.nl
Website: www.fiph.de/koslowski

Printed with the Support of the Fritz Thyssen Stiftung, Köln, and of CIVITAS Gesellschaft zur Förderung von Wissenschaft und Kunst e.V. München

Library of Congress Control Number: 2005921207

ISBN 3-540-24393-3 Springer Berlin Heidelberg New York

Springer is a part of Springer Science+Business Media
springeronline.com

Printed in Germany

Cover design: Erich Kirchner
Production: Helmut Petri
Printing: Strauss Offsetdruck

SPIN 11377641 Printed on acid-free paper – 42/3153 – 5 4 3 2 1 0

Contents

Absolute Historicity, Theory of the Becoming Absolute, and the Affect for the Particular in German Idealism and Historism:
Introduction
PETER KOSLOWSKI 1

Part A

German Idealism's Philosophy of History and its Contemporary Critique

Chapter 1

Schlegel's Theory of History and his Critique of Idealistic Reason
PETER L. OESTERREICH 9

Chapter 2

History as the Control of Speculation:
Schelling's Discovery of History and Baader's Critique of Absolute Historicity
PETER KOSLOWSKI 23

CONTENTS

Part B

The Theory of History in German Historism

Chapter 3

Leopold von Ranke
HELMUT BERDING 41

Chapter 4

Droysen and Nietzsche: Two Different Answers to the Discovery of Historicity
ANNETTE WITTKAU-HORGBY 59

Chapter 5

Philosophy of History and Theory of Historiography in Jacob Burckhardt
EGON FLAIG 77

Chapter 6

Historiography as Political Activity:
Heinrich von Treitschke and the Historical Reconstruction of Politics
KARL H. METZ 98

Chapter 7

Literary Criticism and Historical Science: The Textuality of History in the Age of Goethe – and Beyond
DANIEL FULDA 112

Chapter 8

Social and Philosophical Theory in the 19th Century German Thought
MARIO SIGNORE 134

Part C

German Theory and Philosophy of History Today

Chapter 9

Philosophy of History After the End of the Formative Substantial Philosophy of History: Remarks on the Present State of the Philosophy of History
HANS MICHAEL BAUMGARTNER 149

Chapter 10

Why Kant's Reflections on History Still Have Relevance
HERTA NAGL-DOCEKAL 172

Chapter 11

Rehabilitating the Philosophy of History
JOHANNES ROHBECK 187

Chapter 12

History and Subjectivity – The Relevance of a Philosophical Concept of History in the Kantian Tradition
MATTHIAS LUTZ-BACHMANN 212

CONTENTS

Chapter 13

Towards a New Theory-Based History of Historiography
HORST WALTER BLANKE 223

Chapter 14

Philosophy of History After the Philosophy of History:
Toward a Cultural History with Historical-Philosophical Background
HEINZ DIETER KITTSTEINER 268

List of Authors 283

Index of Names 285

Absolute Historicity, Theory of the Becoming Absolute, and the Affect for the Particular in German Idealism and Historism: Introduction

PETER KOSLOWSKI

German idealism introduces a new understanding of the historical to the history of ideas. The historical becomes absolute historicity and the historicity of the absolute. In this sense, German Idealism is the discovery of historicity in the strong meaning of the term. The ontological quality of the historical as such had already been discovered by the Enlightenment but it is the contribution of German Idealism to attribute historicity to totality and even the absolute. Absoluteness is thereby attributed to the historical. Even God is subjected to history and in the historical process of becoming conscious according to Hegel and Schelling.

The origins of the absolute concept of historicity lie in Schelling's system of identity and Hegel's dialectics of the absolute spirit. Schelling introduces the system of the identity of the absolute subject and the absolute object, of spirit and nature as the basic structure of the totality of being which is being-in-becoming. The world process and being are the becoming conscious of the subject or spirit at the object or nature. All being, even the being of the absolute, is subjected to time and history. There is no supra-temporal realm of being.

Schelling's identity system was taken up by Hegel. Hegel's basic idea is that becoming is the movement from nothingness to being, a process in which the absolute falls from itself into nature ("*der Abfall der Idee von sich*") to become self-conscious absolute spirit in the dialectics of an absolute historical process. Hegel transforms Schelling's identity system furthermore in the direction of a dialectical process of historical totality.

German Idealism dynamizes Spinoza's pantheism. The identity of God and nature is not like in Spinoza being-in-identity but being-in-becoming, an absolute process. It is the history of the progressing consciousness of the identity of absolute subject and absolute object.

At the beginning of his work *Philosophische Untersuchungen Über das Wesen der menschlichen Freiheit* (Philosophical Inquiries into the Nature of Human Freedom) of 1809, Schelling explains his philosophy of the historical absolute and defends himself against the reproach of being a pantheist and atheist. God's being is in becoming but this does not imply that the absolute is identical with every mistaken aspect of being and every accident of history. It is identical with the historical process in total. This dynamic pantheism or one-in-all philosophy does not annihilate the singular and particular, according to Schelling.[1] He does, however, not recognize here yet that the dynamized pantheism will give a new and hitherto unknown value to the particular and unique as a stage of the realization of the absolute in the following decades of historism in the 19th century.

The system of identity as the metaphysical basis of the philosophy of history in German Idealism gives ground to two major ideas: the philosophy of history as the theory of the development of an absolute substrate of temporal or historical being on the one hand and the elevation of the singular and particular to the realization of the absolute in historism on the other hand. The first, the philosophy of history of German Idealism, is a metaphysical theory that claims to understand the laws of development of totality, the second, the philosophical emphasis on the historically singular and particular, forms the core of the Historical School's concern for the uniqueness and importance of every instantiation of the spirit and of culture in every historical period and location, its preoccupation with the particular. Although historism defined itself as a critique of the totalistic philosophy of history in German Idealism it remains still shaped by its pantheistic idea that every historical instantiation is an instantiation of the spirit. The *Geisteswissenschaften*, the human sciences of the spirit, remain, even in their very term, indebted to their origins in the Hegelian philosophy of spirit.

The philosophy of history of German Idealism became subjected to a crisis due to the fact that it could not solve the problem of the relationship between freedom and necessity in the development of history. If the absolute develops according to a metaphysical logic as Hegel assumed, it is not free from this logic and process but subjected to it. The question arises whether an absolute that is not free can be absolute. The necessitarian connotations characteristic of the philosophy of history, be it Hegel's absolute idealism or

1 F.W.J. SCHELLING: *Philosophical Inquiries into the Nature of Human Freedom*, La Salle, Illinois (Open Court) 4th paperback printing 1992, p. 16.

Marx's dialectical materialism, stem from the idea that there are laws of the development of history or a preconceived "logic" in history. The metaphysical philosophy of history is a theory of laws of history. Schelling has been the first thinker to see this Achilles' heel of German Idealism and to criticize Hegel's determinism and dialectical necessitarianism. The thinkers of historism followed Schelling in the emphasis that the historically singular can not be derived from the general.

Not all philosophy of history is Hegelian as several of the contributions to this volume demonstrate. For the present debate on the philosophy of history, the Kantian and Enlightenment traditions have to be considered as well, and they are so in this volume.

With the volume at hand, the Historical School's contribution to the philosophy of history and the theory of history and historiography is approached within a larger project on the Historical School's contribution to the study of society, economy, culture, and politics. The Historical School is characterized by a strong concept of historicity of human society, of its culture, economy, ethics, law, and politics. The Historical School stresses not only the historical character of cultural phenomena in general but their uniqueness and singularity. In its emphatic concept of historicity, the Historical School can not be understood without its metaphysical origins from which it distanced itself but at the same time remained linked to. The discovery of historicity implies a countermovement to the rationalism of the 18th century and its idea of the foundations of ethics and law on reason only. Starting with German Idealism and European Romanticism, the new awareness of the historicity of human culture tried to reconcile the dualism of reason and history.

History is at the centre of the Historical School. Its discovery of historicity was caused by the emphasis on world history and historical development in the philosophy of history expounded in German Idealism. When the German historians after Hegel further developed the historical method they felt the need to give more room to the singular, the unexpected, the unforeseeable, the contingent, and the free then the idealist philosophy of history had provided for. "Historical greatness is", as Droysen put it, "only a piece of dust in the theophany".[2] How even more so is the ordinary historical event only the dust of a piece of dust of the absolute! To recognize the meaning of

---

2 JOHANN GUSTAV DROYSEN: *Grundriß der Historik* (Outline for a Theory of Historiography), Leipzig 2nd ed. 1875, paragraph 90.

history or its laws of development is a difficult task for the historian. The task of a philosophy of history is, as Leopold Ranke put it, unsolvable.

The historical event and the historical actors retain, however, their pantheistic meaningfulness for the realization of the absolute in the historical school. In this sense, it is true for most of the central authors of historism what Gadamer attributed to Wilhelm Dilthey: They were always already on the way to the absolute.[3] Historism emancipates the human sciences from the metaphysics of German Idealism. It criticizes the „grand theory" of world history in idealism and remains also connected to its pantheistic origins. This metaphysical connection can not only be considered a theoretical weakness. It is also a theoretical strength of historism since it gives the human sciences a deeper meaning and metaphysical unity that unifies the cultural sciences as the sciences of the spirit.

The theory of history and of historiography, the methodology of the historical sciences, forms the other major topic of the volume at hand by which it makes the attempt to elaborate the relevance of historism for today's historical and cultural studies.

The Historical School is worth to be reconsidered due to its insight in the historical nature of society, economy, and culture. The cultural sciences must include the determinedness of human culture by history, even if this inclusion of the historical dimension creates an additional difficulty of analysis that unhistorical approaches can avoid. It is open whether the idea of historism that the culture of a historical period and a nation is determined by a „spirit of time" (*Zeitgeist*) and a „spirit of a people" (*Volksgeist*) is a meaningful and sensible question to be asked. The question whether there are common features of an epoch and of a people can not, however, be discarded from the outset as being particularistic and nationalistic.

This volume has been produced as part of the project "The Historical School. Economics, Economic Ethics, Theory and Philosophy of History, Law and Political Science in the German Human and Social Sciences Tradition" supported by the Fritz Thyssen Stiftung. The project tries to throw light on economics and the social sciences, on the study of society and history, from the tradition of German Idealism and Historism and aims at an approach to economics and the social sciences as sciences of culture and of the spirit (*Geisteswissenschaften*).

---

3 HANS-GEORG GADAMER: *Wahrheit und Methode*, Tübingen (Mohr Siebeck) 2. Aufl. 1965, p. 223.

INTRODUCTION

The volume at hand presents the fourth volume on the Historical School after two volumes on the older and younger Historical School and one volume on the theory of capitalism in the German economic tradition.[4] The contributions to this volume have first been discussed in a workshop in Viehhofen near Zell am See, Salzburger Land, Austria, in December 2000 and have been further elaborated since then. The editor and the contributors to this volume express their appreciation to the Fritz Thyssen Stiftung, Cologne, Germany, for their continuous support to this volume and to the entire project on the Historical School.

Historism can be defined by four characteristics.[5] It is first the approach to historize the different branches of knowledge. It is second the attempt to find diachronic laws of history. It is third the recognition that all periods and places of history have their specific and unique meaning and importance that they derive from themselves and not only from their relationship with the historical center of power and meaning. Historism is fourth the readiness and the will to be modest in one's conclusions, to collect and select historical data, sources, and documents. With this will to be modest in one's conclusions comes the concomitant attitude of relativism and modesty connected with historical empiricism. In this sense, historism is a human attitude characteristic to all periods that endeavor to understand history and society.

---

4 Cf. P. KOSLOWSKI (Ed.): *The Theory of Ethical Economy in the Historical School. Wilhelm Roscher, Lorenz von Stein, Gustav Schmoller, Wilhelm Dilthey and Contemporary Theory*, Heidelberg, New York, Tokyo (Springer-Verlag) 1995, reprint 1997, 343 pp.; P. KOSLOWSKI (Ed.): *Methodology of the Social Sciences, Ethics, and Economics in the Newer Historical School. From Max Weber and Rickert to Sombart and Rothacker*, Heidelberg, New York, Tokyo (Springer-Verlag) 1997, 564 pp.; P. KOSLOWSKI (Ed.): *The Theory of Capitalism in the German Economic Tradition: Historism, Ordo-Liberalism, Critical Theory, Solidarism*, Heidelberg, New York, Tokyo (Springer-Verlag) 2000, 587 pp. - In the series "Studies in Economic Ethics and Philosophy has also been published: H.H. NAU and B. SCHEFOLD (Eds.): *The Historicity of Economics. Continuities and Discontinuities of Historical Thought in 19th and 20th Century Economics*, Heidelberg, New York, Tokyo (Springer-Verlag) 2002, 245 pp.

5 Cf. also KARL ACHAM: „Diltheys Beitrag zur Theorie der Kultur- und Sozialwissenschaften", *Dilthey-Jahrbuch für Philosophie und Geschichte der Geisteswissenschaften*, 3 (1985), pp. 9-51.

Part A

German Idealism's Philosophy of History and its Contemporary Critique

Chapter 1

Schlegel's Theory of History and his Critique of Idealistic Reason

PETER L. OESTERREICH

I. 'Death Absolute': Schlegel's Critique of Absolute Reason
II. 'The Idea of the Vivid Word': Rhetorical Anthropology as a Basis of Schlegel's Theory of History
III. 'The Irony of Love': The Three Basic Rules of Conjectural Historiography

The discovery of historicity in German Philosophy is a tale which cannot be told without taking into account the late philosophy of Friedrich Schlegel. In his youth, F. Schlegel, who created the Ironic Idealism of the *Athenaeum*[1], was a prominent 'leader'[2] of the early romantic movement. Hegel's famous system of absolute reason can be interpreted as a negative reaction against Schlegel, whose concept of infinite irony was condemned as "the evil as such"[3] and as "absolute sophistry"[4].

In the wake of the general spiritual turn in late Romanticism, Schlegel began to reconstruct his philosophy. Living in Vienna and in Dresden in his later years, he attempted a new beginning in his philosophical thinking. The

1 H. DIERKES: "Ironie und System. Friedrich Schlegels 'Philosophische Lehrjahre'", in: *Philosophisches Jahrbuch,* 97 (1990), pp. 251–276; and PETER L. OESTERREICH: "'Wenn die Ironie wild wird ...': Die Symbiose von Transzendentalphilosophie und Tropus bei Friedrich Schlegel", in: *Rhetorik: Ein internationales Jahrbuch,* 12 (1993), pp. 31–39.

2 See W. DILTHEY: *Gesammelte Schriften*, XIV, 2, Göttingen (Vandenhoeck & Ruprecht), p. 670.

3 See G.W.F. HEGEL: *Werke*, vol. 7, ed. by E. MOLDENHAUER, K.M. MICHEL, Frankfurt a.M. (Suhrkamp) 1979, p. 279.

4 *loc. cit.*, p. 280.

result was his late *Philosophy of Life*, which he presented in three series of public lectures. This trilogy of philosophical oratory comprises Schlegel's lectures on the *Philosophy of Life* (1827), the *Philosophy of History* (1828) and the *Philosophy of Language and the Word* (1828/29). Due to Schlegel's sudden death in Dresden on January 12th, 1829, his last lectures about the *Philosophy of Language and the Word* remained unfinished.

Within the general evolution of a historical consciousness, Schlegel's late philosophy plays a role which is as significant as Schelling's.[5] On the one hand he critizised the claim of the absolute validity of idealistic reason, which is incorporated in Hegel's system. On the other hand he invented, as a spiritual soul mate of Schelling, a new historical style of thinking. In contrast to Hegel, he emphasized the differences between reason and reality rather than their similarities. Starting from this perspective Schlegel discovered the positiveness of life and the historical character of human existence and culture.

It was already in his *Philosophical Apprenticeship* that Schlegel conceived of history as a synthesis of criticism, religion and rhetoric.[6] The constellation of these three disciplines also characterizes the historical thinking in his late philosophy which comprises, first, a polemics against idealistic reason, second, a new concept of universal history developed from a Christian and spiritual perspective and, finally, a rhetorical concept of historiography.

I. 'Death Absolute': Schlegel's Critique of Absolute Reason

The modern quality of Schlegel's philosophy arises from its critical and ironical self-reflexion which is inspired by the metacritical mentality of a philosophy of philosophies: "The spirit of a philosophy is its being a philoso-

---

5 For the development of Schlegel's late philosophy see: F. LEDERBOGEN: *Friedrich Schlegels Geschichtsphilosophie. Ein Beitrag zur Genesis der historischen Weltanschauung,* Leipzig (Verlag der Dürr'schen Buchhandlung) 1908, pp. 109–151 and "Die Grundlagen der Schlegelschen Spätphilosophy und Idealismuskritik" in: *KA* 8, CVII–CLII.

6 See: *KA* (= *Kritische-Friedrich-Schlegel-Ausgabe,* ed. by E. BEHLER, J.-J. ANSTETT, H. EICHNER, 35 vols., Paderborn/München/Wien/Zürich (Schöningh /Thomas Verlag) 1958ff., 18, 312.

phy of philosophies."[7] This perspective protects the philosopher from unconsciously identifying himself with his own work. It can be described as a metacritical reflexivity which establishes a critical distance to a philosophical system which itself is a construction of dialectical reason.

Schlegel's criticism of German Idealism arises from this metacritical mentality. In his review of Jacobi (1822) he offers a critical characterization of the philosophy of his contemporaries. This critique of the 'outstanding systems of the last epoch of German Philosophy'[8] provides the matrix for the complete criticism of reason which we find in his late *Philosophy of Life*.

Schlegel's attacks on contemporary philosophical systems, which are highly polemical at times, share a profound theoretical background. Schlegel explains that dialectical reason is merely a power of logical synthesis. Described in rhetorical terms, reason is a power of judgement (*iudicium*), not an inventive faculty (*ingenium*). Certainly it is a faculty of indefinite logical thinking and formal construction, "but it cannot invent or produce anything"[9]. In contrast to imagination, reason is no creative faculty. According to Schlegel the lack of poetic power turns reason into something negative – something which is separated from real life. Therefore, the absolute system, as the highest result which can be achieved in an immanent dialectical evolution, can principally never do justice to the positiveness of historical reality. Reason can only produce an absolute phantasma, which Schlegel called 'the dead absolute' (*das todte Absolute*).[10]

In concreto Schlegel's criticism of the contemporary philosophy of systems is founded upon the classical distinction between knowledge and faith. Consequently we can distinguish between two different forms of knowledge:

a) Negative knowledge, which is not connected to faith: It consists of logical or dialectical identities only. Comprising the features of formal perfectibility and absolute necessity this negative knowledge is related to mathematics. In philosophy, however, negative knowledge will necessarily turn into sophistry, because it lacks any connection to the positive facts of real life. It will be nothing more than "dialectical play, and sophistical artificiality"[11].

7 *KA* 18, 37.
8 *KA* 8, 585.
9 *KA* 10, 496.
10 *KA* 10, 524.
11 *Ibid.*

b) Positive knowledge, which is connected to faith: It is partly based on personal convictions and independent assumptions. As an independent and personal knowledge it corresponds to history and real life. Positive knowledge is "the vivid knowledge of life, which is as free as life itself"[12]. Furthermore, it represents the appropriate and apt knowledge of the *Philosophy of Life*, which includes "the most perfect of all positive knowledge"[13].

The distinction between positive and negative knowledge forms the background of Schlegel's main argument against the Idealistic philosophy of systems. This argument is not directed against any specific content, but against the overall negative character of idealistic knowledge, which Schlegel regards as totally inadequate in comparison to historical reality and human existence. Schlegel argues that the systems of Idealism are based on a fundamental methodical error. They arise from the false scientific assumption "to comprehend philosophical truth in the form of mathematical certainty"[14]. Through this fundamental critique Schlegel also attacks Spinoza's *mos geometricus* and the methodical ideal of modern rationalism which had a formative influence on the idealistic systems.

Above all, Schlegel's critique is directed against the "four great 'brains' (*Systemhäupter*) of German Philosophy"[15] by which he meant Jacobi, Kant, Fichte, and Schelling. In his opinion these four 'brains' are allied through a false orientation of their philosophy towards logical and mathematical forms of knowledge. Nevertheless, this error may lead to unexpected results, as can be seen in the cases of Kant and Jacobi on one hand and Fichte and Schelling on the other.

Jacobi and Kant are allied by their insight into the abstract character of negative knowledge that leads to a theoretical scepticism. In their theoretical desperation they seek shelter in a sort of "self-made faith (*selbstgemachter Glaube*)"[16]. This artificial and self-constructed faith, however, should not to be mistaken for a real and lived faith. Being a fiction created by an individual it lacks the positiveness of historical reality. According to Schlegel, Kant's and Jacobi's systems are shaped by the same figure of thought. It can be de-

---

12 *Ibid.*

13 *KA* 8, 590.

14 *KA* 8, 590.

15 *KA* 8, 593.

16 *KA* 8, 590.

scribed as a 'leap' from theoretical scepticism into a faith that is artificial and untrue.

The dogmatic figure of absolute knowledge, on the contrary, is the most important element in the systems of Fichte and Schelling. In Schlegel's opinion the positive and vivid character of their philosophies as well as the divine and the historical reality of mankind, are ruined by the apodictic form of their negative knowledge: The "free and divine knowledge"[17] perishes, because it is exposed to the dead and abstract form of absolute necessity.

Thus, neither dogmatic thinkers, such as Fichte and Schelling, nor sceptics like Kant and Jacobi are able to meet the positiveness of real life. Schlegel even goes further. On the basis of his own theory of consciousness, he gives an explanation for the common errors of Idealistic philosophy. All of the four 'Systemhäupter' start from the assumption of a particular and abstract consciousness. Therefore they are prisoners in the "sphere of a fragmented and abstract consciousness"[18]. In Schlegel's own theory, human consciousness consists of four main faculties: understanding (*Verstand*), will (*Wille*), reason (*Vernunft*), and imagination (*Phantasie*). Schlegel argues that the four great 'Systemhäupter' usually concentrate on only one of these faculties, each in his own way. Kant can be associated with the faculty of critical understanding, Jacobi with moral will, Fichte with ideal reason, and Schelling with speculative imagination. According to Schlegel, Kant "used his critical understanding in vain in all his works"[19]. Jacobi fought "the same never-ending titanic struggle for divine truth by his moral will in all his life"[20]. Fichte's Idealism formed the negative "peak of ideal reason"[21] and, Schelling created his speculative philosophy of nature merely on the "basis of speculative imagination"[22].

Thus Schlegel's critical characterization of the contemporary German philosophy leads to a twofold result. First, all of the four main systems of German Idealism represent only one of the four faculties of human consciousness. Consequently they are regarded as incomplete and lacking any connection to real history. Secondly, all the four systems form a 'closed circle' (*ab-*

17 *KA* 8, 591.
18 *KA* 8, 592.
19 *KA* 8, 592.
20 *Ibid.*
21 *Ibid.*
22 *Ibid.*

geschlossener Zirkel)[23]. Therefore, a philosophy which would be built on the four main faculties of the human consciousness is already exhausted by the four systems of Kant, Jacobi, Fichte and Schelling.

Schlegel's half-polemical critique of Hegel arises from the conviction that the philosophies of Kant, Jacobi, Fichte and Schelling constitute a "artistically closed and completely vanished"[24] circle of systems.[25] In Schlegel's view, Hegel cannot be regarded as an original philosopher, only as a "Fichte developed further"[26]. As can be seen, Hegel plays an extremely negative role in Schlegel's history of modern philosophy. As Schlegel argues, Hegel's philosophical system dissimulates its lack of originality by an "endless influx of empty and abstract knowledge"[27].

In his lectures on the *Philosophy of Life* from 1828 Schlegel repeated his critique of Hegel. Here he elaborated on the historical dynamics of German Idealism which is determined and characterized by the ironical figure of inversion. This "way of inversion (*Gang der Umkehrung*)"[28] began with Kant's opposition against the presumptions of pure reason, then lead to Fichte's and Schelling's affirmation of the absolute rule of reason and finally ended with Hegel's "idolization"[29].

Once again Hegel's system seems to represent the highest degree possible in Idealistic aberration. In Schlegel's opinion Hegel's metaphysical error culminates in his statement that the "absolute idol of reason"[30] is the objective principle of the universe. By emphasizing the negativity of the mind, Hegel's philosophical system corresponds, according to Schlegel, to Lord Byron's poetic description of Lucifer. Thus, Hegel's system constitutes the peak of a mislead Idealism, which will at last enthrone the absolute "evil

23 See: *KA* 8, 593.

24 *KA* 8, 594.

25 For Schlegel's and Hegel's 'mutual destruction' (*Wechselvernichtung*) cf. E. BEHLER: "Friedrich Schlegel und Hegel", in: *Hegel-Studien,* 2 (1963), pp. 241-250.

26 *KA* 8, 595.

27 *Ibid.*

28 *KA* 10, 15.

29 *Ibid.*

30 *KA* 10, 16.

spirit of negativity and contradiction, [...] although being absolutely obscure, in the midst of a confused system"[31].

II. 'The Idea of the Vivid Word': Rhetorical Anthropology as a Basis of Schlegel's Theory of History

Schlegel designed his new *Philosophy of Life* as an answer to the fragmentation of human consciousness which he observed in systems of Idealism. He sought for a spiritual and comprehensive restitution of man's consciousness within a Christian framework, in particular for a "restitution of the lost divine image in mankind"[32]. Schlegel's philosophy does not only aim at an inner 'rebirth' and vivification of the individual consciousness, but also at a new perspective on the history of mankind. Consequently, the *Philosophy of History* forms the core of Schlegel's new departure in philosophy. Within a new spiritual perspective, the history of the world is interpreted as a permanent revelation of the 'lively spirit' and 'personal god'[33].

By overcoming the gulf between reason and imagination, philosophy will be able to reestablish the contact with historical life. This is the reason why in Schlegel's opinion human language is a product not only of reason, but also of imagination. While reason is responsible only for the logical and grammatical structure of language, its "whole figural and pictorial portion"[34] – is created by imagination. In this way Schlegel rehabilitates the figurative aspects of human language, which had traditionally been treated by rhetorical *elocutio*-theory.

The restitution of the original connection between reason and imagination eventually lead Schlegel to a rhetorical anthropology and a *Philosophy of the Word*, on which his whole theory of history depends. Thus, the "original miraculous high dignity"[35] of man is based on the principle of the vivid word. "Man is [...] the spirit to whom – in contrast to all other beings – the word,

31 *KA* 10, 17.
32 *KA* 10, 3.
33 *KA* 10, 56.
34 *KA* 10, 41.
35 *KA* 10, 339f.

the explaining, describing, controlling, mediating and even the commanding word – is being granted, imparted or transferred to."[36] Relying on the "idea of the word"[37] and rejecting all rationalistic reductions, in which man was defined as a mere *animal rationale*, Schlegel emphasizes the original and mutual "link between speaking and thinking"[38]. By regarding man as a creature of the vivid word, Schlegel revives and continues the tradition of rhetorical humanism which had emphasized the original unity of *ratio* and *oratio*. This means that human knowledge in general depends on both discursive and pictural language through which reason and imagination are necessarily connected.

In this context Schlegel generalizes an argument, which Hamann, in his *Metacritique about the Purism of Reason*[39], had already brought forth against Kant's *Critique of Pure Reason*. In Schlegel's version this argument runs as follows: By ignoring the basic connection between reason and language, the speculative philosophers of pure reason deny human limitations and pointlessly try to achieve an "inhuman (*unmenschliches*)"[40], absolute knowledge.

Schlegel, on the contrary, aspires to restitute the imaginary faculty of language and its central position in human knowledge and existence. By focussing on the vivid reality of the word he goes beyond the limits of a logical theory, which would restrict language to the propositional aspect of judgement. Schlegel's theory of the word focuses on the performative qualities of speech. In his lectures about the *Philosophy of History* the philosopher underlined the performative richness of the word, which is familiar to us through our "own experience and from life itself"[41]. In all the different hermeneutic, didactic, erotic, imperative and poetic performances the word appears as a

36 *Ibid.*

37 *KA* 9, 29.

38 *KA* 10, 350.

39 In his *Metacritique about the Purism of Reason* from 1784 Hamann critizised Kant's 'pure reason' as an artificial and fictitious product resulting from three 'purifications': First the 'purification' of consciousness from tradition and faith, secondly from experience and thirdly from language. (See: J.G. HAMANN: *Schriften zur Sprache*, ed. by J. SIMON, Frankfurt a.M. (Suhrkamp) 1967, p. 222.)

40 See: *KA* 10, 42.

41 *KA* 9, 30.

"vivid effective power"[42]. As such it is a persuasive and practical force in human life and culture.

Thus the word has a double position in relation to history. First, the vivid word is a positive fact of our first-hand experience in human life and an event with occurs in real history. "The vivid by communicated, real by articulated word is not only a dead faculty, but a matter of fact, something historically real and given."[43] In this way the word is both a medium of tradition and an object of historical investigation.

Secondly, the vivid word is not only medium and object but also – and this is fundamental of Schlegel's theory of history – the subject and formative principle of history. Allegorically speaking it is "the original root"[44] of the all historical knowledge and human tradition. The underlying principle of Schlegel's *Philosophy of History* is neither economic nor political power, but the convincing force of the vivid word.

Expressed in theological terms Schlegel gives his rhetorically conceived principle of the divine word a particular Christian ring. The motto of his *Philosophy of History* alludes to *Genesis* and the prologue of *St. John's Gospel*: "In the beginning man got the word, and this word was from God."[45] In Schlegel's view the vivid word, which is the formative principle of world history, has a divine origin.

The arrangement of Schlegel's universal history corresponds to this fundamental idea of the principle of the divine word and man's creative power by presenting the history of mankind as a *Historia tripartita*. The plan of a gradual and "general restitution in world history"[46] includes the three ages of the 'word', the 'power' and the 'light'. The first 'epoch of the word' comprises the history of the first revelation of the divine word as well as its degeneration and corruption that was responsible for the splitting of mankind into many nations. Referring to the Chinese, Indian, Egyptian, Hebrew, Greek and Roman cultures, Schlegel characterizes the second 'epoch of power' as the revival of the word. The 'third epoch of light' shows how the original truth of the divine word expanded. It stretches from the Germanic migrations,

42 *KA* 9, 29f.
43 *KA* 9, 29.
44 *Ibid.*
45 *KA* 9, 30.
46 *KA* 9, 3.

the Middle Ages, the Reformation, the Enlightenment and the French Revolution to Schlegel's time.

Schlegel's *Philosophy of History* follows the historical logic of the *Philosophia perennis*, as does Schelling's *Philosophy of the Weltalter*.[47] The history of mankind is conceived of as a story of creation, degeneration, successive revival and the eventual restitution of the lost divine truth. As an example of the "romantic revival of the *Philosophia perennis*"[48] Schlegel's historical thinking incorporates, in the cyclic form of its universal history, the typical Romantic attempt at overcoming the linear progression in history which the Enlightenment had postulated. Furthermore, the specific connection of rhetoric and Christian theology is significant of Schlegel's own philosophical position. By developing the fundamental idea of the vivid word he revived the tradition of rhetorical humanism and Luther's theology of the word.[49]

III. 'The Irony of Love': The Three Basic Rules of Conjectural Historiography

In his presentation of human history in his lectures about the *Philosophy of History*, Schlegel adhered to his own concept of narrative historiography. Again, Schlegel brought history into contact with rhetoric. He opposed the closed form of an apodictic system by using the open conjectural style of historical thinking that he himself preferred. It is not the completeness of logical consequences, which forms the core of Schlegel's historiographical concept, but the "historical course (*der historische Gang*)"[50], which leads to a real understanding of history as a whole. His philosophy of history is a prod-

47 See: W. SCHMIDT-BIGGEMANN: *Philosophia perennis. Historische Umrisse abendländischer Spiritualität in Antike, Mittelalter und Früher Neuzeit*, Frankfurt a.M. (Suhrkamp) 1998, pp. 646ff.

48 *Loc. cit.*, p. 702.

49 See: A. GRÜN-OESTERREICH, PETER L. OESTERREICH: "Dialectica docet, rhetorica movet: Luthers Reformations der Rhetorik", in: P.L. OESTERREICH, TH.O. SLOANE (Eds.): *Rhetorica movet. Studies in Historical and Modern Rhetoric in Honour of Heinrich F. Plett*, Leiden/Boston/Köln (Brill) 1999, pp. 25-41.

50 *KA* 9, 341.

uct not of apodictic but of conjectural reason.[51] In Schlegel's view historiography follows three basic rules which are modelled after the system of classical rhetoric and according to which a story (*narratio*) should exemplify the three virtues of brevity (*brevitas*), perspicuity (*perspicuitas*) and probability (*probabilitas*).[52]

The first basic rule is concerned with the invention of historical contents. This rule is an equivalent to the rhetorical principle of *brevitas*, which demands the clear-cut shortness of a narration. The presentation of universal history requires a methodical selection of the seemingly immeasurable historical material. From the boundless "ocean of singular historical knowledge"[53] one still has to select the important facts.

The second basic rule is related to the arrangement of the historical contents or the form of the 'historical course': "One need not explain everything."[54] This second rule asks for the historiographical courage of leaving a gap in matters which are not so important. This does not question the narrative virtue of clearness at all, because a lack in detail will not hurt the recipient's understanding of the whole. On the contrary, Schlegel points out that an attempt of falsely applying mathematical exactness and completeness to history would lead to "arbitrary and forced hypotheses"[55], which would jeopardize the whole enterprise.

The third basic rule is concerned with probability as a narrative virtue: One must not reject things as impossible or improbable which seem "alien or miraculous at first sight"[56]. The third rule calls for the acknowledgment of the

---

51 For the concept of conjectural reason (*konjekturale Vernunft*) in context with Aristotle's *Rhetoric* see: G.K. MAINBERGER: *Rhetorica I, Aristoteles. Cicero. Augustinus*, Stuttgart-Bad Cannstatt (Fromman-Holzboog) 1987, pp. 15–260. In his metaphysics Nicolaus Cusanus strongly emphasised the role conjectural knowledge, which corresponds to the human mind and its world. "Coniecturalis itaque mundi humana mens forma exstitit uti realis humana" (N. DE CUSA: *De coniecturis/Mutmaßungen*, ed. by J. KOCH, W. HAPP, Hamburg [Felix Meiner] ^{2}1988, p. 6).

52 See: M.F. QUINTILIANUS: *Ausbildung des Redners. Zwölf Bücher/Institutionis oratoriae libri XII*, ed. by H. RAHN, vol. 1, Darmstadt (Wissenschaftliche Buchgesellschaft) 1972, pp. IV, 31.

53 *KA* 9, 11f.

54 *KA* 9, 14.

55 *Ibid.*

56 *KA* 9, 38.

historical otherness. In discussing it Schlegel recalls his early critique of the historical-critical method. In the *Athenäum* fragment 25 the young Schlegel had caricatured this method by ascribing to it a 'postulate of commonness' (*Postulat der Gemeinheit*) and an 'axiom of mediocrity' (*Axiom der Gewöhnlichkeit*): "Postulate of commonness: Everything great, good and beautiful is improbable, because it is exceptional, and at least suspicious. Axiom of mediocrity: The way it is with us and around us, it must have been everywhere, because it is all so natural and normal."[57]

Surveying the realm of human history in his third basic rule, the late Schlegel again warns us against the fallacy of generalising one's own particular consciousness. Thus Schlegel's late *Philosophy of History*, with its acknowledgment of the otherness of history and the plurality of historical worlds, is also influenced by the figure of irony. Its urban and tolerant spirit protects the human consciousness from all sorts of wrong and one-sided claims of absoluteness.

"The true irony ... is the irony of love."[58] It is the figure of the irony of love, which ties together the idea of divine infinity with the finiteness of the contingent and conjectural human spirit. The irony of love, which moulds the historiographical style of Schlegel's late *Philosophy of History*, differs from his early romantic figure of 'infinite irony'. The young Schlegel had extended the rhetorical *tropus* (*ironia verbi*) to the figures of the unlimited irony of life (*ironia vitae*) and the irony of being (*ironia entis*), defining these 'infinite ironies' as the "freest of all licences"[59]: They enable man to experience human existence as a "permanent change of self-creation and self-destruction"[60] and as an "uninterrupted chain of inner revolutions"[61].

The young Schlegel, however, was already aware of the dangers of such an infinite ironic regress. Using irony in an extreme and infinite way can ultimately lead to its self-destruction. Its unhindered application can bring about the fatal situation of ending up as prisoner of one's own irony. One cannot "escape from irony again".[62] Eventually the infinite extension of irony

57 *KA* 2, 149.
58 *KA* 10, 460.
59 *KA* 2, 160.
60 *KA* 2, 172.
61 *KA* 2, 255.
62 *KA* 2, 369.

will evoke the desperate question: "Which gods will save us form all these ironies?"

The answer of Schlegel's late philosophy lies neither in proclaiming the gods of a New Mythology nor in the expectation of a 'coming God'.[63] It is to be found in the personal and living God of Christianity, who has revealed his goodness in real history and is able also to rescue man from the existential precipice of infinite irony. Thus Schlegel's Christian and spiritual turn is the reason for the metamorphosis from infinite to loving irony which can be observed in his work. The new spiritual seriousness suspends the pure poetical concept of infinite irony, which "sublimely hovers over the whole work and everything else, even the whole universe"[64].

In Schlegel's late philosophy the figure of irony does no longer rule unrestrictedly. In addition to the seriousness of spiritual love, which excludes a materialistic or atheistic interpretation of universal history, irony looses its radical negativity. It rather assumes a positive and conciliatory character. The early romantic concept of "the indissoluble conflict of the unconditioned and the conditional"[65] has become more moderate. The new loving irony will not destroy the idea of the infinite; it will, on the contrary, "contribute to her confirmation and reinforcement"[66].

Schlegel's late *Philosophy of History* is thus marked by a spiritual limitation of principle of irony. In the presentation of history the scope of irony is limited by the fundamental idea of a "restitution of the lost divine image in mankind"[67]. Therefore Schlegel's historiographical style can tropologically be described as a combination of negative irony and integrative synecdoche.[68]

It becomes clear that the figure of the irony of love includes a negative as well as a positive element. In principle irony allows for a critical insight into the difference between a literary presentation of history and the manifold facts

---

63 See: M. FRANK: *Der kommende Gott. Vorlesungen über die Neue Mythologie*, Frankfurt a.M. (Suhrkamp) 1982.

64 *KA* 10, 447.

65 *KA* 2, 160.

66 *KA* 10, 357.

67 *KA* 9, 3.

68 For the connection between historiographical styles and rhetorical tropes see: H. WHITE: *Metahistory. The Historical Imagination in Nineteenth-Century Europe*, Baltimore & London (The Johns Hopkins University Press) 1973.

of historical reality. In this way, it permits a new Socratic "smiling of the spirit"[69], which will leave behind the pose of 'anxious systematic omniscience' (*ängstliche systematische Allwissenheit*).[70] Viewed from the angle of an integrative synecdoche, however, all ironic contrasts will finally dissolve into the synthetical perspective "of a gradual approximation to the eternal truth"[71].

---

69 See: *KA* 10, 356.
70 See: *ibid.*
71 *KA* 10, 474.

Chapter 2

History as the Control of Speculation: Schelling's Discovery of History and Baader's Critique of Absolute Historicity

PETER KOSLOWSKI

I. German Idealism as Speculative Philosophy
II. Transfiguration of Philosophy at its Highest Point into History: Schelling's Later Philosophy as History of Being
III. Baader's Critique of German Idealism's Absolute Knowledge

The time of German Idealism is one of the most speculative epochs in the history of philosophy, possibly only comparable with the period of the great speculative systems of the philosophy of the later centuries of antiquity.

I. German Idealism as Speculative Philosophy

In Hegel and the young Schelling, one finds an unbroken confidence that speculative thought is able to answer the most encompassing questions of metaphysics and that it can form a theory of totality that includes not only the present totality but also its genesis, the history of being.

Schelling's system of identity and Hegel's dialectics of the absolute spirit are speculative theories of totality which claim to grasp not only the present being but also its genesis, its history. Schelling introduces the system of the identity of the absolute subject and the absolute object, of spirit and nature as the basic structure of the totality of being which is being-in-becoming. The world process and being are the becoming conscious of the subject or spirit at the object or nature. All being, even the being of the absolute, is subjected to the process of becoming objective in time or history.

Schelling's identity system of totality as the absolute subject-object was given further methodological foundation by the dialectical method which claimed that the logical judgment *(Ur-teil)* is the basic structure of reality. The totality of being is the ontological judgment in which the idea divides itself in nature and forms an ontological conclusion as the synthesis of the idea that returns in itself. The speculative schemes of the absolute identity of subject-object and of the absolute conclusion (*absoluter Schluß*) are not only logical but also ontological schemes. They describe the basic structure of the world.

The genesis of being is the process of the self-objectivation of the absolute subject in Schelling and the conclusion of the absolute spirit in its synthesis with its otherness in nature in Hegel. World history is this process of the self-objectivation or of the self-conclusion of the absolute.

The most general logical structure becomes here the most general ontological structure. The universality of logic seems to support the universal claim of speculative metaphysics. Logic becomes metaphysical and thereby most powerful. Logic creates the appearance of well-foundedness, of the scientific character of speculation based on it. In history and in its process of progress, God realizes himself as subject-object. Schelling explains: "The general world process rests on a universal progress of victories of the subjective over the objective although these victories are alternately always again contested. This victory, this progression is the password (*Losungswort*) of the universal movement whose representation is the science (*die Wissenschaft*)."[1]

1 F.W.J. SCHELLING: *System der Weltalter. Münchener Vorlesung 1827/28 in einer Nachschrift von Ernst von Lasaulx*, herausgegeben und eingeleitet von Siegbert Peetz, Frankfurt am Main (Klostermann) 1990 (=SdW), p. 92.

II. Transfiguration of Philosophy at its Highest Point into History: Schelling's Later Philosophy as History of Being

There are, however, two objections to this logic of being and of history, one from the "logic of freedom", one from the logic of singular historical events. The objection from a philosophy of freedom is made by Schelling against himself in his *Philosophical Inquiries into the Nature of Human Freedom* (*Philosophische Untersuchungen über das Wesen der menschlichen Freiheit*) of 1809[2] in which he states for the first time that the development of the absolute can not be conceived to be a necessary progression but only a sequence of free acts of the absolute. The historical objection against himself he makes in his *Ages of the World* (*Die Weltalter*) of 1813.

In his late philosophy, Schelling turns against Hegel's metaphysical logic and criticizes its only possible character, its character of describing only a structure of possibility lacking historical factualness. He criticizes the infinite lack of being and factualness *(unendliche Mangel an Sein)* in Hegel's system. He calls Hegel's metaphysical logic and dialectics "negative philosophy" that can only describe the possibility but not the facts of the development of the absolute in history.[3]

---

2 SCHELLING: *Ages of the World*, second draft of *Die Weltalter* (1813), Ann Arbor (University of Michigan Press) 1997 (=Ages).

3 SCHELLING: *Philosophie der Offenbarung. Erstes Buch. Einleitung in die Philosophie der Offenbarung*, in: *Schellings Werke*, edited by M. Schröter, Sechster Ergänzungsband *Philosophie der Offenbarung. Erstes und zweites Buch 1858*, München (C.H. Beck & R. Oldenbourg) 1954, Suppl.-Vol. VI, p. 75: The fact that Hegel and the philosophical rationalism are not fond of the word *potentia* demonstrates that in the purely aprioristic rational philosophy only the possibility of entities but not their reality is grasped. (*Daß Hegel und der Rationalismus "dem Wort Potenz nicht geneigt sind", erinnert daran, "daß in der Vernunftwissenschaft, oder, was dasselbe ist, in der rein apriorischen Wissenschaft, nur die Möglichkeit der Dinge, nicht die Wirklichkeit begriffen werden."*) Schelling criticizes, *ibid*, p. 82, that "logical dogmatism which later on Hegel wanted to ground on the purely abstract notion and which is of all dogmatisms the most disgusting one since it is the most petty and narrow-minded one, whereas the dogmatism of the elder metaphysics has still something magnificent". (*"... jener logische Dogmatismus, den später Hegel auf den bloß abstrakten Begriff gründen wollte, der von allen der widerwürtigste, weil der*

He criticizes further that Hegel's negative logic of the development of God, universe, and history does neither correspond to the actual history of the world nor to the history of revelation of the absolute as it is narrated in the religions. Schelling sets out, from his *Philosophical Inquiries into the Nature of Human Freedom* of 1809 to his *Philosophie der Offenbarung* (*Philosophy of the Revelation*) of the year 1814 to 1854 to develop a positive philosophy that is able to incorporate as well the content and facts or world history as the content of the History of Revelation. Positive philosophy, in Schelling's view, must recount the actual history of the absolute as it is narrated in the mythological and religious tradition of humankind, a tradition in which the actual history of the development of the absolute is reflected.

The development from mythology to the revealed religion of Christianity is for him not only the history of human imaginations about the absolute but the development of humankind and God in each other. The absolute is becoming itself in the historical stages of the mind of humankind. The history of mythology and Judaism towards Christianity is a history within history, a sort of higher history, a process of revelation of the absolute in itself, an *Offenbarungsgeschichte*, a "revealing/revealed history" and history of revelation, within the universal history.[4] The history of revelation renders the religious revelation to be the central manifestation of the absolute within the

---

kleinlichste ist, wogegen der Dogmatismus der alten Metaphysik noch immer etwas Großartiges hat." See also *ibid*, p. 151. In contrast to this dogmatism of logic, Schelling wants to develop his positive philosophy and philosophy of revelation as "a metaphysical empirism" (*ibid*, p. 92).

4 SCHELLING: *Philosophie der Offenbarung. Drittes Buch,* in: *Schellings Werke*, edited by M. Schröter, Sechster Hauptband *Schriften zur Religionsphilosophie 1841-54*, München (C.H. Beck & R. Oldenbourg) 1927, reprint 1965, vol. 6, p. 422: The content of the revelation in mythology and religion is a "higher history" (*eine höhere Geschichte*) and "supra-historical history" (*übergeschichtliche Geschichte*), *ibid*, p. 612. - The *Philosophy of Revelation* is not a "revealed philosophy" (*Offenbarungsphilosophie*), but a "philosophy of revelation" (*Philosophie der Offenbarung*), a study of the factual documents of the historical revelation of the absolute in mythology and religion which form the object of this philosophy just as nature, art, history form the object of the philosophies of nature, art, and history respectively (*loc. cit.*, Suppl.-Vol. VI, p. 139). The positive philosophy and philosophy of revelation is not a philosophy of history (*Philosophie der Geschichte*) but a historical philosophy (*geschichtliche Philosophie*) that follows the acts and actualization of the absolute in the higher history of revelation (ibid, p. 138f. footnote).

revelation to be the central manifestation of the absolute within the absolute's general manifestation in the universe.

The objection from the point of view of freedom against the merely logical and speculative identity system is that the absolute cannot be totally dependent on the object. It must be free to accept being or not to accept it.

The historical objection against logical speculation is that it is too universal, too general to explain the actual development of history. It does not justice to the historical events and epochs which are only stations on the way of the absolute to greater self-consciousness, instantiations of the one metaphysical speculative logic of history. In his *Ages of the World*, Schelling transforms philosophy into history to refute this objection against his speculative system. He states: "Science (*Wissenschaft*), according to the very meaning of the word, is history (*historia*)... What is known is recounted, why can what is known of the highest science not be recounted as well, with the candidness and simplicity of everything else that is known?... Can the philosopher never return to the simplicity of history, as did the divine Plato, whose entire work is dialectical throughout, but becomes historical at the summit and point of transfiguration?"[5]

At its highest point, philosophy is transfigured into pure history. It tells the story of being from its beginning in indifference or non-being to its development of conscious being as subject-object. The identity system has grasped the aprioristic structure of world history but not its content and details. It is too general to reach the factual, the facts of the history of being. The identity system has described the process of being only as an aprioristic process and from the point of view of reason. It is, however, necessary to describe this process as a positive-historical one within philosophy.[6] The historical, positive, and narrative philosophy - in contrast to the dialectical, merely rationalist, negative, and conclusive one – has the task to recognize history as the process or path in which the God of the beginning, the first being, *das erste Wesen*, who is above being assumes being.[7] Historical philosophy must make again this path of the absolute through history. It must make this path, which the absolute spirit passed in unconsciousness and which the finite human

---

5 Ages 113, 114, 119.

6 SdW 93.

7 SCHELLING: *Einleitung in die Philosophie* (1830), edited by Walter E. Ehrhardt, Stuttgart-Bad Cannstatt (frommann-holzboog)1989 (=Schellingiana, vol.10) (=Einl.), p. 104.

spirit does not remember, again in an anamnesis and recall this unconscious path to consciousness.[8]

Philosophy becomes a history of the process of being, a recounting of the stages or ages of the world (*Weltalter*). Philosophy becomes a meta-history of history, a story above the stories of world history, a story of the ages through which the absolute assumes being and consciousness. For the philosophical method, this turn to history implies that the philosopher must apply the historical method. "Now, the philosopher finds himself in the same position as another historian. For to find what he wants to know, the latter must also question the testimony of old documents or the memory of living witnesses." Like the historian he needs "considerable skills and discernment, to glean pure facts out of the confusion of reports and to pry apart the true from the false and the authentic from the inauthentic in the available chronicles."[9]

The documents about the ages of the world for the philosopher as historian of being are the documents of the religions as Schelling later explains in his *Philosophy of Revelation*. Like the historian the philosopher must keep distance from his object: "He too urgently requires a separation from himself, a distancing from the present, an abandonment to the past, in order to free himself of the ideas and qualities particular to his time."[10]

Only in the synthesis of the philosophy of freedom and the philosophy of the ages of the world, the history of being (*Seinsgeschichte*) can be understood as what it is: the free self-revelation of the absolute. The history of being is not that necessary dialectical process that the early identity philosophy and Hegel's philosophy of the absolute spirit recount in the language of logic. The philosophy of the history of being recounts being in "a narrative, a history (*Erzählung*) of that sequence of free actions by which God decided from eternity to reveal himself (*sich zu offenbaren*)."[11] Revelation is the making of oneself apparent, the history of being is the process by which the absolute makes itself apparent and visible (*offenbar*).

---

8 Cf. Einl. 42

9 Ages 116.

10 *Ibid.*

11 SCHELLING: *Die Weltalter. Bruchstück.* Aus dem handschriftlichen Nachlaß, 1814 (Schröter IV, 571-720), IV 645: "*Philosophie…eine Erzählung jener Folge freier Handlungen, durch welche Gott von Ewigkeit beschlossen sich zu offenbaren.*" (Philosophy ... a narrative of that sequence of free acts by which God from eternity has decided to reveal himself)

Schelling distinguishes two concepts of revelation for his historical philosophy or philosophy of the history of being.

Revelation is firstly the assumption of being by God (*die Seinsannahme Gottes*), God's revelation in the wider sense in creation and the process of nature or evolution. The sources for this history of being are the holy books of the religions, and the structure of this process is the identity of the absolute subject and object given by the identity system.

Revelation is secondly the revelation of the Jewish-Christian religion as God's revelation in the narrower sense, as his personal revelation in recent history. The history of being as self-revelation of the absolute is not mere progress like in Hegel but a development to the higher stage by returning in itself and by partially retrograding. The fully developed historical philosophy is philosophy of revelation as the historical, positive, and narrative philosophy that recounts the path of God assuming being.[12]

This philosophy is positive since it wants to reach the positive historical facts, the positivity of history, not only the negative logic of history, and strives, at the same time, to render the positive principle of history. It is as well historical empiricism as speculative idea of the principle of history. It is a twofold philosophy, a positive and negative, a historical and purely rational one: As positive philosophy it recounts the revelation of God in nature and in the empiricism of the documents of this process, the narratives of mythology and of the Jewish-Christian revelation and gives the theory of potencies in which being realized itself. As purely rational, dialectical, negative philosophy, it analyses the dialectics of being in a way close to that of traditional metaphysics.

Schelling declares: "I want to give a theory of Christianity in the context of the great history of creation."[13] History is a revelation of its own kind and at the same time the continuation of God's revelation in nature. The historical philosophy of the *Philosophy of Revelation* includes and is the continuation

---

12 SCHELLING: *Philosophie der Offenbarung*. Drittes Buch. Der Philosophie der Offenbarung zweiter Theil, 1842/43 (Schröter VI, 389-726), p. 572.

13 SCHELLING: *Urfassung der Philosophie der Offenbarung*, 1831/32, zwei Teilbände, herausgegeben von Walter E. Ehrhardt, Hamburg (Meiner) 1992 (Philosophische Bibliothek, Bd. 445 a und b), p. 17: „*Ich will das Christentum im Zusammenhange mit der großen Geschichte von der Schöpfung her darstellen.*"

of the philosophy of nature as the theory of God's revelation in nature, the continuation of *Naturphilosophie.*

The cause for this continuation of the revelation in nature and its theory of philosophy of nature or *Naturphilosophie* in history and in its theory, the philosophy of history, is the fall of humankind. Original sin is the origin of history. God's original revelation or assumption of being would have happened without history: "In the human, the primordial principle of nature should have been transformed into spirit and freedom – the natural life should have been the spiritual in the human."[14] The empiricism of revelation gives the stages of the process of the development of consciousness: the stage of the mythologies of the different peoples represents the unfree development of consciousness in the stage of unconsciousness and distortedness of consciousness. The revelation in the narrow sense of Judaism and Christianity is the stage of the free development of consciousness. Mythology and religious revelation are the empirical sources for the history of the world ages as the disclosure or opening-up (*offenbaren*) of God's manifestation in being.

Revelation as self-disclosure, self-evidencing, self-manifestation is not primarily an oral utterance or the sharing of information about truths of reason or reasonable truths. It is basically deed. The knowledge of this deed of self-manifestation is an empirical knowledge, not the understanding of a message. Revelation is, for Schelling, God's deed, not God's teaching. The philosophical recognition of the revelation, the philosophy of revelation (*Philosophie der Offenbarung*) is empirical and historical knowledge, not the obedience to a teaching or the believing of a message. Schelling remains within the idea of German Idealism that absolute knowledge as knowledge of the absolute is possible, and that this absolute task is the goal of philosophy as the theory of the totality of being. He transforms this absolute knowledge into historical empiricism or historism which he also calls metaphysical empiricism by dividing philosophy in a genial way in a logical, dialectical and in a positive, historical part. Only the two sides of the angle that forms the system of philosophy, the historical, positive one and the logical, dialectical one, are able to give a complete knowledge of being.

The claim to absolute knowledge and cognition of totality that Schelling's and Hegel's systems of philosophy make presupposes in both systems that the philosopher can take a standpoint beyond and above being and history and, therefore, beyond and above God. For Schelling is the cognition of God the

14 Einl. 140

cognition of the greatest of all objects. The absolute is the greatest object as absolute subject-object. For being able to say this and to recognize the absolute as an object, the philosopher must have a standpoint and perspective beyond the absolute. This is by definition impossible since it would render the absolute relative, relative to an observer who has an even greater perspective. Goethe made a similar objection against the claim of the philosophy of history to be able to recognize history as a whole: There is no standpoint outside of history for humans from which they could perceive history as a totality. Therefore, philosophy of history as philosophy of the totality of history is impossible. It is impossible as the knowledge of a grand object, as the cognition of the object "totality of history". There might be the possibility of a theological-philosophical cognition of history as a whole but this knowledge can not proceed like the cognition of an oversized, *übergroßes,* object.

III. Baader's Critique of German Idealism's Absolute Knowledge

Ranke held the opinion that Baader and Hegel "were, despite Baader's opposition against Hegel, of the same philosophical school, - only in different labyrinths."[15] This judgment by Ranke does not hold philosophical scrutiny. Ranke underestimated the depth of Baader's criticism of German Idealism and overstated his proximity to Hegel.

The central point of Baader's criticism of German Idealism is that Hegel and Schelling introduced the idea of the becoming absolute, of the God that is subjected to time and history himself and, therefore, a major change in the history of metaphysics. The temporality of the absolute renders the temporal and historical absolute. If even the absolute is historical history is total and all-encompassing, and there is no realm outside of the historical and temporal.

15 L. RANKE: *Letter to Heinrich Ritter*, 4th January 1828, in: *Sämtliche Werke*, Vol. 53/54: *Zur eigenen Lebensgeschichte*, Leipzig (Duncker & Humblot) 1890, p. 185: „Was sagst Du zu der Opposition Franz Baader's gegen Hegel? Sie sind doch fast Einer Richtung, nur in verschiedenen Irrgärten." Vgl. auch D. BAUMGARDT: *Franz von Baader undide philosophische Romantik*, Halle (Max Niemeyer) 1927, p. 368.

By this totalization of the historical, the historicity of history itself that characterized traditional metaphysics is ended. Baader emphasizes that the spirit is not bound to time and space and therefore free of time and history.[16] With the temporalization of the absolute and the making absolute of historicity, German Idealism has changed ontology most deeply. The temporality or non-temporality of the absolute is the most central ontological decision (*Grundentscheidung*) philosophy can make.[17] Baader recognized this as the central ontological change that took place in his time and anteceded the later dominance of absolute historicity in evolution theory. Absolute historicity is opposed to the idea of a free origin of time in creation.

German Idealism understands the beginning of history as a fall of the absolute from itself, as an unfree beginning although Schelling in his later philosophy tries to reintroduce the freedom of the absolute. In the theological perspective, a beginning of the world in a fall of the absolute renders the world to be the consequence of a catastrophe or even sin. According to Baader, the idea of the world and of history in God's fall from himself makes the creation a sin that God should repent since creation is the consequence of his inability to control himself.

The second consequence of the absoluteness of history is that history becomes the absolute court of judgment over the deeds of humankind and of human individuals. Hegel followed Schiller's statement that world history is the world's final judgment. In an ontology in which history is historical itself and the absolute independent of time and history, history is only a relative court of judgment and not the last court of appeal. Baader therefore corrects Hegel's and Schiller's statement to the proposition: World history is only a partial and subordinate court of judgment.[18] History is itself historical, and therefore its judgment not the one of a court without further appeal.[19]

---

16 FRANZ VON BAADER: *Societätsphilosophie*, 1831/32, in: FRANZ VON BAADER: *Sämtliche Werke*, ed. by F. Hoffmann et al., Leipzig 1851-1860, reprint Aalen (Scientia) 1963, vol. 14, pp. 55-160 (=Societ.), vol. 14, p. 55.

17 Cf. FRANZ VON BAADER: *Elementarbegriffe über die Zeit als Einleitung zur Philosophie der Societät und der Geschichte*, 1831, in: *Sämtliche Werke, loc. cit.*, 14, 29-54 (=Elembgr.), vol. 14, p. 29.

18 Societ. 14, 68.

19 Or, as Leo Schestow has stated it, history is the unjust judge to whom, according to the passing on of Russian pilgrims, the fighting parties are forced to turn in pagan countries. LEO SCHESTOW: *Athen und Jerusalem. Versuch einer religiösen*

Hegel's world spirit or *Weltgeist* will be sitting, according to Baader, at the end of history on the ruins of world history in loneliness, and the rubble of history will be formed by the generations of humankind.[20]

The philosophical proposition that history is historical and transient is only possible from a standpoint outside history which would allow the thinker to overlook the entirety of history and to recognize that it is temporal and historical and therefore transient itself. Baader is aware that this requires the theological view on history with the idea of an absolute being independent of time and being the lord of history. From this theological-philosophical perspective, the unity of history can be contended. In contrast, Hegel's and Schelling's claim that they possess a standpoint beyond history that would entitle them to a philosophy of history as a philosophy of the unity of history cannot be founded since they assume everything to be inside of history and since they have no point to look from on history from outside of it and on it as a whole. The idealist philosophy of history tries to develop a philosophy of the totality of history without having a standpoint outside of history. Its phi-

---

Philosophie, Graz (Schmidt-Dengler) 1938, p. 11: "*Die Geschichte ist jener ungerechte Richter, an den, laut überlieferung russischer Pilger, in heidnischen Ländern die streitenden Parteien sich zu wenden gezwungen sind.*"

20 FRANZ VON BAADER: Societ. 14, 112: "*Wohin aber derlei monströse und wirklich abominable Vorstellungen, falls sie consequent durchgeführt und nicht synkretistisch zum Theil wieder dissimilirt werden, in der Philosophie der Geschichte führen, davon können Sie sich in Hegels Grundlinien der Philosophie des Rechts und in seiner dort aufgestellten Ansicht von der Weltgeschichte nach den von ihm angegebenen vier Epochen des orientalischen, des griechischen, des römischen und des germanischen Reichs überzeugen. Eine Ansicht, welche eigentlich das Verhältniss des Schöpfers zum Geschöpf umkehrt (nemlich gegen die bisherigen Ansichten) indem die Philosophen und auch viele Theologen sonst Gott durch seine Einsamkeit und gleichsam Langeweile zur Schöpfung sich bestimmen lassen, wogegen Hegel den Weltgeist, (man weiss nicht ob hierunter der Spiritus dei oder der Spiritus mundi immundi gemeint ist) von unten herauf auf Kosten seiner Geschöpfe und durch alle ihre Gebrechen hindurch sich hinauf arbeitet, hiedurch immer mehr zu sich selber kömmt und sich als Geist substantialisirt, so dass dieser Weltgeist oder Gott nur nach zurückgelegter sämmtlicher Weltgeschichte, und über dem Schutt untergegangener und von ihm mit Recht fallen gelassener Weltepochen und Katastrophen und aller hiezu an die Reihe gekommener Völker und Individuen endlich absolut einsam und ohne alles Geschöpf zurück bleibend seine Absolutheit zu erreichen vermöchte.*"

losophy is a myth and "theology" of history that has no narrative framing the narrative of world history.

The older theological interpretation of the beginning of history in original sin and the fall of humankind in Jewish and Christian religion as well as the myth of the Golden Age in mythology that anteceded the historical age can distinguish between pre-historical and historical time and give historical time a unity that is encircled by non-historical "time". Idealism that conceives only a beginning of history and no end of it can give no principle of unity of history. It is logically impossible to reconcile the idea of the unity of history with the idea of the absoluteness of history. If history is absolute it can not have an end, and might also be very likely, against Hegel and Schelling, that it has no beginning. The absoluteness of history presupposes its eternity. An eternal history might in turn be another *contradictio in adiecto*.

If history has no end it has no unity. The totalization of history is only possible without a teleology of history. A blind or contingent beginning of history implies also a blind and contingent end of history or even no end at all. Hegel's philosophy of the absolute spirit and of world history is a theory of the contingent beginning of history in the fall of the absolute which nevertheless states that history is the realization of freedom and that humans are able to reconcile themselves with the path of history – both statements that are not justified by Hegel's theory about the beginning of history. Hegel takes an intermediate position between the Christian theory of original sin and the big bang theory of the beginning of history: God himself falls and, thereby, originates the world. The fall of the idea from itself implies a fall of the absolute and therefore a being of the absolute before this fall, but it is only this fall that brings the absolute to real existence. The Hegelian Erdmann rightly pointed to the fact that this idea of Hegel is basically Gnostic and reproduces the idea of the fall of the Sophia in Gnosticism on the level of a supposedly logical theory.[21] In both, the Gnostic and the Hegelian, theory of the absolute it is unclear why an absolute the falls will nevertheless return into itself and reach its accomplishment. The return of the spirit into itself (*Zusichkommen des*

---

21 Among the Hegelians, JOHANN EDUARD ERDMANN is probably the only one who openly acknowledged the similarity between Hegel and the Gnostics in the idea of the fall of the Godhead from itself. Cf. J.E. ERDMANN: *Natur oder Schöpfung? Eine Frage an die Naturphilosophie und Religionsphilosophie*, Leipzig (F.Chr.W. Vogel) 1848, p. 112. Gnosticism assumes, however in contrast to Hegel, that not the whole Godhead falls.

Geistes) implies a teleology that is not granted by the origin of the spirit in a fall.[22]

The other objection made by Baader against Hegel and Schelling commences from the idea of a person. Baader develops a personalist critique of the idea of personality in the Idealist philosophy of history. If the personality of the absolute is rejected and the philosophical position taken that the absolute is in an infinite historical development, the concept of the human person becomes unclear as well. The progressism of an infinite historical development or progress excludes the possibility of an accomplished gestalt of a person. Personality is always sublating herself in the theory of permanent sublation, but never achieving a finite gestalt. The other objection from the concept of a person concerns the idea of nature. The person does not sublate (*aufheben*) nature or the real in herself into spirit but conserves nature in herself. The person remains nature and spirit, a real and an ideal being. She is not transformed or sublated into spirit. In the complete person, there are spirit and nature.

A philosophy of history is only possible with the idea of original sin which divides the historical from the non-historical era. This connection was also understood by Hegel and urged him to reinterpret original sin as the fall of the absolute from itself. The beginning of the world coincides with the beginning of history in Hegel's thinking which leads to the equation of being and history. Such a beginning in contingency excludes a teleology of history since the *telos* or goal of history cannot be warranted by a purely contingent process. Hegel's philosophy of history is a "big bang theory" of the origin of history with a teleological concept of history leading to accomplishment in freedom.

The empiricism of history is the control principle of speculation for Baader and the late Schelling. The historian's empirical objection and the theologian's objection from the empiricism of historical religion against the speculative systems are closely connected since both, the historian and the theologian, claim that philosophical speculation must yield primacy to the factual and that philosophy must subject its speculative systems to the empirical test or authority of the facts of history. As Johann Georg Hamann con-

22 A similar problem faces the utopian end of history in Marx's dialectical materialism. Why should a process that produced alienation be able to be overcome to a state of total sublation and end of alienation?

tended[23], experience and history are the authority or the law court for speculative thinking. Schelling tried to follow him in this in his *Philosophy of Revelation*.[24]

Schelling, however, fell from one extreme into the other, from the pure theory of the system of identity into the pure history of the philosophy of revelation which just retells the story of the narratives of mythology and revelation. Between Hegel's absolute theory of metaphysical logic and the late Schelling's absolute empiricism of revelation history, German Idealism seems to have been incapable to find a balance between theory and empirical fact and to fall either in the historicism of absolute logic or in the historicism of the history of the self-revelation of the absolute.

Baader summarized this situation in 1833 as follows: "When today Hegel keeping himself within the negativity (of pure logic, insertions by P.K.) was not able to come to the concreteness of (material) content and (logical) form he was however closer to the solution of the sole problem of philosophy than those who although they put forward the theory of the identity of subject and object cannot conceal their inability to grasp this concreteness (or identity). They believe to conceal this inability by keeping hold of the abstract empiricism, the history as such, within the speculation (or theory) and, according to them, as positive element in speculation." Baader agrees with Philip Marheineke in his critique of Schelling. Schelling fails to understand that revelation

---

23 SCHELLING: *Philosophie der Offenbarung,* loc. cit., Suppl.-Vol. VI, p. 172, quotes Hamann that we know by the authority of our senses, and not by reason, that things exist outside of ourselves. See on Hamann also *Philosophie der Offenbarung*, loc. cit., vol. 6, p. 416.

24 SCHELLING: *Philosophie der Offenbarung,* loc. cit., Suppl.-Vol. VI, p. 61f.: Experience is the control of the speculation of reason: "*Denn eben weil es das Seyende ist, was die Vernunftwissenschaft* a priori *begreift oder construirt, muß ihr daran gelegen seyn, eine Controle zu haben, durch welche sie darthut, daß das, was sie* a priori *gefunden, n i c h t eine Chimäre ist. Diese Controle ist die Erfahrung. [...] Die Vernunftwissenschaft hat also die Erfahrung nicht zur Q u e l l e , wie die ehemalige Metaphysik sie zum Theil zur Quelle hatte, wohl aber hat sie die Erfahrung zur Begleiterin. Auf diese Weise hat die deutsche Philosophie den Empirismus, dem alle anderen europäischen Nationen nun seit einem Jahrhundert ausschließlich huldigten, selbst in sich, ohne darum Empirismus zu seyn.*"

is not a history like any other history.[25] Rather, it still has to be proven that the revelation of religion is history.

A full system of philosophy must be speculative and historical, rational and empirical. It cannot be speculative only or historical and narrative only. The late Schelling is, according to Baader, too servile to the historical and empirical. Those as Schelling who contend that philosophy must be transfigured into history "are not aware of the fact that the servility of an empiricism that looses itself in the subject matter is as bad as the liberalism of abstract theory that has fled the matter. But this exaggerated or forced standing of history in philosophy corresponds only to that forced position which Schelling gives recently, as we have seen, the son of God, i.e. God himself as being subjected to history."[26]

"Forced and unnatural standing of history" (*forcierte Stellung der Geschichte*) is a striking description of the absolute historicity in German Idealism. There is an element of overhistorization in Hegel and Schelling which derives from their historization of the absolute and the absolutization of the historical.

The reminder that history can only be history if it is itself historical and not absolute is the contribution of Baader's philosophical critique of Hegel's speculative logic and Schelling's transfiguration of philosophy into history. It precedes the critique of 19th century's historiography and theory of historiog-

---

25 PH. MARHEINEKE: *Zur Kritik der Schellingschen Offenbarunsgsphilophie*, Berlin (Th. Chr. Fr. Enslin) 1843,reprint Frankfurt am Main (Minerva) 1983, p. 29.

26 FRANZ VON BAADER: *Ueber den Begriff der Zeit und die vermittelnde Function der Form oder des Maasses* (1833), in: *Sämtliche Werke*, loc. cit., vol. 2, pp. 517-534, here p. 530: *"Wenn nun Hegel inner der Negativität sich haltend freilich zu dieser Concretheit des Inhaltes und der Form nicht selbst kommen konnte, so war er doch der Lösung dieses alleinigen Problems der Philosophie näher, als diejenigen, welche, obschon sich zur Identitätslehre des Subjects und Objects bekennend, ihr Unvermögen, diese Concretheit zu erfassen, damit zu verheimlichen meinen, dass sie die abstracte Empirie (Historie) als s o l c h e in der Speculation festhalten wollen, wie sie sagen als positives Element derselben, nicht bedenkend, dass der Servilismus der in die Sache versenkten Empirie ebenso schlecht ist, als der sachflüchtig gewordene Liberalismus der abstracten Theorie. Aber diese forcirte Stellung der Historie in der Philosophie entspricht freilich jener forcirten Stellung, die Schelling neuerlich, wie wir gesehen haben, dem Sohne Gottes, d. i. Gott Selbst als der Geschichte unterworfen gibt."*

raphy on Hegel. Both approaches, Baader's personalist philosophy and the historians' historical theory of history, opposed the absolute historicity assumed in German Idealism. Baader's, Ranke's and Droysen's critique of German Idealism's "forced understanding of history" made visible that the historical standpoint is not identical with the historization of all being and even the absolute or with the totalization or absoluteness of the historical. The historical is not absolute but in itself historical.[27]

27 Cf. to Baader and Schelling also P. KOSLOWSKI: *Philosophien der Offenbarung. Antiker Gnostizismus, Franz von Baader, Schelling*, Paderborn, München, Zürich, Wien (F. Schöningh) 2nd ed. 2001.

Part B

The Theory of History in German Historism

Chapter 3

Leopold von Ranke

HELMUT BERDING

I. Religious Historicism: Every Epoch is Immediate to God
II. Claim to Objectivity
III. In the Name of History: Historical and Political Conservatism

I. Religious Historicism: Every Epoch is Immediate to God

Leopold von Ranke counts among the greatest of historians. His *History of the Popes*, *History of the Reformation in Germany*, *History of France*, and *History of England* – to name only the best known of his great works – are classics. In view of his enormous historiographical work, which comprises fifty-four volumes, to which the nine volumes of *Universal History* are added, Ranke counts far and away as the "greatest German historian," and achieved with enormous creative force and great depictive power a literary accomplishment of the highest rank. With reference to the historical-theoretical content and the methodical principles of his historical writing, Ranke is often called the "father of the objective writing of history" or the "founder of the science of history." Although such acclamations may be fundamentally problematic, Ranke is undoubtedly a central figure in the German discipline of history. He decisively influenced historical-political thought in Germany in the nineteenth century. Occupation with his works has been called, with complete justification, "a decisive part of the self-reflection of German historiography."[1] It also leads to the foundations of our contemporary discipline of history.

---

1 D. GERHARD: *Deutsche Literarische Zeitung*, 1927, col. 2060 (review of L.v. RANKE: *Deutsche Geschichte im Zeitalter der Reformation*, Akademie Edition,

Ranke accomplished the decisive act in the development of German historical thinking by applying the idea of individuality to the political world, "which may perhaps be called Ranke's boldest intellectual achievement."[2] Ranke explained the interpretation of historical individuality – which had already been prepared by Herder and radicalized by romanticism – with all of its postulates of originality, analytical irreducibility, and creative freedom: "The real-mental, which suddenly stands before the eyes in unanticipated originality, cannot be derived from any higher principle. From the particular, one can carefully and boldly move up to the general; from the general theory, there is no way of looking at the particular."[3] In this proposition from the *Political Conversation*, Erich Rothacker saw "the most radical formulation of historicism that I know."[4]

Ranke's idea of individuality is based on assumptions conditioned by his ancestry, the kind of education, and the general, basic, religious-philosophical views of his time. He was born into a devout Protestant family, in which the heritage of a long line of Protestant intellectuals was alive. His father became a lawyer, but without giving up the unshakable Lutheran religiosity of his forefathers. As a lawyer and owner of a small piece of land, he belonged to the persons of rank of the small Thuringian country town of Wiehe on the Unstrut, where Leopold Ranke was born in 1795 (1886 †). From this small-town remoteness, still untouched by the intellectual and social shocks of the turn of the century, Ranke entered the Saxon Prince's School of Pforta ("Schulpforta"). The Lutheran spirit of his parents' home also encircled him here. In addition to classical philology, Christian theology dominated the teaching. Ranke further developed the seeds of Schulpforta during his study of philology and theology at the Universities of Leipzig and Halle from 1814 to 1818. He appeared to return into the theologian's world of his ancestors.

---

ed. P. Joachimsen), cited from R. VIERHAUS: *Ranke und die soziale Welt*, Münster (Aschendorff) 1957, p. 1.

2 T. SCHIEDER: "Das historische Weltbild L.v. Rankes", in: *Begegnungen mit der Geschichte*, Göttingen (Vandenhoeck & Ruprecht) 1962, p. 117.

3 L.V. RANKE: *Sämtliche Werke* (Ranke's collected works, 54 vols., Leipzig (Dunker & Humblot) 1867-90, vol. 49/50, p. 325.

4 E. ROTHACKER: "Savigny, Grimm, Ranke: Ein Beitrag zur Frage nach dem Zusammenhang der Historischen Schule", *Historische Zeitschrift*, 128 (1923), p. 437.

If Ranke was led more strongly by historical than by systematic-theological questions, especially in dealing with the original texts of Luther, this was certainly not because of a lack of faith. Reception – transmitted through Fichte – of the Platonic-Neoplatonic idea that the world is the representation, the phenomenon, the external existence of the divine idea was decisive for his gradual approach to history. The infinite Divine, existing in itself – Luther's "*deus absconditus*" – which evades direct human knowledge, expresses and realizes itself in historical humanity and reveals itself through history. This becomes the hieroglyphic of God, and dealing with the concrete historical phenomenon becomes the religious perception of the Deity: "God dwells, lives, and is to be recognized throughout history ... each moment preaches his name, but most of all ... the context of the great history ... that we for our part reveal this holy hieroglyphic! In this way we also serve God ... ."[5] In such ways of thinking we can glimpse the first stimulus to Ranke's conception of history. History, together with its academic apparatus, which ultimately serves the knowledge of God with the establishment of facts, receives religious inspiration, "which, for Ranke, as the descendent of a line of devout Lutheran pastors, it requires ... ."[6]

With his conception of the unity of the divine idea and human history, Ranke stood in full agreement with the basic historical-theological views of thinkers from Lessing to Schelling and Hegel. As Carl Hinrichs has demonstrated in detail, the "historical theology of the age of Goethe" is the great, universal, epoch-dependent factor of Ranke's historical writing. Its "principal and general thesis"[7] – "Everything is universal and individual spiritual life"[8] – expresses indeed Ranke's belongingness to the historical theology of the time of Goethe; it says nothing, however, about his position within this monstrous, broad, idealistic, total concept, which branched out widely in conflicting directions. The intellectual-historical place and the systematic meaning of Ranke's theory of history become clearer, only when one considers his dispute with Hegel's philosophy of history and with the historical empiricism of, above all, Barthold Niebuhr.

5 *Sämtliche Werke*, vol. 53/54, pp. 89-90.

6 C. HINRICHS: *Ranke und die Geschichtstheologie der Goethezeit*, Göttingen (Muster-Schmidt) 1954, pp. 113-14.

7 F. MEINECKE: *Die Entstehung des Historismus* (*Werke*, Vol. II), Munich (Oldenbourg) 1959, p. 592.

8 *Sämtliche Werke*, vol. 14/15, IX.

Ranke's extraordinarily complex relationship to Hegel[9] was governed by the historian's aversion to the philosopher's speculative and systematic process of "deriving" the particular from the universal by means of the dialectical method. Every attempt to comprehend the historical process from the logic of its laws of motion inevitably has the consequence, for Ranke, that the particular loses its "independent life" and degrades "all human persons" to mere "shadows and shavings."[10] The idea of progress – that "in each epoch the life of humanity elevates itself to a higher level, that consequently each generation completely surpasses the previous one, and thus the latest one is favored, while the preceding generations were only the bearers of the following generations" – contains "an injustice to the Deity."[11]

Ranke reinterpreted the Hegelian dialectic of the inter-penetration of the universal and the particular as a fixed relationship of dependence. Notwithstanding his claims and self-understanding, Hegel approaches a vulgar Enlightenment philosophy and is accused of "scholasticism," in which "life perishes."[12] Ranke's "historically active religiosity," or "religious historicism,"[13] first receives its specific historical character in its opposition to the undialectically interpreted philosophy of history of the Hegelian School.

Ranke reduced his concept of the originality of historical individuality to the classical formula of historicism: "Every epoch is immediate to God." It must be seen as something valid for itself, which has its value in its own existence and is not merely a transition stage in a process of development to a more complete state. From this perspective, the treatment of the individual life in history receives "a completely unique fascination." The task of the historian is to bring to light, first, "the particular tendency" and the "distinctive ideal" that each epoch possesses and, "secondly, also the difference between the individual epochs." In this way historical humanity in its entirety –

9 On the relationship between Ranke and Hegel, see especially E. SIMON: *Ranke und Hegel*, Munich (Oldenbourg) 1928. See also T. STEINBÜCHEL: "Ranke und Hegel", in: *Große Geschichtsdenker*, Tübingen (Wunderlich) 1949, pp. 173-215.

10 L.V. RANKE: *Über die Epochen der neueren Geschichte*, Historical-Critical Edition, ed. T. Schieder and H. Berding, Munich (Oldenbourg) 1971, p. 64.

11 *Ibid.*, p. 59.

12 *Ibid.*, p. 64.

13 G. MASUR: *Rankes Begriff der Weltgeschichte*, Munich (Oldenbourg) 1926, p. 61.

the divine idea in its full richness – comes into view.[14] By their direct relation to the divine, the individual epochs stand in a universal-historical relationship. They are also connected to one another by "an inner necessity of succession"; they are tied to one another "according to laws[!] that are unknown to us, more mysterious and greater than one imagines."[15]

Thus, for Ranke, history does not dissolve into a chaotic plurality of contextless phenomena. It is "not such an accidental state of nations and peoples rushing against one another, attacking one another, and succeeding one another,"[16] as historicism, detached from the foundation of faith and conceived radically to the end, later saw it, which led thinking about history into the theoretical cul-de-sac of relativism. While all later historians failed in avoiding the relativistic consequences of the principle of individuality, Ranke's view found its completion in a very living faith in Providence.[17] And indeed, for Ranke, historical individuality was already not only the starting point and the foundation, but also the ultimate end of historical knowledge. He did place the individual life in a universal-historical context, but as a *direct* relation to the divine, which cannot be comprehended and historically transmitted. He indeed maintained the law-ordered connection of the various epochs to one another, but at the same time denied that the law of motion can be fathomed. Ranke's historical thought is not an understanding consciousness. According to his own words, it is "ultimately sympathy, joint knowledge of the universe."[18]

Ranke, who was unable to accept Hegel's establishment of the unity of world history through the concept of spirit, but instead adhered to the idea of providential history, had to oppose the advocates of the historical school, who, according to a remark of Wilhelm Dilthey, could establish "no relation to universal history."[19] While the philosophy of history puts the significance of the factual and the unique existence of the individual in the system to flight, in specific empirical research, as Niebuhr pursued it, the universal perishes. History as empirical science runs the risk of losing itself in the details. Therefore, one must combine Niebuhr's method of particular research

14 *Über die Epochen der neueren Geschichte*, pp. 59 ff.

15 *Ibid.*, p. 67.

16 *Sämtliche Werke*, vol. 24, p. 93.

17 Cf. MASUR: pp. 66 ff.

18 *Sämtliche Werke*, vol. 53/54, p. 569.

19 W. DILTHEY: *Gesammelte Schriften*, vol. 7, Leipzig (Teubner) 1927, p. 99.

with Hegel's tendency to the universal: "Only one who unites the empirical with idea can refer to the spirit."[20]

According to Ranke's conception, uniting the empirical with the idea, or comprehending the individual event in its universal circumstance, is achieved by a specific historical kind of knowledge: understanding (*Verstehen*). The entirety of a process of development, the guiding tendency of an epoch, the dominant idea of a century, discloses itself to the historian in "divination," through "mental apperception." Through it one attains the view of the total-intellectual reality of an historical individuality.[21] Therefore – if one follows Ranke – historical research defends itself with the help of understanding from the blindness of historical empiricism, which merely registers facts, and simultaneously liberates itself from the philosophy of history's compulsion to construction: "History itself, not a philosophy of history that interprets itself, is called and enabled to elevate itself from the investigation and consideration of the particular to a universal view of events, to the knowledge of an objective, present context."[22]

The science of history, if it wishes to hold its ground against philosophy as an autonomous academic discipline and not be demoted to the insignificance of positivistic empiricism, must understand itself as a hermeneutic science. This conclusion, to be drawn from Ranke's critique of Hegel and Niebuhr, was shared by the historians of the nineteenth century almost without exception. Consequently, efforts to establish a theoretical foundation for the science of history – for instance with Johann Gustav Droysen, Wilhelm Dilthey, or Friedrich Meinecke – coincided to a great extent with philosophical hermeneutics. Ranke, who was no philosopher and never developed the theoretical foundations of his idea of history systematically, was unable to remove the concept of understanding "from the indefiniteness of aesthetic-pantheistic communion" and to formulate his conceptual presuppositions, as the more sharply thinking Droysen later attempted.[23]

For Ranke, understanding was a sort of intuitive comprehension of connections, and neither is capable of nor requires theoretical explanation, but is instead "based on an intellectuality that is present in each person, even if to

20 Cf. HINRICHS, pp. 106-7.

21 Cf. G. G. IGGERS: *Deutsche Geschichtswissenschaft*, Munich (dtv) 1971, pp. 106-7.

22 Cited from STEINBÜCHEL, pp. 187-88.

23 H. G. GADAMER: *Wahrheit und Methode*, Tübingen (Mohr) 1960, p. 199.

highly unequal degrees."[24] Consequently, understanding cannot be acquired methodologically. The central problem of historical knowledge is missing from the methodology of history. This remains restricted purely formally to the critical examination of the determination of facts, which must lead understanding and accompany it. Ranke is not completely innocent of the (profoundly anti-theoretical) attitude of many historians that attention to source-critical principles already guarantees the scientific character of history. What Ranke transmitted to the discipline of history, although in a formal-methodological respect, is fundamental for all serious historical research.

Following Niebuhr's *Roman History*, Ranke made the discipline of history familiar with the critical method of grasping the meaning of sources. The methodological principles of the philological critique of sources, which aim at producing reliable texts, examining their authenticity, and distinguishing that which is independent from that which is derived, were brought to general acceptance by him. They have belonged ever since to every historian's set of tools: "For the critical investigation and confirmation of historical facts, Ranke's method of teaching was effective almost epochally in Germany."[25] It also shaped the beginnings of academic history in the United States through his student George Bancroft, and was influential in England, especially through E. A. Freeman.

II. Claim to Objectivity

The endeavor to attain the objectivity and universal validity of the statement, free of all subjective influences, is the most characteristic feature of Rankean writing of history. The explanation of this concern is the historian's universal-historical interest in discovery. Since, according to Ranke's historical-theological axiom, no epoch contains the divine and eternal completely, but instead that which is not possible in any individual period will happen in all time periods, Ranke had to have the development of the full measure of the life inspired by the Divinity in view, and thus did not let his perspective

24 Cf. IGGERS: *op.cit.*, p. 106.

25 Cf. H.V. SYBEL: "Gedächtnisrede auf Leopold von Ranke", *Historische Zeitschrift*, 56 (1886), pp. 463-81.

be confined to any particular present interest. Ranke is supposed to have accomplished bringing the individual phases into view in empirical approximation by means of the source-critical method. Such an interpretation of the objective character of Rankean historical writing, derived from religious motivation, the universal-historical intention, and the formal historical method, can appeal to the demand for strict objectivity made again and again by Ranke himself.

Already in his book *Critique of Modern Historical Writing* – which appeared as an independent supplement to his first work, *Histories of the Latin and Teutonic Nations: 1494-1514* – Ranke did not assign history the role of "judging the past and telling the present generation how to improve the future," but instead of "merely telling how it really was."[26] In the introductions to his main works, Ranke repeatedly demanded strict objectivity. His *History of Prussia* seeks to "represent events as objectively as possible, without concern for the party attachments and hostilities of the present day."[27] His *History of France* has the goal of "attaining a view of the objective features of the great facts, beyond the opposing accusations of contemporaries and the often restricted view of later generations, through original and reliable sources of information."[28] Finally, in his *History of England*, Ranke writes the famous and oft-cited sentence: "I wanted to extinguish, as it were, myself, and only to let the things talk, to let the powerful forces appear."[29]

Ranke's frequently misunderstood claim to objectivity and the objective character of his historical writing derived from it by his followers are subjected to harsh critique from all sides. Only two years after Ranke's death, Ottokar Lorenz thanked everyone "opposed to the offensive gossip about Ranke's so-called objectivity, that prejudice, which has fed the imbecility of many epigones."[30] It is certainly easy to establish that Ranke's historical sphere and, consequently, also his endeavor for knowledge remained restricted, that he was not able to free himself from his political circumstances and social prepossessions, and that all these subjective conditions influenced his writing of history. Without doubt, the demand for objectivity and its realization diverge widely. Ranke, who was fully aware of this discrepancy, did

26 *Sämtliche Werke*, vol. 33/34, VII.
27 *Sämtliche Werke*, vol. 25/26, IX.
28 *Sämtliche Werke*, vol. 8/9, VIII.
29 *Sämtliche Werke*, vol. 15, p. 103.
30 O. LORENZ: *Leopold von Ranke*, Berlin (Hertz) 1891, p. 127.

not understand his concept of objectivity absolutely: "I establish an ideal here, which I will be told is unrealizable. Once again, this is how it is: the idea is immeasurable; the achievement, by its very nature, limited."[31] Ranke attributed the fact that the reality lags behind the ideal – in remarks that are certainly not well known – to both individually conditioned factors and the "influence of general life."[32] These reservations regarding the possibility of objective knowledge, which were obviously admitted only with regret and were nowhere expressed more carefully, do not essentially alter Ranke's conviction that the historian is quite capable of approaching the ideal of the objective representation of history, if he is guided by the will to objectivity, puts himself in the position of the object of his contemplation, and critically scrutinizes the correctness of the sources of the facts.

The possibility of "objective" historical writing, therefore, is tied to a method that includes a break with "all methods of rationalization and abstraction, of deriving things from conceptually comprehensible ideas,"[33] in other words, the renunciation of a universal theory. The science of history is in fact subject to a methodological restriction, by which both the way of seeing and the way of thinking are limited and the interest in discovery is also steered in a particular direction. Wide regions of historical reality remain excluded from the contemplation of history, so that all objectivity is called into question by the very method that is supposed to guarantee it. The true problematic of Ranke's "objective" writing of history is found here, and not so much in the direct influence of the political in the narrower sense on his picture of history. Ranke's methodological principles and the ideas of historical objectivity derived from them have continued to be influential, while his concrete political convictions, which have likewise become effective historiographically, have met with less sympathy in the German science of history.

Consistently with his methodological premises, Ranke started from the belief that the dominant tendencies or leading ideas of an epoch cannot be "proven, conceptually established," but can "only be described."[34] For this reason, the analysis of the "real-mental" circumstances or structures behind

---

31 *Sämtliche Werke*, vol. 21, p. 114.

32 Cf. G. Berg: *Leopold von Ranke als akademischer Lehrer*, Göttingen (Vandenhoeck & Ruprecht) 1968, p. 193.

33 F. Meinecke: *Die Idee der Staatsräson* (*Werke*, vol. I), 3rd. ed., Munich (Oldenbourg) 1963, p. 450.

34 *Über die Epochen der neueren Geschichte*, p. 66.

the description of the historical event must step back. Indeed, Ranke by no means underestimated the power of long processes. He referred again and again to the "characteristic of things," the "great course of events," the "necessity of things," but did not investigate them. He considered it both unnecessary and impossible to trace political events back to them. His depictions give cross-sections of pictures, not structural analyses. The critique has taken this decisive element of Rankean historiography as its starting point. It has, in so far as it has itself started from idealistic presuppositions, accused Ranke of deficient analysis of intellectual relationships of influence.

Count Paul Yorck von Wartenburg, for instance, called Ranke "a great eye-piece," for whom the stuff of history melts into "a fluctuation of forces increasing in shape."[35] Also Dilthey, who reproached Ranke for standing still "in front of analysis and conceptual thought about the connections that are effective in history,"[36] took aim at the missing analysis of intellectual relationships of influence.[37] This critique experiences a modification when it is conducted from the social-historical perspective. Social-scientifically oriented history complains that the ocular way of contemplating retreats in the face of the analysis of economic-social structures. While the generalizing method of the philosophical contemplation of history and the quantifying method of the social sciences all too easily abstract from that which emphasizes the character of the historical event as a superficial happening, the understanding method of the ocular contemplation of history cuts historical reality short in the aspect of the connections of influence, or structures.

The science of history, which contents itself for methodological reasons, for the sake of objectivity, with reproducing the life that has disappeared, runs into danger in an additional respect, the danger of excluding significant elements of historical reality from its field of vision. By restricting itself to the descriptive representation of singular phenomena, it directs the interest of history towards those historical forces that have gained the advantage in confrontation with others and have stood their ground against them. The dominant tendencies of an epoch become the object of historical description; the forces countering them recede into the background. Because it does not per-

---

35 *Briefwechsel zwischen W. Dilthey und dem Grafen P. Yorck von Wartenburg, 1877-1897*, Halle (Niemeyer)1923, pp. 51 ff.

36 DILTHEY: *op.cit.*, p. 101.

37 Cf. H. FREYER: *Weltgeschichte Europas*, Stuttgart (Deutscher Verlagsanstalt), 2nd ed., 1954, pp. 80 ff.

mit the methodological strictness of empirical-realistic historical research, history must renounce the task of critically distinguish from the wealth of possibilities of an historical situation those that have been realized, of questioning the price of the actual development, and of discussing the alternatives to it.

On the contrary, descriptive historiography assumes that the dominant forces are the only one with historical deep-rootedness. Only they have a claim to legitimacy. This conservative characteristic of the understanding science of history, which does not emerge from its theoretical-methodological assumptions without internal logic, is also conspicuous with Ranke. Nietzsche already attacked his "clever indulgence of strength" and called him, as always bitingly and mockingly, an "*advocatus* of every *causa fortior*."[38] Even the student of Ranke, Jacob Burckhard, opposed the general weakness of the historian: the justification of historical forces, because they exist, and accordingly the justification of historical events, because they happened: "Thus he directly opposed Ranke's view of history, which was based on given facts and justified individual realities by spiritualizing them."[39]

III. In the Name of History: Historical and Political Conservatism

Ranke's historical writing, with a basic disposition that was demonstrably conservative even in theoretical and methodological respects, developed during a time in which awareness of continuity was interrupted and traditional intellectual-political total existence was called into question. In the French Revolution, which was prepared intellectually by the Enlightenment, the attempt was made for the first time to establish an order of reason according to rationally conceived principles in the place of the organic, traditional order. Through the end of the Revolution in France and the defeat of the Napoleonic domination of Europe, political romanticism's conviction that it could not succeed in arranging the world "unhistorically" and according to reason as-

38 F. NIETZSCHE: *Werke*, ed. K. Schlechta, Munich (Hanser) 1955, vol. II, p. 879.

39 E. SCHULIN: *Die weltgeschichtliche Erfassung des Orients bei Hegel und Ranke*, Göttingen (Vandenhoeck & Ruprecht) 1958, p. 291.

serted itself against political rationalism, especially in Germany. History and historical knowledge were called upon and appealed to by the defenders of the old as an intellectual-political power against the idea of the liberal state and constitution.[40]

Even Ranke gave his historical studies, which "actually developed in opposition to the dictatorship of Napoleonic Ideas,"[41] a particular political orientation in the sense of political romanticism. From the beginning, the religiously based change of direction towards history was accompanied by political intentions. After the Neoplatonic-idealist theology of history, political romanticism must be seen as the second great epoch-conditioned factor of Rankean historical thought. Ranke summoned history as an intellectual-political power against the threat to the closed, Lutheran, authoritarian-state life-world of his origin from the French Revolution and its consequences. Everything that threatened to break up the patriarchal-hierarchical structure of society of the pre-revolutionary period was rejected in the name of history.

The fact that history could be called in against the revolutionary changes following the French Revolution is related to two assumptions that Ranke shared with political romanticism. First, the revolutionary upheavals were not traced back to the profound economic and social change that the emergence of bourgeois society hastened as an historical process, but were instead interpreted as consequences of intellectual potencies: as the work of Enlightenment thought. Second, the Enlightenment was not regarded as a current of thought that grew out of the entire historical process, but was instead left out of the tradition-context and understood as an ahistorical power. Ranke did not grant the "mania of improving the people and of the will to destroy everything existing,"[42] which had spread to Germany with Napoleon's rule, the same historical legitimacy as the counterrevolutionary theories of the organic developedness of the historical world. Because the Enlightenment called the traditional order into question and judged it according to its idea of a liberal, bourgeois society, it appeared to him as the "despotism of biased theory."[43] If the revolutionary principle were to gain the upper hand, if monarchy were to fail to "eradicate the destructive tendencies that were washed in from the

40 Cf. SCHIEDER: *op.cit.*, p. 108.

41 *Sämtliche Werke*, vol. 53/54, p. 47.

42 *Über die Epochen der neueren Geschichte*, p. 433.

43 *Sämtliche Werke*, Vol. 53/54, p. 197.

popular principles like a great flood,"[44] then the entirety of European culture and Christianity would be threatened.

Ranke compensated for the deep-rooted fear of revolution, which accompanied him – as well as the entire conservative and also liberal middle class of the nineteenth century – in his political opinions, with his religious faith in history and in the inertia of the old powers. Without ever doubting his conservative position, he also saw a positive factor in the "clash of the two principles, monarchy and sovereignty of the people, with which all other conflicts are connected." It contained "an enormous movement and at the same time a great life-element."[45] Ranke granted the revolutionary principle of the sovereignty of the people, and the related revolutionary principle of national sovereignty as ferment, a partial legitimacy, as long as these principles did not work towards the subversion of what exists, but instead allowed themselves to be "integrated" by the powers of the old order – as did the Prussian Reform Party. The overcoming of the revolutionary principle by the monarchical principle at the time of the restoration was on the whole successful, in Ranke's opinion, even if it was also repeatedly threatened.

Ranke never made a secret of the fact that he stood fundamentally on the side of the Prussian monarchy and the social order embodied by it. After his home city became part of Prussia in 1815, Ranke entered Prussian service as a secondary school teacher in Frankfurt on the Oder in 1818. And after the Prussian state had granted him an excellent social position as a university professor in Berlin in 1825, he felt that in principle agreement with the reigning political and social system of the Prussian monarchy was "necessary for happiness and life."[46] This declaration of belief in the Prussian state meant the Prussia of Friedrich Wilhelm IV in his early years, which was just as remote from the old Prussianness as from the new Prussianness of liberalism and the later "realpolitik."[47] He saw individual liberties and social justice as guaranteed in it by the state – by the social reform policy of the existing government on the basis of its insight into the necessity of social requirements.

Soon after the Revolution of 1830, Ranke took over the editorship of the *Historisch-Politische Zeitschrift*, which was founded by the then Prussian

---

44 *Über die Epochen der neueren Geschichte*, p. 444.

45 *Ibid.*, pp. 441 and 444.

46 L.V. RANKE, *Das Briefwerk*, ed. W. P. Fuchs, Hamburg (Hoffmann & Campe) 1949, p. 308.

47 VIERHAUS: *op.cit.*, p. 19.

Foreign Minister Count Christian Günther von Bernstorff, and which was an organ for the defense of the policies of the enlightened Prussian bureaucracy against the liberal critique of the Left and the reactionary opposition of the *Berliner Politische Wochenblatt*. Although Ranke endeavored "to articulate a third trend, referring to the existing order, between the two opposing trends,"[48] his attacks were almost exclusively against liberalism. He reproached it for applying abstract principles to politics, as he reproached philosophy for applying abstract principles to history. In contrast to liberalism and universal theory, Ranke promoted the idea of individuality: every state has its own inner life and its own principle. It had to follow the direction prescribed by history – thus the path trod by official Prussian governmental policy. It alone embodied the historically legitimated "Prussian Protestant Principle," while the opposing forces, namely the liberal movement, were excluded from the tradition-web of Prussian history and were represented as the embodiment of abstract (i.e. unhistorical) principles. From this conception of individual, historical growth, it followed that liberal institutions that developed elsewhere were useless for Prussia. In France, the unfortunate consequence of grafting on foreign (i.e. English and North American) ideas to traditional institutions has revealed itself. Everything good in Germany since the French Enlightenment originated, not in emulation of, but rather in opposition to, French ideas.[49]

Ranke's basic political views, which had become concretized during his activity as a political commentator in the *Historisch-Politische Zeitschrift* from 1832 to 1836, remained unchanged in principle. After the resignation of Friedrich Wilhelm IV in 1857, Ranke withdrew completely to his historical work and also distanced himself inwardly from Prussian politics, without ever opposing it openly. He lamented the insufficiently strong resistance of the monarchy to the demands of the liberals. Ranke saw the political and social ascent of the middle class as inevitable after 1848, but did not welcome it. Bismarck's alliance with the liberals appeared disastrous to him, since it would sweep aside "all rules that had previously prevented the thronging of a propertyless crowd."[50] Ranke developed an unreservedly positive relationship with Bismarck's nation state, whose emergence he had observed from a cool distance, only after he became convinced "that in Bismarck the power of

48 *Sämtliche Werke*, vol. 53/54, p. 50.

49 *Sämtliche Werke*, Vol. 49/50, p. 41. Cf. IGGERS: *op.cit.*, pp. 99-100.

50 Cited from W. MOMMSEN: *Stein – Ranke – Bismarck*, Munich, 1954, p. 113.

preserving is greater than that of rebuilding and that the Chancellor would once again return to the old conditions of a traditional world."[51]

With the integration of the middle class into the order of the traditional state, and of the German nation state into the concert of the European powers, every break of continuity that had threatened history since the Enlightenment and the French Revolution was once again repaired for Ranke. The mutually inconsistent principles of the time of revolution – monarchy vs. sovereignty of the people and national sovereignty – were brought together. In their mutual intertwining, they could be seen as different developments of the same one and indivisible history, in which the working, divine spirit manifests itself. Ranke seemed once again to be in full agreement with his central historical-theological idea, which grants to every trend in history its legitimacy, which allows rising above the contradiction of the time and bringing the whole of history to view "objectively." He commenced, when the nationalistic historical writing reached its high point, the realization of the universal-historical intentions of his early years and wrote his *Universal History*.

Ranke did not identify his historical writing with absolutized particular interest, as did the liberal-national historians of the Borussian School. He did not understand it as the national-pedagogical mission of creating for the small-German nation state a consciousness of tradition anchored in Prussian history. He was prevented from political historical writing in the national sense or the glorification of the Prussian-German power state by the religious commitments, directed towards universality, of his thought. Although Ranke towered above the national-liberal historians on the basis of his universal-historical perspective and his more cautious and more careful assessment of contemporary political debates, he had at the same time less understanding of and more resolute disapproval of the progressive trends of his time than the national-liberals, because his political ideas remained trapped in the pre-revolutionary European power system of the sixteenth-eighteenth centuries and the political-absolutist and social-patriarchal order corresponding to it. In all periods of his historiographical work, the historical-theological character of his historical thought was overlaid by the political-romantic character, and even suppressed in his theory of the present. For that reason, Ranke depicted the historical, explosive power of the rising bourgeois society only negatively. He saw in the technical-scientific, economic, social, political, and intellectual development of the nascent industrial age only the effectiveness of destructive

51 *Ibid.*, p. 113.

tendencies.[52] In the failure to recognize its positive-progressive significance and in the underestimating of its historical-power are also found the limits of Ranke's historical writing.

Ranke failed to appreciate the significance of economic and social forces in history. The critics of his historical writing have repeatedly made this point. Rudolf Vierhaus has responded to those who have expanded this critique as far as the verdict that the entirety of the economic and social spheres is lacking or appears only peripherally in Ranke. His research has corrected some biases of the traditional picture of Ranke, but is nevertheless unable to change it. Ranke's historical view was primarily directed towards the governmental-political order. Social factors were considered only at particular points, when they intervened visibly in political events and reshaped the political order. They were never the objects of social-historical analysis that would have subtly investigated the social classes and their constant influences on political conditions. The connection between political constitution and social structure remained in the dark.[53] Ranke's disregard of the economic-social sphere was undoubtedly influenced by the kind of sources that he used. Whether it was Venetian relations, *Reichstagsakten*, or documents, the historian was always confronted in them by the political world, and thus by the "public life of the past," whose depiction Ranke saw as the task of history.[54] The choice of sources, however, is not the cause, but the effect of the orientation of Ranke's research interests on the political-governmental order.

Because of the Neoplatonic-idealist and political-romantic presuppositions of his thought, Ranke tied his historical research to a method that prevented him from taking up the remarkable social-historical, constitutional-historical, legal-historical, and economic-historical specialized research that already existed in Germany at that time.[55] In order to overcome the narrowing in perspective of the specialized research and to clear the view of the totality of historical events, he equated historical recognition with understanding. The originally religious motive was penetrated by an aesthetic interest in the richness of historical phenomena, which had to bring the historical depiction to

---

52 Cf. J. RÜSEN: "Technik und Geschichte in der Tradition der Geisteswissenschaften – Geistesgeschichtliche Anmerkungen zu einem theoretischen Problem", *Historische Zeitschrift*, 211 (1970), pp. 529-55.

53 VIERHAUS: *op.cit.*, p. 222.

54 *Ibid.*, p. 131.

55 *Ibid.*, p. 129.

contemplation in artistic after-shaping for the enrichment of the represented subject. Under the influence of this idea of the educated middle class, which was deprived of its religious meaning by Ranke's successors and transformed into the discriminating and exclusive, the writing of history in Germany reached a high point in respect and effect.

The outstanding significance of Ranke for the German science of history and its elevation to the status of a primary force in education is indisputable. Even his critics do not deny this. It is precisely they who tend instead to raise Ranke's position excessively. That is especially true of many Anglo-Saxon and Marxist interpretations. They see, as from a more distant vantage point, the entire official German discipline of history as a unified block, built on the foundation of Ranke's historical thought. Just as the foundation appears from this perspective to be crumbling, so does the building erected on it: theoretically feeble, conservative and authoritarian in terms of history and politics, and without relationship to the economic and social bases of historical movement. Viewed somewhat more closely, the picture looks more complex. As justified as the critique is, Ranke himself deserves a more carefully weighed assessment. His scholarly ethos, his sense of the unique and incomparable aspect of an historical situation that cannot be completely squeezed into uniform and typical historical processes, and his universal-historical orientation to the totality of the historical sequence of events are indispensable elements of historical discovery.

It should also not be overlooked that in addition to the Small-German school, the Ranke renaissance of Max Lenz and Erich Marcks that arose against it, and Friedrich Meinecke's history of ideas movement – currents that can be traced back to a great extent, at least methodologically, to Ranke – the liberal historical writing around Georg Gottfried Gervinus, the economic school around Gustav Schmoller, and the cultural-historical school around Karl Lamprecht in the German discipline of history could hold their own, even if with less resonance. With this reservation, which is certainly significant, one nevertheless cannot deny, when reflecting critically on the history of the German academic discipline of history, that the historical method developed by Ranke, with its idealist-romantic assumptions, its political implications, and its consequences for the relationship of history to economics and social science, has had greater impact than any other influence. Only since the Second World War has the science of history in West Germany begun to distance itself from this tradition and to approach a theoretical-methodological pluralism that opens up new paths to the survey of always-complex economic-social-political reality.

Translated from the German by David W. Lutz

Chapter 4

Droysen and Nietzsche: Two Different Answers to the Discovery of Historicity

ANNETTE WITTKAU-HORGBY

I. Droysen's Concept and Epistemology of the Science of History
II. Nietzsche's Critical Approach to History: On the Use and Abuse of History
III. Strengths and Weaknesses of Droysen's and Nietzsche's Concepts

Since the end of the 18th century, there have been fundamental changes in the political, economic and social order of Western Europe. In Germany especially, many aspects of the political life, social structure, legal system and economic order changed as a result of the French Revolution, the Napoleonic Wars and the subsequent Restoration period.[1] Parallel to the practical experience of such changes and as its theoretical counterpart, European scholars in general and German scholars in particular began to pay more and more attention to the historical dimension of reality. In the 19th century, philosophers and historians, especially in Germany, tried to explain these changes and thus to help cope with the feeling of instability experienced in almost every sphere of life. In 1868, Jacob Burckhardt[2] described the relationship between the experience of a crisis and the increasing interest in history[3] in his famous book "On the Study of History"[4] as follows:

---

1 NIPPERDEY (1983, p. 11).
2 HARDTWIG (1974) and HARDTWIG (1988).
3 RAULET (1996, p. 29).
4 BURCKHARDT (1868).

> The eternal change of time never ceases to carry off with it the forms which shape the outer garment of life. The enormous changes since the 18th century contain something which compels us to look at and investigate former and present conditions [...] A troubled period such as these eighty-three years of the Age of Revolution must create its own counterweight, if it does not want to lose all consciousness.[5]

At roughly the same time, Johann Gustav Droysen and Friedrich Nietzsche[6] were also contemplating the origins and consequences of the increasing interest in history. They were contemporaries, but belonged to two different generations, and they developed two fundamentally different concepts of how to deal with the discovery of historicity.

In this paper I wish to present a rough summary of both concepts (part I and II) and then to compare them (part III). My thesis is that on the one hand both positions contain a certain amount of truth, but that on the other hand they are both deficient in some respects. It is the combination of the two positions in a complementary sense that provides an adequate answer to the discovery of historicity.

I. Droysen's Concept and Epistemology of the Science of History

From the end of the 18th century and the beginning of the 19th century onwards, the investigation of the past became *scientific*. Scholars started to investigate the historical genesis and development of all kinds of cultural phenomena. Historical sources and other historical material relating to cultural phenomena such as economics, law, music and art were used for empirical research. The figure of 'historical development' ('*historische Entwick-*

5 BURCKHARDT (1868, p. 107); "Der beständige Wandel der Zeiten rafft die Formen, welche das äußere Gewand des Lebens bilden, unaufhörlich mit sich." "Die gewaltigen änderungen seit dem Ende des 18. Jahrhunderts (haben) etwas in sich, was zur Betrachtung und Erforschung des Früheren und Seitherigen gebieterisch zwingt ... Eine bewegte Periode wie diese dreiundachtzig Jahre Revolutionszeitalter, wenn sie nicht alle Besinnung verlieren soll, muß sich ein solches Gegengewicht schaffen." BURCKHARDT (1929-1934, vol. 7, p. 11).

6 OEXLE (1996, p. 75).

lung') became an important and widely used type of explanation. In the disciplines of law and economics, the important so-called 'Historical School' emerged in Germany at this time. But in spite of all these scientific approaches to the history of law, economics, music or art in the first half of the 19th century, no *epistemology* of the historical science had yet been developed. In the prefaces to several historical studies, such as those of Ranke, Niebuhr, Savigny and Roscher, there were numerous remarks on how to investigate cultural phenomena in a scientific manner, but a systematic epistemology of the historical science did not yet exist.

In 1857, the historian Johann Gustav Droysen presented a first attempt at such an epistemology of the science of history. In his lecture called *Historik*, published in 1868,[7] he attempted to analyse what it meant to deal with history in the manner of an empirical science.

Droysen (1808-1886) had studied in Berlin under Hegel and August Boeckh. In 1831, he wrote his doctoral dissertation and two years later, in 1833, he submitted his habilitation thesis, thus becoming qualified in the field of classic philology. He received a professorial chair in Kiel in 1840, moving in 1851 to the university of Jena and finally to Berlin, where he was offered a professorial post in 1859.[8] He first delivered his lectures on history as an empirical science in Jena, repeating it frequently in Berlin, 17 times altogether.[9] None of his lectures was delivered as often as this one. But in no other lecture did he have fewer students.[10]

These lectures have been preserved in the shape of Droysen's manuscript as well as of hand-written notes taken by Droysen's students and, finally, in the shape of Droysen's own manuscript intended for printing. These different versions were edited in a critical edition in 1977.[11] And in spite of the fact that Droysen's reflections went almost unnoticed in his time, they formed "a pioneering achievement in science",[12] which was acknowledged with great acclaim several years later. Droysen himself was well aware of the fact that he

---

7 LEYH (Preface to DROYSEN, 1977, p. XIV).

8 Regarding Droysen's biography see the biography written by his son GUSTAV DROYSEN (1919) as well as OBERMANN (1977).

9 LEYH (Introduction to the Critical Edition of DROYSEN's *Historik*, 1977, p. IX).

10 LEYH (1977, p. IX).

11 LEYH (1977).

12 LEYH (1977, p. IX).

was fighting on a completely new front. In the preface to this lecture he writes:

> Everyone has a rough idea of what history and historiography are, of how to study history. But currently our science itself has no more than this rough idea. ... I undertake to present you a discipline which does not yet exist, nor does it yet have a name or precise place among the sciences. We first have to prove that it is possible to treat it scientifically.[13] The '*Historik*' is intended to be the organon of our science, the epistemology for history, as it were ... It must enable us to do those things which are ... already being done instinctively, but now doing them conscious of means and purpose. It must contain the scientific justification of our studies and it has to give answers to those questions which until now were solved in a practical manner, but which it has been left to who knows which disciplines to answer theoretically.[14]

While Burckhardt had argued that it was the rapid change in the "outer garment of life" that had caused the greater interest in history, Droysen chose a different starting point for his reasoning. He basically agreed with Burckhardt that the current changes were probably extraordinary in respect of their speed and, maybe, their fundamental nature. But changes and development, so Droysen argued, were not generally extraordinary. On the contrary, they were necessary and essential to human existence. The actual reason for the growth in historical interest was, therefore, not only to be found in the experience of a crisis, but, even more fundamental, was to be seen as rooted in the experience of the historicity of individual human existence.

---

13 DROYSEN (1977, p. 3). "Jeder hat eine ungefähre Vorstellung davon, was Geschichte und Geschichtsschreibung, was Studium der Geschichte ist. Aber mehr als diese ungefähre Vorstellung hat bisher auch unsere Wissenschaft nicht ... Ich unternehme es, Ihnen eine Disziplin vorzutragen, die bisher noch nicht existiert, noch keinen Namen, keine Stelle in dem Kreise der Wissenschaften hat."

14 DROYSEN (1977, p. 44). "Die Historik soll das organon für unsere Wissenschaft sein, gleichsam die Wissenschaftslehre der Geschichte ...; sie muß uns in den Stand setzten, das, was ... fort und fort instinktmäßig getan wird, im Bewußtsein der Mittel und Zwecke zu tun: Sie muß die wissenschaftliche Rechtfertigung unseres Studiums enthalten und auf die Fragen Antwort geben, die man bisher wohl praktisch löste, aber theoretisch wer weiß welchen anderen Wissenschaften zu beantworten überließ."

Not only man's culture had a history, it was man himself who was actually a historical being. The historian as a human being, so Droysen argued, was deeply connected with history. This connection, however, gave rise to a special relationship between subject and object in the epistemological process. The historian did not only *face* history as an object to be investigated scientifically, *his own life and existence were deeply rooted in history itself.* He "is in history and history is in him."[15] There was an essential relationship between the subject and object of historical perception.

> From the moment of his birth, of his conception even, incalculable historical factors start to influence him (i.e. man). In a still unconscious state, he receives a wealth of influences from his parents, from their physical and mental disposition ... He is born into the whole historical circumstances of his people, language, religion, state and so on. And it is only by taking in and imbibing these factors which he found at birth, learning the infinite, without knowing it – it is only by doing this that he lives more than an animal, a human life.[16]

It was this awareness of the historicity of one's own existence that according to Droysen formed the actual reason for the interest in history.

> Here we have the point which lends our science its specific meaning. We see it dealing with a task which belongs essentially to human nature ... The historical world is essentially the human world ... The human world is of a thoroughly historical nature, and this is what specifically distinguishes it from the natural world.[17]

---

15 DROYSEN (1977, p. 14).

16 DROYSEN (1977, p. 14). "Von dem Moment seiner Geburt, ja seiner Empfängnis an, wirken unberechenbare historische Faktoren auf ihn (d.i. den Menschen) ein, bewußtlos noch empfängt er die Fülle von Einwirkungen seiner Eltern, ihrer leiblichen und geistigen Disposition ... Er wird hineingeboren in die ganze historische Gegebenheit seines Volkes, seiner Sprache, seiner Religion, seines Staates usw.; und erst dadurch, daß er das so Vorgefundene, Unendliches lernend, ohne es selbst zu wissen in sich nimmt und verinnerlicht, ... erst dadurch hat er ein mehr als tierisches, ein menschliches Leben."

17 DROYSEN (1977, p. 14). "Hier haben wir den Punkt, der unserer Wissenschaft ihre eigentümliche Bedeutung gibt. Wir sehen sie mit einer Aufgabe beschäftigt, die spezifisch der menschlichen Natur ... angehört; die geschichtliche Welt ist die wesentlich menschliche ... Die Menschenwelt ist durch und durch geschichtlicher Natur, und das ist ihr spezifischer Unterschied von der natürlichen Welt."

Human nature is essentially an historical one, and thus the consciousness of the historicity of the historian's own existence and the interest in history form a unity. Furthermore, the discovery of the historicity of one's own existence forms, according to Droysen, the presupposition for historical understanding.

> Historical investigation presupposes the insight into the fact that the contents of our personality are also a multiply transposed, an historical result.[18]

This essential connection between the subject and the object of perception constitutes the specific character of historical perception. Historical perception is fundamentally different from those forms of scientific research we know from the natural sciences. The historian cannot analyse the past simply as an object. As he is dealing with materials and thoughts which have been created by human beings, he basically has the task of *understanding* the meaning of those relicts of the past which he is investigating.[19]

> The essence of the historical method is to understand by way of research.[20]

Droysen had already drawn attention to this specific dimension of historical perception.[21] Understanding is in his view the core of historical research. When Wilhelm Dilthey later took up this point, he elaborated in detail the importance of understanding the object for the '*Geisteswissenschaften*', as they were then called. Understanding the past is already an important point in Droysen's concept, but it is nevertheless only one of a number of aspects. In contrast to Dilthey, who placed great emphasis on the fundamental difference between the natural sciences (*Naturwissenschaften*) and the humanities (*Geisteswissenschaften*), Droysen stresses the fact that the general scientific approach to the sciences and to history is the same.[22] For in spite of the fact

---

18 DROYSEN (1977, p. 399). "Das historische Forschen setzt die Einsicht voraus, daЯ auch der Inhalt unseres Ich ein vielfach vermittelter, ein geschichtliches Resultat ist."

19 LEYH (1977, p. XI).

20 DROYSEN (1977, p. 398). "Das Wesen der historischen Methode ist forschend zu verstehen."

21 Droysen talked about this problem explicitly in a separate chapter of his 'Historik'. See DROYSEN (1977, p. 22).

22 OEXLE (1996, p. 42).

that the subject and object of historical perception are inseparably connected, historical perception itself is not arbitrary. According to Droysen, history is nevertheless an empirical science.[23] It is an empirical science because it bases and relates all hypotheses about the past to visible and thus empirical material which is still to be found in the present. This empirical way of treating questions is something that the natural and historical sciences have in common.

> The first step towards a correct historical perception is the insight that historical perception deals with the presence of material. This can be authors, acts, documents, monuments, laws ... material of all kinds, and we know that the origins of this material reach back into the past ... but we still find them in the present. And it is only because they are still present that we can ... use them as material for scientific historical investigation.[24]

Again and again, Droysen stresses the point that the basis of scientific historical research is the existence of historical material in the present times. If no sources or other material were to exist as witnesses of the past, scientific historical perception would not be possible. The past itself is gone. What is left is historical material which has survived up to the present.

> Historical research is aware of the fact that it is dealing with material which is part of the present. This material forms the point from which the historian goes back into the past; or, to be more precise, historical research takes up this point in the present and traces it back into the past by analysing and interpreting the material which has its origins in the past. Thus, historical research draws an imaginary picture of the past which would remain dead if historical research did not take up this point in the present.[25]

In this scientific process of an imaginary reconstruction of the past, the hypothesis is of central importance. In analogy to the natural scientist, the historian develops a hypothesis regarding the past and analyses his material, starting with a concrete question.

> Research is concretely looking for something. It is not merely a question of finding by chance. One has to know what one is looking for,

23 LEYH (1977, p. XII).
24 DROYSEN (1977, p. 9).
25 DROYSEN (1977, p. 9).

> otherwise one cannot find anything. One has to ask things in the right way, then they will answer.[26]

As regards his epistemological concept of history as an empirical science Droysen basically argues in the Kantian tradition. However, he integrates this concept within a Hegelian[27] view of the philosophy of history.[28] He is in no doubt that it is moral ideas which actually constitute the driving force of history.[29]

Thus, as Droysen sees it, the meaning and sense of history are generally intelligible. They do not present major problems. Since Droysen follows Hegel in relation to the philosophical interpretation of history, the science of history does not basically present problems either.

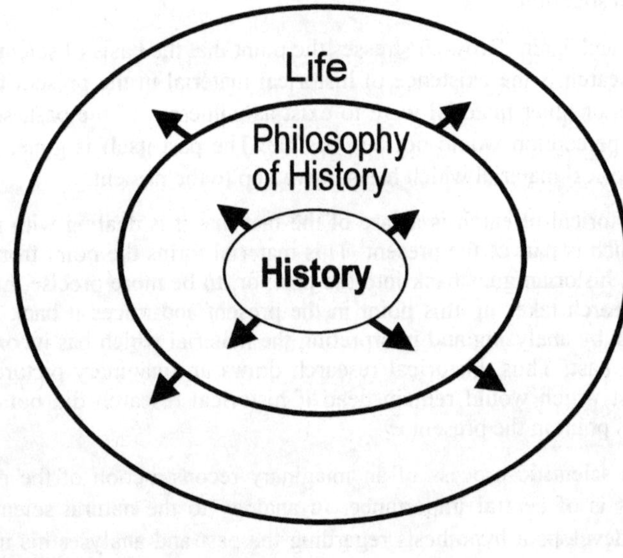

Fig. 1: Droysen's conception of the relationship of history and life

26 DROYSEN (1977, p. 58). "Die Forschung sucht etwas, sie ist nicht auf ein bloß zufälliges Finden gestellt; man muß zuerst wissen, was man suchen will, erst dann kann man finden; man muß die Dinge richtig fragen, dann antworten sie."

27 HARDTWIG (1991, p. 5).

28 DROYSEN (1977, p. 194).

29 DROYSEN (1977, p. 424).

Droysen's epistemological concept of history as an empirical science was itself extremely modern, although it was embedded in the frame of Hegel's philosophy of history, which by that time was already out of fashion.[30] Droysen's epistemology provided the basis for a discussion about the use and abuse of history which started at the beginning of the 1870s and which was to occupy the historical sciences for more than three decades.[31]

II. Nietzsche's Critical Approach to History: On the Use and Abuse of History

Droysen regarded the scientific approach to history as a great achievement. According to him the historical sciences helped to solve problems essential to human existence. Nietzsche did not agree at all in this respect. On the contrary, he regarded the same phenomenon of historicising thought as extremely dangerous. In 1874, only six years after Droysen's publication of the *Historik*, Nietzsche published the second of his *Unzeitgemäße Betrachtungen* under the title of *Vom Nutzen und Nachteil der Historie für das Leben*, 'On the Use and Abuse of History'. Here, he pointed out the negative effects of the scientific approach to history on the practical conduct of life in contemporary society as well as for the lives of the historians.

Nietzsche (1844-1900) had studied theology and classical philology in Bonn and Leipzig from 1864 to 1868. In 1869, at the age of 25 years, he became Professor of Classical Philology at the university of Basle. There he met Jacob Burckhardt who was Professor of History at the same university. In the winter 1870/1871 or 1871/1872, Nietzsche attended Burckhardt's lecture "On the Study of History",[32] which later became popular under the title *Weltgeschichtliche Betrachtungen*. As an admirer of Burckhardt,[33] he was undoubtedly inspired by him to his own thoughts on this problem, and a few years later, in 1874, he published his reflections in the treatise *On the Use and Abuse of History*.

30 WITTKAU (1994, p. 33).
31 WITTKAU (1994, p. 61).
32 GANZ (1982, p. 54) Introduction to BURCKHARDT.
33 GANZ (1982, p. 56).

Nietzsche distinguished clearly between history as an empirical science and the philosophy of history. He showed that there was no relationship between the two which was systematically necessary. Therefore, he looked at both forms of historical understanding separately.

On the one hand, he was critical of the philosophy of history, especially of Hegel's concept. Nietzsche was not convinced by Hegel's philosophy of history at all.[34] He regarded it as both speculative and arbitrary. Nietzsche criticised Hegel's claim that his concept of a philosophy of history was necessary as utter nonsense.[35] His main argument against Hegel's concept was that this philosophy did great damage to practical life because it implied that the climax of history had already been fulfilled by Hegel's own philosophy. The generations after Hegel thus had no choice but to regard themselves as mere epigones. According to Nietzsche this attitude caused an anxiety and uncertainty which prevented people from actively shaping their own historical period.

> For Hegel the climax and final goal of the world process coincided with his own existence in Berlin … In fact, he should have said that all things to come after him would essentially be nothing more than a musical coda to the world history's rondo, indeed that they were to be regarded as superfluous. He did not say this, instead he has instilled in the ... generations after him, made sour by his philosophy, an admiration for the 'power of history' which in effect turns ... into an unconcealed admiration of success and to the worship of reality, of the way things are.[36]

Nietzsche's intention was to completely liberate historical thinking from such philosophical misinterpretation. He detached history as an empirical science from this philosophical framework. Nevertheless, Nietzsche was not

34 NIETZSCHE (1874, p. 304).

35 NIETZSCHE (1874, p. 304).

36 NIETZSCHE (1874, p. 304). "Für Hegel (fielen) der Höhepunkt und der Endpunkt des Weltprozesses in seiner eigenen Berliner Existenz zusammen ... Ja, er hätte sagen müssen, dass alle nach ihm kommenden Dinge eigentlich nur als musikalische Coda des weltgeschichtlichen Rondos, noch eigentlicher als überflüssig zu schätzen seien. Das hat er nicht gesagt: dafür hat er in die von ihm durchsäuerten Generationen jene Bewunderung vor der 'Macht der Geschichte' gepflanzt, die praktisch ... in nackte Bewunderung des Erfolges umschlägt und zum Götzendienst des Thatsächlichen führt."

satisfied with the scientific form of historical perception either, showing that the present form of history as an empirical science was dangerous, too. While Hegel's philosophy of history had the conservative effect of making people admire success and worship reality, Nietzsche's main point of criticism as regards the scientific form of historical perception was that it made people inactive and uneasy. According to Nietzsche, the scientific form of historical perception overwhelmed people with historical facts and material on the one hand,[37] with the practical result that it hindered people from actively shaping their lives in the present. On the other hand, and this was even worse, history as an empirical science had the effect of making values appear relative, thus causing uncertainty in every kind of activity in practical life.

Nietzsche showed that when compared with older forms of history, the modern scientific form of historical perception had started to develop a life of its own. People were no longer asking about the relevance of historical reflection for their present lives, the historians as well as the society in general had simply started to take for granted the fact that historical research was valuable and important.

> Let us take a quick look at our own times! We are amazed ... Where has all the clarity, all naturalness and purity in that relationship between life and history gone? ... Has there been a shift in the constellation of life and history? ...Yes, an enormous star has moved between them. The constellation really has been changed - by science, by the demand that history should be a science. Now it is no longer life itself that rules alone and bridles our knowledge of the past; all boundary posts have been torn up, and everything which once was is now rushing in upon man ... Never has a previous generation seen such an enormous spectacle as that which history, the science of universal development and change, now unfolds.[38]

---

37 Droysen had already noticed this effect, but had not regarded it as dangerous. See DROYSEN (1977, p. 71). "In der Natur der Sache liegt es, daß ... (die) Fülle (der historischen Überreste) unabsehbar ist, da ja alles und jedes, was durch Menschenhand und Menschengeist hindurchgegangen und deren Gepräge trägt, gelegentlich als unmittelbare Quelle benutzt werden kann."

38 NIETZSCHE (1874, p. 268). "Schnell einen Blick auf unsere Zeit! Wir erschrecken ... wohin ist alle Klarheit, alle Natürlichkeit und Reinheit jener Beziehung von Leben und Historie ... Hat sich wirklich die Constellation von Leben und Historie verändert? ... Es ist allerdings ein ... Gestirn dazwischen getreten, die Constellation ist wirklich verändert - durch die Wissenschaft, durch die

Nietzsche pointed out that there were two main differences between history as an empirical science and the older forms of historical understanding. The first was, as shown by Droysen, the fact that the scientific approach to history was based on empirical data. Secondly, it was the fact that the scientific process of historical research was essentially endless. This endlessness of scientific historical perception had the consequence that there were no longer clear criteria for the validity and relevance of historical insight. All facts appeared to be equally important. And it was precisely this aspect of science which according to Nietzsche caused great damage to life.

> Just picture to yourself the mental process which is induced in modern man's soul (through history as an empirical science). Historical knowledge is gushing from ever-flowing sources ... Strange facts without a context fight for our attention, memory has opened all its floodgates ... Finally, modern man is dragging around an enormous number of stones of indigestible knowledge.[39]

But this knowledge remains unconnected to the present practical life. There are no longer valid criteria which could help the historian to distinguish relevant from irrelevant historical information.

> Let us suppose somebody is investigating the works of Democritus. In this case I ask: why did you not choose Heraclitus or Philo or Bacon or Descartes and so on. And why did you take a philosopher? Why didn't you choose a poet ...? And why for heavens sake did you take a Greek, why not an Englishman or a Turk? ... But it does not really matter what people are investigating, as long as history is preserved in an objective manner. Yet, it is *investigated* by people who themselves are absolutely incapable of *making* history.[40]

Forderung, dass die Historie Wissenschaft sein soll. Jetzt regirt nicht mehr allein das Leben und bändigt das Wissen um die Vergangenheit: sondern alle Grenzpfähle sind umgerissen und alles, was einmal war, stürzt auf den Menschen zu ... Ein solch unüberschaubares Schauspiel sah noch kein Geschlecht, wie es jetzt die Wissenschaft des universalen Werdens, die Historie zeigt."

39 NIETZSCHE (1874, p. 268).

40 NIETZSCHE (1874, p. 279).

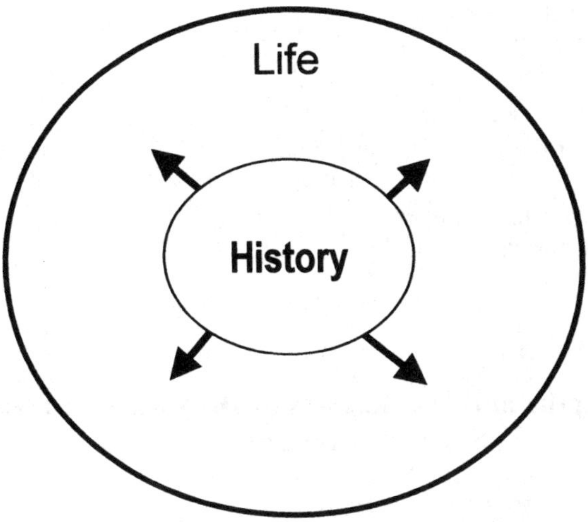

Fig. 2: Nietzsche's conception of the relationship between history and life

Nietzsche was the first one who drew attention to the fact that the scientific attitude towards history might have a dangerous effect on practical life. He showed that scientific historical research not only led to a fixation on the past, but that it also had the effect of generally relativising all cultural phenomena. Historical research made it clear that cultural institutions were normally in a process of development. As soon as cultural institutions came into being, they also began to change continuously; different institutional forms replaced one another in the course of historical development. But this fascinating observation, empirically demonstrated by the historians, had the consequence that it changed the attitude of people towards their own culture, too.

> Like cities which are struck by an earthquake and collapse and lay waste ... so is life itself beginning to collapse and become weak and disheartened when the abstract earthquake embodied by science deprives man of the basis of his security and peace of mind, the belief in continuation and in the eternal.[41]

The discovery that the development of cultural institutions was dependent on how they developed and that they only existed for a relatively short time,

41 NIETZSCHE (1874, p. 326).

made it clear that social acceptance of values was relative. This, however, considerably weakened the respect for the current forms of cultural institutions. As historians convincingly showed that cultural phenomena in general were only of relative value and durability, the contemporary cultural institutions fell under the same suspicion of having a relative value and of being of a temporary nature. Thus, the idea that absolute demands could be made on cultural phenomena was questioned. Summing up, Nietzsche showed that the process of historicising thought inevitably led to the collapse of morals and religion.[42]

III. Strengths and Weaknesses of Droysen's and Nietzsche's Concepts

Droysen and Nietzsche drew attention to completely different dimensions of the discovery of historicity. While Droysen pointed out the strengths of history as an empirical science, Nietzsche concentrated on the dangers accompanying this scientific understanding of history.

The strength of Droysen's concept lay in its epistemological aspect, but a major deficiency of his concept was that he did not take into consideration the possible negative effects of historical perception on daily life. The integration of his concept in Hegel's philosophy of history prevented him from realising the fact that the discovery of historicity was an achievement that might equally cause problems.

Nietzsche, however, chose the opposite approach. His strength lay in his criticism of the practical effects of historical perception on daily life. He pointed out clearly the dangers which accompanied history as an empirical science. But the main weakness of his concept was that he did not see any advantages in a scientific approach to history at all. In his view history could be of 'use' to life only by ceasing to be an empirical science. The three approaches to history that Nietzsche recommended as a remedy against the 'abuse' of history (the so-called 'monumental', 'antiquarian' and 'critical' history)[43] had in common that all of them were *non-scientific* forms of historical perception. Thus, Nietzsche did not really present a solution as to how

42 See also BURCKHARDT (1868, p. 229).
43 NIETZSCHE (1874, aphorisms 2 and 3).

to overcome the negative effects of the modern form of history as an empirical science. On the contrary, in spite of the fact that he had performed an excellent analysis of the practical effects of the discovery of historicity, he finally recommended a pre-modern approach to history.

Nietzsche's critique regarding the use and abuse of history was extended shortly afterwards to the field of political economy by Carl Menger and to that of civil law by Rudolf Stammler. Both claimed that the phenomenon of the historisation of thought had led to a general relativisation of values, causing great damage to the political economy as well as to civil law.[44] From then onwards this accusation was to be heard again and again in the German "*Geisteswissenschaften*" up until the time of Max Weber.[45]

Weber, however, proceeded to show that this charge rested on a false understanding of what science was capable of. He argued that historical knowledge and normative questions were of a completely different nature, epistemologically speaking, and that historical knowledge could therefore neither damage the sphere of values and daily life nor provide ethical concepts.[46] Weber's clear distinction between science and values made Nietzsche's charge that the historisation of thought led to relativism appear unfounded.

Weber made clear that both positions, Droysen's concept and Nietzsche's, contained a certain amount of truth. Droysen was right in claiming that scientific knowledge had to be empirically-based.[47] Nietzsche, on the other hand, was right in arguing that a possible fault of history might lie in it preventing people from developing action programmes focussed on the present. Weber pointed out that empirical science did not deal with the question of 'What should we do?',[48] at the same time showing that Nietzsche's demand for an answer to this question, albeit a non-scientific one, was of vital importance

44 See A. WITTKAU: (1994, p. 61).

45 See A. WITTKAU: (1994).

46 See M. WEBER: „Wissenschaft als Beruf" (1919), in: M. WEBER: *Gesammelte Aufsätze zur Wissenschaftslehre*, 6th edition Tübingen (J.C.B. Mohr/Paul Siebeck) 1985, pp. 582-613.

47 See especially M. WEBER: „Roscher und Knies und die logischen Probleme der historischen Nationalökonomie", in: M. WEBER: *Gesammelte Aufsätze zur Wissenschaftslehre*, 6th edition Tübingen (J.C.B. Mohr/Paul Siebeck) 1985, pp. 1-145.

48 See M. WEBER: „Wissenschaft als Beruf" (1919), in: M. WEBER: *Gesammelte Aufsätze zur Wissenschaftslehre*, 6th edition Tübingen (J.C.B. Mohr/Paul Siebeck) 1985, pp. 582-613, p. 609.

for daily life. By clearly distinguishing between historical and normative knowledge, Weber was able to demonstrate that each type of knowledge had its own sphere of competence,[49] thus doing justice to both of them.

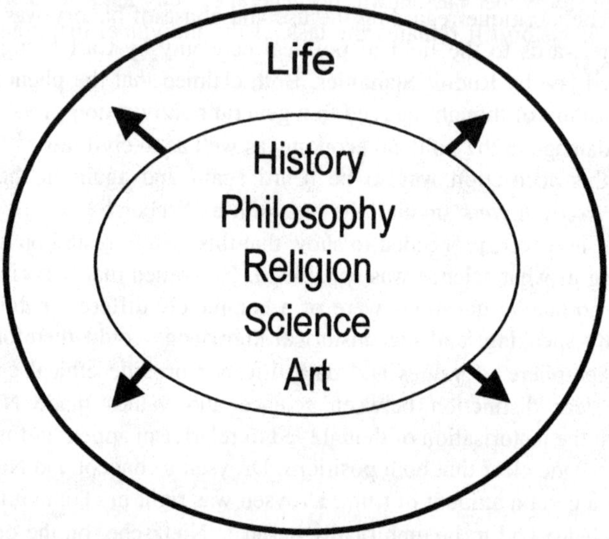

Fig. 3: Weber's conception of the relationship between history and life

In the light of Weber's epistemological approach, the conflict between Droysen and Nietzsche takes on a more pronounced profile. The problem that both concepts over-emphasised one particular aspect of the discovery of historicity can be overcome if we try to see them as complementing one another. Seen thus, Droysen's contribution was that he underlined the strengths and the practical use of history as an empirical science for understanding both human existence and culture. Nietzsche's contribution, on the other hand, was in identifying the potential dangers that might accompany historical investigations. The dangers Nietzsche alludes to do not appear quite so inevitable if we take into consideration Weber's arguments. It is not history itself as an em-

49 See M. WEBER: „Die 'Objektivität' sozialwissenschaftlicher und sozialpolitischer Erkenntnis", in: M. WEBER: *Gesammelte Aufsätze zur Wissenschaftslehre*, edited by J. Winckelmann, 6th edition Tübingen (J. C. B. Mohr/Paul Siebeck) 1985, pp. 146-214.

pirical science that gives rise to the process of relativising values, it is an exaggerated estimation of the importance of history. It is undoubtedly possible to avoid these dangers altogether, if the historian is aware of them. There is, however, as Weber has shown, no general remedy against such forms of the abuse of history. It remains the task of the individual historian to solve this problem.

References

BURCKHARDT, J.: *Über das Studium der Geschichte (1868)*, der Text der 'Weltgeschichtlichen Betrachtungen' nach den Handschriften herausgegeben von Peter Ganz, München (C.H. Beck) 1982.

BIALAS, W., RAULET, G.: *Die Historismusdebatte in der Weimarer Republik*, Frankfurt a.M. (Peter Lang) 1996.

DROYSEN, G.: *Johann Gustav Droysen*, Leipzig (Duncker and Humblot) 1910.

DROYSEN, JOHANN GUSTAV: *Historik*, Textausgabe von Peter Leyh, Stuttgart-Bad Cannstatt (Frommann-Holzboog) 1977.

PETER GANZ (Ed.), JACOB BURCKHARDT: *Über das Studium der Geschichte (1868)*, Der Text der 'Weltgeschichtlichen Betrachtungen' nach den Handschriften herausgegeben, München (C.H. Beck) 1982.

HARDTWIG, W.: *Geschichtsschreibung zwischen Alteuropa und moderner Welt. Jacob Burckhardt in seiner Zeit*, Göttingen (Vandenhoek & Ruprecht) 1974.

HARDTWIG, W.: "Jacob Burckhardt", in: N. HAMMERSTEIN (Ed.): *Deutsche Geschichtswissenschaft um 1900*, Stuttgart (Franz Steines Verlag Wiesbaden GMBH) 1988, pp. 97-112.

HARDTWIG, W.: *Die Verwissenschaftlichung der Geschichtsschreibung zwischen Aufklärung und Historismus*, München (C.H. Beck) 1990, pp. 58-91.

IGGERS, G.: "Historismus im Meinungsstreit", in: O.G. OEXLE, J. RÜSEN (Eds.): *Historismus in den Kulturwissenschaften. Geschichtskonzepte, historische Einschätzungen, Grundlagenprobleme*, Köln/Weimar/Wien (Böhlau) 1996, pp. 7-29.

LICHTBLAU, K.: *Kulturkrise und Soziologie um die Jahrhundertwende. Zur Genealogie der Kultursoziologie in Deutschland*, Frankfurt a.M. (Suhrkamp) 1996.

NIETZSCHE, F.: *Werke. Kritische Gesamtausgabe*, ed. by Giorgio Colli and Mazzino Montinari, Dritte Abteilung, 1. Vol., Unzeitgemäße Betrachtungen I-III (1872-1874), Berlin 1972.

NIEHANS, J.: *A History of Economic Theory. Classic Contributions, 1720-1980*, Baltimore/London (Johns Hopkins University Press) 1990.

NIPPERDEY, T.: *Deutsche Geschichte 1800-1866. Bürgerwelt und starker Staat*, München (Verlag C.H. Beck) 1983.

OBERMANN, W.: *Der junge Johann Gustav Droysen. Ein Beitrag zur Entstehungsgeschichte des Historismus*, (Dissertation), Bonn 1977.

OEXLE, O. G.: *Geschichtswissenschaft im Zeichen des Historismus. Studien zu Problemgeschichten der Moderne*, Göttingen (Vandenhoeck & Ruprecht) 1996.

OEXLE, O. G., RÜSEN, J. (Eds.): *Historismus in den Kulturwissenschaften. Geschichtskonzepte, historische Einschätzungen, Grundlagenprobleme*, Köln/Weimar/Wien (Böhlau) 1996.

RAULET, G.: "Strategien des Historismus", in: W. BIALAS, G. RAULET (Eds.): *Die Historismusdebatte in der Weimarer Republik*, Frankfurt a.M. (Peter Lang), 1996, pp. 7-38.

SCHOLTZ, G.: *Zwischen Wissenschaftsanspruch und Orientierungsbedürfnis. Zu Grundlage und Wandel der Geisteswissenschaften*, Frankfurt a.M. (Suhrkamp) 1991.

WEBER, M.: „Die 'Objektivität' sozialwissenschaftlicher und sozialpolitischer Erkenntnis (1904)", in: MAX WEBER: *Gesammelte Aufsätze zur Wissenschaftslehre*, edited by Winckelmann, Johannes, 6th edition Tübingen (J.C.B.Mohr/Paul Siebeck) 1985.

WITTKAU, A.: *Historismus. Zur Geschichte des Begriffs und des Problems*, 2nd edition, Göttingen (Vandenhoeck &Ruprecht) 1994.

WITTKAU-HORGBY, A.: „Vom Nutzen und Nachteil der Historie für Nationalökonomie und Jurisprudenz. Überlegungen zur Problemgeschichte des Historismus des späten 19. und fröhen 20. Jahrhunderts", in: W. BIALAS, G. RAULET (Eds.): *Die Historismusdebatte in der Weimarer Republik*, Frankfurt a.M. (Peter Lang), 1996, pp. 71-89.

Chapter 5

Philosophy of History and Theory of Historiography in Jacob Burckhardt

EGON FLAIG

I. European Culture is a Continuum
II. The Threatened Continuum of the Occidental Culture
1. The Untameable Sovereignty of the People
2. Political Equality and Class Conflict:
Burckhardt Between Tocqueville and Fustel de Coulanges
III. Culture and War: Aestheticizing History
1. Enhancement of Existence: Heroism Versus Utilitarianism
2. Aestheticizing War
IV. Reshaping the Tasks of Cultural History

I. European Culture is a Continuum

Occidental Culture for Jacob Burckhardt is a singular phenomenon in the History of the planet. Only this culture succeeded in building up a continuous tradition stretching from the Ancient Near East to the 19th century. All non-European cultures remained within a special type of natural history: as they are not interested in one another, they appear and they disappear without being able to create a continuum joining them altogether. In Europe however, by means of a constant cultural effort of remembrance and tradition, the past is kept alive in a sort of historical metempsychosis:

> Das Kontinuum ist höchst großartig. Die Menschheit ums Mittelmeer und bis zum persischen Busen ist wirklich ein belebtes Wesen, die aktive Menschheit χατ′ εξοχη`ν. Hier allein verwirklichen sich die

> Postulate des Geistes; hier allein waltet Entwicklung und kein absoluter Untergang, sondern nur Übergang.[1]

This peculiar culture which is able to perpetuate itself took its origin in Greece. The Greeks developed a mental ability that made them susceptible to an interest in all things ("*Allinteresse*"). This intellectual disposition has guaranteed the survival of their own past in the sublimated form of a highly differentiated tradition and conscious appropriation of past achievements. This disposition is bound up with a curiosity which helps even foreign cultures to survive in the medium of remembrance, by including them into the great tradition initiated by the Greeks.

The Greek culture originates in the Greek myth.[2] The Myth creates a specific notion of the world, which enables the Greek people to take an aesthetic point of view towards all things in the world. This aesthetically impregnated view is the prerequisite for a radically non-utilitarist attitude towards the world.

> So war das Griechenvolk geistig orientiert, welchem im Verlauf der Zeit die allergrößten weltgeschichtlichen Aufgaben zufallen sollten: in seiner mythischen Vorzeit gefangen, zu einer burchstäblichen Geschichte nur ganz allmählich befähigt, in poetischer Bildlichkeit völlig aufgehend - und doch im Verlauf der Zeiten dazu bestimmt, alle Völker zuerst zu verstehen und dies Verständnis der Welt mitzuteilen, gewaltige Länder und Völker des Orients zu unterwerfen, seine Kultur zu einer Weltkultur zu machen, in welcher Asien und Rom zusammentrafen, durch den Hellenismus der große Sauerteig der alten Welt zu werden; zugleich aber durch das Weiterleben dieser Kultur die Kontinuität der Weltentwicklung für uns zu sichern; denn nur durch die Griechen hängen die Zeiten und das Interesse für diese Zeiten aneinander; ohne sie hätten wir kein Wissen von der Vorzeit, und was wir ohne sie wissen *könnten*, würden wir zu wissen nicht *begehren.* Neben dieser endlosen Bereicherung des Gedankens bekommen wir dann noch als Beigabe die Reste ihres Schaffens und

1 „Historische Fragmente", in: JACOB BURCKHARDT: *Gesamtausgabe*, 14 vols., Basel/Stuttgart/Berlin/Leipzig (Deutsche Verlags-Anstalt) 1929-1934, vol. VII, p. 225.

2 JÖRN RÜSEN, JACOB BURCKHARDT, in: H.-U. WEHLER (Ed.): *Deutsche Historiker*, vol. III, Göttingen (Vandenhoeck und Ruprecht) 1972; E. FLAIG: *Angeschaute Geschichte. Zu Jacob Burckhardts 'Griechische Kulturgeschichte'*, Rheinfelden (Schäuble) 1987, pp. 187-250.

> Könnens: Kunst und Poesie. Wir sehen mit ihren Augen und sprechen mit ihren Ausdrücken.[3]

Greek art and poetry are only *external*. The main legacy of Hellenic culture is not the material remnants but the mental disposition, a non-utilitarian curiosity and a non-utilitarian attitude towards life and the world. This is the basis for objective knowledge. Thus science and myth must not be diametrically opposed, instead they both are antagonistic against a mere utilitarian view of the world, a view that is *eo ipso* unable to be interested either in the past or in foreign cultures.[4]

This attitude can best be preserved by art and by keeping ones eyes susceptible for the impressions art does give.

> Vollständige und gleichmäßige Begabung für tiefe und zugleich vielseitige Aufnahme der Kunst ist eine seltene Gabe; was sich jeder davon am besten aneigne und wie, das ist jedes Einzelnen Sache. Die *Hauptvorbedingungen* sind: Daß man nicht blind der Welt der Absichten verfallen, sondern überhaupt einer objektiven Erkenntnis der Dinge offen, d.h. daß man kein gemeines Subjekt sei.[5]

In a very Schopenhauerian phrase he asserts: Aesthetic susceptibility is an ethical quality; one must not submit one's own life totally to 'the world of intentions'. There is always a historical risk that this ability may perish, if there are too few people left who have not succumbed to a utilitarian attitude. Connecting that aesthetic attitude towards the world and the ongoing existence of occidental culture, Burckhardt is able to predict the exact time when the occidental culture will come to its end:

> Die Stunde, da unsere Kultur die großen griechischen Göttertypen nicht mehr schön finden wird, wird der Anfang der Barbarei sein.[6]

The aesthetic attitude is deemed to be the vital condition that the occidental culture may go on. It can disappear during a sharp historical crisis, if all

3 „Griechische Kulturgeschichte", I (*Gesammelte Werke*, Berlin o.J. V), pp. 49f.

4 E. FLAIG: "Ästhetischer Blick und Griechischer Mythos. Wie Burckhardt für Europa einen Ursprung erfindet", in: P. BETTHAUSEN, M. KUNZE (Eds.): *Jacob Burckhardt und die Antike*, Mainz 1998, pp. 27-37.

5 „Die Kunst des Altertums", in: JACOB BURCKHARDT: *Gesamtausgabe*, vol. XIII, p. 27.

6 „Die Kunst des Altertums" (*Gesamtausgabe*, XIII), p. 23.

activities of the European mankind are defeated by material interests. According to Burckhardt's historical diagnosis, this is going to happen in the deep crisis which the European society is undergoing during his own time and the immediate future. Anyway, he sticks firmly to his opinion that the occidental culture in spite of all social transformations may survive and be prolonged into the future. His implicit philosophy of history cuts out the margin for his theory of historiography and determines to a high degree the tasks of cultural history.

But if in Burckhardt's diagnosis the actual crisis threatens the very basis for the continuity of the occidental culture, we have to take a very close look at the peculiarity of this crisis.

II. The Threatened Continuum of the Occidental Culture[7]

Burckhardt's conception of contemporary history revolves around three premises. He postulates, first, that no distinction exists between 'radical' and 'representative' democracy; any kind of 'restraint' that the principle of representation might impose on the will of the masses ultimately fails to be effective due to the basic sovereignty of the people in *all* types of democratic government; secondly, that *political* equality inevitably produces the desire for *social* equality, and that the fight for social equality that ensues throws society into class struggles; and thirdly, that class struggles dramatically lower the moral standard of society as a whole: they generate a historical constellation in which social life falls increasingly under the sway of base material motives that lack any cultural dimension whatsoever; at that point, the danger arises that outright civil wars will tear the very fabric of society into pieces.

1. The Untameable Sovereignty of the People

The cardinal point of reference in the nineteenth-century political debates was of course the French Revolution. Liberals, democrats, Bonapartists, le-

---

7 I am grateful to Ingo Gildenhard and Martin Ruehl for translating the whole second chapter of my article together with all quotations from BURCKHARDT's Griechische Kulturgeschichte.

gitimists or reactionaries – when formulating their political theories, argued their case with reference to this event. The most hotly debated issue was the sovereignty of the people. The great counter-revolutionary thinkers – DeMaistre, Bonald, Donoso Cortés – shared the same fundamental objection to a form of government based on this principle: It would, they thought, result in chaos and the dissolution of society. How so? Quite simply: the sovereignty of the people would bring about the equality of all citizens; political equality would undermine social hierarchies; this, in turn, would destroy the political authority of social institutions and lead to anarchy; and anarchy would plunge society into chaos and civil war. This chain-reaction was bound to happen since a sovereign people was allegedly unable to maintain a stable order. After all, in a democracy, potentially everything is at all times up for discussion, transformation, and repeal - even the constitution itself.

In part, this line of reasoning was a backlash against some of the most widely-read theoreticians of the sovereignty of the people – Rousseau and the Abbé Sieyès – who had developed such radical versions of this concept that one could indeed draw anarchistic conclusions from their ideas. In his famous pamphlet, *Qu'est-ce que le tiers état?*, Abbé Sieyès[8] argued that the "Pouvoir constituant" is not bound to any single will; it may dissolve or reshuffle the "pouvoir constitué," i.e. the government and the constitution, at any time in any way it considers fit. The nation, in other words, may re-create its societal conditions ever anew — when and as it pleases. At the time of the French revolution, the Abbé Mably endorsed the same point of view[9] - precisely the line of thought against which the counter-revolutionary critics of democracy direct their harshest polemics.

In the beginning of the nineteenth century a liberal movement gradually took shape that defined itself against the forces of radical democracy as well as counter-revolutionary Catholicism and conservatism. These Liberals were outspoken proponents of the sovereignty of the people, while at the same time rebutting the ancient model of direct democracy. The best-known advocate of this *via media* is Benjamin Constant, who, in 1819, delivered a speech on "two types of freedom" in the Athenaeum at Paris, in which he drew a sharp distinction between the individual freedom of modernity and the political

8 *Qu'est-ce que le tiers état?* (ed. by R. Zapperi), Geneva 1970.

9 Gabriel Bonnet de Mably: "De la législation ou principes des lois", III 3 and 4, in: *Collection complète des Oeuvres* (par G. Arnoux), vol. 9 (Paris 1794/95); reprinted Aalen 1977, pp. 290-356.

freedom of antiquity.[10] He acknowledged both the principle of sovereignty of the people (which he considered a good thing); yet at the same time he took the edge off its radical implications by claiming that the people should not govern directly, but *via* their elected representatives. Here we have, for the first time, a succinct political formula of modern representative democracy. Constant's writings were highly influential in the decades leading up to the 1848 revolutions.

In many ways, Burckhardt levies a frontal attack on this notion of representative democracy. For him, the ultimate outcome of any democratic form of government, with or without an element of representation, is the tyranny of the masses. Representation in no way prevents those who are being represented from gaining the upper hand over the representing instance - due to the fact that the masses ruthlessly and unconditionally pursue their very own interests:

> Die guten liberalen und selbst radikalen Erwerblinge können lange vor den Volksführern auf die Knie fallen und sie anflehen, keine Dummheiten zu machen. Die Volksführer müssen eben, um wiedergewählt zu werden, die geschreilustigen Schichten der Volksmassen für sich haben, und diese verlangen, daß stets etwas geschehe, sonst glauben sie nicht, daß `Fortschritt' vorhanden sei... Aus diesem cercle vicieux kommt man beim suffrage universel überhaupt nicht mehr heraus. Eins nach dem Andern muß geopfert werden: Stellen, Habe, Religion, distinguierte Sitte, höhere Wissenschaft – so lange die Massen auf ihre meneurs drücken können und solange nicht irgend eine Gewalt drein ruft: Haltet' s Maul! Wozu vor der Hand noch nicht die leiseste Aussicht vorhanden. Und... diese Gewalt kann beinahe nur aus den Bösesten hervorgehen und haarsträubend wirken.[11]

---

10 In: BENJAMIN CONSTANT: *Cours de politique constitutionelle ou collection des ouvrages publiés sur le gouvernement représentatif*, ed. by Edouard Laboulaye, 2 vols., Paris 1872, vol. II, pp. 539-60. Cf. STEPHEN HOLMES: *Benjamin Constant and the Making of Modern Liberalism*, New Haven/London (Yale University Press) 1984, pp. 182-7.

11 *Letter to Alioth, 10. September 1881* (*Jacob Burckhardt Briefe. Vollständige und kritisch bearbeitete Ausgabe. Mit Benützung des handschriftlichen Nachlasses hergestellt von M. Burckhardt*, 9 Bände, Basel 1949ff, vol. VII, pp. 288-9): „The good liberals and even those in a radical way of business, may fall on their knees before the leaders of the people and beseech them not to commit any follies. But

Buckhardt apparently believes that delegates must of necessity yield to the interests of those whom they represent; otherwise, the masses will vote them out of office. In other words, Burckhardt asserts that a state of political equality eliminates the possibility of representation. Succinctly put, he regards representation as an illusion. This premise has drastic consequences for the status and significance of ancient democracy in modern times. The liberal supporters of Benjamin Constant were able to keep the direct democracy as practiced by the Athenian *polis* at a comfortable distance, together with its potentially radical lessons for contemporary politics. With representative democracy offering a viable alternative, the disturbing fact of mass-rule in ancient Athens could safely be filed away in the archives of history, bearing little relevance to current affairs.

By disavowing the efficacy of representation in his own time, indeed rejecting the very principle, Burckhardt all but eliminates the distinction between the ancient type of democracy and alternative modern forms. As a result, Greek democracy is suddenly no longer a thing of the past. The events in fifth-century Athens have gained a burning urgency; rather than being a closed chapter of history, they are frighteningly real. With one strategic stroke, Burckhardt has thus staked out a distinct theoretical space for himself, in which the historiography of ancient Greece turns into a lesson for Europe's political future at the time he was writing. This works both ways: if no fundamental differences exist between ancient and modern democracies, Greek democracy may be analyzed with recourse to ideological schemes articulated in modern political thought; in turn, if these schemes prove their validity in the analysis of the past, they will have acquired greater plausibility when adduced in arguments about the present and future. It is not by accident that the above letter was written just when Burckhardt compiled the final version of the first two volumes of his Greek Cultural History.

---

in order to be re-elected, the leaders of the people, the demagogues, must have the masses on their side, and they in turn demand that something should always be happening, otherwise they don't believe 'progress' is going on. One cannot possibly escape from that *cercle vicieux* as long as universal suffrage lasts. One thing after another will have to be sacrificed: positions, possessions, religion, civilized manners, pure scholarship - as long as the masses can put pressure on their *Meneurs*, and as long as some power doesn't shout: Shut up! - and there is not the slightest sign of that for the time being. And ... that power can really only emerge from the depth of evil, and the effect will be hair-raising." (translated by A. Dru).

2. Political Equality and Class Conflict: Burckhardt Between Tocqueville and Fustel de Coulanges

Unlike Constant, Burckhardt criticizes the direct democracy that was practiced in the Athenian *polis* not by comparing it to the modern version of representative democracy - as we have seen, this was not a viable alternative for him anyway. Rather, he put the stress on the inability of ancient Athens to reconcile a general civic equality with a distinctly political inequality between leaders and the masses:

> Eines scheint in Athen ganz unmöglich gewesen zu sein, nämlich die Einführung eines Systems, das Regierung durch Wenige mit Freiheit für alle verband, einer die Gleichberechtigung der Regierten voraussetzenden Oligarchie… Denn der Mißbrauch der Gewalt wäre zu unvermeidlich gewesen. Thukydides selber sagt: es bedürfe des demokratischen Regiments, damit die Armen eine Zuflucht und die Reichen einen Zügel hätten. Die Griechen haben nie bürgerliche Gleichheit mit politischer Ungleichheit zu verbinden gewußt. Der Arme mußte zu seinem Schutz gegen Unbill Mitstimmen, Richter und Magistrat sein können…[12]

This quotation is taken almost verbatim from Fustel de Coulanges' influential book *La Cité Antique* of 1864, where the relevant passage reads:

> On aurait peut-etre evité l' avènement de la démocratie, si l' on avait pu fonder ce que Thucydide appelle *oligarchia isonomos*, c'est-à-dire le gouvernement pour quelques-uns et la liberté pour tous... Les Grecs n' ont jamais su concilier l' égalité civile avec l' inégalité politique. Pour que le pauvre ne fût pas lesé dans ses intêrets personnels, il leur a paru

12 *Griechische Kulturgeschichte* I (*Ges. Werke*, V) p. 205. „One thing appeared to be entirely impossible in Athens, i.e. the introduction of a system that combined the rule by the few with freedom for all, an oligarchy that would take as its basic assumption the equality of those being ruled… For the abuse of power would have been unavoidable. Thucydides himself says that a democratic regime is necessary so that the poor may have a refuge and the rich a restraint. The Greeks were never able to combine civic equality with political inequality. The poor man had to be able to act as voter, judge and government official in order to protect himself against injustice…"

> nécessaire qu'il eût un droit de suffrage, qu' il fût juge dans les tribunaux, et qu'il pût etre magistrat.[13]

The all but direct quotation is by no means exceptional. In fact, the entire conceptual architecture that Burckhardt employs to explicate the socio-political processes he deemed responsible for the disintegration of the Greek *polis*, he derived from Fustel's great book, changing hardly anything at all in his model.

In his *Greek Cultural History*, Burckhardt explains the decline of the Greek polis with reference to an axiom formulated by Tocqueville, namely that political equality will inevitably lead to ongoing efforts to bring about social equality. Delivering a speech as a delegate in October of 1847, Tocqueville stated:

> La Révolution française, qui a aboli tous les privilèges et détruit tous les droits exclusifs, en a pourtant laissé subsister un, celui de la propriété. .. Aujourd'hui que le droit de propriété n'apparaît plus que comme le dernier reste d'un monde aristocratiqe détruit...c'est à lui seul maintenant à soutenir chaque jour le choc direct et incessant des opinions démocratiques...[14]

---

13 FUSTEL DE COULANGES: *La Cité Antique. Etude sur le culte, le droit, les institutions de la Grèce et de Rome*, Paris [27]1922, p. 387. „Perhaps one could have avoided the turn towards democracy if one had been able to establish what Thucydides calls *oligarchia isonomos*, that is to say sovereignty for some and liberty for all... The Greeks were never able to reconcile civic equality with political inequality. In order to protect the poor man from being abused in his personal affairs, they deemed it necessary that he have the right to vote, that he be judge in the tribunals and that he have the possibility to act as magistrate." Burckhardt indicates in his text that he is following Fustel here (*Griechische Kulturgeschichte*, vol. I, p. 206). Nonetheless, he does not say to what extent he echoes Fustel's formulations. Right after the quotation given above, Fustel argues that it is precisely the enormous control of the *polis* over human life in its entirety that makes everyone want to participate in its power. Burckhardt makes this thought his own.

14 OC (= ALEXIS DE TOCQUEVILLE: *Oeuvres, Papiers et Correspondance,* Edition définitive publiée sous la direction de J. P. Mayer, Paris 1952ff.), vol. XII, pp. 36-7. „The French Revolution which abolished all privileges and destroyed all special rights, however, left one of them intact, the right of property... In our time, when the right of property only appears as the last remainder of a destroyed

Tocqueville here sets up an antagonistic relation between political equality and economic inequality. This alleged antagonism has become crucial both for so-called liberal and for so-called conservative thinkers in their endeavours to play off 'liberty' against 'equality' - a move that is only plausible if one radically depoliticizes the notion of 'liberty'. Burckhardt even goes a step further in suggesting that political equality will eventually result in the breakdown of social stability.

Political equality, in his eyes, had two fateful consequences that kicked in almost immediately after it is set up: it created a new burning desire – the desire to turn political equality into economic equality; and it also created a new instrument to bring this about - political decision-making by majority vote. Burckhardt describes the origins of this fateful nexus thus:

> In der alten Zeit der Geschlechterherrschaft nämlich hatte man die Misere kaum gekannt. Erst die Gleichheit der Rechte machte die Ungleichheit der Lage recht fühlbar. Ein Ausgleich durch Arbeit aber (welche der Reiche bedurft und der Arme gegen Lohn geleistet hätte) war unmöglich wegen der allgemeinen Antibanausie.[15]

He took this line of argument almost directly from Fustel who had taken it, in his turn, from Tocqueville and other commentators on the 1848 revolution in France.[16]

We also find this thought in Tocqueville's notes for February 1848 (revised in 1850).[17] Here we have the origins of Burckhardt's notion that equality of political rights renders long-standing socio-economic inequalities glaringly obvious. Tocqueville built his theory of the revolution around this very

---

aristocratic world...it is its task alone now to bear every day the direct and unceasing brunt of democratic opinions.“

15 *Griechische Kulturgeschichte* I, p. 243. „In the old times when aristocratic families ruled, the misery was hardly felt. Only the equality of rights made the inequality of position truly noticeable. A balancing through labor (which the rich needed and the poor would have provided for wage) was impossible due to the general antibanausia“.

16 „La démocratie ne supprima pas la misère; elle la rendit, au contraire, plus sensible. L` égalité des droits politiques fit ressortir encore davantage l`inégalité des conditions“ (*Cité antique*, p. 397). „Democracy did not eradicate misery; on the contrary, it made it even more strongly felt. The equality of political rights brought the inequality of social conditions even more to the fore.“

17 Cf. Tocqueville's notes for Feburary 1848 (revised in 1850), OC XII, pp. 96-7.

axiom. In Burckhardt, it becomes the motor that keeps the internal struggles within the Greek city-states going until the final breakdown of their civic communities. He argues that the poor citizens, once empowered politically, will start to pursue material interests in their desire to abolish economic inequality as well. In Burckhardt's scenario, this is the moment in time when class struggles dramatically erupt in the political sphere. Being in the majority, the poor employ the popular vote to change the existing distribution of property:

> Jetzt wurde der Arme inne, daß er als Herr der Stimmen auch Herr des Besitzes werden könne...[18]

- again a sentence that has its all but verbatim equivalent in Fustel de Coulanges' *Cité antique*.[19]

For Burckhardt, this thought is absolutely pivotal, the factor around which the entire political process of Greek civilization ultimately revolves. It is also the core of his conception of social order in the modern age. Let us take a closer look at the reasons he gives for the outbreak of the struggle between rich and poor:

> In Griechenland aber begann, als die Gleichheit da war und man nicht mehr um Prinzipien und Rechte zu kämpfen hatte, der Krieg zwischen Reich und Arm, in manchen Städten schon sogleich mit Eintritt der Demokratie, anderswo nach einer längeren oder kürzeren Zwischenzeit der Mäßigung...[20]

---

18 *Griechische Kulturgeschichte* I, p. 243. „Now the poor man realized that as lord of the votes, he could also become lord of property".

19 „Le pauvre avait l'égalité des droits. Mais assurément ses souffrances journalières lui faisaient penser que l'égalité des fortunes eût été bien préférable. Or il ne fut pas longtemps sans s'apercevoir que l'égalité qu'il avait pouvait lui servir à acquérir celle qu'il n'avait pas, et que, maître des suffrages, il pouvait devenir maître de la richesse" (*Cité antique*, p. 398). „The poor man had the equality of rights. But naturally his daily sufferings made him think that the equality of property would have been much preferable. Now, it did not take him long until he realized that the equality which he had could help him gain the one he did not have. As lord of the votes he could become lord of wealth."

20 *Griechische Kulturgeschichte* I, p. 242. „In Greece, the war between poor and rich began when equality had been achieved and one no longer had to fight over principles and rights; in some cities that happened as soon as democracy got established, elsewhere after a longer or short interval of restraint." Again, he took

Burckhardt's explication of the change and decline of the Greek city-states can be summed up as follows: since the polis exercised quasi-total power over its citizens, it could enforce arbitrary expropriations. The masses could not resist the temptation to abuse their majority in the assembly and thus to transform political equality into social equality. Naturally, the oligarchs defended themselves as much as they could. The class war resulting from this socio-political dynamic ruined the Hellenic polis.

> Von der späteren Zeit der demokratischen Polis, seit der Schlacht von Chäronea, wendet sich der Blick bekanntlich gerne ab, es ist aber alles Eine Kette von Ursachen und Wirkungen bis zur gegenseitigen Ausrottung, bis zur Verödung desjenigen Griechenlands wie es die Römer übernahmen, und dieser Krankheitsgeschichte wird sich die Darstellung, sobald sie objektiv verfahren soll, nie entziehen können... Das Hauptübel war, daß sich die Demokratie mit der starken antibanausischen Gesinnung gekreuzt hatte, daß die Gleichheit der Rechte mit der Abneigung gegen die Arbeit zusammengetroffen war, worauf die Nichtstuer die Mittel des Stimmrechts und des Gerichtswesens auf permanente Bedrohung der Besitzenden wandten. Es ist wahnsinniger Mißbrauch der Majorität in einer Sache, welche unvermeidlich auch diese wieder in eine Majorität und Minorität spalten muß...[21]

---

this assessment straight from Fustel: „Lorsque la série des révolutions eut amené l`égalité entre les hommes et qu' il n' y eut plus lieu de se combattre pour des principes et des droits, les hommes se firent la guerre pour des intérêts" (*Cité antique*, p. 397). „When the series of revolutions between men had led to equality between people, and when there was no longer an opportunity to fight with one another over principles and rights, men went to war with one another over interests".

21 *Griechische Kulturgeschichte* I (*GW*, V) p. 254. „It is well known that the later periods of the democratic polis (since the battle at Chaironeia) are usually ignored; but we are dealing with One chain of causes and effects up to the point of mutual annihilation, up to the destruction of that Greece that the Romans took over. And a historical narrative once it strives to be objective can never ignore that chronicle of pathologies... The main evil consists of the merging of democracy with a strong anti-banausic ethos, of a meeting of equality of rights with a dislike of labor, which resulted in the idle turning the devices of the right to vote and the legislature into a permanent threat to the propertied. It is an insane abuse

In other words, civil wars - conceived as wars between the poor and the rich - accelerate the self-destruction of the political sphere. This process is tantamount to an erosion of social cohesion, with a slow, yet comprehensive disintegration of society as such. Once the state itself has degenerated to the point of being a mere instrument for the enforcement of special interests, no instance is left to counterbalance the collision of diametrically opposed desires. Since these desires are material in nature, a compromise is out of the question, for the simple reason that material desires are insatiable.

> Die Wünsche aber sind weit überwiegend materieller Art, so ideal sie sich auch gebärden, denn die Weitmeisten verstehen unter Glück nichts anderes; materielle Wünsche aber sind in sich und absolut unstillbar, selbst wenn sie unaufhörlich erfüllt würden, und dann erst recht.[22]

In his *Greek Cultural History*, this thought recurs in the following guise:

> Die Gier der dotierten Masse hinwiederum war aus innern Gründen unerfüllbar und mußte stets zu neuen Änderungen drängen. [23]

Burckhardt employed the concept of material interests in the same radical sense in which Donoso had used it[24] - as an analytical tool to associate systematically such concepts as 'the masses' and 'the sovereignty of the people' with political catastrophe. Burckhardt here openly peddles a sort of philosophy of history: naked material interests undermine the cultural determinants that should ideally shape our habitual dispositions.

For Burckhardt such a development would prove nothing short of disastrous - unsurprisingly, given the causality he thought would be triggered once

---

of majority in a matter that will inevitably again split this majority into a majority and a minority..."

22 "Historische Fragmente" (*Gesamtausgabe*, VII), p. 432 „The large majority of wishes are of a material nature, even if they are dressed in an idealistic garb, for most people take happiness to mean just that. Material wishes, however, are in and of themselves absolutely unfulfillable, even if they are continuously satisfied - or rather: especially when they are continuously satisfied".

23 „Griechische Kulturgeschichte" I *(GW*, V) p. 200. "The greed of the masses, on the other hand, was inherently unfulfillable and constantly had to bring about new changes".

24 See JUAN DONOSO CORTÉS: *Der Abfall vom Abendland,* ed. by P. Viator, 1849, p. 95 (Letter to Cardinal Fornari, 19 June 1852).

material interests gained the upper hand: once that is the case, human beings cease to follow their intellect and higher ideas; their readiness for self-sacrifice breaks down; and they are no longer concerned with promoting culture: the motives for doing so have been diminished. Once material drives triumph and social interaction within a culture is predominantly oriented towards mercenary profit, the potency "State" declines. Quickly, all struggles turn into struggles over the distribution of wealth. This process will not come to a halt by itself since all material desires are inherently unsatisfiable; in the end, they induce the masses to tear each other to pieces.

This protracted state of war leads to the gradual destruction of the political as well as the social sphere. No institution is able to provide a counterweight to the opposing factions since the state itself has degenerated into a mere instrument for competing particular interests. Burckhardt constructs a relapse into a state of nature slightly reminiscent of Hobbes. Yet whereas in Hobbes everybody is at war with everybody else (*bellum omnium contra omnes*), Burckhardt projects a succession of conflicts between different social groups.

The notion of "material interest" is not merely an analytic tool for Burckhardt; it is a concept that has political value when the stability of social and political order in general is at issue. As always, he is not merely concerned with the analysis of the fall of the Greek polis; in addition, he uses his historiographical narrative to take a stance in political controversies. As contemporary France shows, the lessons of history should better be heeded:

> Erbärmlich und hilflos ist die Lage überall, wo von unten herauf und durch die Presse regiert wird, aber so elend wie in Frankreich geht es doch nirgends. Selbst Boulanger ist nur pétulance und contrefaçon und gar alles ist réclame... Frankreich ... wird von Strebern bis aufs Mark aufgefressen. So kann' s aber noch lange gehen! Die Griechenstaaten haben über zweihundert Jahre so geserbelt, bis die Bevölkerung sich allmählich aufgerieben hatte und die Verödung eintrat, d.h. zwei Drittel der Städte nur noch menschenleere Trümmer waren. Wo Streber gewaltet haben, erhebt sich die Tyrannis nur noch momentan und lokal, und das Strebertum wird immer wieder Meister. Wenn nicht die Römer drüber gekommen wären, hätte auch der Rest der Nation sich aufgezehrt. Also Geduld! Und richte man sich aufs dauernde Elend ein.[25]

---

25 JACOB BURCKHARDT: *Briefe*, vol. IX, p. 125-6. "In every place, where the government is run from below and by the press, the situation is miserable and help-

Burckhardt's prediction about the future of the crisis in contemporary France does not fully converge with his historiographical staging of decline in ancient Greece. For he pinpoints one essential difference between modern times and Greek antiquity. The Greeks did not find a way out of democracy and thus succumbed to ruinous civil wars.

Modern nation-states, however, maintain large standing armies. This is the reason why they will not succumb to the anarchy of civil war that is otherwise the characteristic outcome of a democratic form of government. Rather, their fate will be ruthless military dictatorships after a sequence of serious social upheavals. Here, too, the much-lauded prophet Burckhardt erred.

III. Culture and War: Aestheticizing History

In Burckhardt's eyes, the trend towards democracy threatened to destroy Western civilization since it diminished the human capacity for the creation of "high culture." He thought that democratic forms of government would inevitably lower human motivations to a level so base that it could not sustain cultural production in the higher sense; the fall of society into a state of lawlessness would then always be an imminent possibility. This does not imply that Burckhardt considered any other form of political constitution as inherently conducive for cultural creativity; rather, he endorsed the view that the greatness of an age, i.e. above all its cultural productivity, depends on the quota of individuals who are able and willing to make personal sacrifices. The "willingness to make sacrifices" thus advances to a state of cardinal importance in his implicit philosophy of history. What does this notion signify?

---

less, but nowhere are matters more desolate than in France. Even Boulanger is only pétulance and contrefaçon and everything is réclame... France is devoured to the bones by careerists/ social climbers. But this can go on for years to come! The Greek states have warred until the population gradually wiped itself out and desolation ensued, i.e. two-thirds of the cities were depopulated ghost towns. Where careerists had ruled, tyranny arises only temporarily and locally, and careerism always reasserts itself. If the Romans had not arrived, the rest of the nation would have spent itself as well. Hence, patience! Preparations be made for protracted misery."

Burckhardt asserts that War, if led in a specific manner enhances human existence and creates excellent mental conditions for high cultural achievements.

1. Enhancement of Existence: Heroism Versus Utilitarianism

Burckhardt draws a fundamental distinction between two forms of existence along a dividing-line that appears in Homer and Hesiod: that of the *heros* (i.e. the warrior-hero) and that of the *banausos* (i.e. the utilitarian trader and craftsman). The upshot of his comparison, illustrated with reference to the *Odyssey*, reads as follows:

> Ein stärkerer Gegensatz läßt sich allerdings nicht denken als der zwischen dem Banausen und derjenigen Denkweise, die es darauf ankommen läßt, ob man sterbend dem Feinde Siegesruhm verschafft oder siegend von ihm solchen gewinnt.[26]

Burckhardt considers the willingness to risk a violent death a special form of existence. Untainted by any base and craven consideration of a pragmatic or utilitarian nature, the hero distinguishes himself by his ability to develop and sustain a truly aesthetic outlook on life. Burckhardt elevates the powerful presence of such an aesthetic disposition into the defining feature of Western Culture that accounts for its undeniable superiority over all others. In other words, Burckhardt grants the attribute "fully human" only to those who accomplish something special by raising themselves above the level of "mere existence", far above utilitarian ends and material interests.

In the lectures *On the Study of History* Burckhardt sketched a complete theory of the moral dimension of war. It is important to note that Nietzsche attended some of these lectures, and knew either the manuscript or the main ideas:

> Ein Volk lernt wirklich seine volle Nationalkraft nur im Kriege <, im vergleichenden Kampf gegen andere Völker > kennen, weil sie nur

26 *Griechische Kulturgeschichte* IV (*Ges. Werke*, vol. VIII) p. 42. "It is hard to imagine a starker contrast than the one between the banausos and the mentality of those men who put their life at risk in battle in order to hand in death the glory of victory to the enemy or by emerging victoriously themselves to acquire that glory from him."

> dann vorhanden ist; auf diesem Punct wird es dann suchen müssen, sie festzuhalten; allgemeine Vergrößerung des Maßtstabes.[27]

Here Burckhardt advances the following two arguments: first, war is the ideal medium to raise human existence above the basic impulses of nature. If life has an inherent tendency to strive towards a vital summit, then athletic competition in the sense of the Greek *agon* does not suffice. War mobilizes energies in a much more intensive fashion. Secondly, war sets up standards. The experience of war creates new yardsticks of intensive communication and devotion to a common cause, both in each individual and even more so in the community as a whole. If a people manages to preserve this newly acquired standard of existential intensity, then its ability to muster resources and strive tenaciously for higher goals will result in cultural achievements. In his philosophy of history, a systematic correlation exists between the cohesiveness of a civic community and its cultural productivity.[28]

2. Aestheticizing War

It is not astonishing that Burckhardt shapes the contours of a theory of total war *avant la lettre*.[29] Alongside its moral and social components, war, for Burckhardt, also possessed an aesthetic dimension. At times of war, we witness the "great spectacle" of the "subordination of the entire community under a common goal."[30] What is Burckhardt's rationale for aestheticizing war?

---

27 *Über das Studium der Geschichte. Der Text der ‚Weltgeschichtlichen Betrachtungen' auf Grund der Vorarbeiten von E. Ziegler nach den Handschriften herausgegeben von P. Ganz,* München 1982, p. 344. "Only in war, only in its struggle with other nations, a people does really become aware of its full national force. For this force manifests itself only in war. The task is to keep it at this level; this results in a general enhancement of the standard."

28 He uses this idea to explain the astonishing dynamic of Athenian activities after the Persian Wars. See *Griechische Kulturgeschichte* I (*Ges. Werke* V), p. 208-11.

29 I have elaborated this argument in detail in my essay „Burckhardt, Greek Culture and Modernity" in: ARION (forthcoming).

30 The whole quotation in *Studium der Geschichte*, p. 345: „Sodann enorme sittliche Superiorität des Krieges über den bloßen gewaltsamen Egoismus des Einzelnen: er entwickelt die Kräfte im Dienst eines Allgemeinen und zwar des höchsten Allgemeinen (Der Krieg allein gewährt den Menschen den großartigen Anblick der allgemeinen Unterordnung unter ein Allgemeines), und innerhalb

War as an aesthetic experience becomes only possible when the different moral reasons for individual and collective sacrifice have ceased to be of any great importance.

Hence Burckhardt had to break up the triad of the good, the beautiful, and the true: he historicizes (and thereby relativizes) the good and the true, while exalting the latter as a transhistorical absolute. The beautiful is supposed to be eternally valid. Historiographically speaking, that means that the most disastrous catastrophes offer magnificent spectacles of desperate heroism and total devotion:

> Ganz anders stellen sich zu unserm Gefühl diejenigen Bevölkerungen, von deren letzten Kämpfen und Untergang Kunde erhalten ist: die lycischen Städte gegen Harpagus, Carthago, Numantia, Jerusalem gegen Titus. Solche scheinen uns aufgenommen in die Reihe von Lehrern und Vorbildern der Menschheit in der Einen großen Sache: daß man an das Gemeinsame Alles setze und daß das Einzelleben der Güter höchstes nicht sei. Sodaß aus ihrem Unglück ein herbes, aber erhabenes Glück für das Ganze ensteht.[31]

According to Burckhardt's philosophy of history, catastrophes need to be incorporated into an ideal image, an image of eternal beauty that occidental humanity could hand down from generation to generation through its poets and historians, who are only up to the task when they disregard moral considerations and focus exclusively on the sublime and the consolation that inheres in the beautiful.

No doubt, many of these thoughts could be found in the works of other nineteenth-century authors. An intertextual analysis could easily point up the

---

einer Disciplin, welche zugleich die höchste heroische Tugend sich ent <falten> läßt" („There is, then, an enormous ethical superiority of war vis-à-vis the merely brutal egotism of the individual: war develops forces that are in the service of a more general good [war alone grants men the great spectacle of a collective's complete subordination to a general goal] and that within a discipline which allows the blossoming of the highest heroic virtue.")

31 *Studium der Geschichte*, p. 242. „Those populations whose last struggles and decline have come down to us elicit a completely different feeling in us: the Lycian cities against Harpagus, Carthage, Numantia, Jerusalem against Titus. They seem to belong to the ranks of models for humankind in that they teach us the one great lesson: that one has to devote everything to the common cause and that the individual existence is not the highest of goods. So that their misfortune is transformed into a bitter, but sublime happiness, for the whole."

existing affinities. *For present purposes this is not relevant.* What concerns us is Burckhardt's peculiar synthesis of these thoughts. He articulates the problem of material interests more radically than other contemporary historians and turns war into that social experience which is capable of silencing them - not any kind of war, but total war to which he attributes a cultural significance of the first order. In a war involving the entire existence of a people, as Burckhardt correctly defines total war, it is highly likely that the losers downright vanish. This destruction yields a double profit: the losers rise in their misfortune above their dull determination by natural instincts and assert their spiritual and cultural calling; they reach a moral end; and posterity delights in the sublime spectacle of catastrophe, thereby experiencing a "*herbes aber erhabenes Glück*", a bitter, but sublime happiness. It is difficult not to read these ideas in the context of the aestheticist movement that was gathering momentum in artistic circles in the last third of the nineteenth century and contributed both to the decadent anxieties of the fin de siècle and the vitalist hopes for a cathartic, redemptive war which eventually came in 1914.

IV. Reshaping the Tasks of Cultural History

Three very different factors can work to sustain the occidental culture in its actual crisis. Firstly a strong susceptibility for classical art helps to maintain abilities and dispositions necessary to keep up the cultural continuity of the West, as has been shown at the beginning of this essay. Secondly, war can be a medium for a transformation of culture which is favourable to the occidental tradition. Finally, it is incumbent for historiography to draw conclusions from the historical diagnosis of the actual crisis. As historiography occupies a pivotal place in the cultural tradition, Burckhardt is obliged to reshape the tasks of historical education and historiography and to define its form and content.

In the Introduction to his *Greek Cultural History* Burckhardt lines out a programme of the new tasks that historiography is obliged to, given the 'crisis' of historical education at the universities."[32]

---

32 *Griechische Kulturgeschichte* I (*GW,* V) p. 4.

The verdicts in this "Introduction" result in a sharp break with the premises of the German Historicism. Burckhardt stakes out the objective of his version of 'History of Culture': It has to map out as precisely as possible the cultural conditions of longue durée which made up the framework for that mental dispositions needed by the Occidental Culture – for its coming into existence and for its ongoing continuity.

> Das Interesse an der Geschichte ist in hohem Grade abhängig geworden von den allgemeinen Schwingungen des abendländischen Geistes, von der allgemeinen Richtung unserer Bildung...[33]

As the interest of each generation of 'humanistically educated people' in the past is directly dependent on the "allgemeine Richtung unserer Bildung" (*general direction of our educational culture*), Burckhardt cannot but stress that it is of prime importance to take influence on this 'orientation of our Bildung'. Otherwise we risk loosing the interest itself.

Thus, Cultural History has to become the main locus of historiologic self-reflection; others may care about a million details; but Cultural History has to give account of the "*wirklich Wissenswürdigste*".[34]

In contradistinction to antiquarian research and to the narrativist history of events he maps out the contours of what 'History of Culture' should be. Without rebuffing the antiquarian studies of August Boekh completely, he defines his 'History of Culture' as a clear counter-programme. And in a radical turn against the history of events he underscores:

> Wir dagegen haben Gesichtspunkte für die Ereignisse aufzustellen.[35]

Against both sides he raises Cultural History to the rank of an epistemic instance: it is bound to draw the dividing line between what is necessary to know and what is not, which straightens the coordinates attributing meaning to past events and facts. Modern educated people must be equipped with a well defined interest in knowledge so as to be able to acquire that minimal quantum of knowledge about the past which allows the European cultural continuum to subsist. Therefore, he insists that the prerequisite for a real interest in the Hellenic past is to be equipped with a 'humanistische Bildung'.

---

33 *Griechische Kulturgeschichte* I (*GW*, V), pp. 4f.

34 *Griechische Kulturgeschichte* I (*GW*, V), p. 4.

35 *Griechische Kulturgeschichte* I (*GW*, V), p. 4: "We, on the other hand, have to formulate the criteria for the events".

Mutatis mutandis this equipment is necessary for a deeper understanding of all times of the European past.

Which and what kind of knowledge is worth to be acquired by these interested people? A decision must be taken. The production of knowledge by universities is totally unable to shape semantic criteria which could help to decide. Historians who are snowed-under by the spadework of detail-research do not consider that it needs only small changes within the fragile ensemble of the modern Culture to invalidate our whole historical knowledge and to delegitimize historical research on a large university scale. Some changes within the semantic structure of the modern Culture may be sufficient to bring about this result.

The production of knowledge by universities is totally unable to do this. The status of scientific knowledge is at stake. Burckhardt constructs a pre-knowledge which is able to select what is worth to be known and eliminates what is not. A pre-knowledge is very close to a sort of transcendental scheme of historical understanding. It is not by chance that Burckhardt constructs this pre-knowledge very much like the idealistic philosophy constructed the concept of taste:

> Für Gelehrsamkeit sorgt die jetzige historisch-antiquarische Literatur; - w i r plädieren für ein lebenslang aushaltendes Mittel der Bildung und des Genusses.[36]

Interest in the past and in the heirloom of European Culture cannot be the result of a blind research and proliferation of historical details. It depends on the mental disposition of the educated classes. This mental disposition is intricately bound up with '*Genuß*', aesthetic pleasure. Therefore, it is a special form of aesthetic taste. As a matter of consequence Burckhardt favours the 'dilettant' as the saviour figure of Culture.

His concept of Cultural history is made for 'dilettants' and it seeks to create exactly that 'dilettantic' disposition of mind. This disposition is the modern form of that aesthetic view onto the world which took its origin in Greek Culture.

---

36 *Griechische Kulturgeschichte* I (*GW*, V), p. 9.

Chapter 6

Historiography as Political Activity: Heinrich von Treitschke and the Historical Reconstruction of Politics

KARL H. METZ

I. Introduction: Politics as History
II. Explication: Historicity and Political Action
III. Conclusion: Descending the Mountain of Nebo

I. Introduction: Politics as History

When you hear the name Treitschke,[1] you notice the smell of something like sulphur, you perceive a vague idea of that diabolic moment which sometimes attaches itself to names, to a "Machiavelli" or a "Hobbes". Smell-thinking of this kind is an act of political correctness. It defines public enemies and transforms them into emotional ones against whom we react personally: Give me someone to detest, and I know who I am. In any case, political action becomes a fiery reaction against enemies, and enemies are those who endanger the stability of an established system whose legitimacy they deny. In the Treitschkean perspective, too, politics were a fire giving off light and heat but at the same time posing a threat of destruction. It is the sensation of life you experience when you approach fire, it makes you alive and wide awake. This existential experience of politics forms the political man, and Treitschke

1 There is a political biography of Treitschke by ANDREAS DORPALEN: *Heinrich von Treitschke*, New Haven (Yale University Press) 1957. His work, taken as a historiographical pattern, is analysed by KARL H. METZ: *Grundformen historiographischen Denkens*, München (Fink) 1979, pp. 237ff.

was always more of a political man than a historian. History had to be political history, because the essence of social action was politics, i.e. a struggle for power in an ever-changing context. If, then, politics formed the centre of history, historical writing had to be perceived as political activity, for how could you speak about the fire, if you did not feel its heat?[2] The true historian, therefore, experiencing the political struggles of his time, writes contemporary history, a history that is meaningful to us, because it is still influential, forming the structures of institutions and ideologies which regulate the present. The historian writes about his time, in his time, for his time. He is a messenger of the past for the future, but he approaches the future only through the present. The future is the history of today; if we fail now, we will miss it.

This insistence on the present is significant. It distinguishes the Treitschkean position from the one held by Machiavelli and Hobbes. Adopting the liberal view, Treitschke interprets history as progress and European history as progress towards the nation state. Neither Machiavelli's "Prince" nor the Hobbesian "Leviathan" perceive of the present in this way, despite some Machiavellian dream of a free Italy. To them, history does not change the pattern of politics, analytically understood and, perhaps, geometrically constructed. Exactly this: the "mathematical" mind, armed with a timeless, sceptical perspective, made Hobbes, made Machiavelli a great name in the history of political thought. Treitschke, however, failed. He performed analytical shortcuts, responding to political challenges, presented as polemics. These analytical shortcuts, leading to verdicts, made him influential as well as notorious in his time: they prevented his becoming a great name, stinking of sulphur, but fascinating. Hobbes and Machiavelli outlived the states they had praised, and they survived in fame. Treitschke did not.

II. Explication: Historicity and Political Action

You cannot know what history means, you can only know what you mean when you look at history. No true knowledge can be gained by perceiving

2 METZ, K. H.: *Grundformen*, p. 301; HEINRICH VON TREITSCHKE: *Briefe*, Leipzig 1912–1920, vol. III, p. 178.

history from a distance referred to as objectivity or contemplation. Knowledge results from action or from a mind inclined to action. Knowledge rationalises action. This is a position deduced from historicism and, yet, in opposition to its quietist interpretation posed by Ranke, as Treitschke saw it.[3] If time is change, nothing can be stable - except your decision. Thus, it is not simply continuity that gives legitimacy to action, because a new epochal tendency can break continuity, as it does in the case of the nation which transformed the state, deposing regimes and princes. Legitimacy itself is a historical concept like all social institutions, be it law, economy or the form of social order. To recognise such a tendency and to transform it into politics makes man's social existence meaningful. The social sense thus gained is neither relativistic nor absolute. It is not relativistic, because it performs, so to speak, history's work in the present, and it is not absolute, because it moves before an open horizon that recedes, whenever it is approached. There is no ending of history, no final state, therefore you never reach the future, you only reach out for it. Here is no room for "dream politics" (*Idealpolitik*), i.e. politics that demand utopia, the ideal state and nothing but that. Nor is there a place for standstill politics, performing dead politics for dead days. Instead, a sort of politics is necessary that moves between the extremes: "realistic politics" (*Realpolitik*) pursuing an ideal with a sense of compromise. Treitschke's rejection of dream politics corresponds with his criticism of any "pure" theory of politics, or of society, economy and law. Social theory is always historical, bound to place and time, and so is society.[4] A pure theory would reduce reality to some geometrical construction, just as dream politics does, Jacobinism or Socialism would transform reality into a nightmare. No theory can, therefore, leave the realm of history and neither can any form of politics.[5]

The nucleus of politics is power and the nucleus of power is force, because the dynamics of politics is the struggle for power and its first and last criterion is force: the ability to use it and the ability to prevent its collapse into sheer violence. Politics, perceived as struggle, distinguishes friend from enemy, but historical, "realistic" politics accepts neither eternal enemies nor revolutionary violence, because it rejects the utopian absolutist impulse. An enemy can become a friend and vice versa, which implies that he always

3 *Briefe III*, p. 361; *Briefe II*, p. 351.

4 H. VON TREITSCHKE, *Die Gesellschaftswissenschaft. Ein kritischer Versuch* (1859), Darmstadt (Wissenschaftliche Buchgesellschaft) 1980.

5 *Briefe II*, pp. 124, 301, 345; *Briefe I*, p. 203.

remains human: He may leave us, but not mankind. History, or better historical consciousness, keeps us in balance, shaky and unstable, to be sure, a vague borderline, often approached, sometimes even crossed, but never left behind for good.

This is the Treitschkean paradox: the ambivalence of an activist attitude undermined by relativity. Treitschke himself tried to solve it by using historical relativity as a tool to question the legitimacy of the present and of its establishment, to transform the eternity of the present, as assumed by those who profit from it, into a time of change. Historicity, thus, meant the historisation of the present, it meant its openness towards the future, it meant political commitment as the expression of life. Historicity implied participation, but not in the sense of using it as contemplative knowledge of the past to enrich us as persons, because knowledge was only of value if it led to action. To inspire action, guided by historical knowledge, which made sure that you acted in accordance with a great epochal tendency, was the goal and social justification of historical writing: its indispensable service to society. Only such historically enlightened politics could move towards the future without destroying the past. The destruction of the past led to Dantonian fanaticism and Bonapartist ideology; it led to forms of political consciousness shaking the very foundations of the political community. The French Revolution as a leap into the future was the focus of Treitschke's critique of a political radicalism which reduced history to a heap of citations and gestures to be plundered at will. History, historical consciousness keeps politics within a pattern of continuity, within a pattern of interrelated change. Because "idealism", Treitschke was convinced, "clears up the mystery of history better than anything else",[6] politics had to be primarily politics of consciousness just as historiography had to use the history of social thought as its starting point for its enquiries into social action. Man was an image-maker, he needed justifications, declarations, insinuations, communications. This stress on consciousness as the dominant factor of action and, therefore, on the ideological formation of consciousness as the basic factor of politics, is typical of any activist historiography. The historian as an intellectual, i.e. as a producer of words, explanations, and images, needs a conception of the human as being ordered in his behaviour by reflections and knowledge. Or, to put it more precisely, he needs such a conception if he wants to appeal to convictions and decisions,

6 Cited by W. BUßMANN: „Treitschke als Politiker", *Historische Zeitschrift,* 177 (1954), p. 255.

and the activist historian is not one who whispers to the powerful few, but he is one who cries out to the many.

Historical, or "realistic" politics[7] is, then, the combination of two factors, namely social consciousness and force, reflected upon from a perspective of centuries. History contributes the experience of time, duration and change to the study of politics. History, politically understood, is not fatality: it is freedom which realises itself, whenever one interprets limits as potentials for success and not as walls to be exploded.

You can only understand what you love: this is the first principle of Treitschkean historiography. "Bloodless objectivity", he insists, "is contrary to the true historical sense".[8] Universal love is impossible, because the essence of love is inclusion at the price of exclusion. As in life, so in history. You cannot love all, accept all, or you will miss the true meaning of a historical situation, which is characterised by conflict and decision. Therefore, if you want to understand history, you have to take sides, and if you want to love, you have to opt for one or the other. Historiography makes you vividly alive by pushing you into love and emotion as do political decisions here and now. It seems ridiculous to think "that only those are able to come to an independent political judgement who hardly care about the state," and who stay aloof of political strife.[9] Neither the rigid moralism of an ideal politics, exemplified by liberalism and its representative historians F. C. Schlosser and G. G. Gervinus, nor the moral quietism of a Ranke can help us in our endeavour to face the present and recognise it as a challenge that imbues our social existence with meaning. What we need is a history that combines the moral impulse, indispensable to any guiding idea of social order, with an insight into the contemporary situation, and its potentials and limits. What we need is a kind of historical writing that "narrates and judges".[10] Historiography tells the past as present by looking for constellations in the past that are comparable to present ones. It tells the present as past by asking for the rise of the actual situation and its problems in the course of the last century. All history is,

---

7 Cf. *Briefe II*, p. 437; LUDWIG AUGUST VON ROCHAU: *Grundsätze der Real-politik, angewendet auf die staatlichen Zustände Deutschlands* (1853), ed. by H. U. Wehler, Frankfurt a.M. (Ullstein) 1972.

8 *Briefe II*, p. 351.

9 *Ibid*., p. 72.

10 H. VON TREITSCHKE: *Deutsche Geschichte im Neunzehnten Jahrhundert*, First Part (1879), Königstein (Athenäum) 1981, p. VII.

therefore, contemporary history, asking for the past because it asks for the future. The three great questions of German unification dominate, therefore, Treitschke's historical works before 1871. Should the new Germany be a centralised or a federal state? Should she include Austria or accept Prussian dominance? Should parliament or monarchy be the decisive political factor? Reflecting on the failure of 1848, a personal experience which had deeply moved him, Treitschke concluded: "You cannot storm the entrenchments of Alsen with an ideal spirit of the nation."[11] History shows that ideals must be compromised, or nothing is achieved at all. This was exemplified by the United Dutch Provinces in their struggle with the Spanish or the rise of a free Italy forcing Austria out of the country.[12]

France is the great example of political failure. France tried to destroy history in order to start anew. But Europe was no virgin country, it was imbued with culture and violence, with memories of a thousand years, with acres tilled since time immemorial. In Europe you could not build from the ground, simply because there was no ground, only the foundation walls, ruins, buildings of former generations. In Europe you could not break with history once and for all, you had to accommodate yourself to it, not by denying your ideals, but by adjusting them to a situation that was the result of a long historical process. However, France disturbed him in yet another respect, for it showed that you could, indeed, storm entrenchments with the help of such a thing as the ideal spirit of the nation. Perhaps the French experience - the fall of the Bastille, the ignominious collapse of an ancient monarchy, the terror, Bonapartism - left the deepest imprints of all on his consciousness. The chronic instability of the French state after 1789 was, thus, the result of an act of political madness, of an attempt to have future without history. France became the ideological battlefield of the nineteenth century[13], and by reflecting upon it, Treitschke discovers a new type of politics that springs from a state of broken history: "democratic despotism" or "Bonapartism".[14] Here, history is conceived as waste from which one picks up pieces of decoration, a Roman

---

11 H. VON TREITSCHKE: *Aufsätze, Reden, Briefe*, Meersburg (Hendel) 1929, vol. I, p. 571.

12 TREITSCHKE: „Die Republik der Vereinigten Niederlande"; „Cowour", cf. *Aufsätze, Reden, Briefe*, vol. II.

13 TREITSCHKE: „Frankreichs Staatsleben und der Bonapartismus", cf. *Aufsätze, Reden, Briefe*, vol. II, p. 109.

14 *Ibid.*, pp. 321f.

toga or Ceasar's laurel crown, reminiscences of an old king or a new dictator, all exchangeable at will. Democratic despotism is the result of an understanding of politics that no longer accepts history as experience and limitation. It is remarkable that two intellectuals as different as Treitschke and Karl Marx wrote their most poignant essays on Bonapartism, that novel phenomenon which disturbed them profoundly, since it did not fit into the familiar pattern of conservatism, liberalism and socialism. Treitschke's diagnosis, sharpened by polemics, was that of a history turned upside down by revolution, a history which offered only pieces of decoration, but no legitimacy drawing on some continuity of the political order. Thus, the construct of a "fable convenue",[15] of a political myth for the millions, becomes important. Bonapartism uses this fable in a more cynical way; it reduces politics to a theatre, while Jacobinism, the other ideological output of revolution, transforms it into a sermon preached in a most serious manner. The fatal weakness of Bonapartism lies in its descent from Machiavelli. The Florentine philosopher liberated the state from the church, but he still accepted that ethics was part of the spiritual realm of the church. Therefore, morality and politics were divided and this, Treitschke declares, spells destruction to the community.[16] In Europe, Christianity is the moral code: Christianity interpreted as ethics, not as confession or church. Politics, i.e. the activity of leading the state, produces its own moral obligations, corresponding to Christian principles as long as the basic law of statehood is not questioned, namely the pursuit of the state's self-preservation.[17] Impartial administration of the law, personal liberty, freedom of conscience, local self-government, and avoidance of unnecessary wars are political obligations of this kind. Human rights, the result of a historical process in the West, were also accepted by Treitschke. Historical interpretation of rights implies perceiving them as rights within limits set by culture and societal development. To interpret them as absolute, however, means to explode them, because only history produces cultural meaning.[18] Because of its absolutist pattern, the revolutionary conception of "fraternity" or "equality" leads to death or servitude. "La fraternité ou la mort!" is the beginning of political madness signifying the end of politics. Everything that is cultural, is histori-

---

15 *Briefe II*, pp. 112, 263, 347, 459; *Aufsätze, Reden, Briefe III*, pp. 11, 15.

16 H. VON TREITSCHKE: *Politik. Vorlesungen gehalten an der Universität zu Berlin*, ed. by M. Cornicelius, Leipzig (Hirzel) ^{4}1918, vol. I, pp. 90ff.

17 *Ibid.*, pp. 100ff.

18 *Ibid.*, p. 189.

cal, too. Time is a process in which growth, change, destruction and continuity are mixed up, forming patterns of complex individuality. Treitschke believes in progress, but it is a progress that cannot be described as a homogeneous, uniform development which ends in a final stage, predictable once and for all. Thus, Treitschke moves between historicism and liberalism: he insists on the relativity of values and on the necessity of relating behaviour and judgements to the historical situation in which they were formed.[19] However, he also views history, or better, the history of Europe, as a course of uneven improvement with great losses and great gains, but in the long run moving towards personal liberty as the noble aim of human endeavour. Slavery and bondage, for example, had their historical place. Now they have been abolished forever. This is a good thing, because the idea that one man is the property of another man is contrary to our belief in personal liberty, which again, is fundamental to modern society.[20] Thus, the historicist answer to the relativist dilemma is Treitschke's answer, too, though his is accentuated by activism. It is activism, not voluntarism. It acts, not because it desperately grasps for an experience of life, but it acts in order to do the work of the day, trusting not so much in God, but more in a history that makes sense. His antipathy against the agnostic philosophers of Basel drew its strength from his conviction that agnosticism disappeared, when reasoning was tamed by politics. If you take your point of view high up in the "clouds", you miss life; you cannot do justice to reality and to people who try to master it. Any flight into art and beauty was in vain, not only because it caused the focus of politics to become an issue of secondary importance, but also because it produced a notion of the present as decay and weakened the will to act. Treitschke appreciated Jacob Burckhardt's book on the Renaissance, he was a friend of Franz Overbeck, and he felt the intellectual power of Friedrich Nietzsche, and yet he had to turn against them, knowing that he could not join them without losing his Archimedian point of ethico-practical history.

There is no general theory of politics, there is only a plurality of historical reconstructions, concerning individual developments. Any realistic conception of politics is contemporary history, which draws its relevance from the political commitment of the historian. Machiavelli, for example, wrote contemporary history. If you criticise him, you have to consider the situation in which he experienced politics and in which he gave advice. Apart from the

19 *Ibid.*, pp. 4f., 367.
20 *Ibid.*, p. 169.

basic law of the state, namely its will to survive, there is nothing unchangeable in politics, except perhaps the necessity to balance force and consent, because no state can exist for long if it is not maintained by popular consent.[21] Such a "realistic" conception of politics had been advanced, according to Treitschke, by Alexis de Tocqueville, by Franz Lieber, the promoter of Political Science in the USA, or by Alexander Hamilton, one of the founding fathers of the United States and a contributor to the "Federalist Papers".[22] Now, Hamilton still had argued within the context of natural law, but since then man had seen through the illusory character of such a right, and the Hamilton argument had found its true basis in historical reasoning. Names or titles are semantic illusions, they become meaningful only when they are understood historically, i.e. related to the situation in which they were used. [23] Any general theory, so Treitschke supposes, is just a system of names. In order to communicate ideas you need names. In order to organise information you need them, too. However, names remain labels without content, and only history can make them meaningful. Treitschke uses "names" as signposts showing the way to contemporary history and, thus, to the chances and limits of attempting to realise goals.[24] The aim is a kind of reasoned political activity on the side of the citizens as well as on the side of the statesmen. "Politics is applied history",[25] or better: Politics is the application of historical experience, mainly as formulated by historiography, to the conflicts and problems of the present. Consequently, historical politics cannot be universal. It remains a conception with empty spaces and contradictions. Every present produces its own, specific history, which cannot be predicted by the historical experience of times past. Secondly, no situation of bitter conflict can be resolved into harmony. Theoretically, any collapse of the state is awful, therefore, no political theory can justify revolution or civil war on "moral" grounds, because then it would surrender to religion, fanaticism and the chaos of individual absolutism in moral questions. Yet, history demonstrates the futility of any theoretical rejection of revolution. Revolution is a historical fact, and more than that, it is propelled by some kind of moral reaction against a corrupted

21 *Politik*, vol. II, p. 368.
22 METZ: *Grundformen*, pp. 310, 363ff.
23 *Ibid.*, p. 362.
24 *Ibid.*, pp. 374ff.
25 *Politik*, vol. I, p. 2.

regime that has lost popular consent.[26] Moreover, to resist a ruler who violates conscience is an act that can regenerate the essence of ethics in a man, in a society, and save them from decay. Treitschke thinks of Luther and he offers no answer, but the paradox of a "yes" and a "no" at the same time. Neither historiography nor political action are able to resolve the paradox, but the historian can understand it, while the politician has to fight it. Treitschke, however, was both historian and politician, and this was his strength as well as his dilemma. As long as he remained a critic of official policy, the historian and the political activist were united by a common cause. But when the "prophet" arrived at the promised land, the dilemma became obvious. Satire, perhaps his main intellectual weapon, was reduced to polemics, when he turned from criticism to apology. Finally, German unification was realised by Prussia and yet, there was still quarrel, even strife in this happy new land. The historian Treitschke should have known better, but the activist was angry and understood nothing. Climbing the mountain is tiresome, nevertheless it is full of expectation. But descending the mountain of Nebo is quite another thing, for its easiness is burdened by the loss of hope of the great horizon that waits for us. Treitschkes's controversial attacks on German Jews and on the group of social reformers led by Gustav Schmoller were misguided, because they did not achieve their declared goal, namely to strengthen the new state, and they alienated many friends and collaborators of former times.[27] The critical potential of a politically committed historiography was lost and with it the idea of combining critical history with historicism, the will to act with the reflective power of a historical mind.

III. Conclusion: Descending the Mountain of Nebo

After victory, a political idea is at once verified and nullified, unless one succeeds in transforming it into a policing myth, a "*fable convenue*" defining political correctness. Jules Michelet's historiographic praise of the French

26 *Ibid.*, pp. 131ff.

27 Cf. W. BOEHLICH (Ed.): *Der Berliner Antisemitismusstreit*, Frankfurt a.M. (Insel) 1965.

Revolution[28] became essential for the "*mystique républicaine*" of the new French state after 1871. Treitschkean history, too, played an important role in the formation of correct thinking in the Germany of Prussian descent. This was acknowledged by the allied philosophers in the trench, who fought the First World War as a war of civilisations and who gratefully took Treitschke as a symbol for a political regime that showed how detestable the enemy was, detestable on moral grounds and not simply because he was a rival in the struggle for influence and power.[29] Using his "Politics" as evidence, a text composed of notes put down by students during a lecture, they aimed at agitation. Of course, an Englishman nurtured by Whig history had to be scandalised by many of Treitschke's remarks and judgements, for there was only one true pattern of progress and Macaulay had described it, a description that became a prescription for all who claimed to be civilised. Therefore, not just England and Germany, but Whiggism and Historicism confronted each other. It was more than an intellectual and cultural confrontation: It was a political confrontation, too, because Greater Britain, as well as the Greater United States later in the century, was grasping for a conception of historically justified politics, one which combined the claim to global validity with the glory of the one and unique nation that had created it. The Great and "Greater" Britain was a nation of global possessions and ambitions, a nation justifying her civilising mission in India and Africa with Macaulayan progress. The "Little" Germany of Treitschke's vision, which was close to Bismarck's policy for a "satiated" Germany, did not aim at such a view, she called only for the position of a great power among other great powers. Politics, thus, remained historically and geographically limited, knowledge for here and now, not wisdom for all days nor prescription for mankind.

In his beautiful book on *History and Historians in the Nineteenth Century*, George P. Gooch spoke about Ranke with admiration, even love: Here was a man who had understood that the house of Clio was a temple, not a battlefield. The search for truth, not the call for action is the end of historical

---

28 Cf. K. H. METZ: „Die Resurrektion der Geschichte. Ein Beitrag zum historischen Denken J. Michelets", *Archiv für Kulturgeschichte,* 65 (1983).

29 Cf. E. LEIPPRAND: *Treitschke im englischen Urteil*, Stuttgart (Kohlhammer) 1931; J. MACCABE: *Treitschke and the Great War*, London (Unwin) 1914; E. BARKER: *Nietzsche and Treitschke: the worship of power in modern Germany*, London (Oxford University Press) [4]1914.

writing. For Treitschke, therefore, Gooch felt no sympathy.[30] To look at history from a distance allows one to see the faces of men without feeling the heat of their breath. One experiences the distance as hermeneutic space. Historiography becomes an act of contemplation on men: not on humankind in general, but on a pluralistic universe which has no end nor meaning recognisable to us, but only ends and meanings innumerable. Truth is an answer with many questions, but if you want to act, it is better to arrive at answers and to avoid too many questions. Treitschke tried to demonstrate that it was possible to combine the novel pattern of historical thinking with a position of value-judgement and political participation. Such a synthesis can be achieved best by writing contemporary history, which is knowledge gained by partisanship. If there is just one permanence in social life, it is the permanence of contemporaneity. Man is always a contemporary, he lives within a contemporary framework of conditions, problems and values, he thinks about the past by contemporizing it. Historiography analyses the past in the context of present problems and questions: Not just because this is the only way to understand it, but also because this is the only means to make the historiographical activity useful to society.

If we try to put together the essentials of Treitschkean thought, we could summarize them as follows: First of all, it is characteristic of his thinking that he develops his categories not in an abstract or "mathematical" manner, but in the course of his narrative. Thinking is an activity that forms and alters its analyzing concepts according to the events or structures discussed. These concepts are not defined once and for all, they are produced anew whenever a new situation is under discussion, and they claim meaning only insofar as this situation is concerned. Such an idea of the historicity of words and concepts results from the conviction that everything which is social is historic, too, and because it is historic it is relative to the genetic pattern in which it occurred and relative to the observer who constructs it as a narrative meaningful to him. Contemporary history, being the history of our present mind and state, is the history nearest to our problems and questions: It is the history we need most. Contemporary history is innovation: Those who want to write it are those who want to change it. Therefore, it is no accident that historicism was the intellectual tool of the "Prussian" school of history, i.e. of those who struggled for a "German Revolution" in the sense expressed by Disraeli. His-

30 G.P. GOOCH: *Geschichte und Geschichtsschreibung im 19. Jahrhundert* (1913), Frankfurt a.M. (S. Fischer) 1964, p. 168.

toriographical historicism in the nineteenth century implied a policy of innovation rejecting one of tradition and legitimacy as incorporated by Austria. That Austria did not participate in the great drive towards a historicist perspective of history and politics, that her leading intellectuals defended "mathematical" positions (e.g. in economics or logical positivism) just shows how much historicism reflected a specific political situation. Historicist historiography of the Treitschkean type, however, is emphatic communication urging for a "better future". The result is a text that longs for a reader. To attract him the literary quality of the text is important, and Treitschke knew this. He was not afraid of literature because the literary style was the medium transporting meaning to the public. The message to be transported was the idea of the nation as a cultural entity with political ambitions, i.e. the claim to form a nation state, a claim favourable to Prussia but destructive to Austria.

The present is the provisional finality of history, it is the goal of historical writing. The present time is our lifetime, and life is identified by activity. Activity for activity's sake remains blind, but historiography can enlighten it by pointing to limits and conditions as results of specific historic developments. Conditions that are historic are relative, too. They can be altered within a framework of continuity, breaking which would spell disaster. Acting responsibly, enlightened by historiography, means to realise liberty, and this is the sense of human existence in the polity. It is the Treitschkean message, spoken with the heat of enthusiasm and soaked with prejudice and partisanship, but spoken still.

References

BARKER, E.: *Nietzsche and Treitschke: the worship of power in modern Germany*, London (Oxford University Press) ^{4}1914.

BOEHLICH, W. (Ed.): *Der Berliner Antisemitismusstreit*, Frankfurt a.M. (Insel) 1965.

BUßMANN, W.: "Treitschke als Politiker", *Historische Zeitschrift*, 177 (1954).

DORPALEN, A.: *Heinrich von Treitschke*, New Haven (Yale University Press) 1957.

GOOCH, G.P.: *Geschichte und Geschichtsschreibung im 19. Jahrhundert (1913)*, Frankfurt a.M. (S. Fischer) 1964.

LEIPPRAND, E.: *Treitschke im englischen Urteil*, Stuttgart (Kohlhammer) 1931.

MACCABE, J.: *Treitschke and the Great War*, London (Unwin) 1914.
METZ, K.H.: *Grundformen historiographischen Denkens*, München (Fink) 1979.
METZ, K.H.: "Die Resurrektion der Geschichte. Ein Beitrag zum historischen Denken J. Michelets", *Archiv für Kulturgeschichte*, 65 (1983).
ROCHAU, L.A.v.: *Grundsätze der Realpolitik, angewendet auf die staatlichen Zustände Deutschlands (1853)*, ed. by H. U. Wehler, Frankfurt a.M. (Ullstein) 1972.
TREITSCHKE, H.v.: *Die Republik der vereinigten Niederlande*, Berlin (Reimer) 18XX (Preußische Jahrbücher, Bd. 24).
TREITSCHKE, H.v.: *Briefe*, ed. by. Max Cornicelius, 3 Vol., Leipzig (Hirzel) 1912-1920.
TREITSCHKE, H.v.: *Politik. Vorlesungen gehalten an der Universität zu Berlin*, ed. by Max Cornicelius, Leipzig (Hirzel) [4]1918.
TREITSCHKE, H.v.: *Aufsätze, Reden und Briefe*, ed. by Karl Martin Schiller, Meersburg (Hendel) 1929.
TREITSCHKE, H.v.: *Die Gesellschaftswissenschaft. Ein kritischer Versuch (1859)*, Darmstadt (Wissenschaftliche Buchgesellschaft) 1980.
TREITSCHKE, H.v.: *Deutsche Geschichte im Neunzehnten Jahrhundert, First Part (1879)*, Königstein (Athenäum) 1981.

Chapter 7

Literary Criticism and Historical Science: The Textuality of History in the Age of Goethe - and Beyond

DANIEL FULDA

I. The Texts of History
II. Narrativism and the Origin of 'The One History' in the 18th Century
III. The Contribution of Art to the Shaping of History as Knowledge

Which methods and perspectives of literary criticism can contribute to describe the unique character of historical thought, the epistemological status of historical knowledge as well as the methodology of historical science in its complexity? With the title "Textuality of History", that particular aspect is characterised by which the study of literary criticism primarily presents its observations on history and its discipline. The epistemological potential of such a method of observation, especially for the study of historicism, will be proposed in this article in three steps. After a short explanation dealing with the meaning of 'Textuality of History', the first chapter introduces the consciousness of that textuality already possessed by historicism, when it used the topos of history as a book. The second chapter deals with the systematic explanation of this particular textuality. In this connection, the relation between history and narrative must also be discussed along with the peculiarity of the concept of 'the one History' described by Reinhart Koselleck which emerged in the latter half of the 18th century. The third and simultaneously most extensive chapter undertakes the attempt to explain the 'rise of historicism' as a literary analogous textualisation of historical thought and scientific historical activity.[1]

I. The Texts of History

To conceive history, metaphorically speaking, as a text or as a book to be read is not just one of the oldest but also one of the most relevant topics of historical thought.[2] The starting point of this idea in the method of history should not create much of a problem: In the medium of texts, history at first appears in various sources which are the basis of historical research. Only these sources still give evidence of past actions and social structures on which history attempts to throw light. Even though the past in question is relatively recent and gives one the opportunity to gain insight into it by speaking to contemporary witnesses, the historian is all the same involved with texts, in this case, mainly oral in nature. Even non-textual or semi-textual sources such as various archaeological finds, historical buildings, seals, tables etc. finally come under the regimen of texts in the event of them being subjected to verification and interpretation of sources. We also find history in a textual form wherever the historian puts down his knowledge of history, or, to be more precise, wherever he develops this knowledge, for both, thought and word, cannot be epistemologically separated.[3] The knowledge represented in a text thus cannot be found anywhere else outside that text, in any case it does not possess the same marked character. Eventually, the discipline of history emerges as the historians' collective endeavour only by the exchange of texts, mainly those published, but apart from that, also those oral in nature.

Thus, working with texts as his basis, the historian goes on to produce texts. 'History as text' most certainly means something much more fundamental. It indicates that the structural pattern of History (indicated in the follow-

1 The author would like to refer in part to some of his own research, cf. FULDA (1999). - I am grateful to Shahnoor Sheryari for the translation of this essay.

2 Cf. DEMANDT (1978, pp. 379-92). Forerunners of the topos date back to the *Old Testament*.

3 Notes to philosophy of language, explanations and functional requirements of the knowledge of History by Wilhelm von Humboldt, cf. PRÜFER (1996, pp. 150-7, 164-6).

ing text by a majuscule), with the help of which we organize the past and connect it with the events of the present and the future, is a product of texts. This process of events, which we call History, is not merely represented and appreciated in texts, but at first constitutes itself in texts. Only when written by the historian do these texts give the past that particular structure which clearly identifies it as 'History'. In other words, the term 'history' does not represent a structure in the past, but rather portrays a conceptual pattern borne by texts which only then enables us to see the 'past', along with our present and the expected future, in that specific genetic context familiar to us. The linguistic and epistemological postulates claiming that textuality cannot be circumvented does not, in this regard, simply undermine the 'realistic' referential assumptions of numerous historians.[4] The concept of History by itself appears as a textual construction. This proposition seeks, by introducing two important points, to extend beyond the topos of history as a book. The activity of reading a given text has now been taken over by producing a text. The historical matter meant to be read must first be written down. And the textual quality of 'the' History doesn't merely have the status of a metaphor, but it also represents an epistemological finding.

During the last two decades, the discussion on the textuality of 'History' has played a key role in both, the theory of history as well as literary criticism.[5] However, it has hardly ever been put into question what our interest concerning this particular textuality can do to contribute towards explaining the emergence of modern historical thought ('modern' here refers to the fundamentals developed during the '*Sattelzeit*' (*pivotal period*) around 1800). Even those texts which create a certain meaning of history are conditioned by their historical context and are subject to change. If we want to see at what point in time and in which way historical thought following the concept of the 'one History' has developed, it is necessary to examine those texts in which this process has been effected. To analyse the structure of those texts would then also mean to disclose the structure of what is known to us as 'History'. The reason is that the text which generates the characteristic structure of events and knowledge, viz. History, must have a characteristic structure on its part.

---

4 Cf. WHITE (1989).

5 Cf. VEESER (1989); EGGERT/PROFITLICH/SCHERPE (1990); BERKHOFER (1995); ANKERSMIT/KELLNER (1995); ZAGORIN (1999); FULDA/TSCHOPP (2001).

The history of the *topos* of History as a book indicates that the correlation between History and Text has certainly undergone historical change. As pointed out by Hans Blumenberg, this concept is derived from the previously held perception, existing over the Middle Ages, of Nature as a book, in which God is revealed to mankind.[6] In German-speaking countries, we first come across this transfer by Johann Georg Hamann, later described in detail by Johann Gottfried Herder. Herder perceives "*die Dinge der Welt als Worte eines großen Buches [...], in welchem wir den Sinn des unbekannten Urhebers lesen*" i.e. he sees "the things of the world as words of a great book in which we confront the meaning given by the unknown creator".[7] Applied to history this would mean that the centuries form syllables, the nations "letters and perhaps even punctuation marks" the significance of which can only be concluded from their position in the entity.[8] The framework of this textualization is still theological in nature: History, according to Herder, is the "great book of God".[9] Apart from this idea, he sees man as cooperating in composing this book and definitely as an author of great genius, for only his synthetic observation can behold that which is otherwise only perceived in small fragments.[10] Subsequently, it had become self-evident to historians of the 19th century to speak of the book of history ("*Buch der Geschichte*") in the sense of a literary structure of the past in question.[11] Even the theoretician Johann Gustav Droysen believes it can only be possible to understand the order of things and the meaning of the whole ("*Sinn des Ganzen*") according to the model of those texts which flow from the creative poetic spirit

---

6 Cf. BLUMENBERG (1981, p. 178). Textualization of History in the work of Herder was thoroughly investigated by VOM HOFE (1984).

7 HERDER: *Eine Metakritik zur Kritik der reinen Vernunft* [1799; *Against Pure Reason*], in: HERDER (1998, pp. 303-640, see p. 472).

8 HERDER: *Auch eine Philosophie der Geschichte zur Bildung der Menschheit* [1774; *This, too, a Philosophy of History*], in: HERDER (1994, pp. 9-107, see pp. 105-6).

9 *Ibid.*, p. 106.

10 Cf. HERDER: "Shakespeare" [1773], in: HERDER (1993, pp. 498-521, see pp. 509-10).

11 RANKE: "Über die Trennung und Einheit von Deutschland" (1832; "The Division and Unification of Germany"), in: RANKE (1867-1890, vol. 49/59, pp. 134-72, see p. 172).

("*schöpferischen Dichtergeist*").[12] The literary text offers the point of comparison in order to explain the assumed structure of history. This application of the book-metaphor (i.e. the metaphor of history as a book) does not mean that history is only constructed when it becomes a written text. An important step in that direction is made by Wilhelm Dilthey in whose work the historistic concept of 'History as text' reaches its peak. Dilthey ignores the divine author who had till then confirmed the coherence and significance of such texts.[13] From now on, man writes the text of history himself. This leads the historian to a similar paradox as today when confronted with poststructuralist theories on textuality: History must first be written in order to be known. A major difference is yet to be listed: According to Dilthey, human life has the structure of meaning of a text, so that writing history means less of a purely linguistic construction and more of a spelling-out of anthropological preconditions.

The above discourse has given us a first impression on the metaphoric textualisation of History in the German 'Historical School', which is set in the period from Herder to Dilthey. The development of a topos, of course, does not have much evidential value since it merely reflects the process in question but does not necessarily influence it. I must go back a long way in the realms of historical theory and also be more explicit in order to make my theory more plausible that the modern concept of history has developed in the course of a specific textualisation of human orientation between past, present and future.

II. Narrativism and the Origin of 'The One History' in the 18th Century

Knowledge of the past was not and is not necessarily referred to the framework familiar to us as History. Neither is knowledge of the past always and everywhere referred to this framework. This particular category, History, requires a certain form of historical knowledge, a certain form of texts that reconstruct the past. Since about thirty years, scholars such as Hayden White,

12 DROYSEN (1977 [1857], p. 30).

13 Cf. DILTHEY (1927, pp. 290-91).

Louis Mink, Paul Ricœur and Jörn Rüsen have worked out that we have to view this particular form in narratives. In Analytical Philosophy, narrativity was first examined and identified "as a *kind of explanation* especially appropriate to the explanation of historical, as against natural, events and processes".[14] Fundamental to this explanation is the understandable logical consistency of narratives;[15] in addition to that we have their synthesizing function. The modality of the narration makes it possible to create a specific organization and arrangement of the past and its genetic linkage to the present. In retrospective, past happenings can gain the logic of a coherent and straight history. To tell a history would thus imply following a definite fable and a particular narrative pattern which in turn build the 'depth structure' of this history. With the help of this deep structure, the narrative conducts its own interpretation, i.e. the allocation of a certain significance not contained in its factual elements.[16] To this point, the narrative dominates historical writings as put down in a literal sense by the historian. In Hans-Michael Baumgartner's transcendental philosophy of history, the "basic feature of the narrative" is further identified as an "a priori scheme" on which all reconstructions of history "are based as a condition of possibilities".[17]

In general, narrativism does not work on historical differentiation. The narrative is held to be an anthropological universal and hence a major form of any historical thought. The problem of ahistoricity becomes quite clear in the case of Ricœur when he, along the lines of Augustinus, formulates the problem of 'dissonance' in the human conception of time and finds the 'answer' to this problem in the 'consonant' story long existing as a *myth* in Aristotelian poetics.[18] But this view neglects one important point: the insight gained by such different thinkers as Reinhart Koselleck and Michel Foucault that History, understood as a universal and integrating relation of events and processes having an irreversible development, is a concept that first took shape not before the mid-18th century. Of all the things, this narrativism seems to relieve the history of its historicity.

Let us take a look at the result before proceeding to the main argument. The theoretical narrativity of history is well able to stand the test which is

14 WHITE (1984, p. 7).
15 Cf. DANTO (1965, pp. 233-56).
16 Cf. WHITE (1984, pp. 20-5).
17 BAUMGARTNER (1976, p. 279).
18 RICŒUR (1983-85, vol. 1, pp. 19-136).

signified by the historicity of the term history, and in such a way that the textuality of the modern term of history becomes all the more clearer. Firstly: Given that the concept of the one History were only to be valid in a historically limited period, the more fundamental, anthropologically based connection of narrative and knowledge of the past, as in the works of Ricœur, Rüsen and David Carr among others, is by no means totally dissolved. Narratives and memories of past events can be found in the earliest texts of western civilisation. Carr, in addition, has reason enough to describe that the narrative is that particular implement with the help of which people everywhere have always assured a meaningful coherence of their lives by giving the events in which they have been involved a pragmatic context.[19] These particular stories must of course be clearly distinguished from the narrative organization of all events which we know as History. To understand the past as presented in histories, be it the individual past of one's own life, or be it in the larger sense the past of certain peoples, does by no means imply that the entire past in its relation with the present forms solely one unique History. One single grammatical detail, namely the number of the term 'history', indicates the crucial difference. Although there may be innumerable histories with which people have always conceived their past, on the other hand, the history which covers the civilisations of the ancient world as well as the Chinese Middle Ages and the American Civil War always exclusively exists in the singular. This one single History integrates all the particular histories and hence, using Reinhart Koselleck's accurate expression, can appropriately be termed as a 'collective singular'.[20]

As shown by Koselleck in a detailed study on historical semantics, the appearance of the collective singular in the German-speaking countries exactly coincides with the perception of this History as a total continuum of events and processes.[21] Firstly, the term *Geschichte* referred simply to the object of historical research, and from around 1780 onwards, also to the totality of historical knowledge, which up to then was denoted in German by the Latin word *Historia* which in turn could always be used with the implication of a 'collective singular'.[22] In the respective languages of the leading nations in

19 Cf. CARR (1986, pp. 45-72, ch. 2). In support of this theory from a psychological viewpoint, cf. STRAUB (1998).

20 Cf. KOSELLECK (1992, pp. 38-66).

21 Cf. KOSELLECK (1975, pp. 647-53).

22 Cf. *Ibid.*, pp. 653-8.

historiography, Britain and France, the intellectual turn during the 18th century cannot be established at a similar semantic level as in German. Reason being that in English and French there exists no competition, as seen in German between the borrowed term from Latin, *Historia.* and a word of Germanic origin, *Geschichte*, for these two countries have both maintained that similar word of Latin origin, viz. *history* and *histoire*. Nevertheless the idea of the past seen as being a total continuum that leads to the present gained ground in the field of historical thought in Western Europe, too.[23]

The basic way in which history is supposed to be seen as a text is elucidated by the fact that the new, complex concept of History that emerged in the 18th century owes its existence to a "fusion of poetics and history".[24] Koselleck makes this clear on the basis of German and French source material. Whereas literary composition increasingly stood up to the requirements of historical plausibility, history, to speak in Aristotelian terms, orientated itself towards the more general truth of literature, i.e. towards its inner plausibility.[25] The logical consistency and sufficiency of actions, always a remarkable feature of the poetical *mythos*, became a requirement of historiography as well, and thereafter was passed on to the object of historiography, the connection of events in History.[26] Ever since, history has been seen as a text. Or to put it precisely, only by understanding the entirety of the past in an emphatic sense, namely in the sense of a literary composition as a text, it is constituted as History.

III. The Contribution of Art to the Shaping of History as Knowledge

After passing through the *theory* of history, or to be more precise, the narrative theory of history, we turn to the history of the concept of 'History' (*Begriffsgeschichte*). It cannot be taken for granted that along with the new term we also had the capability to represent its content textually, i.e., in the true

23 Cf. SCHULIN (1994, pp. 337-8).

24 KOSELLECK (1975, p. 661).

25 Cf. *Ibid.*, p. 660.

26 Cf. *Ibid.*, p. 663.

sense of the word 'History'. The concept of 'History' as yet did not create a sufficient condition for the writing of history which was capable of expressing its conceptual implications (continuity, totality, orientation). What this term demanded but did not provide for was the principal possibility as well as the concrete modi not just to think but also to write 'History'.

In the middle of the 18th century, the status of historiography lacks uniformity in the leading European nations. The historians in Britain and France were way ahead of the German development. Worth mentioning among others are, on the French side, Voltaire's and Turgot's philosophies of a coherent history of Ancient China right up to their own period, and Hume's and Robertson's narrative histories on nations and epochs on the British side. Compared to their West-European counterparts, German historians were far less in a position to write history in a way as to appropriately suit the new, 'modern' concept of historical thought.[27] Historians belonging to the Enlightenment in Western Europe had lesser difficulties in representing history as a narrative text for they had the necessary linguistic patterns along with the required literary competency. Conversely, German historians from that period used to work in a lesser developed framework within the national literary scene. This refers to the stylistic repertoire as well as the book market and the views of the public. In spite of that, German historiography at the beginning of the 19th century first acquired a scientific status that required some distancing from foreign purposes of historiography, both philosophical and of a rhetorical-moral nature, and as well required the public organization of research facilities mainly at universities.[28] The above mentioned backlog had been transformed in only a few decades to a head start. This requires further explanation: Which made historiographical methods this exceptional rise possible?

In my opinion, this leap ahead was due to, at first a delayed, but for that an even more thorough acquisition of the concept of history as text. Among German historians, the modern concept of history as being in itself a differing continuum was first proposed in the Göttingen school. A highly ambitious attempt to orientate the writing of history along these lines was undertaken in 1772 by August Ludwig Schlözer in his work *Vorstellung seiner Universalhistorie* (Presentation of His Universal History). Schlözer introduced a con-

27 Cf. BÖDEKER ET AL. (1986); GOTTLOB (1989); BLANKE/FLEISCHER (1990); BLANKE (1991, pp. 111-88); FULDA (pp. 49-58); SÜßMANN (2000, pp. 33-66).

28 Cf. SIMON (1996, pp. 127-30).

ceptual pair in the theory of history which attempts to grasp the new concept of history in a theoretical manner: the contrary of aggregates and systems. The historical aggregate merely consists of *Geschichten* (histories/stories); only the system, in contrast, is in a position to give "a living idea of the whole" ("*eine lebendige Vorstellung des Ganzen*"). Schlözer's ideas are aimed at a universal history; the whole entity means to him "the world", i.e., "humanity" ("*das menschliche Geschlecht*").[29] This expectation inevitably lead to an excessive overtaxing since Schlözer was pushing towards a system which would explain the unity of history. Thus, a structural model, which could neither be sufficiently verbalised nor be symbolically represented, was drawn up. The historians of the Enlightenment period, on the other hand, rejected the narrative as an *implicitly* explanatory process. Schlözer and Gatterer raised the concept of not narrating but rather creating a closed system of cause and effect to a historiographical ideal, because they were oriented towards the mechanical ideals of rationalistic philosophy[30]. Schlözer finds literary composition and historical writings to be antithetically opposing one another. A "novelist" ("*Romanschreiber*") meant to him someone who extracts the efforts of scholarly work. Accordingly, a "*creative* genius" ("*schöpferisches* Genie") was truly someone "who creates his stuff out of nothing". From an epistemological point of view, Schlözer believed objectivity to be possible and thus based his assumption that "the historian creates nothing" ("*der Historiker hingegen erschaffet nichts*").[31] A literary composition in his opinion was, therefore, neither a substantial model nor a medium of reflection of historiographical text production.

Nevertheless, only within a few years' time, the Göttingen historians came to a dead-end. It was not possible to realize a single one of their numerous concepts of universal history.[32] A way out of this dead-end was shown by that particular concept which had before been refuted viz. 'history as (a literary analogical) text'. But now, this was applied to a totally different concept of

29 SCHLÖZER (1990 [1772/73], p. 18), also reprinted in: HORST WALTER BLANKE, DIRK FLEISCHER (1990, vol. 2, p. 670).

30 Cf. GATTERER (1767a, p. 80); FULDA (1996, pp. 59-76).

31 SCHLÖZER (1990 [1772/73], vol. 2, p. 245); cf. GATTERER (1767b, p. 20).

32 Cf. REILL (1975, pp. 46, 101); FULDA (1996, pp. 200-208). As shown by Frank R. Ankersmit in his Gibbon-analysis, the substantialist representation-model in Western European historiography also faced a similar crisis; cf. ANKERSMIT (1995).

history. It was no more the particular history narrated about a definite period in the past, but rather the newly-gained History as a whole. The text, the only mode in which we are able to conduct historical thought, thus gained the function of a transcendental pattern.

This phenomenon is first observed in the case of Herder whom we saw transfer the book metaphor to history. Through more or less direct debates with the Göttingen historians he composed history and historiography according to the structure of a literary text. According to Herder, the structure of these texts always forms a presupposed pattern which adequately enables the historian to connect the disparate particles of historical events. Thus, in a way, we could satisfy the demands of a scientific discipline to maintain a coherence that easily corresponds to human intellectual and linguistic capabilities. In this manner, Herder sets free the microstructural sequence of the cause and effect principle from its mechanistic chains. At the same time, the dramatic plot advances to that macrostructure in which, as Droysen maintains, affairs (*Geschäfte*) become history.[33] To view history as a text is, in these cases, anthropologically founded: As man learns about the world through language, say through texts, any sort of integrating concept of knowledge like, for instance, History must follow textual structures constructed by language itself. These structures are found to be most concise especially in poetry.

What Herder acquires from literature is consequently no more a facultative supplement of historiography that possibly intensifies its effects on the reader, but in fact constitutes its object.[34] The text, structured according to a literary pattern, is the appropriate presentation of 'History' as perceived by historicism since it conveys meaning by both, the whole as well as by the individual components, on a symbolical-microcosmic level "in which an independent whole appears in each detail" ("*wo in jeder Einzelnheit schon so ein Ganzes erscheint*").[35] It can articulate the intrinsic value of peoples and epochs as well as the inseparability of the entire history (which is, of course, never complete). Two epistemological obstacles of the Enlightenment history have thus been taken care of: Firstly, the illustrative quality of historical writing to the past is substituted by historiographical 'fiction'. We must note here

33 Cf. DROYSEN (1977 [1857], p. 69).

34 Cf. SEEBA (1985); KNODT (1990); FULDA (1996, pp. 183-227).

35 HERDER: *Auch eine Philosophie der Geschichte zur Bildung der Menschheit* [1774; *This, too, a Philosophy of History*], in: HERDER (1994, pp. 9-107, see p. 105).

that fiction does not mean inventing stuff but rather perceiving and constructing the narrative. Secondly, the obligation of conformity to the system of the Enlightenment history is resolved, the reason being that Herder conceives historical insight oriented towards the 'liberal' model of understanding a literary text which uses all faculties of the mind and soul.

Herder had the inclination to unite source research, rational knowledge and aesthetic constructions and so there emerged a threat of forgetting the 'epistemological cut' between historiography and literary composition. A clear evidence for that is Herder's enthusiasm for the famous 'historian' called Shakespeare.[36] This overemphasis of *literary* genius was rectified by the reflections on autonomy and interdependence between art and knowledge during the period of the Weimar *Klassik*. It was mainly Schiller who made important contributions towards the development of a narrative historiographical tradition in Germany.[37] This was supported by the historical constructivism of Kant's philosophy of ethics and law, the poetics and the hermeneutic literary history of Friedrich Schlegel, and the poetical hermeneutics of Wilhelm von Humboldt.[38] In addition, Goethe the poet and the authority on aesthetics, had a major influence when Leopold von Ranke, the founder of history as a discipline in the historistic sense, included these aspects. We can follow up in detail the course of developments in Ranke's aesthetic and historical studies at school and later as an academic student.[39] Common to the earlier-mentioned authors is the fact that they proposed convincing reasons to comprehend history as a literary text and to exercise aesthetic thinking in its study. Following this development, historiography adapted these processes of the newly-formed German literature which had gained extraordinary cultural influence. The 'autonomy' which was granted to literature in the same period should not conceal the importance of this transfer. Characteristic for the autonomous literature of the period of Goethe is the fact that it raised the demands of value and also promised to have an integrating character reaching without its very own sphere and being incorporated into historiography which was largely dependent on the integration of happenings and events. In the moulding work of historicism, Ranke's *Römische Päpste* (History of the

---

36 HERDER: "Shakespeare" [1773], in: HERDER (1993, pp. 498-521, see p. 515).

37 Cf. PRÜFER (2000).

38 Cf. SAUL (1984); GOTTLOB (1989); IGGERS/POWELL (1990); PRÜFER (1996), LAU (1999, pp. 147-244, 318-389).

39 Cf. FULDA (1996, pp. 296-343).

Popes) from 1834-1836, we can appreciate, at all possible levels, thought processes and presentation techniques as shaped in the literature of the Goethe period, some of them being e.g. the conversion of historical events into a story form - with a clear tendency to plots similar to those in the *Bildungsroman* - the assigning of ideal tasks to important figures along with the withdrawal of the authorial narrator, the immanent narrative explanation of historical processes, the symbolic concentration of the whole story in deciding situations, as well as incorporating seemingly trivial but nevertheless significant and/or vivid details.[40] Some complementary philological methods by virtue of their intuititive aspects (contemplation, sensitivity, fantasy-analogous divination) go back to the field of aesthetics.[41] In addition, aesthetics was the carrier of the idealism of the material theory of history, the historistic assumption of an ideational nucleus in phenomenal events. Ranke has confessed this quite openly when asking Goethe for assistance:

> If I now understand singular entities and recognize by this virtue the living being of the whole: O if only life were so clear to grasp as life itself has been, if only your spirit would grace me, O you septuagenarian, so that on the steadfast ground of history, the true ideal would emerge: may knowledge unknown emerge from those known forms! That blood may turn to gold![42]

At that point, the theory of historiography was conspicuously underdeveloped. In general, historiographic practice was at the fore. To make it possible was the true merit of the so-called *Ideenlehre* (theory of ideas) since it provided general explanatory terms which assisted in the classification and interconnecting of events and happenings reported in detail.[43] To sum up, let us point out that 'History' is older than historicism, but only after its adaptation

---

40 Cf. METZ (1979); HARTH (1980); FULDA (1996, pp. 374-90); HARDTWIG (1997).

41 Cf. HARTH (1996, c. 861).

42 RANKE (1964-75 [1817], vol. 1, p. 174): "Wenn ich nun das Einzelne fasse und verstehe, und es kömmt mir aus dem Leben desselben das Leben des Ganzen zu Gedanken und Gemüte: o daß die Entwickelung dieses Lebens so klar würde, wie es selbst gewesen ist, daß mich Dein Geist besuchte, Siebzigjähriger, daß sich auf dem festen Boden des Historischen das Ideale wahrhaft erhübe: aus den Gestalten, die da gegeben sind, was nicht gegeben ist, herausspringe! Daß uns Blut zu Gold werde!"

43 Cf. RÜSEN (1993a, p. 56).

of aesthetic procedures did the modern, poetically-constructed term of history get its historiographic realisation; one could almost say: its fulfilment.

As far as certain aspects of this field are concerned, scholars have been well aware of this over a long time. Metonymically speaking, Friedrich Meinecke was of the opinion that "for Ranke to be possible, Goethe simply had to be the predecessor".[44] The study of the history of ideas however appreciated only the material historical theory of historicism as influenced by the *Kunstperiode* of German literature. That mainly meant "the consciousness of individuality, of the inner forces, of their characteristic individual development, and of the common fundament that connected everything together".[45] This aspect is of some importance – especially when it is in connection with the explanation of certain cognitive and socio-theoretical restrictions of historistic thought[46] –, but it 'only' deals with the characteristic highlights embedded in an assumed 'History', not its discoursive emergence: its principal 'writing' which has to precede all kinds of special writing. Similarly, the function of literary-aesthetical procedures will be reduced if only their influence on the 'representational forms' is given any significance. Contrarily, Ulrich Muhlack ascertains that:

> It is essential that the follow-up [-relation of historistic historiography to the literature of the Goethe period, D.F.] does not amount to external relations, for example in the adoption of certain literary techniques. Historiographers instead actually gain the categorial framework from literature in which they fix their newly-gained understanding of historical research.[47]

Analogous to the poesies of literature, 'research' was no longer considered a purifier of written records but was instead practised and understood as the producer of new knowledge.[48] The aesthetisization of history indeed affected the entire process of research, i.e., *conception, cognition, structuralisation, explanation and interpretation of the historical process which had to be recognized as well as the historical narrative which has to be composed.* Aesthetic processes gained a transcendental function in historicism for they

44 MEINECKE (1965, p. 601) (Leopold v. Ranke, Gedächtnisrede [Memorial speech, 1936]).

45 *Ibid.*

46 Cf. IGGERS 1968.

47 MUHLACK (1997, p. 69).

48 Cf. *Ibid.*, pp. 70-1.

possessed consequences in regard to the *Weltbild*, the material historical theories, cognition, hermeneutics and discourse.

The aesthetisization of the Goethe period encompassed all 'factors' of the disciplinary matrix of history (according to Jörn Rüsen's model)[49], although this assumption has not been explored in detail: This ranges right from the fundamental aesthetic concept of education (*Bildung*) as an expected function of historical knowledge through to the seemingly stringent field of positivistic source interpretation. The outlined aesthetisization should, in addition, have considerably facilitated the interaction of the said factors, firstly, because the aesthetic thinking of the Goethe period was generally orientated towards the entirety of things; secondly, because this aesthetisization constantly points out the historiographical aim to the historian. The internal networking and systematization of historical research counts as a definitive indicator for making it into a scientific discipline.[50] To conceive history in analogy to a literary text would accordingly not only have modernized the forms of *writing* history, and would not only have supported the *idea* of *one complete* history, but it would, in addition, have given a tremendous impetus to the uniformity of history as *a university discipline*. The conversion of history into a university discipline which prevented an aesthetisization in the German Enlightenment history would have been achieved with the help of the aesthetisization in historicism.

Subsequently, the more history understood itself to be scientific in nature, the more it was bent to suppress its aesthetic-poetical dependency. Even Droysen, himself a theoretician and considered an exception among his contemporaries, could not get away from these aesthetics. The initial concept of his *Historik* [Principles of History], which by itself is not quite specifically aesthetic but rather anthropological, and its linguistic instruments did not have such an obvious effect but were inevitable as aesthetisizing factors. Droysen's definition of the historical process as 'education' (*Bildung*)[51] continues an anthropological programme which Schiller had combined with an

49 RÜSEN (1993a, p. 32) names the five factors of this matrix as follows: the need for orientation inherent to the present, leading views on the human past, rules of empirical study, forms of historiographical presentation, and functions of historical knowledge. For an English version cf. RÜSEN: "What is Theory in History?", in: RÜSEN (1993b, pp. 15-48, esp. pp. 19-22).

50 Cf. *Ibid.*, pp. 36, 44.

51 Cf. DROYSEN (1977 [1857], pp. 14, 309).

'aesthetic education' through art. In addition, the historical method operates aesthetically when it seeks the spirit of the materialised expression found in the source and when it deals with the historical phenomena as well as their ideational fundamentals.[52] Even the material theory of the history of "moral similarities" (*sittliche Gemeinsamkeiten*) is based on aesthetics. Droysen has developed this theory on the basis of language, to be more precise, on the basis of the two-fold character of language, viz., the material and the non-material character.[53] Language is deliberately implemented in that region of the system which the German *Klassik* originally reserved for art. Droysen says that an 'aesthetic' structure is an inherent attribute of language since this medium represents its non-material or 'spiritual content' by means of a perceivable 'material' expression. Therefore, the linguistic-philosophical concept alone does not explain the existence of the fundamental aestheticity of Droysen's *Historik* but simultaneously also its suppression.

The connection of material historical theory and philosophy with anthropology, epistemology and methodology in the case of the earlier-mentioned authors ought to make it clear that a textualised viewing of the history of historical thought does not just give an insight into what is often called the '*representational* side' of the research of history. (Theoretically this is rather problematic since it is quite reduced.) We have instead examined how the concept of History, which continues to influence our historical thinking too, first came into existence. Accordingly, it had nothing to do with an epiphenomenon but the basis, the central concept of historical thought. Looking at things from an epistemological point of view, history and historiography of the period from approximately 1760 to 1860 verify that German historicism conceives 'History' itself as a text which should be read and interpreted according to literary patterns. The fundamentality of this process corresponds to the range of the results: Without this kind of textualisation, historical thinking in Germany would hardly have acquired the prestige and influence in the middle of the 19th century by which it made an impact on the bourgeois culture (*bürgerliche Kultur*) and replaced literature as a central medium of influence.[54]

Translated from the German by Shahnoor Sheryari

52 Cf. *Ibid.*, pp. 233-4. Cf. FULDA (1996, pp. 418-43).

53 Cf. DROYSEN (1977 [1857], p. 26).

54 Cf. HARDTWIG (1997).

References

ANKERSMIT, F.R.: "Historicism: An Attempt at Synthesis," in: *History and Theory*, 34 (1995), pp. 143-61.

ANKERSMIT, F., KELLNER, H. (Eds.): *A New Philosophy of History*, London (Reaction Books) 1995 (= Critical Views).

BAUMGARTNER, H.M.: "Thesen zur Grundlegung einer transzendentalen Historik," [Basic Theses on the Transcendental Theory of History] in: HANS MICHAEL BAUMGARTNER, JÖRN RÜSEN (Eds.): *Seminar: Geschichte und Theorie*, Frankfurt am Main (Suhrkamp) 1976 (= suhrkamp taschenbuch wissenschaft, vol. 98), pp. 274-302.

BERKHOFER, R.F.JR.: *Beyond the Great Story. History as Text and Discourse*, Cambridge, Mass./London (Harvard UP) 1995.

BLANKE, H.W., FLEISCHER, D. (Eds.): *Theoretiker der deutschen Aufklärungshistorie* [Theorists of the Enlightenment Historiography in Germany], vol. 1-2, Stuttgart-Bad Cannstatt (Frommann-Holzboog) 1990 (= Fundamenta historica, vol. 1.1-2).

BLANKE, H.W.: *Historiographiegeschichte als Historik* [The History of Historiography as Theory of History], Stuttgart-Bad Cannstatt (Frommann-Holzboog) 1991 (= Fundamenta historica, vol. 3).

BLUMENBERG, H.: *Die Lesbarkeit der Welt* [The Readability of the World], Frankfurt am Main (Suhrkamp) 1981.

BÖDEKER, H.E. ET AL. (Eds.): *Aufklärung und Geschichte. Studien zur deutschen Geschichtswissenschaft im 18. Jahrhundert* [The Enlightenment and History. Studies in the Humanities in Germany during the 18th Century], Göttingen (Vandenhoeck & Ruprecht) 1986 (= Veröffentlichungen des Max-Planck-Instituts für Geschichte, vol. 81).

CARR, D.: *Time, Narrative, and History*, Bloomington/Indianapolis (Indiana UP) 1986.

DANTO, A.C.: *Analytical Philosophy of History*, Cambridge (University Press) 1965.

DEMANDT, A.: *Metaphern für Geschichte. Sprachbilder und Gleichnisse im historisch-politischen Denken* [Metaphors Applied to History. Figures of Speech and Similes in History and Politics], München (Beck) 1978.

DILTHEY, W.: *Gesammelte Schriften* [Collective Works], vol. 7: *Der Aufbau der geschichtlichen Welt in den Geisteswissenschaften* [The Construction of History in the Humanities], Leipzig/Berlin (Teubner) 1927.

DROYSEN, J.G.: *Historik* [Principles of History]. *Rekonstruktion der ersten vollständigen Fassung der Vorlesungen (1857)* [A Reconstruction of the First Completed Version of Droysen's Lectures], *Grundriß der Historik in der ersten hand-*

schriftlichen (1857/58) und in der letzten gedruckten Fassung (1882) [Outlines of the Principles of *Historik* in the First Manuscript and in the Final Printed Version], ed. by Peter Leyh, Stuttgart-Bad Cannstatt (Frommann-Holzboog) 1977. (English edition of the *Grundriß*: JOHANN GUSTAV DROYSEN: *Outlines of the Principles of History*. With a biographical sketch of the author [by Hermann Krüger]. Transl. by E. Benjamin Andrews, New York (Fertig) 1967.)

EGGERT, H., U. PROFITLICH, KL. R. SCHERPE: *Geschichte als Literatur*, Stuttgart (Metzler) 1990.

FULDA, D., TSCHOPP, S.S. (Eds.): *Literatur und Geschichte. Ein Kompendium zu ihrem Verhältnis von der Aufklärung bis zur Gegenwart* [Literature and History. A Compendium of Their Interrelation from the Enlightenment to the Present], Berlin/New York (de Gruyter) 2001.

FULDA, D.: " Die Texte der Geschichte. Zur Poetik modernen historischen Denkens," [Historical Texts. On the Poetics of Modern Historical Thought], in: *Poetica*, 21 (1999), pp. 29-60.

FULDA, D.: *Wissenschaft aus Kunst. Die Entstehung der modernen deutschen Geschichtsschreibung 1760-1860* [Knowledge from Art. The Rise of Modern German Historiography], Berlin/New York (de Gruyter) 1996 (= European Cultures, vol. 7).

GATTERER, J.C. (1767a): "Vom historischen Plan, und der darauf sich gründenden Zusammenfügung der Erzählung," [From the Historic Plan and the Interconnection of Narrative Based on It] in: *Allgemeine historische Bibliothek*, 1 (1767), pp. 15-89. Reprinted in: BLANKE/FLEISCHER (1990, pp. 621-62).

GATTERER, J.C. (1767b): "Vorrede von der Evidenz in der Geschichtkunde," [Preface on the Evidence Found in the Study of History] in: FRIEDRICH EBERHARD BOYSEN (Ed.): *Die Allgemeine Welthistorie die in England durch eine Gesellschaft von Gelehrten ausgefertigt worden. In einem vollst?ndigen und pragmatischen Auszuge. Alte Historie* [The History of the World, as drawn up in England by a Society of Scholars. Available in a Complete and Pragmatic Excerpt. Ancient History], vol. 1, Halle (Gebauer) 1767, pp. 1-38. Reprinted in: BLANKE, FLEISCHER (1990, pp. 466-78).

GOTTLOB, M.: *Geschichtsschreibung zwischen Aufklärung und Historismus: Johannes von Müller und Friedrich Christoph Schlosser* [Historiography between the Enlightenment and Historicism: Johannes von Müller and Friedrich Christoph Schlosser], Frankfurt am Main (Lang) 1989 (= Europäische Hochschulschriften. Reihe 3: Geschichte und ihre Hilfswissenschaften, vol. 385).

HARDTWIG, W.: "Historismus als ästhetische Geschichtsschreibung: Leopold von Ranke," [Historicism as an Aesthetic Historiography: Leopold von Ranke] in: *Geschichte und Gesellschaft*, 23 (1997), pp. 99-114.

HARTH, D.: "Biographie als Weltgeschichte. Die theoretische und ästhetische Konstruktion der historischen Handlung in Droysens *Alexander* und Rankes

Wallenstein," [Biography as World History. Theoretical and Aesthetic Constructions of the Historical Plot in Droysen's *Alexander* and Ranke's *Wallenstein*] in: *Deutsche Vierteljahrsschrift für Literaturwissenschaft und Geistesgeschichte*, 54 (1980), pp. 58-104.

HARTH, D.: "Geschichtsschreibung," [Historiography] in: GERT UEDING (Ed.): *Historisches Wörterbuch der Rhetorik* [The Historical Dictionary of Rhetorics], vol. 1-4 [uncompleted to date], Tübingen (Niemeyer) 1992-2000, vol. 3, c. 832-70.

HERDER, J.G.: *Werke in zehn Bänden* [Collective Works in Ten Volumes], ed. by Günter Arnold et al., Frankfurt am Main (Deutscher Klassiker Verlag), vol. 2: *Schriften zur Ästhetik und Literatur 1767-1781* [Writings on Aesthetics and Literature], ed. by Gunter E. Grimm, 1993; vol. 4: *Schriften zu Philosophie, Literatur, Kunst und Altertum 1774-1787* [Writings on Philosophy, Literature, Art and Antiquity], ed. by Jürgen Brummack and Martin Bollacher, 1994; vol. 8: *Schriften zu Literatur und Philosophie 1792-1880* [Writings on Literature and Philosophy], ed. by Hans Dietrich Irmscher, 1998.[55]

IGGERS, G.G., POWELL, J.M. (Eds.): *Leopold von Ranke and the Shaping of the Historical Discipline*, Syracuse, N.Y. (Univ. Pr.) 1990.

IGGERS, G.G.: *The German Conception of History: The National Tradition of Historical Thought from Herder to the Present*, Middletown, CT (Wesleyan UP) 1968.

KNODT, E.: "Dramatic Illusion in the Making of the Past: Shakespeare's Impact on Herder's Philosophy of History", in: WULF KOEPKE (Ed.): *Johann Gottfried Herder. Language, History, and the Enlightenment*, Columbia, South Carolina (Camden House) 1990 (= Studies in German Literature, Linguistics, and Culture, vol. 52), pp. 209-23.

KOSELLECK, R.: "Geschichte," [History] in: OTTO BRUNNER, WERNER CONZE, REINHART KOSELLECK (Eds.): *Geschichtliche Grundbegriffe. Historisches Lexikon zur politisch-sozialen Sprache in Deutschland,* [Basic Concepts of History. An Historical Dictionary of Political-Social Language in Germany], vol. 1-8 (in 9). Stuttgart (Klett) 1972-97, vol. 2 (1975), pp. 593-718.

KOSELLECK, R.: *Vergangene Zukunft. Zur Semantik geschichtlicher Zeiten*, 2nd ed., Frankfurt a.M. (Suhrkamp) 1992 (suhrkamp taschenbuch wissenschaft. 757). English edition: *Futures Past. On the Semantics of Historical Time*, transl. by Keith Tribe, Cambrigde, Mass. (MIT Press) 1985 (= Studies in Contemporary German Social Thought).

55 As a selection in English cf. HERDER, J. G.: *On World History. An Anthology*, ed. by Hans Adler and Ernst A. Menze, transl. by Ernst A. Menze with Michael Palma, Armouk/London (Sharpe) 1997.

LAU, V.: *Erzählen und Verstehen. Historische Perspektiven der Hermeneutik* [Narrating and Understanding. Historical Views in Hermeneutics], Würzburg (Königshausen & Neumann) 1999 (= Epistemata. Reihe Philosophie, vol. 271).

MEINECKE, F.: *Die Entstehung des Historismus*, ed. by Carl Hinrichs, München (Oldenbourg) 1959 (= Werke, Vol. 3). English edition: *Historism. The Rise of a New Historical Outlook*, transl. by J. E. Anderson, with a Foreword by Sir Isaiah Berlin, London (Routledge and K. Paul) 1972.

METZ, K.H.: *Grundformen historiographischen Denkens. Wissenschaftsgeschichte als Methodologie. Dargestellt an Ranke, Treitschke und Lamprecht. Mit einem Anhang über zeitgenössische Geschichtstheorie*, [Basics of Historiographical Thought. History of the Humanities as Methodology. Based on Examples from the Works of Ranke, Treitschke and Lamprecht. With a Supplement on Contemporary Historical Theories] München (Fink) 1979 (= Münchner Universitäts-Schriften. Reihe der Philosophischen Fakultät, vol. 21).

MUHLACK, U.: "Geschichtsschreibung als Geschichtswissenschaft," [Historiography as Historical Disciplin] in: WOLFGANG KÜTTLER, JÖRN RÜSEN, ERNST SCHULIN (Eds.): *Geschichtsdiskurs in 5 Bänden* [The Discourse on History - Five Volumes], vol. 3: *Die Epoche der Historisierung* [The Age of the Rise of History], Frankfurt a.M. (Fischer Taschenbuch Verlag) 1997 (= Fischer Wissenschaft, vol. 11477), pp. 67-79.

PRÜFER, T.: "Wilhelm von Humboldts 'rhetorische Hermeneutik'. Historische Sinnbildung im Spannungsfeld von Empirie, Philosophie und Poesie," [Wilhelm von Humboldt's 'Rhetorical Hermeneutics'. The Construction of Historical Meaning in the Conflict of Empirism, Philosophy and Poetics], in: DANIEL FULDA, THOMAS PRÜFER (Eds.): *Faktenglaube und fiktionales Wissen. Zum Verhältnis von Wissenschaft und Kunst in der Moderne* [Fictional Knowledge and the Belief in Facts. On the Relation between Art and Knowledge in the Modern Age], Frankfurt a.M. (Lang) 1996 (= Kölner Studien zur Literaturwissenschaft, vol. 9), pp. 127-66.

PRÜFER, T.: *Die Identität der Geschichte. Friedrich Schiller, der Historiker, und die Anfänge der modernen Geschichtswissenschaft* [The Identity of History. Friedrich Schiller, the Historian, and the Rise of Modern History], Phil. Diss. Univ. of Cologne 2000.

RANKE, L.V.: *Aus Werk und Nachlaß* [From his Published and Unpublished Works], ed. by Walther Peter Fuchs and Theodor Schieder, vol. 1-4, München/Wien (Oldenbourg) 1964-75.

RANKE, L.V.: *Sämmtliche Werke* [Complete Works], vol. 1-54, Leipzig (Duncker & Humblot) 1867-1890.[56]

56 As a selection in English cf. RANKE, L.V.: *The Theory and Practice of History*, ed. with an Introd. by Georg G. Iggers and Konrad von Moltke. New transl. by

RANKE, L.: *Die römischen Päpste, ihre Kirche und ihr Staat im sechszehnten und siebzehnten Jahrhundert*, vol. 1-3, Berlin (Duncker & Humblot) 1834-36 (= Fürsten und Völker von Süd-Europa im sechszehnten und siebzehnten Jahrhundert [Princes and Peoples of Southern Europe in the Sixteenth and Seventeenth Centuries], Vol. 2-4). English edition: History of the Popes; Their Church and State, transl. by E. Fowler, vol. 1-3, New York/London [1901] (= World's Greatest Literature); New York (Ungar) [1966].

REILL, P.H.: *The German Enlightenment and the Rise of Historicism*, Berkeley/Los Angeles/London (Univ. of California Pr.) 1975.

RICŒUR, P.: *Temps et récit*, Vol. 1-3, Paris (Ed. du Seuil) 1983-85. English edition: *Time and Narrative*, vol. 1-3, transl. by Kathleen McLaughlin and David Pellauer, Chicago (Univ. of Chicago Pr.) 1984-88.

RÜSEN, J. (1993a): *Konfigurationen des Historismus. Studien zur deutschen Wissenschaftskultur* [Configurations of Historicism. Studies in the Humanities in Germany], Frankfurt am Main (Suhrkamp) 1993 (= suhrkamp taschenbuch wissenschaft, vol. 1082).

RÜSEN, J. (1993b): *Studies in Metahistory*, ed. and introd. by Pieter Duvenage, Pretoria (Human Sciences Research Council) 1993.

SAUL, N.: *History and Poetry in Novalis and in the Tradition of the German Enlightenment*, London (Institute of Germanic Studies, University of London) 1984 (= Bithell Studies of Dissertations, vol. 8).

SCHLÖZER, A.L.: *Vorstellung seiner Universalhistorie (1772/73) Mit Beilagen* [Presentation of his Universal History. With Appendices], ed. by Horst Walter Blanke, Hagen (Rottmann) 1990 (= Beiträge zur Geschichtskultur, vol. 4).

SCHULIN, E.: "Der Zeitbegriff der Aufklärung und des deutschen Historismus," [The Conception of Time during the Enlightenment and German Historicism], in: WOLFGANG KÜTTLER, JÖRN RÜSEN, ERNST SCHULIN (Eds.): *Geschichtsdiskurs in 5 Bänden* [The Discourse on History - Five Volumes], vol. 2: *Anfänge modernen historischen Denkens* [The Rise of Modern Historical Thought], Frankfurt am Main (Fischer Taschenbuch Verlag) 1994 (Fischer Wissenschaft. 11476), pp. 333-43.

SEEBA, H.C.: "Geschichte als Dichtung. Herders Beitrag zur Ästhetisierung der Geschichtsschreibung," [History as Poetry. Herder's Contributions towards the Aesthetization of History] in: *Storia della Storiografia*, 8 (1985), pp. 50-73.

SIMON, C.: *Historiographie. Eine Einführung* [An Introduction to Historiography], Stuttgart (Ulmer) 1996 (= UTB. 1901).

Wilma A. Iggers and K.v.M., Indianapolis/New York (Bobbs-Merrill) 1973, or RANKE, L. V.: *The Secret of World History. Selected Writings on the Art and Science of History*, ed. with transl. by Roger Wines, New York (Fordham UP) 1981.

STRAUB, J. (Ed.): *Erinnerung, Geschichte, Identität* [Memory, History and Identity], vol. 1: *Erzählung, Identität und historisches Bewußtsein. Die psychologische Konstruktion von Zeit und Geschichte* [The Narrative, Identity and Historical Consciousness. The Psychological Reconstruction of Time and History], Frankfurt a.M. (Suhrkamp) 1998 (= suhrkamp taschenbuch wissenschaft, vol. 1402).

SÜßMANN, J.: *Geschichtsschreibung oder Roman? Zur Konstitutionslogik von Geschichtserzählungen zwischen Schiller und Ranke (1780-1824)* [Historiography or Novel? About the Formative Logic of Historical Narratives between Schiller and Ranke], Stuttgart (Steiner) 2000 (= Frankfurter historische Abhandlungen, vol. 41).

VEESER, H. A. (Ed.): *The New Historicism*, London/New York (Routledge) 1989.

VOM HOFE, G.: "Die Geschichte als 'Epopee Gottes'. Zu Herders ästhetischer Geschichtstheorie," [History as an 'Epopee of God'. Writings on Herder's Aesthetical Theory of History] in: BRIGITTE POSCHMANN (Ed.): *Bückeburger Gespräche über Johann Gottfried Herder 1983*, Rinteln (Bösendahl) 1984 (= Schaumburger Studien, vol. 45), pp. 56-81.

WHITE, H.: "'Figuring the nature of the times deceased': Literary Theory and Historical Writing," in: RALPH COHEN (Ed.): *The Future of Literary Theory*, New York/ London (Routledge) 1989, pp. 19-43, 411-14.

WHITE, H.: "The Question of Narrative in Contemporary Historical Theory," in: *History and Theory*, 23 (1984), pp. 1-33.

WHITE, H.: *Metahistory. The Historical Imagination in Nineteenth Century Europe*, Baltimore/London (The John Hopkins Univ. Pr.) 1973.

ZAGORIN, P.: "History, the Referent, and Narrative: Reflections on Postmodernism Now," in: *History and Theory*, 38 (1999), pp. 1-24.

Chapter 8

Social and Philosophical Theory in the 19th Century German Thought

MARIO SIGNORE

I. From the Gnoseological and Scientistic Limit to the Horizon of the "Significance". Dilthey-Windelband-Rickert

II. The "Meaning Constitution" from Weber's Subjectively Intentioned Sense to Schütz's Intersubjectivity

III. The Analysis of Social Action in the Horizon of a Double Necessity and the Hermeneutic Opening

In his preface to *Die Entstehung des Historismus*, written in 1936, Friedrich Meinecke, among other things, maintains that "the rise of the historicism has been...one of the main spiritual revolutions that the Western thought has ever produced".[1]

Half a century after that assertion, which in that period could seem partial, if we want to strike the balance of the level of the conceptual elaboration and of its influence on Western European culture, we cannot but confirm Meinecke's conviction.

Moreover, if we want to perceive, without any prejudice or cultural provincialisms the significant influence that the "historicisms" had on the development of the social-historical science, we should go further the above-cited quotation, in order to go through the most significant moments of a debate which had and still has, as landmark, the route which leads from Dilthey to Weber, going through Simmel and Rickert.

1 F. MEINECKE: *Die Entstehung des Historismus* (The Coming into Being of Historicism), in: "Werke", III, Munchen (Oldenbourg Verlag) 1959, Vorwort, p. 1. Italian translation: *Le origini dello storicismo*, Firenze (Sansoni) 1967, p. IX.

This route led, on one hand, to the formulation of a concept of history which was able to use in a constructive and productive way the contribution of the social science and the sociological analysis, and, on the other, to a deep consideration of the social science which has taken it gradually out of the positivistic and Marxist spheres, by opening them to a positive confrontation with contemporary philosophy, according to which phenomenology and hermenutics have the main responsibility on the theoretic turn of such a science.

I. From the Gnoseological and Scientistic Limit to the Horizon of the "Significance". Dilthey-Windelband-Rickert

In this conscious research of the theoretical origins, of course we need to emphasize the role of W. Dilthey's reflection because, among the other things, he was able to start that process of corrosion of the absolute historicism, that in Germany had the most definitive and total expression in the Hegelian system and paved the way to the autonomous development of the historic science, which positively influenced the social science, as well.

Even though the debt of contemporary sociology to W. Dilthey has to be totally defined, it does not seem groundless that just his attention to the human world, the changes which favoured the inner experience, the opening, as risky as courageous to the *Erlebnisse* (experiencing), have put to the social science those questions, that have forced them to revise the old epistemological statutes, in order to reconstruct new ones, maybe less reassuring but also more efficacious in order to get a better understanding of the social behaviour in a concrete-historical situation.

In this direction, J. Habermas seems to have hit the mark, because he has found in Dilthey's thought the essential care to let emerge in the social science the urgency of self consideration, that has been completely naturalized by the positivism and to build a sociological theory of life, as the analysis of the human interaction, in order to integrate and correct Marx's positions.

We should not neglect to notice that "Dilthey takes from the philosophy of reflection the basic model of *Erleben* (experiencing) as the methodological connection, that is expression and comprehension instead of an ingenuous theory of the sympathetic penetration: the spirit has a life of its own because it alienates into objectivations and, in the same time, comes back to thinking itself over its vital manifestations. The history of the human race is linked to this process of the spirit's making. For this reason the everyday experience of the socialized fellows moves in the direction of *Erleben* with expression and comprehension, which represent also the way the science of the spirit proceeds".[2]

If we place ourselves in the right historical perspective, it is not difficult to notice Dilthey's broadmindedness, because he wants to support the spiritual side of the human world and, consequently the spiritual meaning of the human actions. When humans act in society, in fact, they set their thoughts and values, their tensions, intentions and passions in motion before moving as bodies; that means also contemporaneously with their bodies, the object that interacts with its own environment and the other bodies.

All this has become essential for the redefinition of the bounds of social science research and paved the way to a new science which risked to flatten out on the scheme of the classical theories about knowledge and science. And that's not all. This let sociology open inexhaustible spaces to the human "praxis", by forcing it to confront with the human question about "to be", that takes men to look for those trends that determine the construction of the human world without appealing to metaphysical or theological visions of history.

We need all this information in order to recognize the inner limits of the social science and, as we will see later, the necessity to open a multidisciplinary perspective, which can take it out of a proud and self-sufficient isolation where they were shut in, just some decades ago.

In spite of the limits we have to acknowledge that thanks to Dilthey the social-historical science has conquered a new dimension of the universal which does not consist in an objectivity established beforehand of the exact science but, on the contrary, takes place in the permanent relation with the social reality and the history of the community, a history which does not disregard any moment of its experience, whether it is made up from reflection or praxis.[3]

---

2 J. HABERMAS: *Erkenntnis und Interesse*, Frankfurt a.M. (Suhrkamp Verlag) 1968. Italian translation: *Conoscenza e Interesse*, Bari (Laterza) 1973, p. 149. Cf. also W. DILTHEY: *Gesammelte Schriften*, VII Leipzig/Berlin 1927, pp. 86ff. Italian translation: *Critica della ragione storica*, Torino (Einaudi) 1954, pp. 154-55.

3 It would be very interesting to confront H. JOACH: *Haldelnder Mensch und objectivr Geist. Zur Theorie der Geist-und Sozialwisssenschaften bei Wilhem*

Once the gnoseological and scientistic limit, which tried to reduce the epistemological statute of the social science, has been exceeded, and the horizon of the "significance" has been opened, the thematic approach to the value became inevitable, an approach that was the basis of the distinction between natural science and the sciences of the mind, even inside the Methodenstreit, which had involved nearly all the German thinkers, philosophers in particular in the last years of the 19th century and the first decades of the 20th one.

By considering the "value" as the differentiating criterion, Dilthey's distinction between *Natur- and Geisteswissenschaften* undergoes a change and looks for a new characterization, because it cannot support the contrast between nature and spirit, any more. According to this statement, for example, W. Wildelband, since his speech for the Rectorship at Strasburg University in 1894, entitled *Geschichte und Naturwissenschaft* (History and Natural Science), rejects the antithesis in which Dilthey is involved, about nature and spirit, by saying that "it is an objective antithesis which gets a dominant position at the end of the classical thought and at the beginning of the medieval one and that has been rigorously kept until the recent metaphysics from Descartes to Spinoza, until Schelling and Hegel".[4]

All the empirical disciplines, according to Wildelband share the purpose of looking for the laws of becoming, "whether it is a movement of bodies, a transformation of elements, the development of the organic life, or a process of representation, feeling or will".[5]

The empirical science will not be separated and distinguished according to their object, any more: very different objects will be included in the same context of the empirical science.

The only distinction possible is the methodological one, whose principle of division is characterized from the formal aspects of their cognitive aims: the natural science aims at the research of general laws, while the spiritual

---

Dilthey, Meisenheirn a G. 1974. For a more recent discussion about Dilthey's themes, it would be useful to consult F. BIANCO, F. ANGELI: *Dilthey e il pensiero del novecento*, Milano 1985, where there are some more contributions by Italian specialists (F. Bianco, G. Calabrò, F. Tessitore, M. Perniola, G. Marini, A. Izzo, A. Marini), and the significant apports by H.-G. Gadamer, M. W. Orth, O. Pöggeler, H. Boeder, G. Schmidt.

4 W. WILDELBAND: *Geschichte und Naturwissenschaft*, in: "Praludien", II, Tübigen (Mohr) 1924, p. 142.

5 *Op. cit.*, pp. 143f.

science aims at the research of historical facts.[6] After having ascertained that the empirical science aims at the knowledge of reality, it is possible to make a distinction about the "way" reality is perceived: either in the form of the general and natural law, or in the form, determined by history, of the singular fact; according to this distinction the former is a science of law, while the latter is the science of the events. So, whether the former indicates what is normal and regular in reality, the latter indicates what has happened and goes on happening in an unrepeatable way, because it is unique. "The scientific thought - if it is possible to elaborate a new term - is in the first case nomothetic and in the second one ideographic. If we want to follow the usual expressions, we can talk about an antithesis between the natural and the historical discipline, considering that in the methodological sense, psychology has to be included in the sphere of the natural sciences".[7]

The distinction between natural research and history, therefore, begins and is justified only when we use facts with a cognitive aim: only the aim of the research can make a distinction of the facts.

We should not omit the risk to which Wildelband and the *Wertphilosophie* expose themselves, when they subtract the cognitive and generalized purpose from the historical science.

But it seems to us that we can say that such a risk is compensated for by new horizons, opened up to the new science, with the rediscovery, implicit in Windelband, but more and more explicit in the following authors, of the decisive role of the values in the social-historical science, which are one more time forced to revise the method of enquiry of the human-historical and social reality, that is of course the specific sphere where the empirical values can be formulated and carried out.

H. Rickert still moves in this direction, because he accepts as a starting point Windelband's distinction between "nature" and "culture" by insisting that, since the cultural objects are always related to values as "*Wertvolle Wirklichkeiten*" (valuable realities) as well as since the natural objects are absolutely deprived of them, "through the relation to the values, if it is or not, we can... distinguish two kinds of objects of science and we can use it only from a methodological point of view, because any cultural development, apart

6 *Op. cit.*, p. 144.
7 *Op. cit.*, p. 145.

from the value to which it is linked, has also to be considered as related to nature and is therefore nature itself".[8]

Here, the *Beziehung auf Werte* (the relationship to values), while discriminating between natural science and cultural one, imposes itself as a logical-methodological presupposition of the social-historical science, and need the *Verstehen* (understanding) to reveal the value that is related to the cultural event.

According to Rickert, this means that if the natural world is accessible only to the perception (*Wahrnehmen*), "the remaining objects of comprehension are…just abstract significance or making of meaning. Only these ones are immediately caught, in fact, by existing they require from the science a kind of representation different from the one of the objects which can perceive the physical or psychic or material reality."[9]

Moreover we have to say, if we do not want to dissipate Rickert's significant conception of value (*Wertgedanken*) and of the *Beziehung auf Werte*, that "sense and meaning are characterized by a value and for this reason their perception without a reference to the value is scientifically vague".[10]

Obviously also *Verstehen* needs an explanation from which neither Rickert nor we want to escape. So Rickert wonders: "apart from the … "sympathetic reviviscence" (*Nacherleben*) of the psychic being, how far is it right to define history as a science which understands, distinguishing it from the science that clarifies (*erklärende Wissenschaften*)? The term "understands" (*Verstehen*) has a lot of meanings that we do not need to list here, and its theories are so many as the sense of the word…in order that the word does not loose its meaning and importance for the methodological doctrine, we have to conceive the term "understanding" as the knowledge of a particular argument which cannot be totally satisfied or clarified. Everything that has no sense or value is incomprehensible and, therefore, supposed that it is accessible to science, it can be simply described and explained as a senseless and valueless reality…"[11]

---

8 H. RICKERT: *Kulturwissenschaft und Naturwissenschaft,* Tübingen (Mohr) 1899/1926, p. 18; Italian translation: *Il fondamento delle scienze della cultura*, by M. Signore, Ravenna (Longo) 1979, p. 69, chap. IV, *Natura e cultura*.

9 *Op. cit.*, p. 19; Italian translation, cit., p. 70.

10 *Op. cit.*, p. 20; Italian translation, cit., p. 71.

11 H. RICKERT: *Die Grenzen der Naturwissenschaftlichen Begriffsbildung. Eine logische Einleitung in die historischen Wissenschaften,* Tübingen (Mohr)

From this we realize that sense and value are tightly connected and almost coincide, and that value is considered as an "immaterial matter" (sense, to be exact) that requires a historical being which can let it materialize, or a discoverer of the sense hidden in the social-historical reality. Now it is quite easy to catch the effect that this moment of Rickert's philosophical reflection exerts, more or less directly, on the sociological theory, forcing it to an elaboration, that, in our opinion, has not finished, yet, even though it is already possible to catch some of its effects.[12]

II. The "Meaning Constitution" from Weber's Subjectively Intentioned Sense to Schütz's Intersubjectivity

In our approach to the sociological theories which animate, often in a lively way, the current discussion, the first decisive influences of Rickert's elaborations on the contemporary sociological theory meet with Max Weber's ones, because even though he rejected the master's pretence to develop a system of universally valid values and the ability to supply humans with absolute and incontrovertible criteria of orientation, he reconsiders the *Wertbeziehung,* but he uses it in a more worldly way and considers values as unreal and logical instruments with an exclusively heuristic function.

Moreover Weber, in order to avoid misunderstandings about his support to a possible theory of values, insists very much on the moment of the "choice", as qualifying the relationship between the human action and values, and upholds the necessity that every important single action, and rather "life as a whole" (*das Leben als Ganzes*), has not to proceed as a natural event but in a conscious way, because "it represents a concatenation of decisions, through which the soul, as for Plato, *chooses* its own destiny".[13]

1896/1929, pp. 424ff; (IV ed. 1921) for the "Verstehen" problem Rickert refers to Simmel, Spanger, Weber and Jaspers (p. 424, note 1).

12 At the end of his philosophical discourse, Rickert talks about a philosophy of history, in an objective way. For going deeper into the ontologic theory of Ricker's *Weriphilosophie,* see H. RICKERT: *System der philosophie*, Tübingen (Mohr) 1921.

13 M. WEBER: "Der Sinn der 'Wertfreiheit' der soziologischen und okonomischen Wissenschaften" (1917), in: *Gesammelte Aufsätze zur Wissenschafftslehere*,

Weber's position about the "last decisions", which does not want to reduce life only to a natural event, is very much innovative about sociological research, that for the first time, thanks to Weber associates the social behaviours and first of all the social acts, not of rigid and fixed laws, but to the individuals' actions.

This turning point will have a lot of consequences about the redefinition of the roles and the responsibility of the agents, but this is not the right context to deepen this further aspect of the problem.[14]

What we want to notice is the importance of the change, that has to be ascribed to Weber's recovery of the "decision", that refers to the subjective ability of choice and the consequent, even implicit recall to the intentionality of the behaviour, as a new task of the sociological analysis. It is just this element of novelty that links Weber to Husserl, by allowing a sociological use of the phenomenological category of the transcendence of the conscience, which makes the German sociologist the father of modern sociology and the promoter of contemporary sociological theories.

It is not casual that Alfred Schütz, at the beginning of his *Der Sinnhafte Auffbau der sozialen Welt* (The Meaningful Construction of the Social World), wants to make clear the aims of his work and recognizes his intellectual debts: "In this work it has been tried to go back to the origins of the problems of the social science, starting from the fundamental actions of the conscience. In this sense Bergson's and Husserl's research about the sense of the inner time has been fundamental. Only the works by these thinkers, and above all Husserl's transcendental phenomenology, has brought out the basis of the thought which can solve the problem of significance. In order to express to these philosophers my greatest admiration, I am deeply aware of how much this work and all my thought depend very much on their and Max Weber's writings."[15]

Tübingen (Mohr) 1973, IV ed., p. 508. Italian translation: "Il significato della 'avalutatività' delle scienze sociologiche ed economiche", in: M. WEBER: *Il metodo delle scienze storico-sociali*, Torino (Einaudi) 1958, pp. 332-33.

14 For a deeper analysis of this aspect see MARIO SIGNORE: *Senso e Significato in Max Weber*, Lecce 1977.

15 A. SCHÜTZ: *Der Sinnhafte Auffbau der sozialen Welt. Eine Einleitunh in die verstehende Soziologie*, Frankfurt a.M. (Suhrkamp Verlag) 1974, pp. 9ff. Italian translation: *La fenomenologia del mondo sociale*, Bologna (Il Mulino) 1974, p. 4.

Here is shown a well-defined cultural horizon, inside of which A. Schütz tries to elaborate a concept of 'action', that, at least at the beginning had Weber's formula as reference, according to which action is an attitude to which "the actor or actors...associate a subjective meaning",[16] which let them link in an irreversible way, the development of the sociological meaning of the category of the 'significance', even referred to Husserl's phenomenology and to the structure of the social world, which requires the opening of the category of the 'sense' to the supra-individual dimension, and its introduction into the "complex of a more comprehensive constitution has as *realiter* its place without which it becomes unintelligible."[17]

But once this widening of the perspective has been grasped, the "significant constitution" trancends Weber's subjective sense and requires a more adequate consideration of the essential factor which makes it possible a "comprehensive constitution of the meaning" of the social world, that is inter-subjectivity.

In this way we have various possibilities of the discourse that, of course, we cannot reveal immediately, but that have to be taken into consideration for the qualifying influence they have on the sociological theory. The most important of them is the definition of the inter-subjectivity in a different and more complex context, than the one maintained by Weber, who even specifying that "not every kind of contact among men has a social characteristic, but only an attitude that is oriented in view of the others' attitude"[18] in the end simplifies this statement in a limitative way, by defining 'social action' as the attempt of two cyclists (today we would say motorists) to avoid the collision and "the squabble, the resolution or the pacific discussion which comes after the squabble."[19]

---

16 M. WEBER: *Wirtschaft und Gesellschaft. Grundriß der verstehenden Soziologie* 5. Revedierte Auflage besorgt von J. Winckelmann, Tübingen (Mohr, P. Siebek), 1980. Italian translation: *Economia e società*, Edizioni di Comunità, Milano 1968, p. 4.

17 R. BUBNER: *Handlung, Sprache und Vernunft. Grundbegriffe praktischer Philosophie*. Neuausgabe mit einem Anhang, Frankfurt a.M. (Suhrkamp) 1976. Italian translation: *Azione, Linguaggio, Ragione*, Bologna (Il Mulino) 1985, p. 20.

18 M. WEBER: *Wirtschaft und Gesellschaft*, cit., p. 11; it. transl.: *cit*., p. 2.

19 *Ibidem.*

The context in which A. Schütz includes inter-subjectivity, which qualifies social action, comes from Husserl and is the one of the *Lebenswelt,* according the definition that he gives in *Die Krisis der europäischen Wissenschaften und die transzendentale Phanomenologie*[20]. Thanks to this reference the intersubjectivity goes over the reductivity of collision between two fellows, as in Weber's example, and is caught in a whole of relationships, also "constituted in an anonymous way, where we move without having the awareness of the inter-subjectivity which has founded the sense."[21]

But it is not all because Husserl's reference, reinforced by Bergson's classical theories about 'conscience' and 'durèe', allows Schütz to single out the origins of the subjective sense in the consciousness, from which the particular modality of the attention, revolved to past experiences of the ego.

As Bubner underlines, interpreting Schütz, "the sense, that in the simple...flux of the experiences is latent, is the performance of the conscience that the ego achieves with reference to the past experiences. This experience, that has lived in the inner consciousness, is the basis of the phenomenological concept of the sense. In this perspective the actions look like a form of the living attempt".[22]

III. The Analysis of Social Action in the Horizon of a Double Necessity and the Hermeneutic Opening

Here it is clearly shown, at least according to our perspective, the tendency of the analysis and inquiry of social action, that certainly reveals the limits of the empirical sociology because of the necessity to consider the *sphere of our liberties*, as it is defined by F. H. Tenbruck, which otherwise would not have any nomological explanation, that intends to define the sphere of the 'regularity and not the one of the particularity or 'singularity' of the

20 E. HUSSERL: *Gesammelte Werke, Husserliana*, vol. VI, Haag (M. Nijhoff) 1976, in particular paragraphs 33 and 34, pp. 123-138. Italian translation: *La crisi delle scienze europee e la fenomenologia trascendentale*, Milano (Il Saggiatore) 1961, pp. 150-163, by E. Filippini and E .Paci, 1954.

21 R. BUBNER: *Handlung, Sprache und Vernuft*, Frankfurt (Surkamp) 1976, cit. Italian translation: cit., p. 20.

22 *Op. cit.*, p. 22.

social historical aspects. It does not mean that the nomological instance, with its heuristic value and the meaning of systematic objectivity, can be totally taken out of sociological research. It does not seem to us that, in sociology the comparison between 'nomothetic' and 'ideographic' has ever seen winners or losers. But it is just this lack of 'conclusion' that today forces us to live and think of a 'double necessity', that of the regularity and that of particularity, without the useless claim to repeal the one or the other.

Living in the 'double necessity' does not mean to give up developing a science on the solid basis of the 'nomological', but to broaden the critical ability of the enquiry systems, by forcing them to pay attention to one's theoretical statute, that in this way can be dominated without being expelled. Opening our mind to this new "double necessity", means, however, that sociological theory should stand another comparison which allows it to broaden the horizon some more, according to 'comprehension'.

We refer to the inevitable comparison between social theory and interpretative theory that is useful because of its function in the different systems of interpretation, by preventing both of them from acting in a hegemonic way.

We do not demand to face here a comparison which can be full of implications and, of course, be productive with the object of the broadening of the theoretical statute of the social sciences. It is enough to put the question and indicate some of the interrogatives and necessities of the contemporary hermeneutics, which can be a further stimulus to talk about the possibility of the social sciences, that by then is considered part of a comprehensive sociology.

Our theoretic purpose is to prize all the hermeneutical analysis highly, that finds any form of comprehension in the language, as a 'way of being', and that is open to that "architecture of sense, which can be called double or multiple sense, whose role is the one to show, step by step, by hiding"[23] and that, consequently requires "a mental process that consists in deciphering the hidden sense in the visible one, and the implicit levels of significance in the literal ones".[24]

Now, it is clear that by talking about the interpretative instance we should not be any more satisfied with registering that complex system of signs, through which the social actions show themselves, as the individual ones, but, on the contrary, demand to go 'further' the sign, toward the existence that is hidden behind it and wants to come out, even in a never definitive way.

---

23 P. RICOUER: *Il conflitto delle interpretazioni*, Milano (Jaca Book) 1977, p. 26.
24 *Ibidem*.

The interpretative task consists in the laborious effort to fill the gap between the interpreter and the 'thing', not only because of the impossible simultaneousness between the actor and the interpreter of the action as Schütz definitely demonstrated, but also for the variety of the signs and of the meanings hidden behind any sign.

All this requires the courage of the significant proposition, but also the patience to go deeper and deeper, in order to catch that variety of meanings that is the true richness of the human world, and that is often hidden behind the same sign.

It is an engagement that is very much related to the professional sociologist, who should have, among his abilities, that 'interpretative patience' which makes him capable to comprehend the others at the same time he makes the comprehension of his own self deeper, and vice versa. All that cuts off to the sociologist from any chance to reduce the richness and complexity of the human behaviour and of the comprehension of the self, in a sort of dialectics of identification and alienation, which requires the conquest of the self, in order to have a better comprehension of the other.

We do not want now to fall back into that situation of psychologistic solipsism or transcendental idealism. On the contrary, the interpretative instance, applied to the social research can contribute to make us consider how "the immediate consciousness is, first of all, 'false conscience'"[25], and that the social scientist has to become free from this false consciousness, by thinking over the objectivity of the social action, that does not indicate an empty 'self' or a 'vague and invincible truth' or a 'false thought'[26], but a 'self continuously full of existence', connected to a relationship of dependence, that allows to give an objective value to the forms in which this relationship is expressed, from the archaeological to the theological and eschatological ones, which want to show a 'particular existential function'.[27]

The interpretative proposal we have adopted, as in Paul Ricoeur's elaboration, could give more answers to the problems.

If we want to give some examples, the discourse about 'validity', the use of the 'causality' category in sociology, the distinction between the ones who act and the ones who reflect on society, the contrast between daily activities and system, between liberty and nomology, are just some of the problems

25 *Op. cit.*, p. 31.

26 *Ibid.*

27 *Op. cit.*, p. 36.

which could have a resolution by using hermeneutics, such as the one by Ricoeur, that after having been compared with phenomenology, which operates on an experienced level and the linguistic analysis, which operates on an enunciative level, reveals that "phenomenology and linguistic analysis together give life to the same descriptive and analytic discourse, whose unity will be better explained when it is opposed to it…another kind of constitutive and dialectic discourse, the one of the sensible action".[28]

In our opinion, the social science cannot escape from this discourse, because it has to make up for the interpretative instance and the ontological need which prevents it from loosing sight of the original data, revealed by the phenomenological method, that gives prominence to its superiority on the linguistic analysis.

In fact, "phenomenology can understand its own limits, because it defers to its origins the linguistic analysis, but cannot do it because the methodological decision not to know the experience that in its proposition implies the oblivion of the matter of the originally, produces the cancellation of the matter about the origins of the sense".[29]

Sociology is not allowed to neglect this matter, because today it is summoned to examine the 'sensible' action.

---

28 P. RICOUER: *La sèmantique de l'action, primière partie: Les discours de l'action*, Editions du Centre National de la Recherce Scientifique, Paris 1977. Italian translation: *La semantica dell'azione*, Milano (Jaca Book) 1986, p. 169.

29 *Op. cit*, p. 173.

Part C

German Theory and Philosophy of History Today

Chapter 9

Philosophy of History After the End of Formative Substantial Philosophy of History: Remarks on the Present State of the Philosophy of History

HANS MICHAEL BAUMGARTNER†

I. Different Approaches to the Philosophy of History and the Theory of History
II. The Discernability of History as the Essential Problem of the Philosophy of History and Theory of History
III. The Historical Rise and Decline of the Philosophy of History as a Central Discipline of Philosophy

Historical philosophy at the present day appears to be a rather unmethodical area of philosophical thought. The philosophy of history today is not - as it was up to half a century ago - about a firmly laid down canon of retrievable concepts and categories. Nor may it be understood any longer, as it always was heretofore, as an expression of a homogenous historical outlook on life. It reveals itself much more as a reservoir of differing ways of posing questions that are partly dependent on one another, and partly cover the same ground as an ensemble of diverse and in part disparate problems and methods of approach. Therefore, to begin with, an ascertainment of the present position of historical philosophical thought has to be directed at the examination, putting into order and elucidation of the essential facts and problems. The contribution that follows is dedicated to this task.

It deals with three areas of enquiry:

1. The different implications of the philosophy of history. The treatment of this area of enquiry is supposed to serve to distinguish and examine the

multiplicity of historical-philosophical approaches. It concerns itself directly, so to speak, with the present state the philosophy of history.

2. The essential problem of the philosophy of history or the enquiry into the historical process, the process of world history itself and its discernability. Here it concerns the central problem associated with history, the problem which involves first of all a philosophical examination, and is, as an implicit question, at the foundation of all approaches, regardless of how this question is then answered. This chapter is orientated systematically according to its nature and possesses, moreover, a critical function. It deals basically with the essence and the possibilities of historical philosophy.

3. The formative substantial philosophy of history as a historical formation or the historical development of the philosophy of history. This chapter is concerned with the state of the philosophy of history in the past. It sketches out the path it took to become a fundamental discipline, the lode-star of the philosophy at a particular time, but also has to do with its decline and its neutralisation as a discipline. Thus it leads on to a more precise determination of what is to be understood by the philosophy of history after the end of the formative substantial philosophy of history.

I. Different Approaches to the Philosophy of History and the Theory of History

A review of the various meanings of philosophy of history may apply firstly to that 'innocuous' meaning, according to which one speaks in general of a philosophical examination of historical events, historical happenings and historical processes. It is, in this respect, a deliberate examination of history according to maxims and reflections in the face of historical occurrences that are in some way outstanding. Examinations of this kind are familiar. They are to be found in the history textbooks for schools as well as in the relevant literary articles of daily and weekly newspapers. If one were to look for the classical example of this way of looking at things, then without doubt Jakob Burckhardt's *Weltgeschichtliche Betrachtungen*[1] would be cited. With the characterisation of this meaning as 'innocuous', in speaking of history in this

---

1 JACOB BURKHARDT: *Weltgeschichtliche Betrachtungen* (1868), 11 ed., Stuttgart.

manner, it is made clear that no systematic form of philosophical examination of historical happenings is presented but rather a more or less rhapsodic discussion of problems and perspectives which become intelligible to the historian during his work on the research and presentation of a past occurrence but intelligible also to the thoughtful observer of the conjunctures of circumstance. In this first significant area of the philosophy of history it is a matter, therefore, of it being, in the model case, the "historical prudence of wise historians"[2] according to Odo Marquard's formulation.

A second meaning, - basically the core one - adheres to the expression 'philosophy of history', when by it a philosophical theory is indicated or intended as an entire process. In theories of this type, the idea is that one can examine the essence, the origin, the end-purpose and the course of the entire process of 'history'. The philosophically most relevant impressive comprehensive theories of this kind are to be found in the historical-philosophical constructions of the school of German Idealism. The early Schelling's conception of a formative substantial philosophy of history based on reason may serve as an illustrative example[3]. Schelling is the first and probably the most consequential thinker to develop a systematic concept encompassing the whole of history using reason as a guide. He takes his point of departure from the transcendental reflection on the conditions of the feasibility of perception

2 ODO MARQUARD: "Schwierigkeiten mit der Geschichtsphilosophie", in: ODO MARQUARD: *Schwierigkeiten mit der Geschichtsphilosophie*, 2nd ed., Frankfurt a.M. 1982, p. 14.

3 Cf.: FRIEDRICH WILHELM JOSEPH SCHELLING: *Antiquissimi de prima malorum humanorum origine philosophematis genes. III explicandi tentamen criticum et philosophicum* (1792), in the same reference, *Historisch-kritische Ausgabe*, commissioned by the Schelling Commission of the Bavarian Academy of Sciences, edited by Hans Michael Baumgartner, Wilhelm Gustav Jacobs, Hermann Krings and Hermann Zeitner: *Werke*, vol. I, Stuttgart 1976, pp. 47-181; HANS MICHAEL BAUMGARTNER (Ed.): *Schelling. Einführung in seine Philosophie*, Freiburg/München 1975; WILHELM GUSTAV JACOBS: "System und Geschichte. Neueste Forschungsergebnisse zu Schellings frühester Entwicklung", in: DIETER HEINRICH (Ed.): *Ist systematische Philosophie möglich?,* Stuttgarter Hegel-Kongress 1975, Bonn 1977, pp. 165-170; HANS MICHAEL BAUMGARTNER: "Vernunft im Übergang zu Geschichte. Bemerkungen zur Entwicklung von Schellings Philosophie als Geschichts-philosophie", in: LUDWIG HASLER (Ed.): *Schelling. Seine Bedeutung für eine Philosophie der Natur und der Geschichte*, Stuttgart 1981, pp. 175-192.

and leads on to an idea of reason, which establishes itself as a valid base for all our knowledge.

On the model of Kantian philosophy, Schelling conceives this reason as an articulated structure of perceptive functions. In his *Critique of Pure Reason*, Kant had set forth and argued for the following faculties of perception: the faculty of sentience, by means of which all material things are primarily given to us; the faculty of intelligence, that permits us to observe things in time and space according to their properties, to place them into a context of experiences and to identify them as objects. Finally, there is the faculty of reason in its narrower sense, whereby the concrete nature of experience of the world, that is perceived by our intelligence, is brought to an all-encompassing coherence of judgement, i.e. expanded to its totality and thereby to the absolute. From these faculties, from sentience as the faculty of receptivity, from intellect as the faculty of conceptualisation and from reason (in its narrower sense) as the faculty of ideas there flows a systematic corpus of our perception, in so far as these faculties harmonise together of necessity and thus prove themselves to be part impulses for reason (in its wider sense).

It is precisely this reason as the embodiment of human perception with its three functions of material observation, comprehension of the abstract and systematic linkage of our propositions in an integral scientific coherence that is now, for Schelling, the starting point for the establishment of a systematically elaborated, formative substantial philosophy of history. He expands this structure of reason out into time and reads it as a uniform yet at the same time articulated history of human development. The uncovered structural factors of reason become, thereby, highly important epochs of the historical process, in which reason itself becomes materialised. The first stage of the history of mankind is the direct and untroubled state of material perception, the paradise; the second stage marks a condition, in which the ensuing idea disintegrates and destroys the unity of life in the material perception, the stage of the fall from grace. The efforts connected with this stage to reverse this fall from grace, to overcome by reason the disruption of the world and finally to unite again that which had been separated in a perfected condition of reason, lead to the third and last age, to the recovery of the paradisal state at, however, a new and higher level through the mediation of reason that reconciles all things. In this way the history of the world is, on the one hand, a history of the consciousness of humankind as a species, in so far as it moves humankind as a perceptive entity into the central position, and on the other hand at the same time as a history of the liberation of human reason out of the faint existence of sentience to the reflected existence of reason as a unity.

In 1806 Fichte argued for a similar idea[4], as did Hegel in his historical-philosophical scheme in *Phänomenologie, Enzyklopädie* and *Rechtsphilosophie* by founding his philosophy on the structural idea of reason. However, Hegel in a speculative dialectic describes in an essentially more complex manner, both materially and conceptually, the ascent of reason as being a reason that liberates itself to its own unique essence as pure spirit. The comparatively greater proximity to historical reality in this concept is based on the fact that Hegel articulated the ondriving impetus of the negative, that is negativity, essentially more sharply He is able, in this manner, despite the processes of ascent and advance, to diagnose at the same time the factors of the decline and make them comprehensible.

The thinking intrinsic to these philosophical theories and the claim to explain history according to *a priori* points of view were taken up in the following tradition ever and again - from Marx onwards - and it also forms the nucleus of those philosophical universal histories, which no longer refer back to the structure of the reason but seek to grasp the legitimacy of the historical process on the basis of another scheme of construction. All of these philosophical theories, that construe speculatively, allow fundamentally of three approaches to the interpretation of the historical process: -

1. the interpretation of history as a process of ascent, to be located historically in the early and middle periods of the Enlightenment - an optimistic variation of the construction.

2. its pessimistic variation, the interpretation of history as a process of decline, as it develops in the late Romantic period and as it is still to be found in the twentieth century in Oswald Spengler's work[5].

3. the interpretation of history as a process both of ascent and decline, i.e. as an intervention of both variants in the manner of an admittedly still positive balancing of accounts of history, the prototype and example of which is presented by Hegel's dialectic of history.

In this second interpretative field, the philosophy of history is a philosophy of history of a speculative content, i.e. a material philosophy of history.

---

4 Cf. JOHANN GOTTLIEB FICHTE: *Grundzüge des gegenwärtigen Zeitralters* (1806) with an introduction, edited by Alwin Diemer, Hamburg 1979.

5 Cf. OSWALD SPENGLER: *Der Untergang des Abendlandes. Umriß einer Morphologie der Weltgeschichte,* vol. 2, München 1918/22.

Possible criticism of this type of a formative substantial philosophy of history has to pay attention to the manner and way in which the presupposed *a priori* part, for example the concept of reason, is reconciled with the empirical part, the selected and elaborated elements of historical knowledge. It has in particular to clarify what significance is due in each case to the *a priori* scheme of construction, what grounds namely are laid down for its own justification in the field. In the second chapter this will be further discussed.

The third interpretation of philosophy of history includes the different philosophical approaches to the determination and the establishment of historical knowledge. What is meant here by philosophy of history is the formal epistemology of historical knowledge in opposition to the material philosophy of history. Because of the haphazard nature of this field, it seems expedient to take a retrospective glance at the history of the concept as a basis. The first to be recalled is Johann Gustav Droysen, the founder of the modern science of history. His *Vorlesungen über Enzyklopädie und Methodologie der Geschichte*[6] (Lectures on the Encyclopaedia and Methodology of History) cannot count as the founding charter of the speculative nor of the positivist theory of history. They include, however, the opening gambits of the notorious far-reaching disputes, from Dilthey on until the early and mid-20th Century, between the positivist natural sciences and the hermeneutic arts.

In his *Historik*, Droysen posed the question in the Kantian tradition of transcendental philosophy about the prerequisites of historical knowledge, linking several philosophical approaches together with one another. The question of how something that happens in space and time can be understood as a historical event then is, to quote Droysen, how "history arises out of affairs." Posing this problem implies essential and, for historical theory, effectual distinctions, - for one thing, the drawing of a distinction between the course of everyday life and history, between mundane events and "affairs" (in the sense meant by Droysen) and that which contains significance as history, - for another, the distinction between the manifold histories, which present themselves as narratives and *history proper,* through which these histories are registered primarily as an element of history, as an all-embracing process, and finally the distinction between temporality in general and historical time, since not everything that is *in* time or runs a temporal course can straightaway

6 Cf. JOHANN GUSTAV DROYSEN: *Historik. Vorlesungen über Enzyklopädie und Methodologie der Geschichte,* edited by Peter Leyh, Historisch-kritische Ausgabe, vol. I, Stuttgart-Bad Cannstadt 1977.

be called historical. Let us imagine the running down of a mechanism, such as a musical box, which certainly represents a happening within time, but would we view it as history? Droysen's analysis of the processes of the cognition and presentation of history can show that in the knowledge of history it is not only objects and occurrences that are perceived but always, at the same time, the implications of the "moral world" as well, of the moral world that is linked to them. Here, in this way, the category of significance, which occupies central value status in Dilthey's *Aufbau der geschichtlichen Welt*[7], moves to the centre of interest.

Representatives of neo-Kantianism, such as Heinrich Rickert[8] and Georg Simmel have gone back to Kant more uncompromisingly than Droysen. Simmel in particular sets forth in his early works the constructivist composition of our knowledge of history[9]. We do not observe history but construct it. What we observe are events in space and time. The conception of an occurrence as a historical event is enjoined in accordance with a system of interpretation which thereby makes possible a uniform narrative, that links what happens in connection to other happenings under one point of view that bestows uniformity and significance at the same time. Only on the basis of such a system of interpretation can emerge in the end the idea of a union of many stories, that is to the idea of a comprehensive process entitled history.

At the beginning of the 20th century, the theory of history that is transcendental and hermeneutic on the one hand and constructivistically aligned on the other hand is put into question by the philosophy of life and by philosophic anthropology. These philosophical approaches contradict the *a priori* nature of the shaping of events; they interpret history as a product of life, through which the human, as a being with needs, can primarily orientate himself in a world that is of itself in a state of chaos, disburden himself and maintain himself. Thinking about the historical nature of our historical knowledge leads ultimately to the historical nature of human existence itself. It was con-

7 WILHELM DILTHEY: *Der Aufbau des geschichtlichen Welt in den Geistesgewissenschaften,* edited by Manfred Riedel, 2nd ed., Frankfurt a.M. 1981.

8 Cf. HEINRICH RICKERT: *Naturwissenschaft und Kulturwissenschaft,* examined and extended edition, Tübingen 1926, new edition edited by Friedrich Vollhardt, Stuttgart 1986, and HEINRICH RICKERT: *Die Probleme der Geschichtsphilosophie. Eine Ein-führung,* 3d ed., Heidelberg 1924.

9 Cf. in particular GEORG SIMMEL: *Die Probleme der Geschichtsphilosophie. Eine erkenntis-theoretische Studie,* 5th ed., München/Leipzig 1923.

ceived initially in Heidegger's anthropology, and then freed from Heidegger's narrowing constraints and further developed in the universally applied Hans-Georg Gadamer's hermeneutics. It is characteristic for these positions that they prevail in pushing through the idea of the historicity of historical knowledge against both the constructivistic and the transcendental *a priori* approaches. In this way, the hermeneutic theory of its historical nature thus marks the second form of a cognition theory of historical knowledge. In as much as it rests on the understanding and the historical nature of our knowledge, it does not, to be sure, disavow the feasibility of valid knowledge, but, for being able to be held to be valid knowledge, it is required that the reference to the historical dimension be established and that the object on which doubtlessly correct judgements should be passed, be understood as an essentially historical object.

While the cognitive theory approaches presented up to now are still, after all, set off by and large against our knowledge of history, the type of historical cognition theory formed from it subsequently is limited to the historical sciences: "The scientific theory of the historical sciences" is the title which characterises the philosophy of history as a cognitive theory of historical knowledge in a third sense. Its analytical variant applies neither to the historical occurrence itself, nor to our conceptions of history, but to the way and manner, in which we "discourse" about a happening in history. At the centre stands the analysis of sentences and speech. Its purpose is, on the one hand, a grammar of the vocabulary of history and, on the other, a methodology for the explanation of singular sentences. Consequently it repudiates every substantial or material philosophy of history. The problem of the nomological explanation of singular sentences in accordance with the Hempel-Oppenheim system of scientific interpretation opens up a new variant of the "Comprehension(*Verstehen*)-Explanation Controversy" and leads in the end to a widely ramified and in many respects very productive discussion between the hermeneutic, the transcendental and the analytical tradition of the philosophy.

In connection with this, my own attempt - as well as that of Jörn Rüsen - sees in the mediation of analytical, transcendental, anthropological and hermeneutical theorems the task to work out, in comparison with that of Droysen, a "renewed study of history", forming the foundation of a uniform theory regarding our historical knowledge as a whole and, as a consequence, a uniform theory of the historical sciences[10]. Above all, this is a matter of three areas of inquiry: -

1. what constitutes the historical object (occurrences and processes),
2. what are the problems of historical research (heuristic, systematic, interpretative), and
3. which is the form of historical presentation?

The question of the provenance and validity of universal theories of history is one of the central problems, more precisely, as to whether such theories qualify as pure hypotheses or even turn out to be laws of history at all. Primarily, the following questions are posed: Are there laws for the facts of history, which apply universally, or can the laws of history - if there be such things at all - be entitled merely to periodic validity? Are there, consequently, laws of only medium range? And: Do laws have validity, no matter how far they extend, *a priori* and *ex ante* or only *a posteriori, ex post*? Is it *a priori* laws or only empirical normalities that we discover after "history" has taken place and with the help of which we would be able to extrapolate into the future and foretell a future happening in broad outline? In this final question, modern historical theory touches on problems of the substantial philosophy of history.

To sum up this first section: - The expression "philosophy of history" denotes, for one thing, more or less "prudent" reflections and considerations, which are employed in the face of historical research, historical findings from sources and the facts of history. For another thing, one always understands under philosophy of history something as well of the approach to an examination of the process of history as a whole. Finally philosophy of history is a collective concept for the most various epistemological theories, therefore for

10 Cf. HANS MICHAEL BAUMGARTNER: *Kontinuität und Geschichte. Zur Kritik und Metakritik der historischen Vernunft,* Frankfurt a.M. 1972; as well as: "Thesen zur Grundlegung einer transzendentalen Historik", in: HANS MICHAEL BAUMGARTNER, JÖRN RÜSEN (Eds.): *Seminar: Geschichte und Theorie. Umrisse einer Historik,* Frankfurt a.M. 1976, pp. 274-302; JÖRN RÜSEN: "Ursprung und Aufgabe der Historik", in: HANS MICHAEL BAUMGARTNER, JÖRN RÜSEN (Eds.): *Seminar: Geschichte und Theorie. Umrisse einer Historik,* pp. 59-93; HANS MICHAEL BAUMGARTNER, JÖRN RÜSEN (Eds.): *Historische Vernunft. Grundzüge einer Historik I: Die Grundlagen der Geschichtswissenschaft*, Göttingen 1983; HANS MICHAEL BAUMGARTNER, JÖRN RÜSEN (Eds.): *Rekonstruktion der Vergangenheit. Grundzüge einer Historik II: Die Prinzipien der historischen Forschung*, Göttingen 1986.

the posing of reflective questions, which relate to our conversations about history, and our cognition, perception, comprehension, interpretation and presentation of it.

II. The Discernability of History as the Essential Problem of the Philosophy of History and Theory of History

Any debate on the central problem of a philosophy of history, that is the question concerning the historical process and its discernability, has to make allowance for the implied fact that "history" simply does not let itself be perceived. History is not identical with what happens in time and space. History and what has happened are not the same thing. Rather, history demands an interpretative model that allows it to label an event that occurs in space and time as a historical event. Only by such an interpretative system, an incident in space and time transcends to the historic dimension, and its significance is perceptible in the framework of more or less greater associations of occurrences. The "perception" of incidents as historical events and - in even much greater measure - the "perception" of a multiplicity of events as a historical process, assumes firstly, therefore, a peculiar capacity for abstraction, that is dependent on the projection of a system that grants it meaning (or as Rickert would have called it "value"). The historical subject, whether it be an occurrence or a process, is derived from an abstraction, and this abstraction originates in its turn from fashioning a model by which we bring individual facts, individual occurrences into a structure that bestows significance on it, incorporates it into a working model and awards it the appropriate significance. The "history overriding histories", as Droysen once formulated it or history as "collective singular" (in Koselleck's expression[11]) is not something given but a construct.

How now are those models, through which the mundanely significant becomes history, to be determined? Which types of model can one discover, if

11 Cf. REINHART KOSELLECK: „Article Geschichte“, in: *Geschichtliche Grundbegriffe. Historisches Lexikon zur politisch-sozialen Sprache in Deutschland*, edited by Otto Brunner/Werner Conze/Reinhart Koselleck, vol. 2, Stuttgart 1975 pp. 666ff., and REINHART KOSSELLEK: *Vergangene Zukunft. Zur Semantik geschichtlicher Zeiten,* Frankfurt am Main 1979.

one looks back to philosophy of history in its development? It seems that above all there are two basic types, applied to the character of the historical process, that may be discerned. One can be characterised as the "biomorphic" type and the other as the "ratiomorphic" type. From the class of biomorphic conceptions, there are two to be named: firstly the type oriented on plant and growth symbolism, that is considered as a paradigm in Oswald Spengler's morphology of cultures. Spengler explained the origin, the blooming and the evanescence of the various cultures on the model of the laws governing the growth of different plants that are not dependant on one another; just like plants, cultures bloom, become mature and die out according to their own peculiar laws. Secondly, the type that goes back to Augustine and Cicero, which describes the course of world history as analogous to the sequence of the ages of man, - childhood, youth, maturity and old age.

The ratiomorphic model type similarly has several variations, from which those of Kant, Schelling, Fichte and Hegel named above and briefly sketched out can be characterised as the classic ones. By them the structure peculiar to reason acts as a model, which brings to light a history and allows an interpretation, which extends from the first appearance of reason right up to its complete realisation. It is reason which is on the path to itself and is, ultimately, realised and comprehended as a unity of the power of reason. According to this model, history is realised as a history of the spirit. Another ratiomorphic type has been brought into the debate in the 1970s by Piaget, Kohlberg, Habermas and - with another centre of emphasis by Günter Dux[12] as well under the label of "the learning process of the human species." To be sure, these extensions to such learning processes are thrown into relief, being, above all, not conscious learning practices but practices put into operation by way of conditioned reflexes. Nevertheless, the ratiomorphic structure even of these conceptions manifests itself in that the morally responsible individual. This is emphasised in all of them and in an exemplary manner in Piaget, who links it to the ontogenetic development[13]. Habermas, in particular, has transposed the logic of the ontogenetic development of moral consciousness to the phylogenetic level, so that the final stage of the entire sociocultural develop-

12 Cf. GÜNTER DUX: *Die Logik der Weltbilder. Sinnstrukturen im Wandel der Geschichte*, Frankfurt a.M. 1982.

13 Cf. JEAN PIAGET: *Das moralische Urteil beim Kinde*, Frankfurt a.M. 1973.

ment is seen to lie in moral freedom[14]. If in connection with these approaches, the problem still remains open as to how moral responsibility should emerge from receptive learning behaviour, and thus out of natural processes in their widest sense, so is it to be put on record that here too is an entity available that is analogous to the idealistic model of rational history. At the end of the history of development, the individual (and the collectivity) assume responsibility for itself and can perceive and, at the same time, shape the history out of which it proceeded, as the entity of history.

In connection with abstraction and the forming of models, the important question arises as to how models of this kind can be justified philosophically. It has, indeed, to be shown by what right, in one case, world history is interpreted according to the seasons of a man's life, while, in another, humankind's world history should be interpreted according to the concepts of a developing reason that is coming to itself. How then are these models to be justified? That is one of the central questions of the philosophy of history. The conceptions of German Idealism start, as has been noted already, from a concept of reason, which one can ascertain for oneself in terms of cognition-theory. Reason (in the wider sense) as finite reason is the framework of relationships of the cognitive functions, physical perception, concept of understanding and idea of reason, unified in the transcendental apperception of the "I think." As a functional whole of the theoretical as well as of the practical perception of truth, it is the foundation of human self-understanding. Humankind has always made presuppositions in this way, when the individual speaks out about something; concerning history too, the claim of truth is raised. Hence, as an uncontested foundation, a *fundamentum inconcussum,* in such an attempt to reconstruct reason, the self-reflecting, morally responsible man is formulated idealistically by self-awareness.

This connection is illuminating. For it shows that, in all these models, projections and transfers are in play. For one thing, a *fundamentum inconcussum* is sought, that can be claimed and identified as a basis of our knowledge, (for example, reason or life); accordingly in its internal disposition, it is differentiated in itself, developed into a working model and ultimately projected onto history. The transfer of the model to all processes of genesis appears in the

---

14 Cf. LAWRENCE KOHLBERG: *Zur kognitiven Entwicklung des Kindes*, Frankfurt a.M. 1973; JÜRGEN HABERMAS: *Kultur und Kritik*, Frankfurt a.M. 1974; and JÜRGEN HABERMAS: *Zur Rekonstruktion des historischen Materialismus*, Frankfurt a.M. 1976.

course of history then as an intrinsic insight. If one then adds that outstanding occurrences from the "framework" of the model can be included by means of the theorem of the "contemporaneity of the non-contemporary" that dates back to Herder or, as the case may be, "the non-contemporaneity of the contemporary", then the essential elements of the substantive philosophy of history are denominated. Philosophies of history of this type are immune against criticism. They are irrefutable but, because of that, are therefore problematic.

The central problem in regard to this model is the question concerning the clues to its fundamental validity. As a rule, it concerns a concept that is used with reference to the character of humankind. In German Idealism it is defined, by the concept of human reason, as a self-aware and moral character, whereas the concept of the learning process based in the anthropological approaches identifies it as a biological creature of needs exclusively concerned with survival. There is always present in the concepts a sort of information, acting as clues, about the character of what humankind is "in truth", so that what appears as the character of history depends on the self-understanding of humankind. Assuming that humankind is in truth self-awareness, the history of the world becomes the history of reason developing to the point where it realises its essential uniqueness. Assuming, however, that the human is in truth a creature of needs, history is a necessary process of relief and compensation for the survival of this character.

What status is accorded, as a consequence of these models, to the things mentioned above? What cognitive meaning can be awarded to them? It is certain that the question of whether these models make an essential insight possible into the course of history has to be denied. To be sure, they evoke the appearance of containing *a priori* laws governing history. However this alleged *a priori* nature lies, at best, at the level of the model that is cultivated, not at the level of the actual course history takes. Consequently, one will be able to say that these models do not have the status of an *a priori* insight into world history and that the same holds true for the philosophies of history that are orientated towards these models. It seems to me to be just as important, however, that these models are, on these grounds, by no means without meaning. They can serve as heuristic designs for the discovery and interpretation of available historical material. That they do not allow any prognosis is true, but they make it possible to test other alternative models, i.e. to debate the question which sequences of events, measured against which models, are to be revealed and to be made intelligible. In short, they are germane to the heuristics of historical research.

The critique of the material and substantive philosophy of history of this kind, therefore, does not go so far, as to dismiss as being without meaning in itself, as the unreflected fancy imputed here that one could with such models have a grasp of world history. Much more does the philosophy of history perceive its function in the historical sciences, as being that of interpretation in so far as these models furnish heuristic ideas, which can act as projects for the interpretation of the material content of history. If one pursues these thoughts further, then the consequence demonstrates that philosophy of history is possible only as a formal *a priori* theory of historical knowledge[15]. A "transcendental dialectic of historical reason" can show, namely, that, on the one hand, it is by no means meaningless to present the forming of models in the manner described as guides to the process of historical research, yet, on the other hand, no penetration of the essence in history is to be gained thereby. Thus it is shown that history is not an *a priori* recognisable and observable process of development, neither is it a process of evolving the "absolute in the finite", as Schelling claimed in his middle and later periods, nor is it a history of the development of reason, finding its way to itself in the Hegelian sense, nor a process of mankind's self-liberation from all servitude, as in historic materialism. History is much more an open process, in which it depends on every person involved in the action and the conditions of the action. It is an ensemble of histories, which are co-determined by the action of humans and are retrospectively interpreted by the acting persons themselves. Generally speaking, history is a happening occurring freely, and not at anyone's command. It is fate. It is a happening arising out of human liberty, not an *a priori* process leading to liberty. For this reason, it can and must be evoked and be ever newly actualised as a deposit of human destiny.

15 Cf. HANS MICHAEL BAUMGARTNER: "Thesen zur Grundlegung einer transzendentalen Historik" in: HANS MICHAEL BAUMGARTNER, JÖRN RÜSEN (Eds.): *Seminar: Geschichte und Theorie. Umrisse einer Historik*, ibid., pp. 274-302.

III. The Historical Rise and Decline of the Philosophy of History as a Central Discipline of Philosophy

Philosophy contains both fundamental - or central - disciplines and marginal disciplines, "hyphenated philosophies"[16], within its canon of subjects. Even a superficial observation of the history of philosophy allows three central disciplines to be discerned, which one can characterise when looking at Plato or Aristotle and also at late Kant. Philosophy always concerns itself essentially with our thinking, therefore its central discipline is logic. It is also concerned with the objects of our world, at its core it is constantly - to formulate it in Kantian terminology - a metaphysic of nature, or as the case may be, physics as Platonists understand it. Philosophy is always constantly concerned with human actions, looking at those of the single individual and at the social context as well. It is at its core a theory of human activities; it is ethics or - once again in Kant's formulation - a metaphysic of freedom.

These core disciplines shape the basic structure of philosophising, which reifies itself in the course of the historical development of philosophy in variously changing and alternating historical formations. The historical formations of philosophy are determined by the fact that a specific theme, or a particular type of philosophical approach or a special fundamental perspective on the world as a whole, come to the fore, in the breach of which each of the three core disciplines manifest themselves in another light, without their basic elements having been called into question. In this a differentiation is made as to whether logic, physics and ethics, are being thematised in the perspective of the question about existence and, consequently, in the historical constellation of ontology, or whether they stand under the systematic ascendancy of cognition theory, anthropology, linguistic philosophy or even philosophy of

16 "Hyphenated philosophies" means in German all philosophical disciplines formed by linking the object of that discipline by a hyphen to philosophy like "*Geschichts-Philosophie*" or "*Sozial-Philosophie*". Since the English language does not use a hyphen in this case, but links the object of the philosophical discipline to this discipline by the preposition "of" like in "philosophy of history", the term "hyphenated philosophies" should be rendered by the term "philosophies of". By making philosophy the subject of the genitivus objectivus of a field outside of philosophy proper the philosophical endeavour seems to be depotentiated (editor's note).

history, which advanced to become the ruling fundamental philosophy some two centuries ago[17].

For the observer of the history of philosophy the process is extremely illuminating in that philosophical formations of this type are epochal structures, which disappear again from the field of view after a certain period of operation and then are included as hyphenated philosophies in the stock of subjects in philosophy and are "neutralised" into becoming philosophical disciplines alongside others.

A comparable process is characteristic too for the history of the philosophy of history. Philosophy of history nowadays is a formerly dominant fundamental philosophy neutralised into being a marginal discipline. It finds itself, thereby, alongside all the disciplines which are not core disciplines such as logic, physics and ethics, but merely particular perspectives and ways of approach, in comparison to what everyone is interested in at all times in it, being placed in perspective and taken into view. It is at all times interesting, whether and whereby we can think clearly and logically. It is always of interest how we as human beings in nature and the universe should be able to comprehend nature, and it is always of interest which are the fundamental concepts and principles of our actions. It is always of interest, how we respond to other humans and deal with them rationally. Therefore the complex of questions of logic, natural metaphysics (physics) and ethics are of interest at all times. However, the question of existence, the problem of cognition, the theme of history are not of interest at all times, at least not in a comparable way. In ancient days, for example, on the basis of the presentation of cosmic eternal recurrence and of the integrated nature of humankind also in this cosmos, history as an autonomous theme of philosophical observation has been attracted as little attention as, say, problems of cognition, which have drawn the primary attention of philosophy in the new era, with the entry of a new picture of the world and thereby have established gnoseology as a fundamental discipline focusing all other problems. In a similar manner, so too has philosophy of history become a guide both for the reflection and for the philosophical interpretation of reality, only a certain historical constellation. This development asserts the formative substantial philosophy of history as a his-

17 Cf. ODO MARQUARD: "Schwierigkeiten mit der Geschichtsphilosophie", 2nd ed., Frankfurt a.M. 1982, p. 1. Also ODO MARQUARD: "Geschichte/Geschichtsphilosophie", in: *Staatslexikon*, edited by the Görres-Gesellschaft, vol. 2, Freiburg/Basel/Wien 1986, pp. 924-936.

torical formation that, at a fixed time, by its perspective, which as it were transforms everything into history, became simply the guiding perspective of philosophy - became a guiding perspective such as is represented, one may probably claim, at the present time by the *linguistic turn* of the philosophy of language.

The golden age of the formative substantial philosophy of history started with the Enlightenment and the philosophies that followed on after it. It was Voltaire who introduced the concept "philosophy of history" into idiomatic use; at the same time, as Reinhart Kosellek has shown, it was precisely at that period that in speech the collective singular "history" was formed, and thus it was the first time that history as a totality and a separate effective power was marked of from the multiplicity of stories referred from life and to life and was elevated to the central and singular theme[18].

What further circumstances are to be shown for the genesis of formative substantial philosophy of history as the fundamental discipline dominant in its day? Firstly, one will have to refer to some deficiencies, mistaken information and blank spots in the intellectual store house of that time. The idea of an ordered and meaningful cosmos, such as it had been assigned by the Greeks and also by medieval philosophy as the underlying thinking basic to all knowledge and actions, - this idea of a cosmos had been rendered obsolete by the experimental research of the natural sciences. At the same time, metaphysics above all had fallen into disrepute. It had "abdicated" firstly in favour of nominalism with regard to epistemology and later, in respect of its metaphysical content, it had given up in the collapse of theodicy. The question of whether one could justify God in the face of the wickedness and the evil in the world had found its answer in the insight that one would have to basically exculpate God if one then wanted to save Him. This led ultimately - with O. Marquard - to His "abolition" and to the establishment of an "atheism ad majorem Dei gloriam"[19]. Loss of the cosmos - loss of the Absolute. Their place was taken by humankind, who now had to take over and to bear the burden of the absolute and the burden of the role of the cosmos for endowing

---

18 Cf. REINHART KOSELLECK: "Historia vitae magistra. Über die Auflösung des Topos im Horizont neuzeitlich bewegter Geschichte", in: REINHART KOSELLECK: *Vergangene Zukunft. Zur Semantik geschichtlicher Zeiten*, Frankfurt a.M. 1979, pp. 38-66.

19 ODO MARQUARD: "Wie irrational kann Geschichtsphilosophie sein?", in: ODO MARQUARD: *Schwierigkeiten mit der Geschichtsphilosophie*, ibid., p. 70.

meaning. The human then has become an absolute and autonomous being whose areas of experience, action and life have by this time turned into history. History, which the human person moreover makes herself and for which therefore she has also to be responsible, became for the human person an absolute horizon, a horizon at any rate for the endowment of meaning. On this path, formative substantial philosophy of history separated itself from cosmos-orientated metaphysics, and put in a claim to replace it, but the theme of history stepped into the foreground, not only philosophically regarding the history of the mind but also at the political level.

The problem of the *ius gentium* in the framework of the community of states that was being developed, the idea of natural law as a right for all men and the Utopia of the League of Nations denote questions of life, which seem to be soluble only within a historical-philosophical horizon. They are a further condition for the genesis of formative substantial philosophy of history as a historical formation of philosophy.

That it has been the formative substantial philosophy of history that became the dominant philosophy precisely at this moment in history can be made plausible by the following reflection. At all times, it seems to hold true that when the then dominant view of the world, whatever it be, experiences a disturbance, since the basic assumptions giving meaning to it disappear, the deficiency in taken up and compensated for by a suitable substitute. If the natural order can no longer be the background, from which everything is to be ordained and comprehended, if Almighty God is no longer available as an establishing horizon and the notion of the Creator no longer possesses any binding force, then substitutes are, as it were, sought of the necessity, substitutes for the loss of Nature and for the loss of God. The thought of "history", at the relevant time under discussion, offers itself as such a substitute, since it is precisely in "history" that the human can comprehend herself in her autonomy, indeed in her absoluteness, as it seems, in a certain way. It is exactly in this way that both a change of perspective as well as a transformation in style of thinking is accomplished: History now becomes a guiding concept, which can take the place both of the divine cosmos and of the Absolute God; in as much as it occupies this position, it becomes the new symbol of redemption for mankind.

Alongside the conditions sketched out in closer detail, there are more remote ones to be perceived for the origin of a formative substantial philosophy of history as a historical formation. They were rooted in the discussion about formative substantial philosophy of history in particular under the label

"Secularisation of Christian eschatology". This is supposed to imply that the formative substantial philosophy of history in accordance with its distant provenance in Western tradition is to be understood as a product of the secularisation of Christian sacred history. In this sense Karl Löwith expounded the thesis that the eschatology of Christianity has been secularised into becoming, in the course of time, a doctrine of internal expectation of the salvation of man in the framework of history[20]. This thesis, however, does not address the circumstances of the case exactly enough. If the points of correspondence between the Christian eschatology and the assumptions of formative substantial philosophy of history are to be ascertained, then it must not be overlooked that the thought of "history" was shaped in the early Christian era by the fact that the *Eschaton*, the Last Things, was not coming at exactly the point of time it was expected and that the immediately expected Second Coming of Christ had failed to arrive. The thought of "history" is not therefore a concept, which would have been formed in the late Middle Ages or even firstly in the modern era through a secularisation of the concept of the Final Days, the *Eschaton*. Much more was it the failure of the *Parousia* to arrive and the entry of the Church for reasons of the need to bridge time, which led to the development of a historical consciousness of salvation. If, therefore, the discussion is to be about secularisation, then it should not be about a secularisation of eschatology but about ecclesiology becoming more worldly and secularised. Consequently, in considering Karl Löwith there should be a precise definition. The historical conception of salvation of Christendom is the product not of thinking about the Last Days but about the non-appearance of the Last Days. Formative substantial philosophy of history is not, therefore, about eschatology becoming part of the world but about the secularisation of church history.

Thus, so far as it concerns the more remote conditions for the origin of the formative substantial philosophy of history, the origin of historical thinking lies not in the notion of the last days but in the perception of the institution of the Church, in its vocation to be the bridge and the path to salvation. Church history becomes formative substantial philosophy of history at the very moment in which in the face of the Enlightenment's critique, the Church collapses in its authority and, consequently, also in its claim to be the instance

20 KARL LÖWITH: *Weltgeschichte und Heilgeschehen. Die vorausgesesetzten Voraussetzungen der Geschichtsphilosophie*', Stuttgart 1953, reprinted in: KARL LÖWITH: *Sämtliche Schriften*, vol. 2, Stuttgart 1982.

and sacrament of historical salvation. It is precisely Voltaire's critique of the Church that confirms this connection. It does not criticise a false *Eschaton*, but the false claim of the Church to authority. Its criterion is reason. Formative substantial philosophy of history as a historical formation is, on that account, the idea of reason and the idea that reason by its developing historically into the consummation of mankind becomes dominant. An example of this is Schelling's formative substantial philosophy of history of sketched out above.

Why did this formation come to collapse? The first cause is, without doubt, to be seen in the disintegration of the substantialist philosophy of reason of the school of German Idealism. If the reason was the sustaining principle of the Enlightenment and of German Idealism, then, with the end of this philosophy, that which had to appear as its stringent consequence, namely the metaphysical historical philosophy orientated on reason and its self-realisation, had to become invalid at the same time. Despite all the criticism of the absolute power of reason, as it gains shape in the later philosophies of Fichte and Schelling and then, later on, by Marx, Kierkegaard and Nietzsche, there remains, admittedly, the irrefutable realisation that even today we cannot renounce an *a priori* concept of reason. With this, reason is no longer indeed taking the part of an absolute substance of reason in the Hegelian sense, but allowance is made for the fact that without a structural concept of reason comparable with the idealistic, namely transcendentalist concept[21], a philosophy or science is not possible, nor is it to be warranted in its claims to be accepted as true.

The second reason for the collapse of the formative substantial philosophy of history lies in the bewildering experience that history proved to be an ambivalent happening just at that very moment, at which one could at long last be convinced that it lay now in humankind's own hands. This moment was the French Revolution and the crisis that followed directly at its heel, its debacle. This debacle signifies - in principle - the end of the optimism about progress and equally so the end of that pathetic formative substantial philosophy of history which was *a priori* confident of the perfection and of the good ending of the world.

---

21 Cf. in addition H. M. BAUMGARTNER: "Ereignis und Struktur als Kategorien einer geschichtlichen Betrachtung der Vernunft", in: NORBERT A. LUYTEN (Ed.): *Grenzfragen*, vol. 12, Freiburg/München 1982, pp. 175-217.

The rise of the empirical-historical humanist sciences and, as a consequence of that, the gaining of ground in the humanities of theories of cognition and science are to be called in as the third reason for the collapse. Droysen's and Ranke's argument against both, against the positivist writing of history and against German speculative historical philosophy, was successful and of a long-lasting effect. History remains, it is true, the all-embracing reality. However, it is no longer observable through reason's self-reflection.

The fourth reason lies in the parvenu rise of the admittedly naturalistic, yet even so speculative social sciences, being studied as a paradigm of Auguste Comte's "social physics" and in the recurrence of the idea of Nature coming along with it, which is gradually establishing itself in each of its differing modifications as a new powerfully effective counter-concept to history, consequently in the naturalism of the 19th Century, in philosophical anthropology, but also - and primarily - in the new metaphysics of evolution. The cosmos has been scattered into infinity and thus lost. God is dead and now, it must be said, history too is at its end. What consequences this process of the erosion of meaning has for the position of the human person she herself must grasp, moreover since it is no longer possible for the human person to believe on the basis of experience that she herself - as humankind - could take the place of the cosmos, let alone that of God. It is the self-understanding of the human, as a pure being of nature, which emerges from this situation, with all the difficulties, which in particular stem from the fact, that the human as this natural being is not only alive but also acts upon herself and consequently cannot but, at least, assert herself as a morally responsible being. The idea of Nature, after the precedent of Schelling and the Romantic, returns to philosophy; even though it be deprived of potency, it is all the same once more a sign of salvation.

The consequences of the plausible and, however evident it may have become, not unwarranted decline of the formative substantial philosophy of history as a fundamental philosophy may be summarised in three issues:

1. The philosophy of history is neutralised as a discipline to being but one hyphenated philosophy alongside numerous others.

2. Its previously overblown claim leads to a critical restriction of its approach and equally so to a restriction of the assertions claimed by it regarding history in general. Philosophy of history turns into the epistemology of historical knowledge and, where it becomes elevated, into " the critique of historical reason". This title, an expression of Dilthey's, if it is taken up in a

modified form, could probably best characterise the present constitution and conceptual orientation of the discipline of philosophy of history.

3. The pathos originally bound into the formative substantial philosophy of history has departed elsewhere with its decline, firstly into the pathos of the natural sciences and the social utopias that march along with them, later into the consciousness of salvation of a new mythology, into the "Resurrection of Metaphysics", equally so in the myth of "Life" and ultimately too into the philosophy of the identity of evolution. Pathos, thus let free and ending up without an object or master, proves to be the most problematical consequence of the neutralisation of the formative substantial philosophy of history.

The fate of the human that has become autonomous and settled in herself as being absolute, becomes apparent in the eventualities discussed for the philosophy of history and the fate of the formative substantial philosophy of history as a historical formation. Just like the formative substantial philosophy of history, so too does the human person fail with the excessive demands she makes on herself and on the hybrid claim, that she is able to assure for salvation and historical-philosophical perfection and able to take control of it by means of the history made by humankind itself. Is there, therefore, only educated scepticism left to be with us? This question is to be answered in the affirmative, as far as it refers to the result, the stages and even the beginning of history. Scepticism has, however, to be refuted, when considering - which despite all the arguments is still possible - the self-perception of the human person, as a finite being of reason, as a creature of nature, who is capable of perception and has to bear moral and practical responsibility.

What therefore does the philosophy of history consist in after the end of the formative substantial philosophy of history? What can it be? Firstly, a critique of the speculative formative substantial philosophy of history in its manifestly always recurring overblown claim. Secondly, a theory of historical reason, a critical study of history that discusses the possibilities of our historical knowledge and also fixes the structures and significance of the perceptions of historical science with the result that our knowledge of history is only appropriate for orienting our responsible activity, not for anticipating it. Lastly, the perception of the non-dispositional character of history and the character of destiny within it. The philosophy of history following the end of the formative substantial philosophy of history is a critique of historical reason. It has reference to *history itself* as a regulative idea of history, like our self-understanding and our action. It is an initiation into self-perception.

However, it is no longer an occasion for self-deception or an inducement to human arrogance.

Chapter 10

Why Kant's Reflections on History Still Have Relevance

HERTA NAGL-DOCEKAL

I. The Idea of Historical Progress
II. Three Paradigmatic Objections to Philosophy of History
III. Why Kant's Reflections on History Remain Untouched by the Current Critique
IV. Philosophy of History: An Indispensable Project

I. The Idea of Historical Progress

Is philosophy of history still possible today? Before addressing this question, I first need to clarify exactly what the term 'philosophy of history' means. A quick review reveals that the term has been used in a number of very different ways. In more recent debates, the following issues - to mention only a few variants - have been discussed under the rubric 'philosophy of history': the question of the scholarly status of history as a discipline; the fundamental ontology of the historicity of human beings; the analysis of narrative constructions of history by means of the philosophy of language; as well as reflective observations in the form of maxims and reflections (what Odo Marquard, in his inimitable style calls the „historical wisdoms of wise historians"[1]).

In spite of this, there does appear to exist wide-spread agreement about the core of the term's original meaning: the expression 'philosophy of history' – which, according to etymological research, was used for the first time in

1 MARQUARD, ODO: *Schwierigkeiten mit der Geschichtsphilosophie*, Frankfurt a.M. (Suhrkamp) 1973, p. 14.

1764 by Voltaire in his review of Hume's *Complete History of England*[2] – refers primarily to the project of interpreting the development of humanity as a whole. It is revealing that the collective singular 'history' (*die Geschichte*) arose approximately contemporaneously to Voltaire's coining of the term.[3] This original understanding of the expression 'philosophy of history' designates, in terms of its argument, the conception of humanity's progressive improvement, as was characteristic in Enlightenment thought and the theoretical tradition emerging from it.[4] Historians of philosophy remain divided as to whether we should regard this project as a genuinely modern one[5], or whether we must, on the contrary, trace it back to a transformation of the eschatological thought of the Judeo-Christian tradition (as Karl Loewith[6], Jakob Taubes[7] and other representatives of the secularization thesis have argued). However, the agreement that the philosophy of history's central thematic was initially located in the idea of progress is untouched by this controversy.[8] There are many indications that the terminological expansion mentioned above only arose in connection with the increasing critique of this original conception and with the numerous attempts to place other projects in its place.[9] In order to avoid ambiguity, I will use the expression 'philosophy of history' in the

---

2 See the entry "Geschichtsphilosophie" written by U. DIERSE and G. SCHOLTZ in: *Historisches Wörterbuch der Philosophie*, vol. 3, Darmstadt (Wissenschaft-liche Buchgesellschaft) 1974, pp. 416-439.

3 KOSELLECK, REINHARD: "Historia Magistra Vitae. Über die Auflösung des Topos im Horizont neuzeitlich bewegter Geschichte", in: KOSELLECK: *Vergangene Zukunft. Zur Semantik geschichtlicher Zeiten*, Frankfurt a.M. (Suhr-kamp) 1979, pp. 38-66.

4 For a detailed account of the development of the concept of historical progress see ROHBECK, JOHANNES: *Die Fortschrittstheorie der Aufklärung. Französische und englische Geschichtsphilosophie in der zweiten Hälfte des 18. Jahrhunderts*, Frankfurt a.M./New York (Suhrkamp) 1987.

5 E.g. BLUMENBERG, HANS: "Die Legitimität der Neuzeit", *Philosophische Rundschau,* 15 (1968) pp. 195-201.

6 LOEWITH, KARL: *Weltgeschichte und Heilsgeschehen*, Stuttgart (Kohlhammer) 1953.

7 TAUBES, JAKOB: *Abendländische Eschatologie*, Berlin (Mattes & Seitz) 1947.

8 See ANGEHRN, EMIL: *Geschichtsphilosophie. Grundkurs Philosophie*, vol. 15, Stuttgart/Berlin/Köln (Kohlhammer) 1991.

9 For a well informed summary of these developments, including a very useful bibliography, see the lexicon entry quoted in note 2.

following reflections to refer to this original idea of progress. However, does such an understanding not relegate the term to philosophical history? Haven't we learned to regard this original project as having failed?

It is a received opinion today that the idea of progress has been definitively overcome. However, it is precisely here that I would like to take up the issue once again. In the first part of my presentation, I will rehearse three characteristic objections to the philosophy of history (for obvious reasons, I can proceed here only in an exemplary fashion). Following this, I will consider whether these objections do, in fact, justify the complete dismissal of the philosophy of history which has become so widely accepted.

II. Three Paradigmatic Objections to Philosophy of History

The rejection of the idea of progress is almost as old as the idea of progress itself. We could recall, for example, Herder's objections to Voltaire and Hume, which were published in 1774[10]. However, I will limit myself here for reasons of topicality to objections which have been raised in the 20th century. The first of my three examples is Karl Popper's critique of the philosophy of history – levelled from the perspective of the philosophy of science. Popper's argument is the following: Insofar as the philosophy of history takes as its subject human history as a whole, it also speaks about the future; and it does this in a way which makes it impossible for us to test the empirical validity of those statements. Consequently, Popper argues, the philosophy of history belongs in the domain of prophecy and not that of science.[11] It is clear that this train of thought only signifies a repudiation if conceptions of the philosophy of history are actually formulated, as Popper presumes here, with the self-understanding of empirical science. In what follows, we must question whether this is always the case and, at the same time, investigate whether

10 HERDER, JOHANN GOTTFRIED: "Auch eine Philosophie der Geschichte zur Bildung der Menschheit", in: HERDER: *Sämtliche Werke*, ed. by B. Suphan, Hildesheim (Olms) 1967, vol. 5, p. 524.

11 POPPER, KARL: *The Poverty of Historicism*, London (Routledge & Paul) 1944/45, chapter 2; and POPPER, KARL: "Prediction and Prophecy in the Social Sciences", in: GARDINER, PATRICK (Ed.): *Theories of History*, Glencoe (The Free Press) 1959, p. 276.

statements about the future which are not intended to be empirically verifiable or falsifiable can, in fact, only have the character of a 'prophecy'. In doing so, we will take into consideration Kant's concept of „a divinatory historical narrative of things imminent in future time"[12]. We must bear in mind as well the fact that while Popper's critique was articulated in the language of the philosophy of science, its actual driving force lay in the thesis that totalitarian systems of the 20th century have their theoretical roots in the mode of thought of the philosophy of history. This thesis is also shared by the two other critics of the idea of progress whom I will consider here. The following objection is characteristic of Critical Theory – my second example: the philosophy of history gives rise to claims by a particular group that they are currently, to speak in the terminology of Hegel, „managing directors of the world spirit" (*Geschäftsführer des Weltgeistes*)[13] – in other words, that they alone are in a position to know what must be done and what steps are necessary in order to lead humanity to a better future. Anyone pursuing other goals appears, from this perspective, to be the enemy. In this way, the philosophy of history legitimates repression and terror.

According to Walter Benjamin, the victims suffer twice here: first, through their actual death, and then through the fact that historical narrative, which has adopted the perspective of the victors – that is, the self-appointed carriers of progress – remains silent about them as victims. Benjamin stated that „even the dead will not be safe from this enemy, if he is victorious."[14] In a similar way, although from different presuppositions, Nietzsche had already polemicized against the philosophy of history, accusing it of being „idolatry of the factual" (*Götzendienst des Tatsächlichen*[15]). In this regard, Benjamin argued that we must attempt – both in our dealings with history as well as in

12 KANT, IMMANUEL: "An Old Question Raised Again: Is the Human Race Constantly Progressing?", in: KANT: *On History*, ed. by Lewis White Beck, Indianapolis (Bobbs-Merrill) 1963, p. 137.

13 HEGEL, GEORG WILHELM FRIEDRICH: *Vorlesungen zur Philosophie der Weltgeschichte*, Frankfurt a.M. (Suhrkamp) 1970, p. 46.

14 BENJAMIN, WALTER: "Über den Begriff der Geschichte", in: BENJAMIN: *Illuminationen. Ausgewählte Schriften*, Frankfurt a.M. (Suhrkamp) 1977, p. 253.

15 NIETZSCHE, FRIEDRICH: "Vom Nutzen und Nachteil der Historie für das Leben", in: NIETZSCHE, FRIEDRICH: *Sämtliche Werke*. Kritische Studienaus-gabe, ed. by Giorgio Colli and Mazzino Montinari, Berlin-New York (De Gruyter) vol. 1, 1980, p. 309.

our actions – to live up to the messianic expectations which have been passed on to us – the living – from the victims of the past. In Benjamin's eyes, incorporating the disappointed hopes of the victims into our own demands requires letting go of the notion of historical progress „in the consciousness of blasting the continuum of history"[16]. Benjamin's famous metaphor of taking a „tiger's leap into the past"[17] is to be read from this perspective.

In their *Dialectic of Enlightenment* (written in 1947), Horkheimer and Adorno also argue that the philosophy of history unavoidably takes the side of the victor, when they object that progressive thought amounts to „scorn for the weak"[18]. Horkheimer and Adorno, however, pay particular attention to the identification of historical progress with technological innovation – an identification which is still common today – arguing that the domination of nature can easily turn into its opposite: „No universal history leads from savages to humanity, but very well from the catapult to the atom bomb. Universal history ends in the total threat of organized humanity against organized humans... Through this, Hegel is at the same time horribly verified and turned upon his head."[19]

The objections raised by Jean-François Lyotard – my third example – are viewed by many authors as the definitive „point of no return" for the philosophy of history. In his study „The Postmodern Condition," Lyotard uses the expression „grand narrative"[20] (*grand récit*) in order to characterize the object of his critique referring at the same time to the thought of Kant, Hegel and Marx. Lyotard points, above all, to two problems here. The first lies in the erasure of diversity. In terms of motif, Lyotard picks up here – albeit without thematizing it – on a reservation first expressed by Herder: If past realities are considered solely from the perspective of their significance for later developments, then their richness and heterogeneity are lost from view.

---

16 BENJAMIN (*loc. cit.*, p. 259).

17 *Ibid.*

18 HORKHEIMER, MAX and ADORNO, THEODOR W.: *Dialektik der Aufklärung*, Frankfurt a.M. (Suhrkamp) 1969, p. 263.

19 *Ibid.*, p. 312.

20 LYOTARD, JEAN-FRANÇOIS: *Das postmoderne Wissen. Ein Bericht*, Theatro machinarum, 3/4, 1982, p. 32.

In this context, Lyotard pleads for a multiplicity of „small narratives."[21] Lyotard's second point refers to the practical consequences of the homogenization which occurs through „grand narratives." According to this argument, the philosophy of history is also a „narrative of legitimation"[22] providing a justification for the repression or even the destruction of the existing variety of life forms. Here, Lyotard sees the danger of a „terror of homogenization"[23] and demands, in opposition to this, the free play of differences. Thus, his rejection of the philosophy of history can be seen as providing the theoretical presuppositions for dealing with a series of contemporary issues - in particular, for the program of recognizing difference, as this has been expounded, for example, in regard to ethnic, religious and cultural differences. Lyotard's argumentation intersects here with contemporary debates of other origins, in particular with communitarian-inspired critiques of the intellectual tradition of liberal legal theory. In short, insofar as Lyotard connects the philosophy of history to the levelling pressure characteristic of the contemporary world, his critique has been welcomed by many as the definitive and long-overdue departure from concepts of progress.

III. Why Kant's Reflections on History Remain Untouched by the Current Critique

Is it possible, nevertheless, that this evaluation is incorrect? The question leads to the next part of my reflections. Here, I would like to investigate whether the image of the 'enemy' so emphatically rejected does actually coincide with all of the variants of the Enlightenment's philosophy of history. It is conspicuous that such objections are usually formulated in an indiscriminate manner and assume that Hegel's conception of world history as „progress in

21 See LYOTARD, JEAN-FRANÇOIS: "Le nom et l'exception", in: NAGL-DOCEKAL, H. and VETTER, H. (Eds.): *Tod des Subjekts?*, Vienna-Munich (Oldenbourg) 1987, pp. 43-53.

22 LYOTARD: *Das postmoderne Wissen*, *loc. cit.*, p. 60.

23 "Ödipus oder Don Juan? Legitimierung, Recht und ungleicher Tausch. Ein Gespräch zwischen J.-F. Lyotard und J. P. Dubost", in: LYOTARD, JEAN-FRANÇOIS: *Das postmoderne Wissen*, 3. ed., Vienna (Passagen) p. 147.

the consciousness of freedom“[24] is paradigmatic for the philosophy of history. It seems appropriate, therefore, to consider more closely Kant's reflections on the matter. As I will attempt to demonstrate, Kant's thought remains untouched by all three of objections presented above.

It is not in his philosophy of knowledge that Kant systematically examines the question as to whether there has been progress in the history of humanity, but rather in his theory of practical reason. The question arises in the course of Kant's explanation of the consequences which result from the fundamental principle of morality – as that principle is presented in the theory of the categorical imperative. Thus, it is the conception of the self-legislation of practical reason which forms Kant's starting point. In regard to this, he investigates the question: What precisely is required, if we intend to follow the imperative „So act that you use humanity, whether in your own person or in the person of any other, always at the same time as an end, never merely as a means“?[25] Kant derives the following fundamental thought from this practical principle: If all humans should be regarded and treated as persons who are capable of deciding about their own ends – in distinction to 'things' which do not dispose over such a capacity and thus may be instrumentalized – then it is at least necessary that all individuals are granted their own space to act, that is, they must have 'external'[26] freedom. This demand by no means expresses all of the implications contained in the categorical imperative, but it does indicate the necessary first step. (It should be noted that the concept of moral duty includes not only the prohibition of using other humans as mere means, but also the command to assistance, which Kant expounds under the title „duties of love“[27]). However, the initial consequences arising from the moral law should not be underestimated: it is at this point that Kant begins his legal-philosophical considerations. The idea of law is derived from the categorical imperative insofar as it aims at protecting the freedom of all individuals. Thus, the idea of law rests upon the „concept of freedom in the external rela-

24 HEGEL: *Vorlesungen zur Philosophie der Weltgeschichte*, *loc. cit.*, p. 32.

25 KANT, IMMANUEL: *Groundwork of the Metaphysics of Morals*, ed. by Mary Gregor, Cambridge, UK (Cambridge University Press) 1998, p. 38.

26 KANT, IMMANUEL: *The Metaphysics of Morals*, ed. by Mary Gregor, Cambridge, UK (Cambridge University Press) 1991, p. 56.

27 KANT: *Groundwork of the Metaphysics of Morals*, *loc. cit.*, p. 38.

tions among men."[28] Here, Kant´s concern is, in fact, an „idea": He does not begin with a discussion of concrete legal conditions as they have evolved throughout history, but rather develops a general concept of law. According to Kant, the central task of the state lies in guaranteeing the „greatest freedom".[29] Of course, this task cannot be performed by allowing the 'capacity for choice' (*Willkür*)[30] to unfold in an unrestricted manner: there is always the danger that individual humans or specific groups will, in expressing their ´capacity for choice´, impinge upon the freedom of others, or even render completely impossible the freedom of others – this is precisely the reason why the institutionalization of justice is required. It proves necessary to establish limitations to provide sanctions for such infringements. At this point, the concept of 'equality' moves into the foreground of Kant's thought. Kant argues that the freedom of individuals to enact their 'capacity for choice' should be limited equally – however only as far as is absolutely necessary so that „the action of one can be united with the freedom of the other in accordance with a universal law"[31].

With the idea of law, history moves into Kant's focus. While it is the moral duty of every individual human to work for the establishment of a completely just constitution, this task can, when considered as a whole, be implemented neither by individuals nor even by a single generation, but rather „only in the race".[32] The idea of law functions as a critical measure, according to which each generation must confront anew existing conditions, in order to uncover injustices and work to overcome them. Thus, we have, from a moral-philosophical perspective, the following view of history: the practical imperative inherent in reason sets a goal, and every generation has the duty to make their contribution to the gradual attainment of this goal. In this way, progress in history is a moral demand.[33]

---

28 KANT, IMMANUEL: "On the Proverb: That May be True in Theory, But Is of No Practical Use", in: KANT, IMMANUEL: *Perpetual Peace and Other Essays*, ed. by Ted Humphrey, Indianapolis (Hackett) 1983, p. 72.

29 KANT, IMMANUEL: "Idea for a Universal History from a Cosmopolitan Point of View", in: KANT: *On History*, *loc. cit.*, p. 16.

30 KANT: *The Metaphysics of Morals*, *loc. cit.*, p. 42.

31 *Ibid.*, p. 56.

32 KANT: "Idea for a Universal History", *loc. cit.*, p. 13.

33 The mode in which Fichte further develops Kant's moral-philosophical concept of history investigates: FERRY, LUC: *Political Philosophy*, vol. 2*: The System of*

Interpreters who see in Kant a naive enlightener – one who understands humans as beings of pure reason – might be inclined to attribute a descriptive claim to this conception of progress. According to this view, Kant would believe that the history of humanity does, in fact, represent a process of increasing justice that is based upon moral motivations. However, such a reading cannot be reconciled with Kant's own texts. Kant himself initiates no 'grand narrative' according to which the human race – as the subject of history – continually works toward the realization of its moral tasks. This becomes clear as soon as one takes into account the entire scope of Kant's oeuvre: Kant not only develops a theory of reason; he is also an anthropologist and a precise observer of the realities of human relations. From this perspective, Kant saw that the actual course of history has not been determined primarily through actions guided by the moral principle, but rather through the antagonism of particular interests and its violent consequences. He notes in regard to humans of the past: „One cannot suppress a certain indignation when one sees men's actions on the great world-stage and finds, beside great wisdom that appears here and there among individuals, everything in the large woven together from folly, childish vanity, even from childish malice and destructiveness. In the end one does not know what to think of the human race, so conceited in its gifts.“[34] For the future as well, Kant does not expect that humans will allow themselves to be directed completely by the moral law. He thus doubts whether the task of establishing a „perfectly just civic constitution“[35] can ever be realized completely. The metaphor which Kant chooses in this context is unambiguous: „from such crooked wood as man is made of, nothing perfectly straight can be built.“[36]

It is here that the question with which Kant's reflections on the philosophy of history in the more narrow sense of the term are concerned first arises: Can progress in the direction of justice – toward which it is our moral duty to work – be thought of as being possible at all? In the face of the course of history to date, the impression might arise that humans find themselves caught in an *aporia*, namely that justice is absolutely demanded, but, at the same time, completely unrealizable. With this, the question arises as to the mean-

---

Philosophies of History, Chicago/London (The University of Chicago Press) 1992.

34 KANT: "Idea for a Universal History", *loc. cit.*, p. 12.

35 *Ibid.*, p. 16.

36 *Ibid.*, pp. 17-18.

ingfulness of our engagements for the abolition of injustice – engagements which themselves are often very risky. In view of this problematic, Kant explains that there is a path other than that of morality which leads to the increasing institutionalization of justice. Here, he characterizes the human being initially in anthropological terms through his „unsocial sociability": through his aim „to achieve a rank among his fellows whom he cannot tolerate but from whom he cannot withdraw".[37] In other words, everyone primarily follows his own particular interests, even at the cost of others. This, however, results in an antagonism which ultimately escalates into a state of violence in which everyone is threatened. What is decisive here is that Kant sees a basis for overcoming this misery not only in practical reason – in the direction of a morally motivated reciprocal recognition of human beings –, but also in the pragmatic understanding of humans, a faculty which individuals use to calculate their own interest from a long-term perspective. If individuals begin to make a sober cost-benefit analysis of the spiralling violence, they will recognize that it is to their own advantage if they confine themselves within the „preserve"[38] of a civic union and engage in improving its laws. Incidentally, it is not only internal conflicts, but also international conflicts (which even in times of peace give rise to an arms race) which provide the occasion for such agreements. In this context, Kant sketches out his conception of a league of nations.[39] His point that there is an alternative foundation – one other than morality – for the implementation of the principle of justice has validity in regard to the international dimension as well. Kant formulates this point in a rather graphic form when he notes: „As hard as it may sound, the problem of organizing a nation is solvable even for a people comprised of devils (if only they possess understanding)."[40] Analogously, we could say: „As hard as it may sound, the problem of establishing international justice is solvable even for a world comprised of devils (if only they possess understanding)."

As the limiting phrase „if only they possess understanding" indicates, Kant's view is that the possibility he has just sketched of a „society driven together by their natural feelings" (*„eine pathologisch-abgedrungene Zu-*

---

37 *Ibid.*, p. 15.

38 *Ibid.*, p. 17.

39 *Ibid.*, p. 19.

40 KANT, IMMANUEL: "To Perpetual Peace. A Philosophical Sketch", in: KANT: *Perpetual Peace and Other Essays, loc. cit.*, p. 124.

sammenstimmung")[41] also does not guarantee progress for humanity. History offers many examples, as Kant notes with „a certain indignation" in the passage cited above, that humans do not always follow their own pragmatic understanding, but rather seek their advantage in short-sighted ways. Nevertheless, Kant evaluates the prospects here more favorably, indeed with a view to what we would call today the material constraints: he presumes that the antagonism of particular interests will lead repeatedly to such great suffering that it will finally „force"[42] humans to concede to legal rules. Within individual states as well as on an international level, this antagonism will drive humans „finally, after devastations, revolutions, and even complete exhaustion ... to that which reason could have told them at the beginning and with far less sad experience".[43] Admittedly, we cannot expect that, on the basis of a rational calculation of well-understood individual self-interest, humanity will ever be in a position to implement the idea of justice completely: „Only the approximation to this idea has been imposed upon us by Nature" (*„Nur die Annäherung zu dieser Idee ist uns von der Natur auferlegt.*").[44]

What are the consequences of all this for historical representations of the past? It is clear that these considerations referring to pragmatic understanding – like those emerging from the concept of practical reason – do not lead to the formulation of a 'grand narrative' which is supposed to demonstrate humanity's continuous development. Rather, Kant formulates a project which marks out laborious excavation work: we must examine whether there is anything at all in the past – „something, but very little"[45] – which points to an increase in justice. It is in this context that Kant develops his much discussed conception of „an historical sign"[46], with which he characterizes as paradigmatic the

---

41 KANT: "Idea for a Universal History", *loc. cit.*, p. 15. See: "Idee zu einer allgemeinen Geschichte in weltbürgerlicher Absicht", in: *Kants gesammelte Schriften*, ed. by Königlich Preussische Akademie der Wissenschaften, vol. 8, Berlin 1912, p. 21.

42 *Ibid.*, p. 17.

43 *Ibid.*, pp. 18-19.

44 KANT: "Idee zu einer allgemeinen Geschichte", *loc. cit.*, p. 41. (This passage is missing in the English translation used here.)

45 KANT: "Idea for a Universal History", *loc. cit.*, p. 22.

46 KANT: "An Old Question Raised Again: Is the Human Race Constantly Progressing?", *loc. cit.*, p.143.

„mode of thinking of the spectators,“[47] who throughout Europe have followed the events of the French Revolution with an attitude of „a wishful participation that borders closely on enthusiasm“[48]. Thus, Kant's thoughts on the philosophy of history result in a guiding thread for a new kind of historiography. While, as Kant observes, historians have always preferred to spend time in the camp rather than in the cabinet,[49] they should now investigate „what the various nations and governments have contributed to the goal of world citizenship, and what they have done to damage it.“[50]

Kant's reflections also do not result in a „narrative of legitimation.“ Rather, the connection between the philosophy of history, historiography and practice which Kant has in mind is the following: the philosophy of history is able to demonstrate that the progress – to which we have a moral duty to contribute – is also historically possible. In particular, given the pragmatic calculations which we can expect from our understanding, we recognize that we must not regard working to increase justice as hopeless from the beginning. The philosophy of history, in making plausible that humans see themselves forced to institute legal rules – although usually only after many painful experiences –, thus opens up „a consoling view of the future“.[51] Admittedly, the „consolation“ which Kant speaks of here is only accorded to humans as agents. With reference to the future, Kant does not imagine history as proceeding according to a kind of natural law. Rather, future increases in justice can be predicted only under the condition that „the deviner himself creates and contrives the events which he announces in advance“[52]. With regard to Popper's critique, we must insist here that for Kant the philosophy of history's statements about the future do not in any way have the character of „prophecies“ which cannot be regarded as knowledge. Rather, they have the status of declarations of intention for an individual's own actions. In addition to this, they represent an anthropologically informed estimate with regard to the chances of emancipatory action.

---

47 *Ibid.*, p. 143.

48 *Ibid.*, p. 144.

49 "Die Geschichtsschreiber sind immer lieber im Lager als dem Kabinett". KANT, IMMANUEL: "Reflexionen zur Anthropologie, Nr. 1400", in: *Kants gesammelte Schriften*, *loc. cit.*, vol. 15.2., p. 610.

50 KANT: "Idea for a Universal History", *loc. cit.*, p. 26.

51 *Ibid.*, p. 25.

52 KANT: "An Old Question Raised Again", *loc. cit.*, p. 137.

A historiography which adopts the notion of progress as its guiding thread has enlightening significance. While such a historiography investigates the increase in justice brought about in the past – on the level of the 'mode of thinking' as well as on the level of institutional reforms –, it also directs our view of the present to the central tasks of engaging and acting in the public domain. In this way, it can itself „be regarded ... as contributing to"[53] historical progress. However, that does not mean, conversely, that we can legitimate our actions by pointing to their agreement with historical progress. Such a legitimation would accord with the principle of the end justifying the means – a principle which is incompatible with Kant's moral philosophy. According to Kant, a justification of practice can only follow from the categorical imperative, and this means (even for an action „from a cosmopolitan point of view") that we must in each case test whether our action is in agreement with the moral law, or whether we have instrumentalized humans in an improper way. Thus, the practical engagement for freedom and equality which Kant advocates is not a consequence of the philosophy of history, but rather – insofar as such an action evokes a problem of meaning – is its presupposition. In addition to this, we must also bear in mind that Kant, for his part, points out that an action which we seek to justify solely through its contribution to historical progress is identical with a „terrorist manner of representing human history". In order to illustrate this point, he notes: „the pious enthusiast ... is already dreaming of the restoration of all things and a renovated world after the time that this one will have perished in flames."[54]

IV. Philosophy of History: An Indispensable Project

With this brief sketch, I have attempted to demonstrate that the objections to 'the' philosophy of history outlined at the beginning of my presentation do not do justice to Kant's thought – a thought which can be characterized neither as a conception of linear continuity from the perspective of the victor, nor as a „narrative of legitimation." However, if the stated objections miss their target, then isn't it possible that Kant's reflections still have relevance

53 KANT: "Idea for a Universal History", *loc. cit.*, p. 29.

54 KANT: "An Old Question Raised Again", *loc. cit.*, pp. 139-140.

today? In response to this question, my own thesis is: Philosophy of history is not only possible today; it is indispensable. This is an issue which directly concerns all of us. Whoever works to increase justice here and now, can do so only if he or she believes this undertaking is not completely hopeless. As actors who are to some extent rational, we do not engage in something which we are convinced is completely futile. However, if our commitment for an abolition of injustice is supported by an even limited confidence, this means then that we have adopted *in nuce* a philosophy of history in Kant's sense, even if we do not explicitly admit this.

At the same time, I would also like to point to the fact that the perspective of consolation which Kant presents here is thoroughly limited. Kant develops no utopian images which would result in any kind of self-redemption of humanity. Even with all the increase in justice which might occur, humans will continue to be made from „crooked wood". Thus, the objection that the notion of progress implies the thesis that we can construct the future as we choose does not touch Kant's argument. This objection would be justified, for example, in regard to the „principle of hope" formulated by Ernst Bloch. Bloch was concerned with a conception of a world in which the conditions of freedom were themselves supposed to be transcended, so that – extending the Marxist perspective of a naturalization of humans and a humanization of nature – even death would be overcome.[55] Kant, on the contrary, chooses a clearly different path: his philosophy of history has no eschatological dimensions. The question of the meaning of human life cannot be completely answered through our efforts to increase justice, even if they are successful. In regard to this aspect, Kant's historical thought points beyond history – his philosophy of history leads here to the philosophy of religion. Kant develops this thematic in connection with the concept of 'happiness': With our moral actions – and thus with our engagement for emancipation and justice as well – we can only attempt to be worthy of happiness. We cannot, however, expect that our hopes for happiness will be redeemed within history. Reason, rather, sees itself forced to postulate „a wise author and ruler" for whom it is possible to reconcile morality and happiness in „an intelligible world"[56]. In this way

55 BLOCH, ERNST: *Das Prinzip Hoffnung*, Frankfurt a.M. (Suhrkamp) 1973, p. 1382.

56 KANT, IMMANUEL: *Critique of Pure Reason*, ed. by F. Max Müller, Garden City, N.Y. (Doubleday) 1966, p. 519.

Kant's reflections on history merge into his doctrine of god and immortality as postulates of pure practical reason.[57]

57 An earlier German version of this paper was read at the Austrian Academy of Sciences in Vienna on December 12, 1999.

Chapter 11

Rehabilitating the Philosophy of History

JOHANNES ROHBECK

I. The Relevance of the Enlightenment
II. Technology, Culture, and History
III. Media Images of History
IV. Paradoxes of Globalization
V. The End of Industrial and Work Society?
VI. Radicalizing the Modern

The philosophy of history is a problem child of modernity. Since its inception, it has been one of the most controversial disciplines in philosophy. As the secular theory of universal history, the philosophy of history was only able to establish itself late – around the middle of the 18th century. It had hardly asserted itself against theological traditions, on the one hand, and methodological reservations within the Enlightenment, on the other, before it was permanently confronted with critics who denied its very legitimacy. The most important stages of this history include the following: the rejection of the idea of progress and the retreat through historicism to historical methods; the secularization debate (in which the philosophy of history was interpreted as secularized salvation history); and the critique of the philosophy of history within the framework of the 'dialectic of Enlightenment'. At least since the post-modern has settled accounts with the 'grand narrative', the philosophy of history appears to have become definitively obsolete.

What remains now? If the philosophy of history is today a topic at all, then only in a radically reduced form. While Odo Marquard once spoke of "a reduction in stages" (*Schwundstufen*) of the philosophy of history, Hermann

Lübbe has recently recognized only "left-over functions".[1] Relief, therefore, is called for. However, faced with this situation, it no longer makes sense to dispute whether such reflections about history can be called 'philosophy of history' at all. And whoever continues, in spite of all this, to speak of the philosophy of history, can do so only in paradoxes, such as Odo Marquard's "*Beitrag zur Philosophie der Geschichte des Abschieds von der Philosophie der Geschichte*" (*Contribution to the Philosophy of History of the departure from the Philosophy of History*) or Hans Michael Baumgartner's "*Philosophie der Geschichte nach dem Ende der Geschichtsphilosophie*" (*Philosophy of History After the End of the Philosophy of History*).[2] Whatever the formulations might be, they indicate that we have left behind the historical formation 'philosophy of history'. Too little to continue living, too much to be able to die: the end of the philosophy of history is presented as a never-ending death. It would be pointless to want to add something to these continuous obituaries.

1 ODO MARQUARD: *Schwierigkeiten mit der Geschichtsphilosophie*, Frankfurt am Main (1973), pp. 23ff.; HERMANN LÜBBE: *Geschichtsphilosophie. Verbliebene Funktionen*, Erlangen and Jena (1993). These include the critique of philosophy of history in its older form, in particular its teleology; in addition to this, the return to normative premises and to elementary orientations; finally, the limitation to the methods of historical research and representation. Herta Nagl-Docekal has recently reconstructed the individual 'stages of reduction'. See HERTA NAGL-DOCEKAL: "Ist Geschichtsphilosophie heute noch möglich?", in: HERTA NAGL-DOCEKAL (Ed.): *Der Sinn des Historischen*, Frankfurt am Main (1996), pp. 7ff.

2 ODO MARQUARD: "Beitrag zur Philosophie der Geschichte des Abschieds von der Philosophie der Geschichte", in: R. KOSELLECK, W.-D. STEMPEL (Eds.): *Poetik und Hermeneutik V. Geschichte – Ereignis und Erzählung*, Munich (1973), pp.241ff; H.M. BAUMGARTNER: "Philosophie der Geschichte nach dem Ende der Geschichtsphilosophie. Bemerkungen zum gegenwärtigen Stand des geschichtsphilosophischen Denkens", in: H. NAGL-DOCEKAL (Ed.): *Der Sinn des Historischen*, pp. 151ff. Baumgartner's paper is printed in this volume above on pp. 149-171 in the English translation and in a version revised by H.-M. Baumgartner before his death in 2000 (editor's note).

I. The Relevance of the Enlightenment

It is at this point that I begin my reflections on a *rehabilitation of the philosophy of history*.[3] I would like to undertake the untimely attempt of reviving not simply left-over functions, but, in addition to this, several motifs of the philosophy of history which have repeatedly been pronounced dead. In order to rehabilitate this type of theory, I return to the beginnings of modern philosophy of history and re-examine the often unknown or misunderstood epoch of the Enlightenment – by this, I mean French, English and German thinking about history in the second half of the 18th century.[4] My concern here is not to conserve a philosophical tradition, but rather to continue and revise this theory as it relates to our own current historical situation. If theoretical relief has been called for repeatedly for the philosophy of history, then we should perhaps again impose a greater burden on historical reason. I have been guided thematically in my presentation by the following basic considerations.

The central focus of the Enlightenment's philosophy of history was the emergence of *the modern* and the process of *modernization.* It presumed a fundamental experience, one which also formed the conceptual framework of its theory: the experience of an accelerated and organized social transformation, a transformation which was marked in its central domains by an increase of scientific knowledge, the growth of technological capacities and economic wealth, and the transcendence of spatial and social boundaries. This *process of civilization* in the domains of science, technology and economy thus also formed the basis for the idea of progress. This idea combined an evaluation of the course of history up to that time, a self-examination of the contemporary situation, and particular expectations about the future.

This topic and this conception of the problem are still relevant today. Coping with technological transformations – including both their desired and undesired effects – has become increasingly urgent: It is, today, one of our central concerns. Whatever one may think of 'progress' as a guiding idea, the question inherent in that idea about the historical dimension of technological

3 For more detail on this, see my book: *Technik – Kultur – Geschichte. Zur Rehabilitierung der Geschichtsphilosophie*, Frankfurt am Main (2000).

4 I refer here to authors such as Turgot and Condorcet in France, Adam Smith, Ferguson or Millar in England; see J. ROHBECK: *Die Fortschrittstheorie der Aufklärung*, Frankfurt/ New York (1987).

civilization remains undeniable. It is clear today that this process has been able to assert itself with a force which could not even have been imagined earlier. What the thinkers of Enlightenment in the 18th century could only conjure as speculation has become reality: in the rise and fall of nations, and in the catastrophes of our century as well, scientific, technological and economic developments have not merely continued unabated; they have accelerated. And while the thinkers of Enlightenment recognized the first signs of a world trade in the course of colonization, the slogan 'globalization' is used today by everyone to refer to a phenomenon of the world market, international division of labor and worldwide communication. In short, this domain has far exceeded the expectations formulated in earlier universal histories. No other sphere of human life has demonstrated such continuity.

But beyond mere factualness, there is also a *discoursive* argument which speaks for this kind of rehabilitation. Since the philosophy of history's inception, there have been very different reactions to the civilization process outlined above. When the idea of progress is called into question today, the mistrust expressed does not refer to the central domains of scientific-technological and economic developments, but rather to their consequences for human life. Critics doubt that this 'progress' can achieve prosperity for all humans, or create social justice, freedom and peace, better health and developmental possibilities for all individuals. In other words, when one rejects the idea of progress, one is usually, at the same time, silent about the fact that one accepts the existence of scientific-technological and economic progress – regardless of whether one evaluates this as good or bad. Even the most radical critiques confirm precisely this. One complains, in other words, not about the failure of progress, but rather about its success. However diverse the various positions might be, they all assume – either explicitly or implicitly – the modern civilization process as their measure of reference. Technological civilization forms the point at which all of these perspectives – whether affirmative, critical or ambivalent – converge.

In particular, *critics* of the philosophy of history have remained attached to the philosophy of history's models of thought. One cannot deny that Rousseau's critique of civilization itself has the status of a philosophy of history, although Rousseau understood scientific-technlogical progress as a process of decline.[5] In the same way, the *Dialectic of Enlightenment*, whose authors believed that they recognized seeds of downfall in the very first technological progress, must be regarded as a "negative teleology" and thus itself as a veritable philosophy of history.[6] This well-known argument, which until now has been associated with critical theory, is further radicalized by the philosophy of the posthistoire. Of secondary importance is the speculative objection that claims about the 'end of history' are themselves statements about history in general. Rather, it is scientific-technological and economic processes which stand at the center of such arguments, so that they indirectly affirm 'progress' and even exaggerate it.[7] Through these various positions, we can clearly see how the different discourses about the philosophy of history are oriented around the historical macro-unit '*technological civilization*'.

Given these empirical and discursive arguments, I believe I am justified in emphasizing the *continuity* of the civilization process, because I perceive the continuity of typically modern developmental tendencies even amid the current upheavals. Such breaks have stood in the foreground for so long that I have permitted myself to compensate for this by emphasizing the continuities instead. Thus, I strive for a philosophy of history of *middle range*, by concentrating initially on the process of technological civilization. The history which is approached in this way begins in the 'middle' and is open-ended – without

---

5 JEAN-JACQUES ROUSSEAU: *Discourse on the origin of inequality*, translated by Franklin Philip, edited with an introduction by Patrick Coleman, Oxford, New York (Oxford University Press) 1994.

6 MAX HORKHEIMER and THEODOR W. ADORNO: *Dialectic of enlightenment*, translated by John Cumming, New York (Herder and Herder) 1972; see C.F. GEYER: *Aporien des Metaphysik- und Geschichtsbegriffs der kritischen Theorie*, Darmstadt 1980, p. 180.

7 ARNOLD GEHLEN: "Über kulturelle Kristallisation", *Studien zur Anthropologie und Soziologie*, Neuwied 1963, pp. 322f.; see also GEHLEN: "Ende der Geschichte? Zur Lage des Menschen im Posthistoire", in: O. SCHATZ (Ed.): *Was wird aus dem Menschen*, Graz, Vienna, Cologne 1974, pp. 61ff.; GÜNTHER ANDERS: *Die Antiquiertheit des Menschen*, vol. 2, Munich (1987), pp. 273, 279; JEAN BAUDRILLARD: *Symbolic exchange and death*, translated by Iain Hamilton Grant, London (1993); PAUL VIRILIO: *Speed and politics: an essay on dromology*, translated by Mark Polizzotti, New York, NY, USA (Columbia University) 1986; VILÉM FLUSSER: *Nachgeschichte. Eine korrigiert Geschichtsschreibung*, in: S. BOLLMANN, E. FLUSSER (Eds.) Frankfurt am Main (1997), p. 134.

any notion of origins or teleology. In proposing this, I support a *radicalization of the modern.*

From these considerations, I draw the *methodological* consequence that we may once again speak about *historical contents*. For it is doubtful that limiting ourselves to cognitive processes and forms of representation is really as compelling for a philosophy of history as the contemporary consensus seems to assume. This kind of historical continuity is, of course, not an empirical fact, but rather functions as a theoretical construct or a 'regulative idea', one which, admittedly, does not completely lack a referent, but rather relates to the empirical substrate of technological civilization.[8] Thus, my goal is to develop a philosophy of history which is *methodologically reflective* and, at the same time, *material.*

II. Technology, Culture, and History

Given this factual and methodological background, the question arises as to how it is possible that 'progress' is recognized, from very different perspectives, as the self-understood guiding thread of history, but that, at the same time, this very same process is categorically denied, at least since the posthistoire, historicity of any kind. For claims that 'history has ended' do not mean that nothing will happen in the future. Rather, they mean that this end – the future course of history – has no historical meaning or produces no specifically historical meaning. Such claims originate in the presumption that technological civilization suppresses not only older traditions, but also obstructs new experiences in the life-world and in the social world. For this reason, technological civilization ostensibly leads to a loss of experience, reality and

8 I do not find the accusation of 'substantalism' justified here, as other forms of a substantive philosophy of history – i.e. not strictly formal -- are also possible; A.C. DANTO: *Analytical philosophy of history*, Cambridge (1968). – With the idea of continuity, I follow Michael Baumgartner in part, without, however, understanding this idea as trancendental; it is, in any case, an 'historical *aporia*' which must be made concrete; H.M. BAUMGARTNER, *Kontinuität und Geschichte. Zur Kritik und Metakritik der historischen Vernunft*, Frankfurt am Main (1973).

history, losses for which we are supposed to compensate by returning to older values.[9]

Considered more precisely, there is actually a double loss of meaning here. Initially, that meaning which is rooted in the life-world of earlier cultures is lost. The increasingly expansive process of modern civilization interferes with and suppresses cultural traditions, which as a result gradually disappear. This leads to the frequently observed return to particular, ethnic and cultural origins. But more important and farther reaching than this is the conclusion - which remains implicit here - that technological civilization itself is incapable of producing a life-meaning of its own. The development of a specifically modern 'meaning', one which would be understood as the cultural consequence of technological civilization, is excluded as a possibility. As with arguments about the development of the 'two cultures', a chasm emerges here between an historical culture which is oriented around religious and national traditions, on the one hand, and an ostensibly ahistorical technological culture, which produces a loss of history, on the other.[10] Posthistoire culminates in the claim that technological civilization has no culture and consequently no history.

Against claims that technological civilization leads to a loss of culture and history, I would like to demonstrate, on the contrary, that modern technologies do not merely destroy culture, but that they themselves create and alter their own cultures. In order to do this, I will have to unfold the significance of technological action for the world and for the self-understanding of human beings. Should I succeed in demonstrating this, then it would be possible, conversely, to attribute an historically formative dimension to technological culture. Because the continuity of technological development has been empirically demonstrated and is discursively undisputed, we can establish – presupposing that this process contains normative and reflexive potentials –

9 Hermann Lübbe offers the most detailed account here, although he is not a representative of the posthistoire: HERMANN LÜBBE: *Zeit-Verhältnisse. Zur Kulturphilosophie des Fortschritts*, Graz (1983), pp. 33, 49ff.; HERMANN LÜBBE: *Der Lebenssinn der Industriegesellschaft. Über die moralische Verfassung der wissenschaftlich-technischen Zivilisation*, Berlin, Hamburg, New York (1990), pp. 45, 68ff., 72ff., 82ff.

10 On the 'two cultures', see C.P. Snow's book of the same title. The title referred here to the division between natural sciences and the humanities: C.P. SNOW: *The Two Cultures* , New York (1993).

its relevance for history. Because the beginnings of a cultural theory of technology have developed recently, we can take this opportunity to use the new philosophy of technology to reflect upon the philosophy of history.

The Enlightenment's philosophy of history already contained *in nuce* a model of enlightenment which addressed not only the dynamics of technology, but also provided insights into the cultural aspects of technological action. In providing a detailed description of science, technology and economics, historiographers of the 18th century came to the theoretically momentous conclusion that the objective means of available technology contained different – and greater – possibilities of application than had been initially intended or expected.[11] According to this position, technological means always contain a creative *surplus potential*, a potential which expands our horizon for the possibilities for action. This is true of scientific knowledge and technological discoveries, as well as for the successive stages of the economy. In our context, it is decisive to note that, with these expanded possibilities of action, the horizon for *new ends or goals* opens up as well.

This thesis can be expanded in a cultural-theoretical direction.[12] Tools, machines and systems do not only fulfil technological functions, but produce non-technological effects as well. They open up new horizons for spatial and temporal experience, for our ideas of goals and values, and, not least, for the historical understanding of human beings. Objective means contain specifically *cultural surpluses*, surpluses which can neither be predicted nor intended during planning and production. Thus, in dealing with technological objects, humans develop new purposes and goals of action. These surplus potentials are realized through the fact that they are transferred onto other contexts of human action. It is in these *processes of transference* that the surpluses of technological means emerge.

Even today, such an approach can be developed in a number of promising ways. Philosophers of technology today now agree that technological means are not value-neutral, but rather embody more or less limited use-purposes – including the value-decisions inherent in them as means. To this degree, they

11 See J. ROHBECK: *Die Fortschrittstheorie der Aufklärung*, Frankfurt am Main (1987), pp. 158ff.

12 On this subject, see J. ROHBECK: *Technologische Urteilskraft. Zu einer Ethik technischen Handelns*, Frankfurt am Main (1993), in particular pp. 219ff.

also have a normative dimension.[13] In addition to this, we can now show that these means not only exhibit historically assumed purposes, goals and norms, but that they also contribute through the dynamic of production and use to the formation of new needs and values. Because dealing with such means contributes to the *formation of purposes and meanings*, this process also contributes to cultural history in general – indeed provides an independent contribution which should not be underestimated. Through new technologies of transportation and information, for example, the desire for mobility and worldwide communication first arises and then develops into a value in itself. Conversely, the goal of conserving nature first arises as a consequence of technologically produced threats to nature. This demonstrates the life-meaning and the specifically historical significance of modern technology. This is the *obstinacy* of technology.

This is also the way in which I understand the aforementioned thesis about a *radicalization of the modern*, a radicalization which implies dimensions of *continuity* as well as *discontinuity*. On the one hand, the process of civilization has shown itself to be so resistant that it is not even questioned by its critics. On the other hand, the civilization process produces a reflective potential, through which essential characteristics of the modern emerge for the first time. In what follows, I will attempt to demonstrate in an exemplary manner the connection between *radicalization* and *self-reflection* in three domains: first, the example of the new media's influence on the experience of *non-simultaneity*; second, discussions on *globalization*; and third, the repeated claims of an epochal threshold from an *industrial and work society* to a so-called information and knowledge society.

---

13 K. BAYERTZ: "Wissenschaft, Technik und Verantwortung. Grundlagen der Wissenschafts- und Technikethnik", in: K. BAYERTZ (Ed.): *Praktische Philosophie. Grundorientierungen angewandter Ethik*, Reinbek 1991, pp. 173ff; CHISTOPH HUBIG: *Ethnik der Technik. Ein Leitfaden*, Heidelberg 1993, pp. 20f.; G. ROPOHL: *Ethik und Technikbewertung*, Frankfurt am Main 1996, pp. 89ff.; P. JANICH: "Informationsbegriff und methodisch-kulturalistische Philosophie," *Ethik und Sozialwissenschaften*, 9 (1998), pp. 2, 169ff.

III. Media Images of History

When the critics of civilization complain today about a loss of experience, reality and history, they refer not infrequently to the new *communication technologies*.[14] According to this interpretation of technology, the abrupt increase of travel speed and, in particular, the simultaneity of telecommunications have destroyed time and space, thereby affecting our system of coordinates for history. In addition to this, virtual worlds and the immense flood of data inhibit not only our consciousness of contemporary reality, but, above all, our memory of the past as well. Finally, the experience of simultaneity, according to modern cultural critics, destroys the notion of diachronic history which arose during the Enlightenment.[15] On the other hand, however, against this, we can show that it was precisely the experience of the simultaneity of non-simultaneous cultures in the 18th century which gave rise to the theory of history. It remains, therefore, unclear how this same experience today - in a technologically advanced form – is supposed to have destroyed historical thought.

With the idea of *universal history*, Enlighteners developed a program which sought to record the history of all humans in all places and at all times. The fact that they did not intend this as mere abstraction, but rather as a concrete process of universalization is evident in their accounts of mass migrations, conquests and defeats, colonial discoveries and a world trade developing in stages. And the fact that this idea not only presupposed the tendency – observed since the beginnings of human history – to transgress spatial boundaries is demonstrated in the particular historical situation of the late Enlightenment. At the end of the 18th century, voyages of discovery had come to an end due to geographical conditions.[16] It was this context of exceeding boundaries and, at the same time, of marking boundaries which made possible the philosophy of history.

---

14 PAUL VIRILIO: *Speed and politics: an essay on dromology*; VILÉM FLUSSER: *Nachgeschichte. Eine korrigierte Geschichtsschreibung*, pp. 74ff.

15 WOLF SCHÄFER: *Ungleichzeitigkeit als Ideologie*, Frankfurt am Main 1994, pp. 9, 135f., 150; BRUNO LATOUR: *Wir sind nie modern gewesen. Versuch einer symmetrischen Anthropologie*, Berlin 1995, pp. 102f.

16 This context is particularly clear in GUILLAUME RAYNAL and DENIS DIDEROT: *Histoire philosophique et politique; Des Établissemens & du Commerce des Européens dans les deux Indes*, Amsterdam 1770.

These apparently superficial spatial and temporal expansions led, from the perspective of progress, to the path-breaking discovery that different cultural levels were not only temporally successive at single location, but could also be found simultaneously in different locations. Summarizing this insight, Turgot wrote: "Even today, the earth provides us with a view of the entire history of the human race, by showing us the traces of all its stages and providing testimony of its levels, from barbarism, which still continues among the American peoples, up to the civilization of the most enlightened peoples of Europe."[17] What Turgot described here theoretically would later be called the *simultaneity of the non-simultaneous*.[18] However, this kind of simultaneity still referred to non-simultaneous cultures in different, far removed parts of the earth, so that they could only be investigated with significant temporal delay. During the epoch of the Enlightenment, individual cultures were still regarded as homogenous: they could only be shown to be *non-simultaneous* through inter-cultural comparison.

The simultaneity of the non-simultaneous has not only remained relevant for our present. In addition to this, it has become radicalized and, through this, has become reflective. While modern broadcasting technologies practically allow us to communicate synchronically, the simultaneity of non-simultaneous cultures can now be experienced on a single – and potentially arbitrary – location.[19] Simultaneity and non-simultaneity come together spatially as well. Here, one could speak of a *simul-locality of multiple locations* (*Gleichörtlickeit des Vielörtlichen*). Our image of history is affected by a non-simultaneity which has been radicalized in spatio-temporal terms. In addition to this, audio-visually mediated confrontation, cohabitation in the metropolis and migration have made evident to everyone that cultures belong to different historical levels and continually mix with each other. From this, one becomes conscious that one's own culture has always already consisted of a *melange* and that it has been constructed or constituted from non-simultaneous compo-

17 *Turgot on Progress, Sociology and Economics*, translated, edited and with an introduction by R.L. MEEK, Cambridge 1973, p. 123.

18 See REINHARD KOSELLECK: *Vergangene Zukunft. Zur Semantik geschichtlicher Zeiten*, Frankfurt am Main 1984, pp. 130ff.

19 NIKLAS LUHMANN: "Gleichzeitigkeit und Synchronisation", in: NIKLAS LUHMANN (Ed.): *Soziologische Aufklärung* 5, Opladen 1990, pp. 95ff.; WILLIAM J. MITCHELL: "Die Ökonomie der Präsenz", in: S. MÜNKER, A. ROESLER (Eds.): *Mythos Internet*, Frankfurt am Main 1997, pp. 15ff.

nents.[20] In this way, the simultaneity of the non-simultaneous has become part of our everyday understanding of history. Just as we must avoid the 'ideology of non-simultaneity', that is, measuring all cultures according to the same criteria of technological progress, we must also avoid an 'ideology of simultaneity', which ignores those still existing or newly created non-simultaneities. Because these newly created non-simultaneities frequently signify displacement and backwardness – that is, exclusion and poverty – we must retain the critical impetus within the concept of non-simultaneity. Neither simultaneity nor non-simultaneity erase the temporal sequence and, with this, historical consciousness. On the contrary, they continue to presuppose the idea of continuity – a historical continuity which orients itself around an accelerated civilization process.

Summarizing this understanding of a culture of technology from the perspective of the philosophy of history, the relationship between radicalization and self-reflection becomes clear. Initially, modernity is *radicalized* in the sense that global arenas are expanded, consolidated and become specialized through transportation and information technologies. In particular, telecommunications – de-coupled from the transportation system – continue the process of synchronization all the way up to the point at which simultaneity is experienced as immediate. However, contrary to the critiques of civilization cited earlier, spaces, times and realities are not destroyed through these technologies, but rather are altered within a continuous development. We have, in other words, reached neither the 'end' of the modern nor the 'end' of history. Just as the formulation 'the simultaneity of the non-simultaneous' constituted the philosophy of history in the 18th century, we cannot exclude the possibility today that through this experience of historical non-simultaneities an altered understanding of history might also arise.

However, at the same time, these technologies contain *reflective* conditions which allow for the possibility of a new consciousness of space, time and reality, one which, in turn, would affect our consciousness of history. It is precisely at this point that the discontinuity and reflectivity of technological developments become evident. What had always been practiced and known in the course of the modern suddenly becomes directly visible

20 ROLAND ROBERTSON: *Globalization: Social Theory and Global Culture*, London 1992, pp. 173f.; JAN NEDERVEEN PIETERSE: "Der Melange-Effect", in: ULRICH BECK (Ed.): *Perspektiven der Weltgesellschaft*, Frankfurt am Main 1998, pp. 94; ULRICH BECK: *Was ist Globalisierung?*, Frankfurt am Main 1997, pp. 85, 90f.

through telecommunications and computer technology. Communication – completed in 'real time' – transforms synchronization into an experience which, admittedly, is technologically mediated, but precisely because of this is also immediate. While in the 18th century, simultaneity merely had to be calculated, demonstrated and constructed, today it has become something which we can ourselves experience directly. It takes place before our own eyes. Simultaneity becomes, to a certain extent, visualized. Technologically produced sense certainty has not extinguished reflection. On the contrary, this experience opens up new reflective potential.

IV. Paradoxes of Globalization

If the 'paradoxes' of *globalization* are frequently a subject of discussion, a more profound paradox lies in the fact that the cultural dimension of globalization is denied in such discussions. While technological-economic civilization is, in fact, subjected to enormous systemic integration, it is described from cultural-critical perspectives as a process of disintegration, specialization and, at best, as individualization. While electronically mediated simultaneity and the abundance of information make available increasing funds of knowledge about the entire earth, there is a constant talk of confusion (*Unübersichtlichkeit*) and loss of orientation. And while the continents continue to move closer together, an image of total disintegration arises. If Habermas once spoke of a "new confusion," one speaks today of an "end of clarity," of an "uncertainty" and of the "disorder of the new world."[21] Occasionally, it seems as if one simply does not want to admit globalization. The real world and the representational world appear manifestly at odds with one another.

Considered superficially, this distanced attitude is perhaps justified if it is understood as a reaction to globalization. When we are warned of the dangers and, in particular, of the levelling tendency of globalization, these are gener-

21 JÜRGEN HABERMAS: *Die Neue Unübersichtlichkeit*, Frankfurt am Main 1985, p. 143; ULRICH BECK: *Was ist Globalisierung?*, p. 90; ROBERT ROBERTSON: "Glokalisierung: Homogenität und Heterogenität in Raum und Zeit", in: U. BECK (Ed.): *Perspektiven der Weltgesellschaft*, pp. 192ff.

ally attempts to oppose a new myth of globalization. This critique does accord with real counter-movements, in which entire peoples, regions and social groups return to their cultural origins and, in particular, mobilize their traditions.

But in this case, too, we can perceive behind these understandable reactions a separation of the world into 'two cultures'. Since globalization is economically driven and is mediated through broadcasting and information technologies, the indisputable homogenizing tendencies appear to support a worldwide suppression of established cultures, or even to destroy them, while technological civilization, at the same time, is denied any cultural potential of its own. The 'systemic world' is said to lack a 'symbolic world' which could create meaning. In short, global civilization has no culture.

Summarizing the current globalization debate in simplified form, we can identify two extreme models and a mediating model. We find the *global* standpoint expressed in the model of a "capitalist world system," a model expounded, for example, by Immanuel Wallerstein.[22] The *local* standpoint is represented by a model of "polycentric politics, technology and culture," a model which is favored by English supporters of *cultural theory*.[23] Mediating between these two extremes, we have the model of 'glocalization' developed by the sociologist Roland Robertson.[24] According to this model, the universal and the particular are not mutually exclusive; rather, homogenizing and 'heterogenizing' tendencies interpenetrate one another. The global and the local are thought together, that is, the "local in the global" and the "global in the local."

---

22 IMMANUEL WALLERSTEIN: *One World, Many Worlds*, New York 1988; for a similar position, see ELMAR ALTVATER and BIRGIT MAHNKOPF: *Grenzen der Globalisierung. Ökonomie, Ökologie und Politik in der Weltgesellschaft*, Münster 1996, pp. 120f. – For a critique, see ULRICH BECK: *Was ist Globalisierung?*, pp. 64f.; ROLAND ROBERTSON: "Glokalisierung: Homogenität und Heterogenität in Raum und Zeit", p. 205; N. LUHMANN: *Die Gesellschaft der Gesellschaft*, Frankfurt am Main 1997, vol. 1, p. 159.

23 J. ROSENAU: *Turbulence in World Politics*, Brighton 1990; see BECK: *Was ist Globalisierung?*, pp. 67ff.; U. MENZEL: *Globalisierung versus Fragmentierung*, Frankfurt am Main 1998, pp. 40ff.

24 R. ROBERTSON: *Globalization: Social Theory and Global Culture*, pp. 173f. – See JAN NEDERVEEN PIETERSE: "Der Melange-Effect," p. 94; ULRICH BECK: *Was ist Globalisierung?*, pp. 85, 90f.; ALTVATER/MAHNKOPF: *Grenzen der Globalisierung*, pp. 30, 95

Admittedly, this sounds more harmless than originally intended. "Glo*c*alization" turns out to be a systems-theory argument. Niklas Luhmann has already pointed to the fact that 'world society', to the extent that it is regarded as a social system, produces specialization, particularization, and localization.[25] Thus, globalization itself gives rise to tendencies which are, in part, localizing. We must bear in mind here that "glo*c*alization" now means *globalization of the local*, without the reverse being true. We can explicate this rather abstract thesis relating to the domains of economics, politics, culture, and ethics.

The concept of "glo*c*alization" was originally developed from *economics*, or more precisely from the practices of business management, as Robertson himself candidly admits. It was developed through so-called micro-managing, in order to be able to separate goods and services on a global (or almost global) level for local markets. The local is marketed according to the motto 'variety sells better'. With this, the danger of the 'McDonaldization' of everything would appear to be averted. However, at the same time, we can also observe an opposing tendency: that models arise which are at once replicated and uniform. Even when local suppliers sell their goods on the world market, they are forced to integrate their regional products and thus to adapt them to global demand. This results in a standardization of the specific goods offered. Globalization thus produces standardized variety.

If we consider the consequences of globalization for *politics*, we can observe a decline in the significance of bipolar foreign relations in favor of a dependency on the *political system of world society*. Through this development, the particularities of individual nation-states come to exert an increasing influence on the global system of nations.[26] World society and nation-states do not form an opposition; rather the global system of states has become constitutive for individual states. And this, in turn, has consequences for the nation-state. While national cultures continue to exist, they become increasingly compatible with one another. In a best case scenario, this would result in a gentle pressure towards democratization. In this way, the political

25 NIKLAS LUHMANN: *Die Gesellschaft der Gesellschaft*, vol. 1, pp. 162f.; R. ROBERTSON: "Glokalisierung: Homogenität und Heterogenität in Raum und Zeit", pp. 193, 208.

26 ALEXANDER WENDT: "Der Internationalstaat: Identität und Strukturwandel in der internationalen Politik", in: U. BECK (Ed.): *Perspektiven der Weltgesellschaft*, p. 386.

system of world society can produce increased levelling or mutual adaptation among national-political cultures.

We can also observe a similar phenomenon with *cultures*, which have traditionally been considered within the framework of nation-states. The globalization of cultures has become the predominant theme in current cultural sociology. The experiential background for this is the migratory movements (made possible by travel technologies) of emigrants, refugees, tourists and guest workers, who now live and work together not only in larger cities. In addition to this, a simultaneity of communications has developed through television and the internet. This kind of expansion and consolidation produces the paradoxical global-local effect mentioned earlier that numerous cultures of the world can be lived and experienced simultaneously on one location. Individual cultures, however, are not untouched by this 'simul-locality': they are also affected by the globally mediated interplay. Migrants form a different image of their homeland than they would have if they had remained there. In the inter-cultural milieu in which various life habits mutually affect each other, these immigrants develop new conceptions of their own culture and of other cultures. Such images are then further filtered and strengthened through the mass media.[27] Thus, the *system of cultures* produces not only differences, but also models of compatibility and translatability. Such discourses about oneself and about others are carried out within a global context.

The contradictory process of globalization also affects the domain of *ethics*. Moral norms and values – themselves indisputably a part of cultural tradition – have also been subjected to the opposing tendencies of universalization and particularization. If there are repeated calls today for a *global ethos*, there is also a consensus that this cannot mean a uniform world morality. We can also see the influence of a re-culturalization and regionalization of morality, in which the differences among moralities in the world – above all, religiously grounded differences – have been emphasized. Insofar as we regard a mediation of such differences to be desirable in this case as well, we cannot exclude the possibility that attempts at intercultural understanding will tend to a standardization of interpretive models.[28] However, we must distinguish between

27 ARJUN APPADURAI: "Globale ethnische Räume", in: U. BECK (Ed.): *Perspektiven der Weltgesellschaft*, pp. 11ff.

28 JÜRGEN HABERMAS: *Die Einbeziehung des Anderen. Studien zur politischen Theorie*, Frankfurt am Main 1996, pp. 11ff; KARL-OTTO APEL: "Ethnoethik und universalitische Makroethik: Gegensatz oder Komplementarität?", in: W.

whether the particular moral criteria are reflected upon in relative isolation and according to the logic of individual cultures, or whether they come into practical confrontation with other cultures and competing normative ideas.[29] Through the latter, a completely new social situation arises, one in which different moral criteria adapt to one another. While they are not reduced to a single morality, we do find mutually influenced conceptions being used in the dialogue.

If we attempt to generalize these phenomena, then globalization proves to be a contradictory process, a process in which the universal and particular are refracted in a number of ways. First, there is a convergence of cultures: cultural variety is homogenized and levelled in a direct way – a tendency which is regarded affirmatively in theories of modernization, and critically in those of the posthistoire. In contrast to this, we can also observe a reactive tendency of 'heterogenization' and re-localization – a presupposition which makes the phenomena of globalization practically acceptable and theoretically interesting. These opposing tendencies ultimately culminate in a *localization which is mediated through the system of world society*. The local is re-formed globally. There is not *one* global economy, politics, culture and morality; the system does allow for differences, but these differences are, in this very process, also limited. Formulating it paradoxically, we could say: globalization universalizes the particular.

The example of globalization allows us to demonstrate once again the continuity and the discontinuity of the modern. On the one hand, there is a *radicalization*, in that old boundaries are transgressed while, at the same time, new boundaries are experienced. We have seen, in particular, that the universalization of the modern – in the face of the opposing tendencies of globalization and localization – turns out to be a contradictory process, but one which is ultimately all-embracing.

On the other hand, the radicalized modern reaches a *decisive point* at which particular characteristics become recognizable for the first time. If the

---

LÜTTERFELDS, T. MOHRS (Eds.): *Eine Welt – Eine Moral?*, Darmstadt 1997, pp. 60ff.; JULIAN NIDA-RÜMELIN: Über die Vereinbarkeit von Universalismus und Pluralismus in der Ethik", in: *Eine Welt – Eine Moral?*, pp. 104ff.; WILHELM LÜTTERFELDS: "Sind Universalismus und Kontingenz der Moral miteinander verträglich?", in: *Eine Welt – Eine Moral?*, pp. 177ff.

29 RAINER DÖBERT: "Welche Weltsysteme/ Weltbilder überleben den diskursiven Test?", in: *Eine Welt – Eine Moral?*, p. 78.

expansion of arenas of action has stood in the forefront since the modern voyages of discovery, it is now the experience of network consolidation as well as the experience of boundaries which have led to an expanded awareness of globalization. While up to the 20th century nations and cultures were regarded as original, we now recognize that cultures have always already been constituted by reciprocal mixings, adaptations and typologies.

V. The End of Industrial and Work Society?

When we hear pronouncements today that we currently stand upon an epochal threshold, this usually means, from a cultural-critical perspective, that a 'work ethos' appears to have survived. Against this position, I will attempt (connecting up with the Enlightenment) to reformulate the social and normative implications of technology, labour and production from the perspective of the philosophy of history. My intention here is not to cast doubts upon sociological facts or the current transformation of modern societies. However, I would like to raise the critical philosophical question as to whether this transformation is adequately characterized by the substitute terms 'information society' or 'knowledge society'.

In this case as well, we can observe an instrumental narrowing. While sociologists have claimed an "end of industrial and work society," Jürgen Habermas, generalizing this, has spoken of "the obsolescence of the production paradigm," and Jean Baudrillard of the "end of production."[30] Many critics of modern civilization explicitly welcome such an 'end of work', because they see in this a liberation of individuals from the compulsions of technological-economic reality.[31] Implicit in such an understanding is the

30 RALF DAHRENDORF: "Wenn der Arbeitsgesellschaft die Arbeit ausgeht?", *Krise der Arbeitsgesellschaft? Verhandlungen des 21. Deutschen Soziologientages in Bamberg 1982*, Frankfurt am Main, New York (1983), pp. 25ff.; JURGEN HABERMAS: *The philosophical discourse of modernity: twelve lectures*, translated by Frederick Lawrence, Cambridge, Mass. (MIT Press) 1987; JEAN BAUDRILLARD: *Symbolic exchange and death.*

31 MANFRED RIEDEL: "Arbeit als Lebenssinn?", in: G. ROPOHL (Ed.): *Arbeit im Wandel*, Berlin 1985, pp. 18ff.; ANDRÉ GORZ: *Kritik der ökonomischen Vernunft. Sinnfragen am Ende der Arbeitsgesellschaft*, Berlin 1989, pp. 18, 44; OSKAR

conception of an instrumental reason which serves only as a means for realizing external purposes. According to this argument, if work is understood not merely as a condition, but rather as the basis of life, then the means-ends relationship becomes reversed: work has become an independent means, or an end in itself. Thus, according to this argument, the more that gainful employment is limited, the more space humans have for individual autonomy and for activity which is free from all purposes. However, instead of rashly claiming of an 'end of work society', I would prefer to speak of a *structural transformation of human labour* and attempt to focus on the philosophical dimension of this. This transformation exhibits the following general characteristics.

First, the relation of work and vocation has changed.[32] Because knowledge becomes obsolete with increasing rapidity, work has been de-coupled from trained vocations.

The relation between *physical labor and intellectual labor* – the latter of which now consists, to a great degree, in data processing – has also been transformed. This does not mean that work has been replaced by knowledge. Rather, it is intellectual labor which produces knowledge and which processes already existing knowledge. The fact that this is not merely a question of definition can be seen in a double tendency. On the one hand, industry has over the long-term become *increasingly scientific* – a process which began already in the 19th century. On the other hand, the reverse process – the *industrialization of science* – has also developed as a result.[33] This industrialization of science – a repercussion of industry becoming increasingly scientific – is frequently overlooked by scientists. Contrary to the notion that artificial intelligence is primarily an issue of designing intelligent programs, we must

---

NEGT: *Lebendige Arbeit, enteignete Zeit. Politische und kulturelle Dimensionen des Kampfes um die Arbeitszeit*, Frankfurt am Main 1984, p. 42.

32 H. DAHEIM and G. SCHÖNBAUER (Eds.): *Soziologie der Arbeitsgesellschaft*, Weinheim, Munich 1993; CLAUS OFFE: *'Arbeitsgesellschaft'. Strukturprobleme und Zukunftsperspektiven*, Frankfurt am Main 1984, p. 28; ULRICH BECK: *Risikogesellschaft*, Frankfurt am Main 1986, pp. 121ff., 220ff. – The following aspect is forcefully described by RICHARD SENNET: *The corrosion of character: the personal consequences of work in the new capitalism*, 1st ed. New York (Norton) 1998.

33 ROLF KREIBICH: *Die Wissensgesellschaft*, Frankfurt am Main 1986, pp. 9ff., 70ff.; MATTHAIS WINGENS: *Wissensgesellschaft und Industrialisierung der Wissenschaft*, Wiesbaden 1998, pp. 235ff; this is a critique of DANIEL BELL: *The coming of post-industrial society; a venture in social forecasting*, New York 1973.

bear in mind the equally important circumstance that such programs would not be possible at all without a material world.[34] In the programmer's heaven of pure symbolic processing, it might appear as if modern technology now consists solely of communicated symbols, while older forms of industry decline to secondary importance. In reality, however, human thinking shifts increasingly to information-technology machines, machines which not only offer improved conditions for this, but which also pre-form thinking in terms of both form and content. We stand, in other words, on the threshold of the *industrialization of human thought*.

At the same time, the spatial and temporal system of coordinates has changed, as businesses have been decentralized and the resulting organizational components have been globally networked. On the one hand, work has, through this, lost its clearly definable location. If work segments are now coordinated through information technologies, a work process may then arise at the same time in a number of different locations. In a certain sense, this process takes place everywhere. In this way, human labor becomes spatially un-bounded. This, in turn, has consequences for the social character of work. Sociologists speak of the fact that the spatial and the social have drifted apart. This is true for human labor as well: work and location no longer form an inseparable unity. On the other hand, work time has become more flexible, as the length of the workday as well as the hours worked have come to vary greatly. As a result, the boundaries between 'work time' and 'life time' have been erased.[35] The separation between the social spheres of work and non-work has become increasingly blurred.

In addition to this, work is no longer assigned to particular *agents or actors*, when – for example, as with tele-banking – it is performed with increasing frequency by consumers. Labor moves between producers and consumers, and we often cannot determine unambiguously who is actually working. Work has thus lost its social system of reference in terms of production and con-

---

34 GÜNTER ROPOHL: *Ethik und Technikbewertung*, Frankfurt am Main 1996, p. 85.

35 CLAUS OFFE: *'Arbeitsgesellschaft'. Strukturprobleme und Zukunftsperspektiven*, 1984, p. 340; OSKAR NEGT: *Lebendige Arbeit, enteignete Zeit. Politische und kulturelle Dimensionen des Kampfes um die Arbeitszeit*, 1984, pp. 97ff; K.H. HÖRNIG, A. GERHARDT, M. MICHAILOW: *Zeitpioniere. Flexible Arbeitszeiten – neuer Lebensstil*, Frankfurt am Main, p. 25ff.

sumption.[36] Marx already overcame the rigid separation between production and consumption by assuming a 'dialectical' relationship, within which production and consumption were mutually entangled. On the one hand, the producer is already a consumer, because he uses raw materials and foodstuffs. On the other hand, the consumer is also a producer, because he reproduces his own labor power.[37] But with so-called shadow labor, these spheres disappear, so that this dialectic no longer applies. This new confusion, however, does not mean that work has disappeared completely. What is new, rather, is the fact that the division and distribution of labor has become more ambiguous. Human work has lost its traditional frame of reference.

As a whole, work has, through the new information technologies, become *more communicative*. These circumstances have far-reaching consequences for a new concept of work. We can no longer maintain the familiar separation between the work-world and the life-world. Precisely those people who speak of the "obsolescence of the production paradigm" continue, in principle, to hold onto the traditional concept of work, while at the same time invoking a new concept of communication which is supposed to be separate from work. However, we should bear in mind that there are always social components inherent in human labor. Already Aristotle's separation of *poiesis* and *praxis* proved to be problematic, and this is true even more for the distinction between "work, production and action" in Hannah Arendt, and for the distinction between "labor and interaction" in Habermas.[38] In the face of the new media technologies, this familiar critique can now be reversed and sharpened. Communication not only has strategic-instrumental dimensions; it has also come to be mediated increasingly through technology – in many cases, communication is first made possible through such products of human labor. This is an additional and relevant reason why work and communication do not form an opposition.

---

36 In the United States, the term 'prosumption' has been used to describe this phenomenon. – See ULRICH BECK: *Was ist Globalisierung?*, p. 220; CLAUS OFFE: *'Arbeitsgesellschaft'. Strukturprobleme und Zukunftsperspektiven*, 1984, pp. 141ff.

37 KARL MARX: *Grundrisse der politischen Ökonomie*, Frankfurt am Main, Vienna (no date), pp. 10ff.

38 HANNAH ARENDT: *The Human Condition*, Chicago 1958; JÜRGEN HABERMAS: *The philosophical discourse of modernity: twelve lectures*; J. ROHBECK: *Die Fortschrittstheorie der Aufklärung*, pp. 35ff., 146ff., 281f.

All in all, technological civilization expands our horizon for a self-understanding of the modern, a self-understanding which questions particular *idealizations of human labor*. Since the inception of the modern, the myth of the creative human has been widespread: The human who as an engineer, statesman or scientist sets his own goals and knows how to realize them. However, at the same time, since the beginnings of the modern, an opposing insight has also been recognized: that technological means often cause unintended effects, effects which could not have been predicted ahead of time. Since the 1920's, the natural dynamics of technology has itself become a topos. New technological systems and global networking have reinforced the awareness of this contingency. In this way, the self-estimation – and probably the overestimation – of the human's creative capacities has also been transformed. In the place of this long predominant myth of creation, a sober judgment of existing possibilities of action has emerged.

Finally, the debate over the ostensible 'end' of industrial and work society is philosophically loaded insofar as such proclamations of an 'end' also lay claims to an epochal threshold. There is an implicit philosophy of history in such claims, as we can see in the example of Ulrich Beck. According to Beck, we are, at our current stage of human history, experiencing a transition from an "old" modern to "another modern" or a "second modern." Behind this claim is the belief "that industrial society, in the process of establishing itself – in other words, on the quiet soles of normality – has left the stage of world history down the back stairs of its side effects."[39] When Beck further diagnoses an "immanent contradiction between the modern and the anti-modern" or the "contradictions of a modern torn at the foundations of industrial society," he constructs the modern as a movement of return and completion. Beck's sociology of the modern, in other words, contains a hidden philosophy of history.

Behind the talk about the 'end of industrial and work society' and of the transition to 'a knowledge society', there is yet another presupposition of the philosophy of history. With such discussions, one often has the impression that that individual types of society can simply be lined up successively like a string of pearls. Against such a linear image of history, however, it is important to point out that the so-called developing countries – to which a great portion of industrial production has currently been shifted – are only now

39 ULRICH BECK: *Was ist Globalisierung?*, p. 15; on the following, see pp. 14, 18f., 178ff.

beginning to undergo a process of industrialization. From a global perspective – which everyone claims to assume – it is clear that human labor has not disappeared as a criterion for understanding the world, but rather that labor has been redistributed. Thus, in reality we are dealing with a non-simultaneity of history – a non-simultaneity which is produced in the course of globalization and which also effects our own society. This means, however, that industry and work society have not left the stage of world history, but rather continue to be present – next to service, science, information and communication – as integral components of modern societies. They continue to exist in a radically altered form.

Thus, the example of human labor also indicates a connection between radicalization and reflection. The modern is *radicalized* through the industrialization of knowledge. The modern becomes *reflective* in that we now recognize the historicity of work – significantly since the so-called work society has been in upheaval. If Marx still presupposed work to be an anthropological constant, it now becomes clear that work represents a particular historical formation, a formation which can arise and unfold its 'ethos' only under certain social conditions. Today, because the meanings of work and life have multiplied and exist in an increasing number of locations, times and spheres, we must attempt to construct a new relationship between work and life-meaning. Technological civilization thus does not simply erase meaning. It can also lead to new cultural orientations.

VI. Radicalizing the Modern

When I endorse the thesis of a *radicalization of the modern*, I do not mean this merely in terms of the continuity of technological civilization. Radicalization also means rapid increase, exponential growth and, along with this, increased acceleration. This includes decisive breaks, such as those evident in the de-coupling of information networks from transportation systems or in the introduction of a transnational, global division of labor. But in our context, I am interested, above all, in the *reflective* levels of this radicalization which are made possible through *discontinuity*. Just as a later historical stage can allow for a better understanding of earlier stages, the radicalized modern permits us to recognize essential characteristics of modern civilization. This process of reflection was initially revealed in the example of *non-simultaneities* in the modern. In addition to this, *globalization* – intensified through media technologies – opens up the possibility of new forms of reflection about the phenomenon of cultures which are non-simultaneous and systematically mediated. In the same way, *industrial and work society* has been radicalized, bringing the historical and normative dimensions of human labor into view. Through these processes of radicalization, the modern has not been overcome, but rather has been repeatedly reformulated according to new points of view.

With my reference to the reflective potential of technological civilization, I am not attempting to play off the normative side of the modern against its instrumental side. Rather, I would like to draw our attention to the cultural and normative dimensions of technological-instrumental action. New technologies contain their own reflective surplus, a reflective surplus in which typical processes of the modern become recognizable. It is not only communicative action which contains reflective potential; instrumental action contains such reflective potential as well. Formulated pointedly, we could speak of the *self-reflection of poietic reason* – a poietic reason which combines instrumental as well as communicative dimensions.

This, however, should not to be confused with a blind instrumentalism or with an apology for technology, because the surplus character of technological action excludes neither the conscious appropriation nor the rejection of new possibilities of use. Basically, it is a matter of reflectively connecting technological 'possibilities' back to relations in human life. This requires dealing with the expanding possibilities of action in a cunning way. There is nothing we can do except to sound out the new maneuvering spaces and attempt to use them creatively. I suggest, therefore, that we approach the subject 'technology and history' with neither technological euphoria nor fears of alienation, and, at the same time, that we attempt to hold onto the idea of emancipation.

The culture of technological civilization is of decisive importance for the philosophy of history, because the former constitutes the indisputable continuum of history. If one eliminates technology from considerations of history, then history necessarily appears as the eternal rise and fall of cultures. The philosophy of history finds itself in a dilemma here. If it concentrates on the civilization process, it can presume a continuum, but then opens itself to the rebuke that history is insufficient as a cultural and therefore specifically historical phenomenon. If, on the contrary, it orients itself according to traditions such as religion and politics, it begins with phenomena which are indisputably cultural, but must then give up the idea of a continuous course of history. We can resolve this dilemma through a synthesis of technology and culture, a synthesis in which the historical continuum becomes history in an emphatic sense.

Translated from the German by Tom Lampert

Chapter 12

History and Subjectivity - The Relevance of a Philosophical Concept of History in the Kantian Tradition

MATTHIAS LUTZ-BACHMANN

I. The Postmodern Privatization of the Past
II. Foucault's Attack on the Concept of History
III. Arguments for a Philosophical Concept of History

I. The Postmodern Privatization of the Past

As is already evident from the title of one of his essays, Frank R. Ankersmit observes an increasing tendency both in the current science of history, and in the way past events are dealt with in the public sphere, to appropriate and remember events on a "private" basis. Here, Ankersmit makes explicit reference to the methodological self-understanding of the "Annales" School of History, and its rejection of the historiographic principle formulated by Leopold von Ranke that, in the interests of the objectivity of the historian's representation of history, s/he must remain absent from past events. This principle – according to Ankermit – was based on an understanding of history as a single, though largely uncharted, nexus of events comparable to a "world map containing a number of white areas that future research would fill in, in due course".[1] Yet as Allan Magill writes, due to the plethora of historiographic discourses that have since accumulated, the "single history" once

---

1 R. ANKERSMIT: „Die postmoderne ‚Privatisierung' der Vergangenheit“, in: H. NAGL-DOCEKAL (Ed.): *Der Sinn des Historischen*, Frankfurt am Main (S. Fischer Verlag) 1996, p. 204.

postulated by the science of history, the latter itself being understood as an autonomous and coherent discipline, has now become a gigantic amorphous mass through which historians can burrow without ever coming across their colleagues of the present or the past, and without knowing in which direction the results of their work are pointing with reference to "history as a whole".[2] This development, which is reflected in the methodology of the Annales School, renders obsolete not only history as the autonomous and coherent discipline which had emerged in the nineteenth century as a "community of historians ... working on a common project, with each historian playing his own part in building the cathedral of our knowledge of the past".[3] It also renders obsolete the notion of "a specific historic reality which exists independently of the historian", i.e. an "objective" reality with reference to which the results of research can be measured. In that bygone era of historiography, the notion of an objective historical reality as a "reality in its own right" was cognate with the further assumption of a "collective cognitive subject embodied in the discipline as a whole". This because, as Ankersmit puts it: "To the extent had all historians speak more or less the same language, apply more or less the same methods, share a more or less common understanding of what is important and what is not, and are trained in a way which more or less guarantees that they have all these things in common, we can speak of a pseudo-Hegelian "subjective mind" acting as a repository of the joint results of historians' work, penetrated by the mysteries of objective historical reality".[4] In Ankersmit's view, however, once the assumption of a single, objective reality is rendered obsolete then so too is the notion of a single subject within the discipline of historical science: "The image of historiography as a cathedral to which each historian contributes his own bricks and mortar for the greater glory of the edifice as a whole has given way to an image of historiography as a metropolis in which each follows his own path in the light of his own concerns, with little regard to what all the others are doing."[5]

This is the process which Ankersmit terms the "postmodern privatisation" of the past. It follows in the wake of the "disintegration of the past as an

2 See A. MAGILL: „'Grand Narrative' and the Discipline of History", in: R. ANKERSMIT, H. KELLNER (Eds.): *A New Philosophy of History*, Chicago (Chicago University Press) 1995, pp. 151-173.

3 R. ANKERSMIT (p. 204).

4 R. ANKERSMIT (p. 203).

5 R. ANKERSMIT (p. 204).

autonomous and coherent, though complex reality" and the "dissolution of the quasi-collective cognitive subject".[6] These assumptions are superseded by the private reading of any individual historian, a shift which Ankersmit sees "most clearly reflected in the sudden dominance of the term 'memory' in the current historical consciousness. [...] The term 'memory' relates to the way in which we as individuals recall to mind our personal past, whilst the term 'history' is traditionally reserved for our collective past. [...] The fact that the word 'memory' is now being required to do what the word 'history' used to do is a sure sign of the 'personalisation' or 'privatisation' of our relationship to the past."[7] This privatisation of the past goes hand-in-hand with a further shift namely the departure of historians from the collective narratives of national, social and economic history. Without exception, these collective narratives presuppose "that the past was in large measure shaped by forces that went beyond the will and capability of individual actors".[8] According to Ankersmit, the prototypes of these now largely obsolete constructs of past collective agency or anonymous, but generally efficacious structures were the philosophies of history of Hegel and Marx, and the subsequent national histories which, from the perspective of their respective interests in the present, projected onto the past collective agencies such as the French, German or British people. Accepting Ankersmit's proposed substitution of the term 'history' by 'memory', not only the aforementioned notion of a single subject of historiography, but also the assumption of a single historical agenda is thus rendered obsolete. Thematically, the attitude of 'memory' corresponds to "that which in the past was marginalized, repressed or ignored by the collective, and therefore could not reach the public sphere of what was collectively known and acknowledged and has always constituted the proper domain of 'history' in the traditional sense".[9] The logical consequence of this is that postmodern historical consciousness, which is indebted to the methodological programme of 'memory' that has superseded the idea of 'a single history', has turned to address the history of private life and the history of mentalities, the paradigm case of such historiographic practice being the Annales School.

This 'privatisation' of the past and the 'memory' of it do not, in Ankersmit's view, involve the rehabilitation of any – compared to the older con-

6 *Ibid.*
7 R. ANKERSMIT (p. 207).
8 R. ANKERSMIT (p. 202).
9 R. ANKERSMIT (p. 208).

cept of 'history' – new notion of the individual as subject. Ankersmit in the first instance adopts the arguments of the French sociologist Maurice Halbwachs and his interpretation of memory as a collective construct, which the latter deployed against Henri Bergson (and against René Descartes): "As long as an individual is enclosed in a solipsistic, presocial world" and possesses no language with which to access the world, the individual is also without memory. As Ankersmit puts it, "memory is always shaped by the social categories which determine its operations, and communication on memory (including communication between the memory and itself), and determine what we project unconsciously onto memories".[10] Just as 'memory' can only ever be conceived of as socially mediated, the individual must also be spoken of as an "interface of countless social forces which constitute society". It is not society, but the individual which is an abstract construct. In developing this line of argument Ankersmit not only follows the exponents of French post-structuralism and deconstructivism (such as Jacques Derrida, whom he expressly emphasises), he also draws on Gilbert Ryle's critique of the Cartesian notion of mind and on Richard Rorty. According to Ankersmit, this "assault" on the philosophy of the subject based on the theory of mind is conducive to our taking the view when reading Descartes and Kant "that we should not be seeking the individual (or his/her memory) beyond or beneath the domain of publicly observable, accessible phenomena".[11] In opposition to structuralism and its paradoxical partisan stance in favour of a subject-free, objective historical text, and thus a "past in itself", Ankersmit insists on the necessity of an appropriation of the past mediated by personal memory. However, Ankersmit's prognosis is that this will gradually dissolve the old discipline of historical science and lead "to a greater acceptance of the presence of the historian in his/her writings".[12]

10 R. ANKERSMIT (p. 211).

11 *Ibid.*

12 R. ANKERSMIT (p. 232).

II. Foucault's Attack on the Concept of History

In his essay *Nietzsche, Genealogy, History* published in 1971,[13] Michel Foucault makes a plea – as he calls it – for "real history" as opposed to the traditional interpretation of history. This work stands midway between the earlier, so-called archaeological studies of the sixties such as *Folie et déraison* (Madness and Civilisation), *Naissance de la clinique* (The Birth of the Clinic), *Les mots et les choses* (Words and Things), and *L'archéologie du savoir* (Archaeology of Knowledge), and his later works dealing with the aesthetics of existence published in the eighties, and the four-volume *Histoire de la sexualité* (History of Sexuality). The titles of these books already demonstrate Foucault's pronounced interest in the history of science and knowledge, which also links him to the studies of mentality generated by the Annales School of History. In his essay *Nietzsche, Genealogy, History*, which is all I wish to deal with here, Foucault reflects upon his advocated programme of historiography in the tradition of French 'anti-humanism', which was initially able to draw on traditions as mutually divergent as Martin Heidegger's *Brief Letter of Humanism* and the structuralism of Gaston Bachelard. In his short text published in 1971, however, Foucault identified Nietzsche's philosophy as his philosophical frame of reference, in which context he refers less to Nietzsche's own early engagement with the historical science of his time in *Thoughts out of Season*, and more to Nietzsche's idea of a genealogical critique past *Human, all too Human*. The programme put forward here of deconstructing the notion of truth and morality inherent in the philosophical tradition, at least as Nietzsche understands it, serves as a model for Foucault in his critique of the traditional notion of history and its subject. Here we see a number of philosophical ideas reformulated, or anticipated, which we encountered in our reading of Frank R. Ankersmit in the context of a self-reflection of methods and tasks within the historical disciplined in the tradition of the Annales School.

In his early works, Foucault was already at paints to expose the problematic epistemological status of those disciplines in which the human being, understood in the traditional sense, is present at once as both the 'object' and the 'subject' of epistemology. These included alongside the linguistics of the

13 M. FOUCAULT: „Nietzsche, die Genealogie, die Historie", in: *Von der Subversion des Wissens,* Frankfurt am Main (S. Fischer Verlag) 1987.

sixties, which was dominated by structuralism, the disciplines of medicine, sociology and criminology, as well as all the humanities in the broader sense. The aim of this critique is to lay bare the humanism prevailing in the humanities, which Foucault, along with Nietzsche and Heidegger, understands as the philosophical programme formulated by Plato of subjugating all cognitive operations to the principle of the theoretical human. In the works of Plato, this took the form of a philosophy of being which sought to derive the identity of things from their (ideal) principles, their conceptual essence or, as Foucault also puts it, their origin, in other words from 'the pre-cedent', and what Nietzsche declared to be the programme of metaphysics: the interpretation of reality and the identity of things from a 'world beyond'. Foucault's aim is to deploy the method of genealogy to expose, and thus deconstruct this theoretical rationale stretching back ultimately to Plato. Unlike the historical disciplines, this genealogy does not trace what has arisen back to its 'origin', moving from the 'latter' back to the 'former'. Its aim is rather, according to Foucault, to narrate its ignoble 'descent' from the base, its derivativeness from the corporeal. As Foucault puts it: "The genealogy of values, of morality, of the ascetic and of knowledge must not seek to trace their origins (as would be the intention of the historicist approach) [...] It must rather sojourn amidst the details and chance occurrences of their beginnings: it must pay scrupulous attention to their risible malevolence".[14] This approach consists in the first instance in explaining all conceptions of the world and self-interpretations of humankind as humanist praxis, as strategies of mastery of world and social self-assertion. At the same time, these practices are not acknowledged as such, due to the dominance of the Platonic-metaphysical conception of 'theoretical man', and by virtue of this the metaphysicians' being and truth claims are exposed as malicious. In Foucault's view, even the historic decomposition of the old metaphysics generated by its implicit relativity is nourished by the pathos of truth, i.e. the relativity of tracing the latter back to its true former origin, and thus continues the programme of metaphysics, or rather humanism, in the form of traditional historiography. In opposition to the Western conception of epistemology, Foucault follows Nietzsche in putting forward the methodology of genealogy. Yet that methodology itself is dependent on historiography, albeit in a highly specific sense: "Genealogy needs history in

---

14 *Ibid.*, p. 72.

order to cast out the chimera of the origin, just as the good philosopher needs the physician to war off the shadows of the soul.[15]

Foucault argues in favour of replacing traditional historiography, which remains obsessed by origins and truth, by so-called 'real history' laid bare through the method of genealogy. This 'real history', he writes, "has, unlike the historian, no stable ground under its feet. Nothing in the human being – not even her body – is so stable that an understanding of other human beings of a recognition of one's own self in them as other would be possible. Everything which has lent support to the notion of history as an accessible whole, allowing it to appear as a patient and continuous motion, must be systematically shattered. The consoling game of re-cognition must be unearthed. In the historical domain, knowledge does not mean 'recovery', and most certainly does not mean 'recovery of ourselves'.[16]

III. Arguments for a Philosophical Concept of History

Foucault develops this idea by stating that history will become 'real' to the extent "that it introduces the discontinuous into our own being. It will dismember our emotions, it will dramatise our instincts, it will replicate our body and hold up to the corporeal self her own image. It will tolerate no reassuring stability of life or nature above itself ... Because knowledge is a tool not of understanding, but of dissection".[17] In performing its diagnostic and therapeutic role, 'real' history will direct its 'gaze' not towards the grand ideas, the ideals or the intentions of the actors on the stage of world history emphasized in Hegel's philosophy of history, but like a physician will direct its gaze "towards the immediate – the body, the nervous system, the functions of nutrition and digestion, the energies". This directing of the gaze is not, however, designed once again to access a new and prime true reality (as in classical psychoanalysis or in materialism), but "to brusquely tear free from that and

15 *Ibid.*, pp. 72f.
16 *Ibid.*, pp. 79f.
17 *Ibid.*, p. 80.

keep at a distance that which is most immediate: the body (as the physician lowers his gaze to establish the differential diagnosis.)"[18]

Foucault's intention is to seize control of the empowering tools and artefacts of historiography. It is, as he says, "to make oneself master of history", and "make genealogical, which is to say strictly anti-Platonic use" of it. In this way, 'real' history will be able to liberate itself from the 'historic purpose' postulated by 'meta-historic history writing', which Foucault identifies with traditional historiographic practice. More precisely, there are three ways in which 'real' history is used to oppose the traditional view of history. These are: 1. "The parodic deconstruction of reality contests traditional history as memory or recovery. 2. The dissociation of identities contests the assumptions of continuity or tradition underlying traditional history. 3. The sacrifice of the subject of knowledge and truth opposes the traditional view of history as knowledge". Foucault associates with the third use of 'real' history the task of the traditional notion of truth, and a truth-seeking subject of knowledge identical with itself. "Foucault certainly aims "to liberate history once and for all from the metaphysical and anthropological model of memory. The goal is to make of history a counter-memory, and develop within that a quite different modality of time."[19]

In today's debate, Ankersmit and Foucault are certainly not alone in their critique of a single nexus of past events and a corresponding notion of the subject. They reflect the spirit of the postmodern age in their rejection of 'single histories', and their favouring of difference and non-identity in the sense of an unavailable freedom. Acknowledging the provisional nature of what I am about to say, I would now like to conclude with some remarks concerning the critique I want to outline. First of all a few systematic arguments. We can confidently state that the arguments put forward constitute a qualitative innovation, vis-à-vis the debate conducted in the mid-nineteen-seventies concerning the potentials of the philosophy of history. Whereas the points then at issue were the possibility, and possible significance, of the philosophy of history, today the question needs to be addressed more radically than ever before of whether and to what extent we can engage in historiography on the basis of a sound epistemological rationale. The fact that the systematic discussion of this issue already constitutes a first positive answer to the question of the possibility of the philosophy of history today, was

18 *Ibid.*, p. 81.
19 *Ibid.*, p. 85.

pointed out by Hans-Michael Baumgartner in his essay "The philosophy of history after the end of the philosophy of history", published in 1996. Here, as in the nineteen-seventies, Baumgartner speaks of a contemporary form of the philosophy of history as a "theory of historical reason" or as a "critical historiology, which explores the possibility of our historical knowledge, and identifies both structures and the significance of historiographic cognition".[20]

I share with Baumgartner not only this definition of the tasks of the philosophy of history, but also his rejection of the speculative philosophy of history as proposed by the German idealists, not least the early Schelling, and especially Hegel. The latter modify in a problematic fashion the definition of the philosophy of history and its status put forward by Kant, in two keys respects: Kant addresses the issue of the philosophy of history first of all in the context of his theory of knowledge, i.e. in terms of the issue of how the matter of historical narratives and the abundance of historical reports can be organised. In this epistemological context, Kant offers the heuristic of 'teleology', understood merely as a 'regulatory' rational notion. This is to say that he justifies the philosophy of history as an epistemological attitude which systematically organises and observes the matter generated by historical tradition "as if" there had been progress for the better within it. The decision as to "whether" this progress has taken place or not falls neither within the purview of historical science, nor within the purview of theoretical epistemic reason. In Kant's view, this can only be decided by practical, i.e. normative reason in the face of the reality of the state constitutions embodying the rule of law which people have put, or may put, in place. The standard of judgement here is generated solely by practical reason, in its application to the sphere of external, i.e. intersubjective action. The idealist philosophy of history put forward by Hegel presupposes that history itself has a rational structure, however, which leads to an abandonment of the two points of view which were crucial to Kant: 1. the regulatory status of the teleological notion of progress as an epistemological proposal for the organisation of reason in its theoretical use, and 2. the normative practical use of the philosophy of history, i.e. its use relative to (intersubjective) action, which we encounter in the form of the

20 H.-M. BAUMGARTNER: „Philosophie der Geschichte nach dem Ende der Geschichtsphilosophie“, in: *Der Sinn des Historischen*, ibid., pp. 151-172, p. 176. - Baumgartner's paper is printed in this volume above on pp. 149-171 in English translation and in a version revised by H.-M. Baumgartner before his death in 2000 (editor's note).

unconditional postulate of jurisprudential reason that demands the creation of republican frameworks, the renunciation of martial violence, and the creation of a world order for peace.

Yet it is precisely in this respect that the critics of the traditional notion of history such as Ankersmit and Foucault agree with Hegel – whom they reject: Neither of them is able to appropriate the notion of 'history' in terms of either its theoretical status as a regulatory concept of reason, or its normative, practical dimension. This is quite evident in the case of Foucault who, as we have seen, accuses history (and indeed all the humanities) of constructing original identities. The charge of metaphysics which Foucault lays at history's door leaves him blind both to the regulatory status of the notions of historical knowledge which generate a single picture, and to the specific practical dimension of those notions. Disregarding the fundamental *aporia* in which Foucault, along with Nietzsche and Heidegger, becomes caught up with respect to his positions on knowledge, truth, and the subject; disregarding also the paradoxical charge of humanism (of which Foucault himself might be accused), my response to Foucault's proposed 'real history' can be summed up as follows: He not only draws an entirely inadequate picture of the work of traditional historiography, he also fails to embrace any appropriate notion of 'history'.

Ankersmit's description of the work of the traditional historical disciplines also displays deficient traits. However, unlike Foucault Ankersmit avoids becoming entangled in the *aporias* of a radical critique of reason and truth in their entirely. Nevertheless, he does ascribe to the science of history, without justification, the claim to an idealistic interpretation of a 'single history' and a single 'subject of knowledge'. In doing so, Ankersmit overlooks the fact that these concepts are applied if at all in German idealism, but not in the historiography that emerged from the very critique of Hegel. However, if historical science is to hold on to the notion of 'history' in the singular – as I believe it must – then it must do so for the methodologically well-founded reason that this is apparently the only feasible means to create (objective) scope for comparative historiography, and critical historiography. The 'privatisation' of the past which Ankersmit in part describes, and in part advocates, would ultimately lead to historical enquiry having to renounce its objective knowledge claims. Hence, if there is to be objective and verifiable knowledge of the past, then we must embrace a notion – albeit a regulatory one – of 'history' in the singular as a definition of the object of historical enquiry, though not a single grand history at the expense of other histories. This implies a first notion of 'the subject' as the historiographic community, i.e. a 'subject of history' construed epistemologically. This should at the same time be construed as a practical 'subject of history' to the extent that the past events which are the object of historical enquiry are to be understood not primarily in terms of a theoretical enquiry into the causal nexus, but in terms of a practical enquiry into the nexus of subjective interactions. This is history understood, as Baumgartner put it, as "an open process, in which each agent and the conditions of actions are crucial".[21] Historical science is only conceivable as this retrospective interpretation of the interactional nexus, even where – as Marx put it – prehistory prevails, i. e. in settings where the external liberty of people is constrained by natural or societal constellations. Only within this dimension of practical rationality can the significance of 'personal memory' around which Ankersmit's position revolves be justified at the supra-individual level; only here can a claim to joint learning, which is clearly Ankersmit's intention, be upheld. This, however, presupposes a notion of practical subjective agency which neither the private appropriation of history nor the discipline of historiography can do without. Advocacy of the unrenounceability of the notions of 'history' and 'the subject' is a prime task of a philosophy of history.[22]

Translated from the German by John Cochrane

21 *Ibid.*, p. 163.

22 See M. LUTZ-BACHMANN: *Geschichte und Subjekt*, München/Freiburg (Alber Verlag) 1988.

Chapter 13

Towards a New Theory-Based History of Historiography

HORST WALTER BLANKE

I. Types and Functions of the History of Historiography
1. Types
2. The Functions of the History of Historiography
II. Between Criticism and Creation of Tradition:
History of Historiography and its Conception of Itself
as a Reflection upon Fundamental Theoretical Problems
III. Provisional Results and Conclusion:
The Rebelliousness of the History of Historiography.
The Systematic Reconstruction of Scientific Paradigms:
A Research Programme
IV. Building Stones of a New History of Historiography:
The *Gender* Aspect – Interdisciplinarity – References to
Day-to-Day Life – European and Non-European Perspective
V. Preview

> "All existing histories, and my own work is no exception, belong to a pre-scientific phase, as it were."[1]

1 GEORG G. IGGERS: „Probleme einer Geschichte der deutschen Geschichtsschreibung", in: JAN BROCKMANN, JAN KNOPF (Eds.): *Konkrete Reflexion* (Festschrift Hermann Wien), Den Haag (Nijhoff) 1975, pp. 135-54, cit. p. 138. - The present paper is based on three articles: HORST WALTER BLANKE: „Typen und Funktionen der Historiographiegeschichtsschreibung. Eine Bilanz und ein Forschungsprogramm", in: KÜTTLER ET. AL.: *GD* (see footnote no. 120), vol. 1, 1993, pp. 191-211; *ibid.*: „Theorieprobleme der Historiographiegeschichte", in: KONRAD H. JARAUSCH ET. AL. (Eds.): *Geschichtswissenschaft vor 2000.*

The history of historiography is a comparatively young affair. Together with the development of history as an independent discipline it dates back to the late Enlightenment, with L. Wachler's *History of Historical Research and Art*[2]; it also stands in direct relation to the increasingly scientific subject of history: Although there have been numerous *historiae historiae* during Humanism and poly-history - examples would be, on the one hand, the comprehensive works of La Popeliniere and G. J. Vossius, and on the other, the little volume *The Character of a Historiographer. Illustrated by the Life and from the Works of Abbot Claudius Fleury* by Chr.E. Simonetti -, they will have to be regarded as preliminaries to the genuine, yet to be written, history of historiography[3]. The publications that date from that period are thus to a certain extent explications - if not mere illustrations - of timeless-beyond-temporal norms of historiography. During the late Enlightenment, the historian J.Chr. Gatterer from Goettingen, one of the standard-bearers of the increasingly scientific subject of history, discusses in his essays *On Herodotus' Plan* and *On Trogus' Plan and His Abbrevator's Justin*, and eventually also in his *Treatise on the Position and the Point of View of the Historiographer, or the*

Perspektiven der Historiographiegeschichte, Geschichtstheorie, Sozial- und Kulturgeschichte (Festschrift Georg G. Iggers), Hagen (Rottmann) 1991, pp. 185-213; *ibid.*: „Zum Verhältnis von Historio-graphiegeschichte und Historik. Eine Analyse der Tagungsbände *Theorie der Geschichte* und *Geschichtsdiskurs*“, *Tel Aviver Jahrbuch für deutsche Geschichte*, 29 (2000), pp. 55-84. See these original articles for a more complete bibliographical account. - English translation by Nadja Rosental.

2 LUDWIG WACHLER: *Geschichte der historischen Forschung und Kunst seit der Wiederherstellung der litterärischen Cultur in Europa*, 5 parts in 2 vols., Göttingen (Röwer) 1812-20. - Most of the titles mentioned below (up to footnote no. 59) are discussed in detail in: HORST WALTER BLANKE: *Historiographiegeschichte als Historik*, Stuttgart (Frommann-Holzboog) 1991.

3 HENRI LANCELOT VOISIN, SIEUR DE LA POPELINIÈRE [published anonymously]: *L'Histoire de Histoires...*, Paris (Orry) 1599; GERHARD JOHANN VOSS: *De historicis Graecis*, Leiden (Maire) 1624; *ibid.*: *De historicis Latinis*, Leiden (Maire) 1627; CHRISTIAN ERNST SIMONETTI: *Der Character eines Geschichtschreibers. Entworfen in dem Leben und aus den Schriften des Herrn Abts Claudius Fleury...*, Göttingen (Schmid) 1746 [reprinted in: HORST WALTER BLANKE, DIRK FLEISCHER: *Aufklärung und Historik. Aufsätze zur Entwicklung der Geschichtswissenschaft, Kirchengeschichte und Geschichtstheorie in der deutschen Aufklärung*, Waltrop (Spenner) 1991, pp. 348-69].

German Livy timeless-beyond-temporal standards of historiography[4]; however, structural changes of thought reveal themselves in this context in so far as scientific phenomena, which are also understood and interpreted in their respective temporal context, relate for the first time to the urgent question of contemporary academic *historics* (theory of history). Until that time - and Vossius is only one example of many - *ars historica* and *historia historiae* stood side by side relatively unconnected. This is about to change. Ever since Wachler, or even since G. F. Creuzer's *Greek Historical Art, its Origin and Continuation*[5] the history of historiography is characterized by a more theoretical bent; *historics* and the history of historiography now constitute two different aspects or poles of meta-theoretical reflection. This can be traced back from the comprehensive scientific-historical works of M. Ritter, G. von Below and J. Haller to F. Meinecke and H. Ritter von Srbik to the theoretical works of J. Kocka and H.-U. Wehler[6]; in fact, Ritter's lecture on the history of historiography, published under the name of *The Development of the Science of History Illustrated by the Leading Works*[7] in a revised edition, was for a time announced as a systematic *Historics*. At the turn of the last century, K. Lamprecht and K. Breysig propagated a re-orientation, or paradigm shift, within the traditional discipline of history. Although they ultimately failed in their attempt, they took as a starting point the contemporary theoretical discussion (which they themselves in part provoked) and tried to critically reappraise the history of historiography in the light of the intense debate about the foundations of the subject[8]. In the case of F. X. von Wegele (who was no

4 JOHANN CHRISTOPH GATTERER: „Von dem Plan des Herodots", *Allgemeine historische Bibliothek*, 2 (1767), pp. 46-126; *ibid.*: „Vom Plane des Trogus und seines Abkürzers des Justins", *ibid.*, 3 (1767), pp. 18-193; *ibid.*: „Abhandlung vom Standort und Gesichtspunkt des Geschichtschreibers oder der teutsche Livius", *ibid.*, 5 (1768), pp. 3-29 [reprinted in: HORST WALTER BLANKE, DIRK FLEISCHER (Eds.): *Theoretiker der deutschen Aufklärungshistorie*, vol.1, Stuttgart (Frommann-Holzboog) 1990, pp. 452-66].

5 GEORG FRIEDRICH CREUZER: *Die historische Kunst der Griechen in ihrer Entstehung und Fortbildung*, Leipzig (Göschen) 1803.

6 For references see below footnotes nos. 7, 46, 29, 30, 50, 51, 57 resp. nos. 49, 55.

7 MORIZ RITTER: *Die Entwicklung der Geschichtswissenschaft an den führenden Werken betrachtet*, Munich/Berlin (Oldenbourg) 1919.

8 To name but a few: KURT BREYSIG: „Die Historiker der Aufklärung", *Die Zukunft*, 19 (1897), pp. 295-305, 343-55; KARL LAMPRECHT: „Individualität, Idee

expert in meta-theoretical reflections as his *History of German Historiography since Humanism*[9] clearly indicates) and Ed. Fueter (who deliberately excluded the history of *historics* in his *History of Recent Historiography*[10] and only dealt with historiography and historical research), detailed analyses of their histories of historiography reveal that they indeed tended towards an ideal of modern historiography: Wegele attempted to develop the specifically German national peculiarity on the basis of national historiography - German academic history appears as the medium of its individual nationality; Fueter's ideal of a modern science of history is that of history as „sociology".

While there is an obvious theoretical relevance to most of the works within the history of historiography, they touch upon different aspects of it. From a theoretical point of view the traditional scientific histories of the historical discipline can be divided into ten types and two major functions.

In the following, I will consider only that part of the literature that is concerned with history as a specialist subject. The extensive literature on the historiography of antiquity, on Assyrian or Indian historical thought, will be ignored. Similarly, I will largely leave aside the literature on the development outside Germany. I will thus not deal with the most prominent new publication of the past twenty years, i.e. E. Breisach's work *Historiography. Ancient, Medieval, & Modern*[11]. The types that I have (re)constructed nonetheless have a wider range than the examples of which they are abstractions.

I. Types and Functions of the History of Historiography

Although the types cannot really be separated from the functions, for reasons of systematicity I will nevertheless make an attempt. While the examples from the enormous body of literature have not been chosen at random they should nevertheless not be regarded as an empirically complete list of even

und sozialpsychische Kraft in der Geschichte", *Jahrbücher für Nationalökonomie und Statistik*, 68 (1897), pp. 880-900.

9 FRANZ XAVER VON WEGELE: *Geschichte der Deutschen Historiographie seit dem Auftreten des Humanismus*, Munich/Leipzig (Oldenbourg) 1885.

10 EDUARD FUETER: *Geschichte der neueren Historiographie*, Munich/Leipzig (Oldenbourg) 1911 (^{3}1936).

11 Chicago/London (Univ. of Chicago Press) 1983 (^{2}1994).

the most important works: The point is a typologisation, not a bibliographical record of the literature on the history of historiography.

1. Types

(1) Probably the most common form of work in the history of historiography is a personal portrait: Individual, mostly prominent, historians are placed within the history of the subject, be it in the form of an essay, or a comprehensive monograph. Their intellectual biography is traced, their theoretical œuvre is acknowledged, and usually they include observations on the history of the responses to the historian's work. G. Hübinger's *Georg Gottfried Gervinus. Historical Judgment and Political Critique*[12] can be considered a fundamental work on this historian of classical historicism who did not conform to *realpolitik* and was thus gradually pushed into the role of an outsider. Such works either deal with the life and work of an historian, or with individual problems. Depending on the particular historian's status, such works often go beyond his person. This may be the case when the subject matter represents a radical change within the subject of history as is the case with Hübinger and also with B. vom Brocke's monograph *Kurt Breysig. History between Historicism and Sociology*[13] as well as Schorn-Schütte's monograph on Lamprecht monograph[14]. H. Dickerhof's work on I. Schwarz[15], a Jesuit historian of the Enlightenment, is a reconstruction of the conditions and development of a specifically catholic historiography in an increasingly scientific age.

(2) Secondly, there is the type: 'history of historiography as the history of a work'. In this case, the history of the subject is told, as it were, as the history of a particular literary genre. This is probably the most common form of general description. Apart from the works by Wegele, Fueter, Below and Srbik, I would particularly like to refer to Ritter's, where the title itself ("a

---

12 GANGOLF HÜBINGER: *Georg Gottfried Gervinus. Historisches Urteil und politische Kritik*, Göttingen (Vandenhoeck & Ruprecht) 1984.

13 BERNHARD VOM BROCKE: *Kurt Breysig. Geschichtswissenschaft zwischen Historismus und Soziologie*, Lübeck/Hamburg (Matthiesen) 1971.

14 LUISE SCHORN-SCHÜTTE: *Karl Lamprecht. Kulturgeschichtsschreibung zwischen Wissenschaft und Politik*, Göttingen (Vandenhoeck & Ruprecht) 1984.

15 HARALD DICKERHOF: *Land, Reich, Kirche im historischen Lehrbetrieb an der Universität Ingolstadt (Ignaz Schwarz)*, Berlin/W. (Duncker & Humblot) 1971.

study of the most prominent works") refers to his procedure[16]. Apart from H. White's plea for a tropological interpretation of the history of historiography in *Metahistory. The Historical Imagination in Nineteenth-Century Europe*[17], this type does of course not have questions of literature or poetry as a genre as its main focus, but rather it discusses subject matter, models of interpretation and methods of the subject of history, using the succession of the "great" works as a background. Questions of the history of the institutions are only touched upon in passing.

(3) Textbooks containing overviews of the current state of research intended as introductions to a history degree or to its individual areas can only be classified as belonging to the history of historiography in a very limited sense. Such overviews usually refer exclusively to the contemporary state of research or strive for relative bibliographical completeness. Although they are not to be counted as history of the subject in the strictest sense they are important preliminary works and as such, for reasons of systematicity, should be mentioned as an independent type. Examples are the relevant passages in the textbooks by E. Bernheim, C. Wachsmuth and G. Wolf[18], as well as the individual volumes of the *Oldenbourg Outline of History*[19].

(4) Last but not least, the disciplinarity of history is apparent from its institutions. Works on the development of individual historical institutions form a separate type within the history of historiography. This type unites several heterogeneous subject areas. Examples are: K.D. Erdmann's history of international conferences on history[20], H. Heiber's comprehensive work on *Walter Frank and his Reichsinstitut for History of the New Germany*[21], Th.

16 RITTER (1919, no. 7).

17 Baltimore/London (Johns Hopkins Univ. Press) 1973.

18 CURT WACHSMUTH: *Einleitung in das Studium der alten Geschichte*, Leipzig (Hirzel) 1895, pp. 1-66; ERNST BERNHEIM: *Lehrbuch der Historischen Methode und der Geschichtsphilosophie...*, Leipzig (Duncker & Humblot) ^{6}1908, pp. 21-43, 206-50, 685-735; GUSTAV WOLF: *Einführung in das Studium der neueren Geschichte*, Berlin (Weidmann) 1910, pp. 1-15, 172-243.

19 See e.g. vol. 13: DIETER LANGEWIESCHE: *Europa zwischen Restauration und Revolution 1815-1849*, Munich (Oldenbourg) 1985, esp. pp .113-71.

20 KARL DIETRICH ERDMANN: *Die Ökumene der Historiker. Geschichte der Internationalen Historikerkongresse und des Comité International des Sciences Historiques*, Göttingen (Vandenhoeck & Ruprecht) 1987.

21 HELMUT HEIBER: *Walter Frank und sein Reichsinstitut für Geschichte des neuen Deutschlands*, Stuttgart (Deutsche Verlags-Anstalt) 1966.

Schieder's essay *German Historical Studies as Reflected in the Historische Zeitschrift,*[22] works on the Historical Commission,[23] individual university seminars,[24] etc.

(5) The history of historical methods has so far rarely been analyzed in the form of a monograph[25] but rather it has been dealt with in another context, like in Ritter's *History of Historiography* or in H. Bresslau's *History of the Monumenta Germaniae historica.*[26] Nevertheless, such works can be interpreted as a separate type of history of historiography. J. Wach's *History of Hermeneutic Understanding*[27] belongs to this type as much as J. Goldfriedrich's assessment of the (historicist) doctrine about the importance of historical ideas[28].

(6) The focus of the sixth type of history of historiography is not so much method, favoured subject matter or different models of interpretation, but rather the trends within intellectual history that carry these. Such works can,

---

22 THEODOR SCHIEDER: „Die deutsche Geschichtswissenschaft im Spiegel der Historischen Zeitschrift", *Historische Zeitschrift*, 189 (1959), pp. 1-104.

23 FRANZ SCHNABEL et al.: *Die historische Kommission bei der Bayerischen Akademie der Wissenschaften 1858-1958*, Göttingen (Vandenhoeck & Ruprecht) 1958.

24 PAUL EGON HÜBINGER: *Das historische Seminar der Rheinischen Friedrich-Wilhelms-Universität zu Bonn. Vorläufer - Gründung - Entwicklung. Ein Weg deutscher Universitätsgeschichte*, Bonn (Röhrscheid) 1963; HARTMUT BOOCKMANN, HERMANN WELLENREUTHER (Eds.): *Geschichtswissenschaft in Göttingen. Eine Vorlesungsreihe*, Göttingen (Vandenhoeck & Ruprecht) 1989.

25 HORST WALTER BLANKE: „Aufklärungshistorie, Historismus und historische Kritik. Eine Skizze", in: HORST WALTER BLANKE, Jörn RÜSEN (Eds.): *Von der Aufklärung zum Historismus. Zum Strukturwandel des historischen Denkens*, Paderborn (Schöningh) 1985, pp. 167-86; *ibid.*: „Die Kritik der Alexanderhistoriker bei Heyne, Heeren, Niebuhr und Droysen. Eine Fallstudie zur Entwicklung der historisch-philologischen Methode in der Aufklärung und im Historismus", *Storia della storiografia*, 13 (1988), pp. 106-27.

26 HARRY BRESSLAU: *Geschichte der Monumenta Germaniae historica*, Hannover (Hahn) 1921.

27 JOACHIM WACH: *Das Verstehen. Grundzüge einer Geschichte der hermeneutischen Theorie im 19. Jahrhundert*, 3 vols., Tübingen (Mohr) 1926-33.

28 JOHANN GOLDFRIEDRICH: *Die historische Ideenlehre in Deutschland. Ein Beitrag zur Geschichte der Geisteswissenschaften, vornehmlich der Geschichtswissenschaft und ihrer Methoden im 18. und 19. Jahrhundert*, Berlin (Gaertner) 1902.

but not necessarily have to, relate to history as an academic subject. Quite often they deal with the structures of historical thought as part of the cultural heritage. The most famous example is F. Meinecke's later work *The Origin of Historicism*[29]. The work deals with the genesis of the idea of development and individuality, as well as the origin of historicism (understood as a specific history of philosophy and *weltanschauung*) interpreted as a triumphant progress of these two theoretical concepts and their synthesis to a new whole. Even Srbik's *Mind and History from German Humanism to the Present*[30] is more of a take stock of intellectual history, of the influential traditions of German historiography (transfigured into an apologia for his own ideological position, which had come under fire after the collapse of the 'Third Reich'), than a critical chronological account of history's methods and problems.

(7) A large area of interest within the history of historiography are the "problem histories". These touch upon a number of different subject areas: the histories of individual sub-disciplines of history (e.g. the history of Ancient history[31]), the history of the relationship between disciplines (e.g. the relationship between academic history and sociology in general[32] or the relationship between ancient history and social anthropology in particular[33]), the study of the reception of individual historical events (e.g. the revolution of 1848/49[34]), and finally the relationship of different national historiographies to each other (e.g. the image of France in German historiography and the

---

29 FRIEDRICH MEINECKE: *Die Entstehung des Historismus*, Munich/Berlin (Oldenbourg) 1936 (^{3}1959; = *ibid.*: *Werke*, vol. 3).

30 HEINRICH RITTER VON SRBIK: *Geist und Geschichte vom deutschen Humanismus bis zur Gegenwart*, 2 vols., Munich (Bruckmann)/Salzburg (Müller) 1950/51.

31 KARL CHRIST: *Von Gibbon zu Rostovtzeff. Leben und Werk führender Althistoriker der Neuzeit*, Darmstadt (Wissenschaftliche Buchgesellschaft) 1972; *ibid.*: *Römische Geschichte und deutsche Geschichtswissenschaft*, Munich (Beck) 1982; *ibid.*: *Neue Profile der Alten Geschichte*, Darmstadt (Wissenschaftliche Buchgesellschaft) 1990.

32 WINFRIED SCHULZE: *Soziologie und Geschichtswissenschaft. Einführung in die Probleme der Kooperation beider Wissenschaften*, Munich (Fink) 1974.

33 WILFRIED NIPPEL: *Griechen, Barbaren und "Wilde". Alte Geschichte und Sozialanthropologie*, Frankfurt a.M. (Fischer) 1990.

34 FRANZJÖRG BAUMGART: *Die verdrängte Revolution. Darstellung und Bewertung der Revolution von 1848 in der deutschen Geschichtsschreibung vor dem Ersten Weltkrieg*, Düsseldorf (Schwann) 1976.

image of Germany in French historiography[35]). This type also comprises the history of particular myths or of a literary topos. An example is G. Krumeich's study *Jeanne d'Arc in History. Historiography - Politics - Culture*[36], even though it deals not so much with history as an academic discipline, but rather with the specific social, political and cultural functions that historical thought perceives.

(8) A separate area within the history of historiography is the analysis of historiography's social function from a scientific-historical perspective as it is perceived in different ways. There are indeed a number of works which primarily deal with this (e.g. V. Dotterweich's monograph *Heinrich von Sybel. Historical Studies with Political Intention, 1817-1861*[37]). Most of the time, however, such questions are dealt within the context of a much broader problem. Very often, such works are not limited to historians, but rather include all the academic faculties. Examples are K. Schwabe's *Science and War Ethics. German University Lecturers and the Fundamental Political Issues of the First World War*[38] as well as R. vom Bruch's *Science, Politics and Public Opinion. Scholarly Politics in Wilhelminian Germany (1890-1914)*[39].

(9) The penultimate type of work within the history of historiography concerns the subject area of 'history of historiography as social history', or rather the historians' social history. Such questions have not yet been analyzed satisfactorily. As far as the historical profession in Germany from 1850 to 1970 is concerned, the second chapter of W. Weber's *Priests of Klio*[40] is, as far as I

---

35 HEINZ-OTTO SIEBURG: *Deutschland und Frankreich in der Geschichtsschreibung des neunzehnten Jahrhunderts*, 2 vols., Wiesbaden (Steiner) 1954/58.

36 GERD KRUMEICH: *Jeanne d'Arc in der Geschichte. Historiographie - Politik – Kultur*, Sigmaringen (Thorbecke) 1989.

37 VOLKER DOTTERWEICH: *Heinrich von Sybel. Geschichtswissenschaft in politischer Absicht 1817-1861*, Göttingen (Vandenhoeck & Ruprecht) 1978.

38 KLAUS SCHWABE: *Wissenschaft und Kriegsmoral. Die deutschen Hochschullehrer und die politischen Grundfragen des Ersten Weltkrieges*, Göttingen (Musterschmidt) 1969.

39 RÜDIGER VOM BRUCH: *Wissenschaft, Politik und öffentliche Meinung. Gelehrtenpolitik im Wilhelminischen Deutschland (1890-1914)*, Husum (Matthiesen) 1980.

40 WOLFGANG WEBER: *Priester der Klio. Historisch-sozialwissenschaftliche Studien zur Herkunft und Karriere deutscher Historiker und zur Geschichte der Geschichtswissenschaft 1800-1970*, Frankfurt a.M. (Lang) 1985.

can see, the most comprehensive investigation from a systematic point of view.

(10) The final independent type of the history of historiography is the attempt to capture the development of the discipline within the history of its meta-theoretical reflection.[41] One could view the history of the subject as merely a special case of the "problem histories" as characterized above (7), although that would, in my opinion, not be exhaustive. Precisely because meta-theoretical reflection upon scientific practice is distinct from the practice itself, precisely because it is often characterized by a utopian surplus over the normality of this practice, the history of the discipline opens up possibilities of reconstruction of past realities of a professionally structured history. In particular, it can point out the missed possibilities and mention them as such.

2. The Functions of the History of Historiography

As a rule, the history of historiography serves as an ascertainment of scientific standards, or, often related to the former in content, as an ascertainment of ideological position. That is, apart from those cases where the presentation of the history of the subject merely serves particular educational purposes[42], the history of historiography, more or less consciously, refers to current scientific practice.

What do such references look like? What are the associated intentions?

In the main, we can distinguish two main functions: (1) an affirmative function and (2) a critical function.

(1) The affirmation of the official historical ideology is an important, if not the most important aspect of historical reconstruction. An example would be the academic activities of the so-called real socialism as it had developed in the former GDR. The affirmative element is influential in many publications that purport to be outside of the ideological bias. One example of many

---

41 See the surveys by HORST WALTER BLANKE ET AL.: „Historik als akademische Praxis. Eine Dokumentation der geschichtstheoretischen Vorlesungen an deutschsprachigen Universitäten von 1750 bis 1900", *Dilthey-Jahrbuch für Geschichte und Philosophie der Geisteswissenschaften*, 1 (1983), pp. 182-255; *ibid.*: „Theory of History in Historical Lectures. The German Tradition of *Historik*, 1750-1900", *History and Theory*, 23 (1984), pp. 331-56.

42 To give a harmless example: C. W. CERAM [*i.e.* KURT W. MAREK]: *Götter, Gräber und Gelehrte. Roman der Archäologie*, Hamburg (Rowohlt) 1949.

would be L. Ranke's obituary of Gervinus[43], which was written for the sole purpose of leaving behind the political ideals that Gervinus had fought for and thus to legitimize the *real*-political status quo ideologically. The affirmative aspect is also dominant in the works of A. H. Horawitz; in his essay *National Historiography in the Sixteenth Century*[44] the recent *kleindeutsch* foundation of the empire is placed in a venerable tradition with reference to some humanist historiographers - it thus appears as the redemption of a century-old legacy. Similarly, some National Socialists attempted to place Nazi racial politics into a supposedly respectable line of tradition by referring to some anti-Semitic remarks by H. von Treitschke[45]. In retrospect, such remarks on the history of historiography often seem rather odd; the affirmative intention, however, does not necessarily have to be drawn up as in the works mentioned above, nor even as in Below's overview *German Historiography from the Wars of Liberation to the Present Day*[46], where everything is geared towards one single tradition. Below's history of historiography is essentially a political polemic: he campaigns against liberalism, against the ideas of the Enlightenment, against the institutionalization of sociology as an independent discipline, and instead advocates a state-centric view of history and neoromantic thought; Below thus identifies the positions he himself passionately defended with those that would have proved themselves from a scientific point of view. The history of the discipline thus appears, as it were, in a Darwinian sense as the *survival of the fittest*; the historiographico-historical "derivation", i.e. the traditional insurance of a scientific and political position which has to be held on to, and the systematic as well as paradigmatic explication of that position, go hand in hand and mutually substantiate each other[47]. Below's history of historiography had a polarizing effect. This is in

43 LEOPOLD VON RANKE: „Georg Gottfried Gervinus", *Historische Zeitschrift*, 27 (1872), pp. 134-46.

44 ADALBERT HEINRICH HORAWITZ: „Nationale Geschichtschreibung im sechzehnten Jahrhundert", *Historische Zeitschrift*, 25 (1871), pp. 66-101.

45 WILHELM GRAU: „Heinrich Treitschke und die Juden", *Die Zeitwende*, 11 (1934), pp. 82ff.; WILHELM BAUER: „Treitschke und die Juden", *Weltkampf*, 1944, pp. 68-77.

46 GEORG VON BELOW: *Die deutsche Geschichtschreibung von den Befreiungskriegen bis zu unseren Tagen. Geschichtsschreibung und Geschichtsauffassung*, Munich/Berlin (Oldenbourg) ^{2}1924.

47 See in this context also: GEORG VON BELOW: *Historische Encyclopädie (Einführung in das Studium der Geschichte)*, transcript of B,'s lecture in Tübingen WS

contrast to G. Wolf's treatise *Dietrich Schäfer and Hans Delbrück / National Goals of German Historiography since the French Revolution*[48], which was published towards the end of World War I. It is the subjectively honest as well as, in subject matter and objective, failed attempt to pronounce as irrelevant the immense political differences within the narrower academic discipline by developing common grounds. He did this at a time when the consensus amongst German historians as to the question of the German war aims had long been broken.

It seems that a fundamentally sceptical outlook towards the idea of affirmation is essential; and indeed, a certain critical rebelliousness does seem to me to be an indispensable part of a contemporary history of the subject. Any theoretical position however requires positive traditions if it is to survive in the long run. And indeed, apart from the criticism of traditions that are now questionable the dominating effort is to show that historians that had fallen into oblivion are actually forerunners of the conception of history that is exclusively claimed to be progressive. This is true even for the essays in Wehler's *German Historians*[49] and especially for the account on O. Hintze[50]. Kocka's anthology *Max Weber, the Historian*[51] can also be read in this sense.

(2) The exact opposite of the concept of affirmation is the effort to write the history of historiography with the intention to criticize ideological principles: the aim here is to critically overthrow established but now questionable world views and political implications. This is the intention of the late-Stalinist historian W. Berthold in his book "... *to starve and to obey*"[52], where

---

1902/03 by Fritz WEIZSÄCKER (Library of the University Tübingen, Handschrift Mh II 427).

48 GUSTAV WOLF: *Dietrich Schäfer und Hans Delbrück / Nationale Ziele der deutschen Geschichtschreibung seit der französischen Revolution*, Gotha (Perthes) 1918.

49 HANS-ULRICH WEHLER (Ed.): *Deutsche Historiker*, 9 vols., Göttingen (Vandenhoeck & Ruprecht) 1971-82.

50 JÜRGEN KOCKA: „Otto Hintze“, in: WEHLER 1972 (no. 49), vol. 3, pp. 41-64.

51 *Ibid.* (Ed.): *Max Weber, der Historiker*, Göttingen (Vandenhoeck & Ruprecht) 1986.

52 WERNER BERTHOLD: *"... großhungern und gehorchen." Zur Entstehung und politischen Funktion der Geschichtsideologie des westdeutschen Imperialismus untersucht am Beispiel von Gerhard Ritter und Friedrich Meinecke*, Berlin (GDR) (Rütten & Loening) 1960.

he mercilessly criticizes the political role of G. Ritter: Ritter as an ideologue of a revanchist NATO militarism.

The critical function of the history of historiography can of course be perceived in very different ways: (a) as the explicit criticism of traditional standards, i.e. the destruction of a particular tradition that is regarded as dubious and outdated, and (b) the (re)discovery of actual or supposed outsiders, and the recognition of forgotten forerunners of ones own position.

(a) The exposition and destruction of bourgeois history was for a long time the most important task of the history of historiography in the GDR. The above mentioned work by Berthold is just one of many examples. Its West German counterpart is I. Geiss' essay *A critical Retrospective View of Friedrich Meinecke*[53]. While Geiss' essay is a reckoning with Meinecke (his intellectual history is dismissed as historicizing shamanism, and his role as a political and cultural guide and the associated social claim to leadership is negated), who used caricature as a stylistic device, G. G. Iggers' main piece of work *The German Conception of History. The National Tradition of Historical Thought from Herder to the Present*[54] is phrased in a much more moderate way while it is no less critical. Iggers' work should be regarded as the best analysis of historical studies in Germany to date; it is the fiercest criticism of historicism within the framework of a general account. While Iggers did not produce an exhaustive history of historical practice within historicism, he did deal with three nonetheless central questions: the theory of the state, the philosophy of values and the theory of historical knowledge.

(b) The attempt to substantiate a non-conformist theoretical position by appeal to outsiders that were marginalized or even excluded from the academic community could be regarded as a special form of argumentation against the received tradition. At first sight this type of argument seems follow entirely along traditional lines, analogous to the concept of affirmation as developed above (1) - after all, the argument involves an affirmation of the

53 IMANUEL GEISS: „Kritischer Rückblick auf Friedrich Meinecke“, *Das Argument*, no. 70 (1972), pp. 22-36; cf. MANFRED ASENDORF (Ed.): *Aus der Aufklärung in die permanente Restauration. Geschichtswissenschaft in Deutschland*, Hamburg (Hoffmann & Campe) 1974; *ibid.*: *Geschichte und Parteilichkeit. Historisches Bewußtsein in Deutschland*, Berlin/W. (Verlag für Ausbildung und Studium [Elefanten Press]) 1984.

54 GEORG G. IGGERS: *Deutsche Geschichtswissenschaft. Eine Kritik der traditionellen Geschichtsauffassung von Herder bis zur Gegenwart*, Munich (Deutscher Taschenbuch Verlag) ^{2}1972 (reprinted: Vienna (Böhlau) *et al.* 1997).

positions of these "heretics" -, this re-affirmation, however, always takes place in opposition to the established positions. The historians' portraits in Wehler's anthology *Historical Social Science and Historiography. Studies on the Tasks and Traditions of German Historical Studies*[55] fulfill these functions as much as many of the articles in his *German Historians*[56]. The discussion about the scientific achievement of E. Kehr (in particular about his conception of the primacy of home affairs as opposed to Ranke's primacy of foreign politics), Hintze and M. Weber[57] have played an important role for the reorientation of history as studied in West Germany.

(3) Thirdly, the history of historiography is sometimes seen as having an exemplary function - as being empirical illustrative material for theoretical reflection. The contributions in the six-volume *Theory of History*[58] carry out this function; J. Rüsen's essay *The Historian as a "Supporter of Destiny". Georg Gottfried Gervinus and the Concept of Objective Bias in German Historicism*[59] is an attempt to resolve the fundamentally tense relationship

55 HANS-ULRICH WEHLER: *Historische Sozialwissenschaft und Geschichtsschreibung. Studien zu Aufgaben und Traditionen deutscher Geschichtswissenschaft*, Göttingen (Vandenhoeck & Ruprecht) 1980, pp. 227ff. Cf. HANS SCHLEIER: *Die bürgerliche deutsche Geschichtsschreibung der Weimarer Republik. I. Strömungen - Konzeptionen - Institutionen. II. Die linksliberalen Historiker*, Berlin/GDR (Akademie Verlag) 1975, pp. 257ff.

56 Cf. footnote no. 49.

57 At first JÜRGEN KOCKA: „Karl Marx und Max Weber. Ein methodologischer Vergleich", *Zeitschrift für die gesamte Staatswissenschaft*, 122 (1966), pp. 328-57; cf. *ibid.*: *Sozialgeschichte. Begriff - Entwicklung - Probleme*, Göttingen (Vandenhoeck & Ruprecht) 1977 (^{2}1986).

58 *Theorie der Geschichte. Beiträge zur Historik*, 6 vols., Munich (Deutscher Taschenbuch Verlag) 1977-90. Vol. 1: REINHART KOSELLECK *et al.* (Eds.): *Objektivität und Parteilichkeit in der Geschichtswissenschaft*, 1977; vol. 2: KARL-GEORG FABER/CHRISTIAN MEIER (Eds.): *Historische Prozesse*, 1978; vol. 3: JÜRGEN KOCKA/THOMAS NIPPERDEY (Eds.): *Theorie und Erzählung in der Geschichte*, 1979; vol. 4: REINHART KOSELLECK *et al.* (Eds.): *Formen der Geschichtsschreibung*, 1982; vol. 5: CHRISTIAN MEIER/JÖRN RÜSEN (Eds.): *Historische Methode*, 1988; vol. 6: KARL ACHAM/WINFRIED SCHULZE (Eds.): *Teil und Ganzes. Zum Verhältnis von Einzel- und Gesamtanalyse in Geschichts- und Sozialwissenschaften*, 1990; hence cited as: *TG*.

59 JÖRN RÜSEN: „Der Historiker als 'Parteimann des Schicksals'. Georg Gottfried Gervinus und das Konzept der objektiven Parteilichkeit im deutschen Historismus", in: *TG* I, pp. 77-124 [reprinted in: *ibid.*: *Konfigurationen des Hi-*

between academic objectivity and political bias using Gervinus' historiography (and his theoretical reflections in *Essential Features of Historics*).

In the following section (II) we will take a more detailed look at this question.

II. Between Criticism and Creation of Tradition: History of Historiography and its Conception of Itself as a Reflection upon Fundamental Theoretical Problems

Since the late 1960's there has been a bitter theoretical debate that called traditional axioms into question. According to the controversial interpretation of some of those involved, the debate accompanied and in part helped to establish the paradigm shift from 'historicism' to 'historical social science'[60].

The discussions, which were supported by the Reimers-Foundation in Bad Homburg, created a new dimension of theoretical debate. Following a suggestion by Schieder and R. Wittram, between 1975 and 1988 a group of researchers met for six conferences in order to discuss such central questions of history as the relationship between objectivity and party bias and the significance of historical processes[61]. The aim was not explicitly to develop a comprehensively and systematically laid out science of history but rather to „set different and mutually informally complementing focal points within the wide subject area and the different levels of historical theory". The results of these colloquia are published in the six-volume *Theory of History. Contributions to Historical Studies*.

(1) Despite its heterogeneity regarding most areas the discussion group of the Reimers circle was marked by relative uniformity in some aspects: There was agreement concerning the most important problems and also concerning the general direction in which their solutions were to be sought. To mention just one example: with regard to the problem of historical objectivity the research group was in agreement that (methodologically controlled) objectiv-

storismus. Studien zur deutschen Wissenschaftskultur, Frankfurt a.M. (Suhrkamp) 1993, pp. 157-206].

60 See BLANKE (1991, no. 2, pp. 673ff.) citing further literature.

61 Cf. JÖRN RÜSEN: „Forschungsprojekt *Theorie der Geschichte*", *Jahrbuch der historischen Forschung*, 2 (1975), pp. 148f.

ity and (mostly politically motivated) bias did not in principle exclude each other[62]. There was no consensus about how objectivity and bias were to be related to each other in such a way that the need for orientation (as a result of an interested participation in current events) would be recognized as legitimate and important but at the same time constrained by methodology.

The group did not try to conceal the fact that no unanimous position was reached, but rather this became a focus of the discussion: The *Contributions to Historical Studies* contains either a separate category called *Discussion and Criticism*[63] or various critical opinions about some of the published essays; K.-G. Faber for instance questioned the justification of the Rüsenian Gervinus interpretation and criticized it as being de-Zionist[64].

(a) The volume's contributions can be divided into three different types: strictly systematic discussions, historical stock-taking of the discipline and case analysis, mostly gathered from the history of historiography. What is the function of the contributions relating to the history of historiography that make up about a third of the entire volume? What do they achieve that strictly systematic contributions cannot achieve?

The fact that this cannot be stated precisely is the immediate result of the composition of the group, to be precise: it is due to the fact that some of the people that reinforced the core of about 15 historians, specialists and those with a general interest, did not seriously involve themselves with the questions that were set. For the second volume, Chr. Meier drew up a programme on *Questions and Theses towards a Theory of Historical Processes* (which was sent to all conference participants)[65]. He supplemented the programme with a case analysis using Herodotus' and Thukydides' historiographies in

62 See REINHART KOSELLECK: „Standortbindung und Zeitlichkeit. Ein Beitrag zur historiographischen Erschließung der geschichtlichen Welt“, in: *TG* I, pp. 17-46 [reprinted in: *ibid.*: *Vergangene Zukunft. Zur Semantik geschichtlicher Zeiten*, Frankfurt a.M. (Suhrkamp) 1979, pp. 176-207], p. 27; WOLFGANG J. MOMMSEN: „Der perspektivische Charakter historischer Aussagen und das Problem von Parteilichkeit und Objektivität historischer Erkenntnis", in: *TG* I, pp. 441-68, here p. 446.

63 See esp. *TG* III, pp.17ff („Eine Kontroverse“ [between Hans-Ulrich Wehler and Golo Mann]); *TG* IV, pp. 607ff.

64 RÜSEN 1977 (no. 59); KARL-GEORG FABER: „Gervinus oder: Das Elend der Geschichtsphilosophie. Ein Diskussionsbeitrag“, in: *TG* I, pp. 125-33.

65 CHRISTIAN MEIER: „Fragen und Thesen zu einer Theorie historischer Prozesse“, in: *TG* II, pp. 11-66.

order to show the limits and implications of the category of process[66]. At least two of the other five contributions on the history of historiography are entirely unrelated to Meier's programme: one of them investigates the artists' biographies of the Florentine humanist Vasari[67]; the other analyses the profound transformation that took place within historical thought during the step from Humanism to Enlightenment: the replacement of the classical cycle theory (Bodin) with a one-dimensional belief in progress (Fontenelle)[68]. In the one case the idea of process is used to describe the development of art during the Renaissance, i.e., the word is used in a pre-theoretical, every-day sense of the word and not even explicated using Vasari's historiography (which would have been related to the subject matter)[69], the other is a presentation of some previously published theses on literary studies[70]. R. von Thadden presented a brilliant account of Tocqueville[71] where he explicitly refers to N. Elias' concept of process (something Meier also dealt with)[72]. But even Thadden did not refer to the programme. The list could be extended.

The examples from the history of historiography have been taken from various contexts: A small number of the contributions deal with the prescientific period of historiography: classical antiquity[73], the Middle Ages[74],

66 *Ibid.*: „Prozeß und Ereignis in der griechischen Historiographie des 5. Jahrhunderts und vorher", in: *TG* II, pp. 69-97.

67 HANS BELTING: „Vasari und die Folgen. Die Geschichte der Kunst als Prozeß?", in: *TG* II, pp. 98-126.

68 JOCHEN SCHLOBACH: „Die klassisch-humanistische Zyklentheorie und ihre Anfechtung durch das Fortschrittsbewußtsein der französischen Frühaufklärung", in: *TG* II, pp. 127-42.

69 See *e.g.* BELTING (1978, no. 67, pp. 100, 112, *pass.*).

70 Cf. JOCHEN SCHLOBACH: *Zyklentheorie und Epochenmetaphorik. Studien zur bildlichen Sprache der Geschichtsreflexion in Frankreich von der Renaissance bis zur Frühaufklärung*, Munich (Fink) 1978.

71 RUDOLF VON THADDEN: „Geschichte als Prozeß im Denken von Alexis de Tocqueville", in: *TG* II, pp. 143-56.

72 *Ibid.*, p. 144. Cf. MEIER (1978, no. 65, esp. pp. 21-25, also 15 and 40, *pass.*).

73 MEIER (1978, no. 66).

74 GERT MELVILLE: „Wozu Geschichte schreiben? Stellung und Funktion der Historie im Mittelalter", in: *TG* IV, pp. 86-146; *ibid.*: „Kompilation, Fiktion und Diskurs. Aspekte zur heuristischen Methode der mittelalterlichen Geschichtsschreiber", in: *TG* V, pp. 133-53.

Humanism and early Enlightenment[75]; the majority, of course, deal with the large historiography of the nineteenth century, and only later did the history of the late Enlightenment[76] and of the 20th century[77] become the focus of attention. The German history of the subject is the focus of most of the studies, and only occasionally examples are drawn from the English and French history of the subject[78]. The discussion of the theoretical problems is dominated by modern historiography; research contributions to ancient history are an exception[79], and none of them deal with medieval studies. The discussion on Marx, Braudel, Foucault and Polanyi form a special case[80]: no doubt,

---

75 BELTING (1978, no. 67); SCHLOBACH (1978, no. 68); ECKHARD KESSLER: „Das rhetorische Modell der Historiographie", in: *TG* IV, pp. 37-85. Cf. *ibid.*: „Geschichte: Menschliche Praxis oder kritische Wissenschaft? Zur Theorie der humanistischen Geschichtsschreibung", in: *ibid.* (Ed.): *Theoretiker humanistischer Geschichtsschreibung*, Munich (Fink) 1971, pp. 7-47.

76 KOSELLECK (1977, no. 62); PETER HANNS REILL: „Das Problem des All-gemeinen und des Besonderen im geschichtlichen Denken und in den historiographischen Darstellungen des späten 18. Jahrhunderts", in: *TG* VI, pp. 141-68. - Cf. in this context: HORST WALTER BLANKE: „Die Wiederentdeckung der deutschen Aufklärungshistorie und die Begründung der Historischen Sozialwissenschaft", in: WOLFGANG PRINZ/PETER WEINGART (Eds.): *Die sog. Geisteswissenschaften: Innenansichten*, Frankfurt a.M. (Suhrkamp) 1990, pp. 105-33 [reprinted in: BLANKE/FLEISCHER 1991 (no. 3), pp. 274-95].

77 WINFRIED SCHULZE: „Der Wandel des Allgemeinen: Der Weg der deutschen Historiker nach 1945 zur Kategorie des Sozialen", in: *TG* VI, pp. 193-216. Cf. *ibid.*: *Deutsche Geschichtswissenschaft nach 1945*, Munich (Oldenbourg) 1989.

78 THADDEN 1978 (no. 71); WINFRIED SCHULZE: „Narration und Analyse. Beobachtungen zur Historiographie der Englischen Revolution", in: *TG* IV, pp. 290-319; URSULA A. J. BECHER: „Methodenkonzeption und politische Funktionalisierung der Geschichtsschreibung Frankreichs im 19. Jahrhundert", in: *TG* V, pp. 181-99; LUTZ (1982, pp. 320-52); KALLWEIT (1988, pp. 267-99).

79 CHRISTIAN MEIER: „Zum Begreifen des Notwendigen. Zu Theodor Mommsens *Römischer Geschichte*", in: *TG* IV, pp. 201-44; WILFRIED NIPPEL: „Sozialanthropologie und Alte Geschichte", in: *TG* V, pp. 300-18. Cf. *ibid.*: *Griechen, Barbaren und „Wilde". Alte Geschichte und Sozialanthropologie*, Frankfurt a.M. (Fischer) 1990.

80 HEINZ-DIETER KITTSTEINER: „Objektivität und Totalität. Vier Thesen zur Geschichtstheorie von Karl Marx", in: *TG* I, pp. 159-70; HELMUT FLEISCHER: „Zur Analytik des Geschichtsprozesses bei Marx", in: *TG* II, pp. 157-85 (cf. *ibid.*: *Marxismus und Geschichte*, Frankfurt a.M. (Suhrkamp) 1969); HEINRICH LUTZ:

these important historical thinkers represent a counter-model to the „classical writers“ writing about German history.

(b) A clear shift of examples from the history of historiography occurred during the course of the individual conferences. The works on the history of historiography in the first volume deal with the objectivity/bias problem in Ranke, Gervinus, Sybel and Treitschke as well as Marx. Ranke on the one hand and Sybel/Treitschke on the other are appropriately introduced and discussed as representatives of two different movements of historiography (as the „objectivist“ and „subjectivist“ variant respectively). W.J. Mommsen critically examines Sybel's and Treitschke's position, calling it a "systematic crossing of borders“ and "uncritical dogmatism“[81]; nonetheless it is not Mommsen's objective to defame these two great historians but to illustrate a fundamental problem that is inherent in any historiography[82]. Rüsen's account of Gervinus also takes up German academic history's conception of itself: Gervinus, who occupied the role of an outsider in the nineteenth century while sharing several fundamental assumptions with his contemporaries, is the subject of a special treatise because the analysis of his work enables the development of structural properties of (not merely) historistic historical thought: Essentially Rüsen's objective is "a modification of historicism that is contemporary today“[83].

Rüsen has already provoked a programmatic criticism by Faber for whom it was not clear how Rüsen distinguished between „interpretation, idealized forward projection and criticism of the interpreted“; he thought it questionable that historiographic-historical reconstruction, meta-theoretical reflection and the systematic foundation of a scientific paradigm could be related to each other this closely[84]. The objective was essentially to give the historical social science a theoretical underpinning (at least that is how I understand

„Braudels *La Mediterranèe*. Zur Problematik eines Modellanspruchs“, in: *TG* IV, pp. 320-52; HILMAR KALLWEIT: „Archäologie des historischen Wissens. Zur Geschichtsschreibung Michel Foucaults“, in: *TG* V, pp. 267-99; NIPPEL 1988 (no. 79), pp. 303-9.

81 *E.g.* WOLFGANG J. MOMMSEN: „Objektivität und Parteilichkeit im historiographischen Werk Sybels und Treitschkes“, in: *TG* I, pp. 134-58, esp. pp. 140f., 145; cf. also pp. 138, 156, 158.

82 *Ibid.*, p. 158; cf. MOMMSEN (1977, no. 62).

83 RÜSEN (1977, no. 59, esp. pp. 84, 120ff.).

84 FABER (1977, no. 64, p. 127 [citation] and p. 133).

Rüsen's demand for a "contemporary" modification of historicism)[85]; in this context, the most important traditional strands of the subject were critically examined. The historical social science is the transformation of historicism: it is based upon it; in some respects, it represents a partial modification and expansion, and in others, of course, an explicit criticism of historicism. Thus the old opposition of understanding and explaining, which was one of the axioms of classic historicism, is dissolved and now "understanding" and "explaining" are interpreted as mutually fruitful research strategies[86].

The first volumes of *Theory of History* stressed the critical analysis of the great historians of classical historicism. Those however that were excluded from the mainstream of the subject (the so-called outsiders) received a very positive review in the sense of a belated reception of formerly missed chances. This form of traditional insurance gained more and more acceptance and was then no longer rejected as heretical (as it was still the case during the Lamprecht-dispute[87]), rather it was accepted as a serious interpretation. Superficial apologia for historicism, however, are entirely absent from the first few volumes. (Critical comments on contemporary criticisms of historicism are expressed only in the later volumes - more than ten years after the establishment of the new paradigm[88].) This type of traditional insurance is in effect a creation of tradition; new heroes are discovered and built up systematically: Max Weber has long been established as a new identity figure[89].

This new type of history of historiography is reminiscent of forgotten traditions; for example, it discovers early predecessors of a modern history of

85 Explicitly in JÖRN RÜSEN: *Für eine erneuerte Historik. Studien zur Theorie der Geschichtswissenschaft*, Stuttgart 1976, p. 5, *pass.* - Cf. KOCKA (1977, ^{2}1986, no. 57); WEHLER (1980, no. 55).

86 WOLFGANG J. MOMMSEN: „Wandlungen im Bedeutungsgehalt der Kategorie des 'Verstehens'", in: *TG* V, pp. 200-26, esp. p. 226.

87 For more details, see HORST WALTER BLANKE: „Selbstreflexion im Umbruch. Historiographiegeschichte bei Karl Lamprecht und seinen Schülern", in: *ibid.* (Ed.): *Transformation des Historismus. Wissenschaftsorganisation und Bildungspolitik vor dem Ersten Weltkrieg. Interpretationen und Dokumente*, Waltrop (Spenner) 1994, pp. 112-53; BLANKE (1991 no. 2, pp. 439-74).

88 ULRICH MUHLACK: „Zum 'Verstehen' im frühen Historismus. Ein Diskussionsbeitrag", in: *TG* V, pp. 227-32. Cf. *ibid.*: „Leopold von Ranke", in: NOTKER HAMMERSTEIN (Ed.): *Deutsche Geschichtswissenschaft um 1900*, Stuttgart (Steiner) 1988, pp. 11-36.

89 See *e.g.* MOMMSEN (1988, no. 86, p. 209); cf. KOCKA (1986, no. 51).

everyday life as early as in the Enlightenment[90]. One's conception of oneself is critically examined - like when the uncomfortable truth is pointed out that social history is not a new invention of the post-war period but rather that is has its roots in a decidedly National Socialist interpretation of history[91].

(2) It remains to deal with the predominant texts. The examples I will use are Rüsen's *The Four Types of Historical Narration*[92] and R. Koselleck's *Change of Experience and Method. A Historico-Anthropological Outline*[93].

(a) After publishing his essays *Historiography as a Theoretical Problem of History. Outline of the Historical Background of the Current Discussion*[94] and *Remarks on Droysen's Typology of Historiography*[95], Rüsen developed his own systematic typology of historical narrative, for which he claimed universal validity. He distinguishes four historical narrative styles, which are interdependent and synthesized in concrete historiography in different relations to each other. These are the traditional, the exemplary, the critical, and the genetic narrative[96]. According to Rüsen, these four narrative styles form a hierarchical structure in their logical sequence[97], which has its historical counterpart in the temporal model of course of events[98]. As far as the traditional, exemplary and genetic narrative styles are concerned, Rüsen was right.

---

90 REILL (1990, no. 76, p. 165).

91 Explicitly SCHULZE (1990, no. 77, p. 210), but too sharply. Cf. in this context WILLI OBERKROME: *Volksgeschichte. Methodische Innovation und völkische Ideologisierung in der deutschen Geschichtswissenschaft 1918-1945*, Göttingen (Vandenhoeck & Ruprecht) 1993.

92 JÖRN RÜSEN: „Die vier Typen des historischen Erzählens", in: *TG* IV, pp. 514-605 [reprinted in: *ibid.*: *Zeit und Sinn. Strategien historischen Denkens*, Frankfurt a.M. (Fischer) 1990, pp. 153-230, 273-83].

93 REINHART KOSELLECK: „Erfahrungswandel und Methodenwechsel. Eine historisch-anthropologische Skizze", in: *TG* V, pp. 13-61 [reprinted in: *ibid.*: *Zeitschichten. Studien zur Historik*, Frankfurt a.M. (Suhrkamp) 2000, pp. 27-77].

94 JÖRN RÜSEN: „Geschichtsschreibung als Theorieproblem. Eine Skizze zum historischen Hintergrund der gegenwärtigen Diskussion", in: *TG* IV, pp. 14-35 [reprinted in: RÜSEN (1990, no. 92, pp. 135-52, 270-73)].

95 *Ibid.*: „Bemerkungen zu Droysens Typologie der Geschichtsschreibung", in: *TG* IV, pp. 192-200 [reprinted in: RÜSEN (1993, no. 59, pp. 267-75)].

96 RÜSEN (1982, no. 92, pp. 536ff.).

97 *Ibid.*, p. 542.

98 *Ibid.*, pp. 586ff.; cf. also p. 582 on Gervinus.

The critical narrative[99], however, which had a special status in his own systematic account[100], cannot be classified as easily from an academic historical view point. In my opinion, this is at least partly due to the fact that Rüsen uses the term 'critical' in more than one sense: as a technical term for a particular form and as a term for a particular function of narration[101]; neither does he distinguish strictly between the methodical operation of source-critical analysis on the one hand[102] and the critical decomposition of passed down views of history on the other[103]. All these aspects are of course closely linked, but nonetheless it seems necessary to separate all these factors in an analytically precise way. To scientifically classify the critical narrative as located in the Enlightenment as a mere „medium of transition" from the exemplary to the genetic narrative style does not seem satisfactory[104]. While the „genetic" narrative is a historicism-specific narrative style, it is not the style of historicism alone. Empirically well informed analyses will have to prove the use of Rüsen's analysis for questions in the history of historiography.

(b) Koselleck also refers to examples from the history of historiography in his treatise *Change of Experience and Method,* in particular to Herodotus, Thukydides, Polybius, Niebuhr and Ranke, occasionally to Marx and Weber[105]. The heuristic use of his categorical differentiation of the historical term 'experience' into three types - a short-term surprise experience, a generation-specific experience and a long-term experience[106] - requires a more thorough investigation; it is doubtful however that it is a necessary condition of a good historian to belong to the defeated just because "an inexhaustible potential of knowledge lies in being defeated"[107]. There are not nearly enough sources to justify such a thesis that demands absolute validity.

---

99 *Ibid.*, pp. 551ff.

100 See esp. *ibid.*, pp. 569ff.

101 *Ibid.*, pp. 539, 563, 580.

102 *Ibid.*, pp. 569f, 577.

103 *Ibid.*, pp. 554, 570f.

104 *Ibid.*, p. 590.

105 See the references to Herodotus: KOSELLECK (1988, no. 93, pp. 17, 22, 27, 29, 30, 31, 34, 35, 39, 40); the suggestive comparison between Marx and Weber: p. 60.

106 *Ibid.*, pp. 19ff.

107 *Ibid.*, p. 60.

(3) The contributions concerning the history of historiography in the first volumes of the theory group take up and go beyond the German historians' understanding of their own subject as it is concisely portrayed in Ritter, Below, Meinecke and Srbik[108]; in contrast, they attempted to develop their own, deviant position. An examination of Iggers' work played an important role in this process, which was referred to again and again[109]. They thus succeeded in substantiating the historical social science scientifically. As a rule, however, only individual aspects were covered, which means that the substantiation of the new paradigm was sporadic rather than systematic. Neither could it be said that the history of the subject was investigated systematically within the framework of the most urgent theoretical questions. Important questions have so far not been raised at all. The Lamprecht-dispute for instance is in urgent need of a new interpretation. Most recently, even the historical social science has been critically examined, thus creating the need for further systematic research if not an entirely new general interpretation.

III. Provisional Results and Conclusion: The Rebelliousness of the History of Historiography. The Systematic Reconstruction of Scientific Paradigms: A Research Programme

The discussions at the conferences of the Reimers-Foundation in Bad Homburg have solved a number of theoretical problems to a certain extent; in the wake of these discussions and the resulting conference proceedings a number of systematic works on historical theory followed: the most ambitious undertaking is probably the three-part *Outline of Historics*, which Rüsen presented in the years 1983-89[110]; in this context, further publications should

108 See above footnotes nos. 7, 46, 29, and 30.

109 See *TG* I, pp. 64, 79, 122, 127, 135, 144, 272. - IGGERS' book: see above footnote no. 54.

110 JÖRN RÜSEN: *Historische Vernunft. Grundzüge einer Historik I: Die Grundlagen der Geschichtswissenschaft*, Göttingen (Vandenhoeck & Ruprecht) 1983; *ibid.*: *Rekonstruktion der Vergangenheit. Grundzüge ... II: Die Prinzipien der historischen Forschung*, Göttingen (Vandenhoeck & Ruprecht) 1986; *ibid.*: *Lebendige*

be mentioned as well[111]. While this did not render the theory debate superfluous, other deficits became more and more obvious: Ever since Iggers' criticism of the *German Conception of History*, which appeared for the first time in 1968, there has been no attempt at a general presentation of German history of historiography, never mind one that was Europe-wide or even world-wide. This deficit was to be dispelled with the *Historical Discourse* project that was connected to the Bielefelder Centre for Interdisciplinary Research (*ZiF*). This was originally initiated under the title: „Modern Historical Studies - Structures, Forms and Functions from an Historical Perspective "; the succinct term *Historical Discourse,* however, soon gained acceptance.

The three main terms 'structures', 'forms' and 'functions' are drawn from Rüsen's scientific matrix model[112].

The term 'structures' refers to the important conceptions (for historical thought of the modern age) of 'history' as an object of knowledge and the methodological strategies of historical research that correspond to these conceptions. These historical concepts can also be called 'theories', and these together with 'methods' form something like the cognitive structure of historical knowledge as they are manifested in different ways in the course of the development of history as a science. They should be mentioned and inter-

---

Geschichte. Grundzüge ... III: Formen und Funktionen des historischen Wissens, Göttingen (Vandenhoeck & Ruprecht) 1989.

111 JOSEF MERAN: *Theorien in der Geschichtswissenschaft. Die Diskussion über die Wissenschaftlichkeit der Geschichte*, Göttingen (Vandenhoeck & Ruprecht) 1985; HANS-JÜRGEN GOERTZ: *Umgang mit Geschichte. Eine Einführung in die Geschichtstheorie*, Reinbek bei Hamburg (Rowohlt) 1995; also: RICHARD VAN DÜLMEN (Ed.): *Das Fischer Lexikon Geschichte*, Frankfurt a.M. (Fischer) 1990; WINFRIED SCHULZE: *Einführung in die Neuere Geschichte*, Stuttgart (Ulmer [UTB]) 1987, esp. pp. 216ff.

112 The disciplinary matrix is developed by JÖRN RÜSEN (1983, no. 110, pp. 23ff.). It has been proved for the history of historical studies: *ibid.*: „Von der Aufklärung zum Historismus. Idealtypische Perspektiven eines Strukturwandels", in: BLANKE/RÜSEN (1985, no. 25, pp. 15-57). [reprinted in: RÜSEN (1993, no. 59, pp. 29-80)]. Cf. BLANKE (1991, no. 2, pp. 29-47, esp. pp. 36ff.); JÖRN RÜSEN: „Historismus als Wissenschaftsparadigma. Leistung und Grenzen eines strukturgeschichtlichen Ansatzes der Historiographiegeschichte", in: OEXLE/RÜSEN (1996, pp. 119-37).

preted within the framework of an appropriate theory-like analytic set of questions[113].

The aspect 'forms' takes into account the latest developments in the reflection on peculiarity and function of historical thought and historiography in general: ever since the pioneering works by H. White[114] and the debate about narrativity of historical knowledge the question of the historiographical form of representation as a fundamental question of the science of history and the history of historiography has been raised.

'Functions' denotes history's place in everyday life, its role in public life, and the interests that enter into its cognitive process, as a deciding factor of its particular form and change[115].

These three aspects should be investigated and demonstrated in their inner systematic coherence. In addition, there is another point of view, which is currently being discussed widely: the gender-specific differentiation of historical thought.

The „historical perspective" comprises the development of historical thought as a science and the corresponding historiographical presentations. Historical examinations of this kind primarily focus on demonstrating phases of development, and epochs should be defined and described using types accordingly. The subject matter should not just include the German historical subject, but rather the subject in general; the main focus however should be on western European (i.e. English/Scottish and French) and German development. The USA and Eastern European countries should also be included. According to the project plan, China was to serve as an example of an intercultural comparison in order to precisely develop the specifically Occidental phenomena of the modernization of historical thought.

It was clear that such an investigation had to proceed along interdisciplinary lines: experts from the following disciplines were to work together: history of historiography, history, philosophy, literary studies, scientific sociology and philosophy of science.

---

113 See the articles in *TG* I and *TG* V, also in *TG* II and *TG* VI.

114 HAYDEN WHITE: *Metahistory*, *loc. cit.*; *ibid.*: *Tropics of Discourse. Essays in Cultural Criticism*, Baltimore, Md. (John Hopkins Univ. Press) 1978; *ibid.*: *The Content of the Form. Narrative Discourse and Historical Representation*, Baltimore, Md. (John Hopkins Univ. Press) 1987.

115 See the articles in *TG* I.

Compared with the *Theory of History* project, the extensions are obvious; they are largely conceptual. In *Theory of History* examples were also taken from Ancient and Medieval history[116]; the analysis was not entirely limited to German historiography, French and English national historiography was also included[117]. These comparative examples, however, were casual references without method. A non-European perspective was missing altogether. While interdisciplinary approaches can be detected, they are also casual rather than methodical[118]. Furthermore: day-to-day references of historical thought were discussed, but again not systematically. And finally: a gender perspective was completely absent[119].

IV. Building Stones of a New History of Historiography: the *Gender* Aspect - Interdisciplinarity – References to Day-to-Day Life - European and Non-European Perspective

First of all I will present an overview (1) of the conferences and the publications that arose from it; as a second step (2) I will systematically recapitulate some peculiarities of the *Historical Discourse* project.

116 See above with footnotes nos. 66, 79 and 74.

117 See above with footnote no. 78.

118 *E.g.* KARL ACHAM: „Über Parteilichkeit und Objektivität in den Gesellschaftswissenschaften", in: *TG* I, pp. 393-424; *ibid.*: „Über den Zusammenhang von Erwartungshaltung, Wirklichkeitskonzeption und Darstellungsweise in den Sozialwissenschaften", in: *TG* IV, pp.353-414; *ibid.*: „Teil und Ganzes, Differenzierung und Homogenität. Überlegungen zu Gegenstand und Methode der Soziologie und der historischen Sozialwissenschaften", in: *TG* VI, pp. 72-107; HANS ULRICH GUMBRECHT: „'Das in vergangenen Zeiten Gewesene so gut erzählen, als ob es in der eigenen Welt wäre'. Versuch zur Anthropologie der Geschichtsschreibung", in: *TG* IV, pp. 480-513.

119 *E.g.* KARL-GEORG FABER: „Zur Instrumentalisierung historischen Wissens in der politischen Diskussion", in: *TG* I, pp. 270-316; MELVILLE (1982, no. 74); KOSELLECK (1977, no. 62).

(1) Altogether there are five volumes[120], which appeared after the conferences at the Bielefelder *ZiF*, from March 1991 to July 1997; they were published by the three historians W. Küttler, Rüsen and E. Schulin (later on their number rose to six[121]). The project started in the late eighties, „when there were still two German states, but scientific communication had already started taking place "[122]. The project's aim was to write „a new type of history of science"[123]. The focus was mostly on European historiography of the modern age - history with a claim to scientific reliability, but not it alone.

(a) The goal of the fist conference was to bring about a clarification of the general concept and to make a contribution to the group of scientists that were supposed to carry the entire project of the conference[124]. The procedure, which was already employed to a certain extent during the *Theory of History* conferences was to send the contributions to all the participants beforehand in order to facilitate discussion during the conference. (This did not of course work out like that in every case.)

The focus was decidedly theoretical: the development of systematic criteria for the modernity of academic history and the (so-called „postmodern") criticism of the modern age[125]. The discussion was to include the main ep-

---

120 WOLFGANG KÜTTLER ET AL. (Eds.): *Geschichtsdiskurs*, vol.1: *Grundlagen und Methoden der Historiographiegeschichte*, Frankfurt a.M. (Fischer) 1993; vol.2: *Anfänge modernen historischen Denkens*, Frankfurt a.M. (Fischer) 1994; vol.3: *Die Epoche der Historisierung*, Frankfurt a.M. (Fischer) 1997; vol.4: *Krisenbewußtsein, Katastrophenerfahrungen und Innovationen 1880-1945*, Frankfurt a.M. (Fischer) 1997; vol.5: *Globale Konflikte, Erinnerungsarbeit und Neuorientierungen seit 1945*, Frankfurt a.M. (Fischer) 1999; hence citated as: *GD*.

121 Co-editors of vols.4 and 5: GANGOLF HÜBINGER, JÜRGEN OSTERHAMMEL and LUTZ RAPHAEL.

122 WOLFGANG KÜTTLER ET AL.: „Vorwort der Herausgeber", in: *GD* I, 1993, pp. 11-13, here p. 13. Cf. WOLFGANG KÜTTLER ET AL.: *Historiographiegeschichte als Methodologiegeschichte* (Festschrift Ernst Engelberg), Berlin, GDR (Akademie-Verlag) 1991.

123 KÜTTLER ET AL. (1993, no. 122, p. 11).

124 Cf. BLANKE (1993, no. 1).

125 *GD* I, pp. 17-93: „Herausforderungen durch die Postmoderne". Cf. also JÖRN RÜSEN: „Postmoderne Geschichtstheorie", in: JARAUSCH *et al.* 1991 (no.1), pp. 27-48 [reprinted in: *ibid.*: *Historische Orientierung. Über die Arbeit des Ge-*

ochs within the development of modern academic history and its influential criteria within periodisation through the comparative study of the different national historiographies[126], i.e. French[127], English[128] and German[129]. And finally, the *Strategies of the History of Historiography* were to be discussed[130].

An important realization emerged from the discussion of the second set of problems, namely that it makes little sense to talk of clearly recognizable general turning-points within the modern field of history[131]. Within the individual national historiographies, too, there is a juxtaposition of entirely distinct movements; there is in any case no intellectual uniformity of individual phases, no absolute predominance of particular paradigms[132]. There was an emphasis on diversity[133], not in the sense of randomness but rather leading to a pragmatic approach towards finding solutions. The interpretational framework was determined by three poles, national-historical creation of meaning, scientific research and literary ambitions[134]. They identified five different epochs within French historiography since the late Enlightenment, and four within German historiography[135]. There was no well-founded suggestion along similar lines for British historiography. In his pioneering study, J. Osterhammel distinguished three main epochs from a Europe-wide perspec-

---

schichtsbewußtseins, sich in der Zeit zurechtzufinden, Cologne *et al.* (Böhlau) 1994, pp. 188-208].

126 *GD* I, pp. 97-188: „Epochen der Geschichtsschreibung".

127 LUTZ RAPHAEL: „Epochen der französischen Geschichtsschreibung", in: *GD* I, pp. 101-32.

128 JÜRGEN OSTERHAMMEL: „Epochen der britischen Geschichtsschreibung", in: *GD* I, pp. 157-88.

129 HANS SCHLEIER: „Epochen der deutschen Geschichtsschreibung seit der Mitte des 18. Jahrhunderts", in: *GD* I, pp. 133-56.

130 *GD* I, pp. 191-290: „Strategien der Historiographiegeschichte".

131 ERNST SCHULIN: „Vorbemerkung zum Periodisierungsproblem", in: *GD* I, pp. 97-100, here p. 99.

132 See esp. RAPHAEL (1993, no. 127, pp .101, 101f. Cf. also SCHLEIER (1993, no. 129, p. 136).

133 SCHLEIER (1993, no. 129, p. 153).

134 RAPHAEL (1993, no. 127, p. 125).

135 (1) 1750-1815; (2) 1815-1890; (3) 1890-1960, (4) 1960ff.

tive[136], with regard to their subject-matter, the different models of interpretation, the relationship between scientific rigour and the public (i.e. respective status of history in public life), the relationship to other disciplines, political instrumentalization, and finally the historians' social standing.

The suggestion that the history of historiography is the structural history of historical thought[137] was much disputed. As a kind of counter-model White's tropology as model of analysis was suggested for the history of historiography. J. Burckhardt's *Culture of the Renaissance in Italy* was used as an example to answer the question: To what extent can history be understood as text? Eventually, however, the question of applicability was passed back from literary studies to history: „It [tropology] systematically dismantles the body of texts in order to see what it is that holds it together inside. It is up to the interpreting historian (Hippokrates or Frankenstein ...), what he does with the knowledge thus gained."[138] The aim to find out about alternative forms of history of the subject was pursued in a contribution on the relationship between history of historiography and social history[139] and by reflections upon the (sociologically influenced) history of the subject.

The inclusion of a gender-specific point of view was one of the main points of the *Historical Discourse* project[140]. Among the contributions to the first conference was an enthusiastic speech for a feminist science of history

136 (1) The „long" Enlightenment: c. 1750-1860; (2) thrust of professionalization: c. 1860/70-1930; (3) pluralistic consolidation: since c. 1930; OSTERHAMMEL (1993, no. 128, pp. 168-81).

137 Esp. BLANKE (1993, no. 1).

138 IRMGARD WAGNER: „Geschichte als Text. Zur Tropologie Hayden Whites", in: *GD* I, pp. 212-32; the analysis of Burckhardt: *ibid.*, pp. 219-29; cit. p. 229. Cf. HANS-JÜRGEN LÜSEBRINK: „Tropologie, Narrativik, Diskurssemantik. Hayden White aus literaturwissenschaftlicher Sicht", in: *GD* I, pp. 355-61.

139 RÜDIGER VOM BRUCH: „Historiographiegeschichte als Sozialgeschichte. Geschichtswissenschaft und Gesellschaftswissenschaft", in: *GD* I, pp. 257-70. On the term 'historian' see HANS-JÜRGEN PANDEL: „Wer ist ein Historiker? Forschung und Lehre als Bestimmungsfaktoren in der Geschichtswissenschaft des 19. Jahrhunderts", in: *GD* I, pp. 346-54.

140 WOLFGANG KROHN: „Die Wissenschaftsgeschichte in der Wissenschaft. Zu einer Historiographie der Wissenschaftsgeschichtsschreibung", in: *GD* I, pp. 271-90.

along with the development of a separate research programme; one of the five subject areas was the criticism of the male dominated field of history[141].

This part of the proceedings, not unlike the volumes of the *Theory of History* series, contains a *Commentary* section with altogether seven, mostly short, contributions[142] as well as an *Afterword*[143]. From an ancient history scholar's point of view the focus on modern history was seen as fundamentally problematic although at the same time understandable as it followed directly from the subject's tradition; the strict divide between history during the Enlightenment and historicism was questioned vehemently[144]. Others lamented the pointed emphasis on the academic discipline and the exclusion of other forms of historical culture[145].

(b) The second conference was originally announced under the title *The Thrust of Modernization within Historical Thought.* Individual contributions and especially the discussions showed however that there is not one single thrust of modernization but rather a diverse number of *beginnings of modern* (that is scientifically drawn up) *historical thought*[146].

The contributions to the second conference can be divided into five major groups: *hypotheses of modernization*[147], *innovations of the early modern age*[148], *non-European perspectives*[149], *Paradigms of the Enlightenment*[150] and *predominant developments*[151]; an *afterword* completes the volume[152].

141 HERTA NAGL-DOCEKAL: „Für eine geschlechtergeschichtliche Perspektivierung der Historiographiegeschichte", in: *GD* I, pp. 233-56; the research programme inspired by feminism: *ibid.*, pp. 244ff.; the 5th point: *ibid.*, pp. 248ff.

142 *GD* I, pp. 293-361: „Kommentare".

143 ERNST SCHULIN: „Nach der Postmoderne", in: *GD* I, pp. 365-69.

144 WILFRIED NIPPEL: „'Geschichte' und 'Altertümer'. Zur Periodisierung in der Althistorie", in: *GD* I, pp. 307-16, esp. p. 312.

145 GEORG G. IGGERS: „Das Programm einer Strukturgeschichte des historischen Denkens. Anmerkungen zu H. W. Blanke", in: *GD* I, pp. 331-35, esp. p. 331.

146 See WOLFGANG KÜTTLER *et al.*: „Vorwort der Herausgeber", in: *GD* II, pp. 11-13, here p. 11.

147 *GD* II, pp. 17-91: „Hypothesen der Modernisierung".

148 *GD* II, pp. 95-161: „Frühneuzeitliche Innovationen".

149 *GD* II, pp. 165-215: „Außereuropäische Perspektiven".

150 *GD* II, pp. 219-91: „Paradigmen der Aufklärung".

151 *GD* II, pp. 295-377: „Übergreifende Entwicklungen".

152 WOLFGANG KÜTTLER: „Die Anfänge der Geschichtswissenschaft und die Ambivalenzen der Moderne", in: *GD* II, pp. 381-89.

The first problem area is of a fundamental nature. The topic is Foucault's concept of *archéologie*[153], the relationship between the natural sciences and the science of history in the late 18th and early 19th century[154], and finally *The Emergence of the Science of History as it is Reflected in the History of Historiography*[155]. The second problem area attended to the point of view virtually demanded by W. Nippel: the significance of antiquarianism (which had far-reaching consequences that are often underrated) for the emergence of the modern field of history[156]. The third area concerned the non-European aspect: Chinese and Islamic historical thought during the (European) early modern era[157] as well the integration of „new worlds" during European historiography in the same period[158]. The fourth problem area were case analyses,

153 HILMAR KALLWEIT: „Zur 'anthropologischen' Wende in der zweiten Hälfte des 18. Jahrhunderts - aus der Sicht des 'Archäologen' Michel Foucault", in: *GD* II, pp. 17-47. Cf. *ibid.*: „Archäologie des historischen Wissens. Zur Geschichtsschreibung Michel Foucaults", in: *TG* V, pp. 267-99.

154 PETER HANNS REILL: „Die Historisierung von Natur und Mensch. Der Zusammenhang von Naturwissenschaften und historischem Denken im Entstehungsprozeß der modernen Naturwissenschaften", in: *GD* II, pp. 48-61.

155 HORST WALTER BLANKE: „Die Entstehung der Geschichtswissenschaft im Spiegel der Historiographiegeschichte", in: *GD* II, pp. 62-66; cf. HANS SCHLEIER: „Fragen zum Wissenschaftsprozeß der modernen Geschichtswissenschaft. Kommentar zu Horst Walter Blanke", in: *GD* II, pp. 67-72.

156 HENNING WREDE: „Die Entstehung der Archäologie und das Einsetzen der neuzeitlichen Geschichtsbetrachtung", in: *GD* II, pp. 95-119; WOLFGANG WEBER: „Zur Bedeutung des Antiquarianismus für die Entwicklung der modernen Geschichtswissenschaft", in: *GD* II, pp. 120-35 (the summary p. 132); WOLFGANG ERNST: „Antiquarianismus und Modernität. Eine historiographische Verlustbilanz", in: *GD* II, pp. 136-47.

157 HELWIG SCHMIDT-GLINTZER: „Die Modernisierung des historischen Denkens im China des 16.-18. Jahrhunderts und seine Grenzen", in: *GD* II, pp. 165-79 (cf. CHANG-TZE HU: „Exemplarisches und fortschrittliches Geschichtsdenken in China. Ein Diskussionsbeitrag", in: *GD* II, pp. 180-83); ULRICH HAARMANN: „'Ein Mißgriff des Geschicks'. Muslimische und westliche Standpunkte zur Geschichte der islamischen Welt im achtzehnten Jahrhundert", in: *GD* II, pp. 184-201.

158 JÜRGEN OSTERHAMMEL: „Neue Welten in der europäischen Geschichtsschreibung (ca. 1500-1800)", in: *GD* II, pp. 202-15.

Gibbon's historiography for instance[159]. It was an attempt at a typology of the different historiographical narrative styles during the French Enlightenment[160] as well as a clarification of the role of the theory of history during the emergence of modern historical thought[161]. And finally, the fifth area reflected upon the socio-historical anchoring of historical thought in the late Enlightenment[162], again there were contributions on the gender-specific perspective[163], and reflections upon the various concepts of time during the Enlightenment and within German historicism as well[164] as upon the relationship of historical method and religious meaning during the process of rationalization[165].

The focus of the second conference was the threshold to modernity: The answer was sought by comparatively relating different countries to each other and by discussing different aspects of the emergence of modernity (scientific practice, paradigmatic literary form of representation, meta-level of history, cultural frame factors, social conditions etc.). Special aspects like the meaning of rhetoric, the development of the concept of method and the develop-

---

159 WILFRIED NIPPEL: „Gibbons 'philosophische Geschichte' und die schottische Aufklärung", in: *GD* II, pp. 219-28 (also: HARRO MÜLLER: „Einige Erzählverfahren in Edward Gibbons *The Decline and Fall of the Roman Empire*", in: *GD* II, pp. 229-38); cf. WILFRIED NIPPEL: „Der Begränder der modernen Althistorie: Edward Gibbon", in: HORST WALTER BLANKE *ET AL.* (Eds.): *Dimensionen der Historik. Geschichtstheorie, Wissenschaftsgeschichte und Geschichtskultur heute* (Festschrift Jörn Rüsen), Cologne *et al.* (Böhlau) 1998, pp. 209-20.

160 HANS-JÜRGEN LÜSEBRINK: „Subjektivität in der Geschichtsschreibung. Zur Modernisierung historiographischer Erzählweisen in der französischen Aufklärung", in: *GD* II, pp. 249-66.

161 HORST WALTER BLANKE: „Die Rolle der Historik im Entstehungsprozeß modernen historischen Denkens", in: *GD* II, pp. 282-91.

162 HANS ERICH BÖDEKER: „Die Entstehung des modernen historischen Denkens als sozialhistorischer Prozeß. Ein Essay", in: *GD* II, pp. 295-319.

163 HEIDE WUNDER: „Überlegungen zum 'Modernisierungsschub des historischen Denkens im 18. Jahrhundert' aus der Perspektive der Geschlechtergeschichte", in: *GD* II, pp. 320-32.

164 ERNST SCHULIN: „Der Zeitbegriff in der Geschichtsschreibung der Aufklärung und des deutschen Historismus", in: *GD* II, pp. 333-43.

165 JÖRN RÜSEN: „Historische Methode und religiöser Sinn. Vorüberlegungen zu einer Dialektik der Rationalisierung des historischen Denkens in der Moderne", in: *GD* II, pp. 344-77.

ment of the ancillary sciences were also touched upon. Finally, using China and the Islamic world as examples for cultural comparisons, the characteristic features of European modernity were developed, that is, questions such as what 'autochthonous' processes of modernization there were, were its boundaries lay and what the reaction to Occidental thought were. The question of what the long-term effects of Occidental modernization of historical thought were on the articulation of historical identity of non-European cultures was also discussed in this context. The main results were on the one hand the need to historicize the idea of 'scientific rigour'[166], and on the other to take the different national developments sufficiently into consideration[167].

(c) The volume that records the third conference brings together 26 contributions, which deal with the epoch when historical thought in Europe gained central importance for cultural orientation and, at the same time, got established as an academic discipline, in other words, they discussed 'historicism'[168]. The contributions are divided into seven blocks and once again alternate between detailed case analyses and longitudinal section analyses; the most important paradigm is Germany, although there are comparisons with other European national cultures.

The main topics were foundations, content, developmental phases and forms of historicism. The latter was mainly introduced as an international and interdisciplinary phenomenon, in its meta-theoretical foundations (*historics*)[169] and in its critical relation to the philosophy of history[170]. The de-

---

166 SCHLEIER (1994, no. 155, pp. 67f.).

167 See esp. NIPPEL (1994, no. 159, p. 226).

168 OTTO GERHARD OEXLE/JÖRN RÜSEN (Eds.): *Historismus in den Kulturwissenschaften. Geschichtskonzepte, historische Einschätzungen, Grundlagenprobleme*, Cologne *et al.* (Böhlau) 1996; GUNTER SCHOLTZ (Ed.): *Historismus am Ende des 20. Jahrhunderts. Eine internationale Diskussion*, Berlin (Akademie Verlag) 1997; WOLFGANG BIALAS/GÈRARD RAULET (Eds.): *Die Historismusdebatte in der Weimarer Republik*, Frankfurt a.M. *et al.* (Lang) 1996.

169 JÖRN RÜSEN: „Historik - Überlegungen zur metatheoretischen Selbstauslegung und Interpretation des historischen Denkens im Historismus (und außerhalb)", in: *GD* III, pp. 80-99.

170 WOLFGANG BIALAS: „Das Geschichtsdenken der klassischen deutschen Philosophie. Hegels Geschichtsphilosophie zwischen historischen Erfahrungsraum und utopischen Erwartungshorizont", in: *GD* III, pp. 29-44; FRIEDRICH JAEGER: Geschichtsphilosophie, Hermeneutik und Kontingenz in der Geschichte des Historismus", in: *GD* III, pp. 45-66.

velopment of historicism in Germany, which is often regarded as classical but is at the same time viewed critically, was recognized as an important stimulus for the development of historical thought, while it was also relativized within international and interdisciplinary contexts. The predominant theme was the scientification of the historical, and just like during the second conference on the beginnings of historical thought, the relationship to history during the Enlightenment was one of the topics of discussion (Schulin's essay on *The Threshold between Enlightenment and Historicism*, which is an attempt to make plausible the French revolution as a key experience, should receive particular emphasis)[171]. The second main theme, which at the same time created a connection between the academic discipline and historical culture, was the growing importance of the *Historicization of Literature and Art*, which was examined by looking at the development of drama, novel[172] and architecture[173]. Finally, the discussion was about *The Historical Construction of the Nation*, i.e. on the one hand the relationship between historiography and nationalism (using the French historian Michelet as an example)[174] and on the other the role of historical thought and the science of history, the development of national identities (as for example the Jews in Germany)[175] as well as particular forms of nationalistic expressions like the formation of myths[176]. The fourth problem area was made up of „specific topics of historicization", like the relationship between educational theory and historical theory by drawing a comparison between France and Germany[177], the reception of classical antiquity[178], the historicization of the individual in the exam-

171 ERNST SCHULIN: „Die Epochenschwelle zwischen Aufklärung und Historismus", in: *GD* III, pp. 17-26.

172 HARRO MÜLLER: „Thesen zur Geschichte des Historischen Dramas und des Historischen Romans (1773-1888)", in: *GD* III, pp. 121-31.

173 ROBERT-JAN VAN PELT: „Geschichte als Feigenblatt. Einige Überlegungen zum Verhältnis von Historismus und Architektur", in: *GD* III, pp. 132-55.

174 HANS-JÜRGEN LÜSEBRINK: „Französische Geschichtsschreibung im 19. Jahrhundert. Das Beispiel Michelet", in: *GD* III, pp. 218-26.

175 ERNST SCHULIN: „Nationalismus und jüdische Geschichtsschreibung in Deutschland", in: *GD* III, pp. 198-217.

176 WULF WÜLFING: „Mythen und Legenden", in: *GD* III, pp. 159-72.

177 FRITZ RINGER: „Bildungs- und Geschichtstheorien in Frankreich und Deutschland im 19. Jahrhundert", in: *GD* III, pp. 229-43.

178 WILFRIED NIPPEL: „Philologenstreit und Schulpolitik. Zur Kontroverse zwischen Gottfried Hermann und August Böckh", in: *GD* III, pp. 244-53. Cf. *ibid.*. (Ed.):

ple of the biography genre and the relationship to the peoples of Africa, which now, unlike during the Enlightenment, were regarded as having no history[179]. The development of the historical science was put into a wider cultural-historical context by comparing it with the historicization of other disciplines like geography[180], jurisprudence[181] and political science[182], at the same time more attention was paid to the connections with day-to-day orientations and practical socio-political problems (*Vormärz*, revolution of 1848/49 etc.). The sixth subject area was *Alternatives and Controversies of Historicization*. The focus was on forms of historicization of social thinking that are opposed or complementary to idealist historicism and on sciences that deal with society and culture like theories of structure and development, positivism, Marxism and independent approaches to cultural history[183]. In a final discussion the initial problem of the threshold between Enlightenment and historicism was taken up again and critically compared with the results of the individual discussions, particularly with regard to the relation between scientification, professionalisation and the day-to-day function of historical thought. „In place of an afterword" Iggers put forward some „modest reflections towards a synthesis", were he particularly concerned himself with F.

Über das Studium der Alten Geschichte, Munich (Deutscher Taschenbuch Verlag) 1993.

179 CHRISTOPH MARX: „Die „Geschichtslosigkeit Afrikas" und die Geschichte der deutschen Afrikaforschung im späten 19. Jahrhundert", in: *GD* III, pp. 272-81.

180 JÜRGEN OSTERHAMMEL: „Geschichte, Geographie, Geohistorie", in: *GD* III, pp. 257-71.

181 JOACHIM RÜCKERT: „Vom Umgang mit der Geschichte, juristisch und historisch", in: *GD* III, pp. 298-320.

182 GANGOLF HÜBINGER: „Wissenschaftliche Politik und Historismus", in: *GD* III, pp. 340-52.

183 WOLFGANG KÜTTLER: „Gesellschaftstheorie, Ökonomie und Geschichte. Karl Marx im gesellschaftlichen und wissenschaftsgeschichtlichen Kontext der Modernisierung des Geschichtsdenkens", in: *GD* III, pp. 377-95; HANS SCHLEIER: „Kulturgeschichte im 19. Jahrhundert. Oppositionswissenschaft, Modernisierungsgeschichte, Geistesgeschichte, spezialisierte Sammlungsbewegung", in: *GD* III, pp. 424-46 (cf. GANGOLF HÜBINGER: „Konzepte und Typen der Kulturgeschichte", in: *GD* IV, pp. 136-52).

Jaeger's and Rüsen's book on historicism, which had appeared in the meantime[184].

(d) The fourth volume of the conference proceedings contains 19 contributions; just like its three predecessors, it is an attempt to sum up an epoch's fundamental structures, forms and functions of historical thought; it deals with a phase within the history of the subject „where the history of ascent, development and success of European-American, or 'Western', historical thought and its scientification increasingly blend with the many and diverse symptoms of crisis, of loss, and of the questioning of the wider perspectives“[185]. The contributions are divided into five blocks: *Tendencies and Innovations*, *The „Mega-catastrophe of the 20th century“ and its Consequences*, *History in Art*, *Non-Western Cultures: Indigenous Traditions and European Influences*, *Previews*. The contributions to this volume, too, alternate between case analyses and longitudinal analyses; the non-European perspectives now assume an important standing. I would particularly like to refer to the well-informed and knowledgeable essay by A. Mittag on *China's Modernisation and the Transformation of Chinese Historical Thought under Western Influence*, which convincingly divides into periods the main developmental strands between 1840 and 1935[186]. Although P. Sorlin's contribution *The Cinema - a Challenge for the Historian* is situated outside the volume's narrower spectrum of subjects, it is a brilliant outline of the ways in which films can (or even should) be analyzed within the framework of a modern science of history – films are an integral contribution to history[187].

At first, the innovations of the historical discipline of the time were discussed independently of the latest political experiences, innovations that be-

184 GEORG G. IGGERS: „Historisches Denken im 19. Jahrhundert. Überlegungen zu einer Synthese“, in: *GD* III, pp. 459-70; cf. *ibid.*: „Historismus im Meinungsstreit“, in: OEXLE/RÜSEN (1996, no. 168, pp. 7-27). Cf. FRIEDRICH JAEGER/JÖRN RÜSEN: *Geschichte des Historismus. Eine Einführung*, Munich (Beck) 1992.

185 WOLFGANG KÜTTLER *et al.*: „Vorwort der Herausgeber“, in: *GD* IV, pp. 11-15, here p. 11.

186 ACHIM MITTAG: „Chinas Modernisierung und die Transformation des chinesischen Geschichtsdenkens unter westlichem Kultureinfluß“, in: *GD* IV, pp. 355-80.

187 PIERRE SORLIN: „Das Kino - eine Herausforderung für den Historiker“, in: *GD* IV, pp. 276-303; cf. *ibid.*: „Fernsehen: ein anderes Verständnis von Geschichte“, in: *GD* V, pp. 314-33.

gan before the turn of the century and carried on into the twenties with a certain momentum of its own. Especially L. Raphael's contribution made it very clear that the previous assessments of the innovations were coloured by the methodological and occasionally political debate in the seventies between traditional political history and modern social history and especially by an overestimation of the speed of innovation in the western historical sciences. The newly developed standards in the arts subjects and cultural history help to recognize the meaning and limits of the new approaches that emerged at the turn of the century and that were neglected in favour of economic and social history[188]. The second main subject area dealt with the exceptional experiences of World War I and its far-reaching consequences for historical thought and the new position of the science of history, namely Soviet rule and National Socialism. Both, the disintegration of the Soviet Union and the long-term effects of the disastrous events between 1914 and 1945 have brought about new assessments. New research about generation specific group experiences and the formation of myths gave a new standing to contemporary historical and historico-philosophical explanatory attempts. The third subject area was the most innovative of the entire conference: M. Gottlob, W. Schwentker and A. Mittag talked about the development of the historical discipline in non-western cultures: in India, Japan and China. It is interesting to note that within the sequence of historical discourse these developments were raised before the end of the second world war, at a time, that is, when they were visibly independent. Rather these issues were raised in the context of the fourth conference, at a time when the discussion was about European influences. For Japan, which, despite its willingness to learn, was self-confident and rationalist, this was a crucial period of a highly organized academic history. In China and India, on the other hand, one in upheaval and the other in chaotic conditions, only a few periods or literary forms provided any information on changing historical thought[189]. - The final discussion pointed

188 LUTZ RAPHAEL: „Die 'Neue Geschichte' - Umbrüche und Neue Wege der Geschichtsschreibung in internationaler Perspektive (1880-1940)", in: *GD* IV, pp. 51-89. Cf. *ibid.*: *Die Erben von Bloch und Febvre. 'Annales'-Geschichtsschreibung und 'nouvelle histoire' in Frankreich 1945-1980*, Stuttgart (Klett-Cotta) 1994.

189 MICHAEL GOTTLOB: „Indische Geschichtswissenschaft und Kolonialismus", in: *GD* IV, pp. 314-38; WOLFGANG SCHWENTKER: „Zwischen Weltaneignung und

to the necessity of an in-depth treatment of the turning-point of 1945, at the beginning of the next and final conference[190].

(e) The fifth conference deals with historical thought of the second half of the twentieth century; it also takes up the topics of the 1991 conference, methods, foundations and epochs of the history of historiography in general and is an attempt to give a perspective stock-taking. The first subject area deals with the experiences of catastrophe and crises[191]. The Holocaust was the central theme. It serves as paradigmatic example for the critical-historical reflections on the experiences of catastrophes in the modern age[192]. The example of Japan before and after World War II clarified the conflict-laden encounter of this experience and the reflections that followed within modern western historical thought with the traditions of historical orientation and remembering that are based on different cultural and religious foundations[193]. Another main focus was the examination of the past of state socialism, in particular Stalinism in the Soviet Union as well as the dangers that arise in this context from the current situation of its successor states, in particular Russia[194]. The second section concerns the question of the outer and inner conditions of historical thought and the historical science in the second half of the twentieth century in the context of the dominant global conflicts: the East-West conflict, or the conflict of systems, and the North-South conflict together with the associated intercultural oppositions and interconnections[195]. These discussions, which tended to be marked by extra-scientific impulses, were followed by third subject area: the introduction of important historical innovations and changes in this period, each time related to current trends and foundational discussions[196]. For disciplinary and interdisciplinary reasons the

---

Selbstdeutungszwang. Entwicklungstendenzen der Geschichtswissenschaft in Japan 1860-1945", in: *GD* IV, pp. 339-54; MITTAG (1997, no. 186).

190 See RÜDIGER VOM BRUCH: „Schlußbemerkungen", in: *GD* IV, pp. 399-407.

191 *GD* V, pp. 15-72: „Erinnerungsarbeit".

192 SAUL FRIEDLÄNDER: „Auseinandersetzung mit der Shoa: Einige Überlegungen zum Thema", in: *GD* V, pp. 15-29.

193 SHINGO SHIMADA: „Formen der Erinnerungsarbeit: Gedenken der Toten und Geschichtsdiskurs in Japan", in: *GD* V, pp. 30-45.

194 JUTTA SCHERRER: „Das postsowjetische Rußland: Erinnerungskultur oder Vergangenheitspolitik?", in: *GD* V, pp. 46-72.

195 *GD* V, pp. 75-187: „Globale Konflikte".

196 *GD* V, pp. 191-263: „Innovationen".

example chosen was historical anthropology (in particular ancient history)[197]. The contribution on historical sociology and macro-history as a dominant feature between the 1950s and 1970s was, however, missing, due to the speaker cancelling (it was not included in the proceedings either)[198]. The essay relating to the fourth subject area, on the role of historical mediation and the media, drew attention to the growing importance of this area as well as to its increasingly precarious relationship to the development of the science[199]. The subject areas of the fifth and final section were the problems of the philosophy of history in the last decades as well as generally a retrospective and pre-view on the development of historical thought since the beginning of the modern age. On the one hand this was a summing-up of the effects of the linguistic turn on the foundations of the subject of history, which was illustrated by the example of White as one of the outstanding representatives of these new developments. On the other hand, questions of historical meaning-formation in relation to the modern age in general and from the point of view of the end of the twentieth century in particular were discussed[200].

The basic aspects were to be considered according to important epochs and in international comparison, in their complexity as well as in its historical change. Apart from the central developments in Germany, France and Great Britain, the USA and later Eastern Europe as well as the encounters with non-European cultures and their own traditions were increasingly also topics of discussion. Modern historiography was not only examined from inside, as it were, but also in comparison with pre-modern epochs and cultures with re-

197 EGON FLAIG: „Historische Anthropologie und Alte Geschichte", in: *GD* V, pp. 238-63. Cf. *ibid.*: „Geschichte ist kein Text. 'Reflexive Anthropologie' am Beispiel der symbolischen Gaben im römischen Reich", in: BLANKE ET AL. (1998, no. 159, pp. 345-60).

198 Cf. ACHAM (1990, no. 118); CHRISTIAN MEIER: „Notizen zum Verhältnis von Makro- und Mikrogeschichte", in: *TG* VI, pp. 111-40; in this context also ALEXANDER VON PLATO: „Zum Stand der Oral History in Deutschland", in: JARAUSCH ET AL. (1991, no. 1, pp. 418-39).

199 *GD* V, pp. 267-333: „Vermittler und Medien". See e.g. HANS-JÜRGEN PANDEL: „Auf der Suche nach 'neuer Tradition'. Das Geschichtsbuch in der Diskussion nach 1945", in: *GD* V, pp. 267-83.

200 *GD* V, pp. 337-92: „Geschichtsphilosophie"; pp. 337-59: FRANK ANKERSMIT: „Wahrheit in Literatur und Geschichte"; pp. 360-77: JÖRN RÜSEN: „Sinnverlust und Sinnbildung im historischen Denken am Ende des Jahrhunderts"; pp. 378-92: ERNST SCHULIN: „Herrschaft und Geschichtswissenschaft".

gard to their later reception, from the point of view of gender history and other areas of culture (philosophy, literature, art). It was thus not a coincidence that the main focus during the course of the conference and in the proceedings shifted from specific questions of the development of the discipline to socio-cultural contexts from historical and current perspectives.

(2) The five volumes, which have been available for a year and a half, unite 64 authors and their 109 contributions on more than 2000 pages. (The conferences were attended by almost 100 researchers, and the individual seminars were attended on average by 30.)[201] From the beginning, the venture was shaped by the attempt to give the circle of participants the necessary continuity that allows a fruitful discussion in the long-run. Although this was successful on the whole, there are, in my opinion, individual cases where this was not the case. For some areas, for instance, it proved to be extremely difficult to find the suitable experts who were also prepared to take part in several consecutive conferences and make their own contributions. The gender perspective in particular, which had already been developed as a central theme in the conference programme, was difficult to implement in this respect; there was thus much fluctuation, which, although understandable in the individual cases, was not beneficial for the project on the whole: despite several first-rate essays on the topic of gender[202] the subject was not introduced to the extend that would have been desirable.

But let us now go through the main questions as they were developed above, i.e. let us judge the venture in its own terms, by its programme. In summary one could say that for the reasons mentioned above (a) the gender perspective did not receive its fair share of contributions. In my opinion, the aim of tackling the various problems (b) not just in a mono-disciplinary way but rather multi- or even inter-disciplinary was achieved: the individual repre-

201 By comparison: In the *Theory of History* series included 110 contributions by 59 authors on nearly 2700 pages. Only six of the scholars are present in both series of publication (KALLWEIT, KÜTTLER, MUHLACK, NIPPEL, REILL and RÜSEN); Rüsen is the person connecting the two series.

202 NAGL-DOCEKAL (1993, no. 141); WUNDER (1994, no. 163); KAREN OFFEN: „Die Geschlechterpolitik in der französischen Frauengeschichte des 19. Jahrhunderts", in: *GD* III, pp. 100-17; SUSANNE VON FALKENHAUSEN: „Geschichte als Metapher - Geschlecht als Symptom. Die Konstruktion der Nation im Bild", in: *GD* III, pp. 173-97; MARIA GREVER: „Die relative Geschichtslosigkeit der Frauen. Geschlecht und Geschichtswissenschaft", in: *GD* IV, pp. 108-23.

sentatives from literary studies[203], philosophy[204], theology[205] and jurisprudence[206] have made themselves heard and relativized some supposed truisms. Finally, the relationship between history and geography[207] and history and political science[208] for individual periods of the history of the science has been systematically resolved. With regard to the question of interdisciplinarity *Historical Discourse* went one step ahead of *Theory of History* (although some questions remain open and some were not posed at all).

This is also true for the attempt to consider not just recent history, to write the history of the subject as a history of the exploration of the modern age exclusively. The inclusion of (c) Ancient history[209] and Medieval studies[210] was indeed successful: The results were several important corrections; from this perspective, the history of the subject appears more varied and much less uni-linear. The contributions on archeology[211], art history[212] and the history

---

203 WAGNER (1993, no. 138); LÜSEBRINK (1993, no. 138); MÜLLER (1994, no. 159); LÜSEBRINK (1994, no. 160); MÜLLER (1997, no. 172); WÜLFING (1997, no. 176); MÜLLER (1999, no. 212); also LÜSEBRINK (1997, no. 174); ULRICH MUHLACK: „Geschichtsschreibung als Geschichtswissenschaft“, in: *GD* III, pp. 67-79.

204 BIALAS (1997, no. 170); JAEGER (1997, no. 170).

205 KURT NOWAK: „Historische oder dogmatische Methode? Protestantische Theologie im Jahrhundert des Historismus“, in: *GD* III, pp. 282-97; FRIEDRICH WILHELM GRAF: „Geschichte durch Übergeschichte überwinden. Antihistoristisches Geschichtsdenken in der protestantischen Theologie der 1920er Jahre“, in: *GD* IV, pp. 217-44. Cf. RÜSEN (1994, no. 165).

206 RÜCKERT (1997, no. 181); EGON FLAIG: „Volkssouveränität ohne Repräsentation. Zum *Römischen Staatsrecht* von Theodor Mommsen“, in: *GD* III, pp. 321-39.

207 OSTERHAMMEL (1997, no. 180); also OSTERHAMMEL (1994, no. 158).

208 HÜBINGER (1997, no. 182).

209 NIPPEL (1993, no. 144; 1994, no. 159; 1997, no. 178); FLAIG (1999, no. 197); cf. also MÜLLER (1994, no. 159); FLAIG (1997, no. 206).

210 DIETER BERG: „Mediävistik - eine ‘politische Wissenschaft’. Grundprobleme und Entwicklungstendenzen der deutschen mediävistischen Wissenschafts-geschichte im 19. und 20. Jahrhundert“, in: *GD* I, pp. 317-30.

211 WREDE (1994, no. 156).

212 SUSANNE VON FALKENHAUSEN: „1880-1945: Wie kommt die Geschichte ins Bild? Warum verschwindet sie daraus? Und taucht sie wieder auf? Eine Skizze“, in: *GD* IV, pp. 247-75. On the historical novel: HARRO MÜLLER: „Stalingrad und kein Ende. Zur Präsentation des Zweiten Weltkrieges in drei historischen Romanen“, in: *GD* V, pp. 297-313.

of architecture[213] also contributed to the dissolution of this essentially unreflected one-dimensionalism.

The *Theory of History* volumes were unmistakably marked by a German-centrism; it was part of the programme of the *Historical Discourse* to avoid this bias by considering a non-German, i.e. first of all (d) a European dimension: this was achieved by including the national historiographies of England[214] and France[215] and finally by attempting a Europe-wide perspective[216]. The contributions on the development of the historical subject in the United States of America[217] and Eastern Europe (Russia)[218] should also be mentioned in this context.

But that is not enough. *Historical Discourse* did not stop in Europe, it expanded into (e) a non-European dimension[219], especially with reference to Chinese historical thought[220]. In addition, the Islamic world/Arabic countries[221], Africa[222], India[223], Japan[224] and Latin America[225] were also con-

213 VAN PELT (1997, no. 173).

214 OSTERHAMMEL (1993, no. 128); ECKHARDT FUCHS: „Positivistischer Szientis-mus in vergleichender Perspektive. Zum nomothetischen Wissenschafts-verständnis in der englischen, amerikanischen und deutschen Geschichtsschreibung", in: *GD* III, pp. 396-423; also NIPPEL (1994, no. 159).

215 RAPHAEL (1993, no. 127); LÜSEBRINK (1994, no. 160; 1997, no. 174); RINGER (1997, no. 177); CHRISTIAN SIMON: „Gesellschaftsgeschichte in der ersten Hälfte des 19. Jahrhunderts. Frankreich und Deutschland", in: *GD* III, pp. 355-76; also OFFEN (1997, no. 202).

216 OSTERHAMMEL (1994, no. 158); cf. RAPHAEL (1997, no. 188).

217 MATTHIAS WAECHTER: „Die 'Progressive Historians' und die Modernisierung der amerikanischen Geschichtswissenschaft", in: *GD* IV, pp. 124-35.

218 SCHERRER (1999, no. 194).

219 Cf. JÜRGEN OSTERHAMMEL: „Vorbemerkung: Westliches Wissen und die Geschichte nichteuropäischer Zivilisationen", in: *GD* IV, pp. 307-13.

220 CHANG-TZE HU: „Modernität in China und historische Identitätskrise", in: *GD* I, pp. 85-93; SCHMIDT-GLINTZER (1994, no. 157); HU (1994, no. 157); MITTAG (1997, no. 186). Cf. HELWIG SCHMIDT-GLINTZER/ACHIM MITTAG: „'Aufklärungshistorie' in China?", in: BLANKE *et al.* (1998, no. 159, pp. 313-30); HELWIG SCHMIDT-GLINTZER: „Chinesisches Geschichtsdenken", in: Jörn RÜSEN *et al.* (Eds.): *Die Vielfalt der Kulturen* (*Erinnerung, Geschichte, Identität*, vol. 4), Frankfurt a.M. (Suhrkamp) 1998, pp. 115-44.

221 HAARMANN (1994, no. 157); ULRIKE FREITAG: „Nationale Selbstverge-wisserung und der 'Andere'. Arabische Geschichtsschreibung nach 1945", in: *GD* V, pp. 142-61.

sidered. The range of participants and contributors was certainly partly determined by chance; the above mentioned continuity problems of the research group also became noticeable. For instance, a scheduled contribution on China (subject: historical perception of non-European cultures) had to be cancelled for the third conference. But nevertheless: despite all the possible and necessary criticisms, the non-European dimension was introduced in a unique way. Even in the popular encyclopaedias of historians, a type of text, where it is easiest to follow a multi-national perspective (because the procedure would be purely additive), this factor has so far not been considered as consistently as in *Historical Discourse*[226]; in a more recent „foundational introduction" to the history of historiography the non-European aspect does not merely play no important role, it is simply ignored[227].

The subject of history is not merely characterized by the fact that it is a academic specialization with its own particular methods, but also by being linked to (f) the public life in general. This matter, too, was taken into account; the status of history in public life was a predominant subject of discussion. The problem was already formulated as a central theme during the de-

---

222 MARX (1997, no. 179); ANDREAS ECKERT: „Historiker, 'nation building' und die Rehabilitierung der afrikanischen Vergangenheit. Aspekte der Geschichtschreibung in Afrika nach 1945", in: *GD* V, pp. 162-87; cf. also HANS-JÜRGEN LÜSEBRINK: „Zur Genese afrikanischer Geschichtsschreibung im kolonialen Kontext", in: *GD* IV, pp. 381-89.

223 GOTTLOB (1997, no. 189). Cf. MICHAEL GOTTLOB: „Auf der anderen Seite der Globalisierung. Indische Rückfragen an die westliche Geschichte", in: BLANKE ET AL. (1998, no. 159, pp. 287-300; *ibid.*, „Kommunalismus, Nationalismus, Säkularismus. Historisches Denken in Indien vor dem Problem der kulturellen Vielfalt", in: RÜSEN *et al.* (1998, no. 220, pp. 510-41).

224 SCHWENTKER (1997, no. 189).

225 JOCHEN MEISSNER: „Dependenztheorie und lateinamerikanische Geschichtsschreibung", in: *GD* V, pp. 106-41.

226 Cf. RÜDIGER VOM BRUCH/RAINER A. MÜLLER (Eds.): *Historikerlexikon. Von der Antike bis zum 20. Jahrhundert*, Munich (Beck) 1991 (^{2}2001); VOLKER REINHARDT (ed.): *Hauptwerke der Geschichtsschreibung*, Stuttgart (Kröner) 1997; THEO STAMMEN ET AL. (Eds.): *Hauptwerke der politischen Theorie*, Stuttgart (Kröner) 1997.

227 CHRISTIAN SIMON: *Historiographie. Eine Einführung*, Stuttgart (Ulmer [UTB]) 1996.

velopment of the research project[228]; in the course of the project the question took on a momentum of its own.

From the beginning, the conference sequence was intended to be (g) dominated by discussions. The idea to send out discussion papers in advance and to introduce only a thesis at the conference could not always be realized. All in all, however, the discussions turned out fruitful. Conference contributions and conference proceedings do not always coincide. Although, as is common in cases like these, the occasional essays to the presented papers are missing, the proceedings often contain important remarks in the form of developed commentary: thus casual remarks during discussion often produced independent contributions to the book.

Historical Discourse started as a (h) meta-theoretical project; the expression 'structural history of historical thought' emphasizes this aim. The aim itself however was repeatedly critically examined as is exemplified in the sceptical remark: „What does a structural history of historical thought look for: preservation of tradition or critical research?“[229] Even though not all the researchers got involved with this problem, the final result is not just history of the subject for its own sake but rather applied to the foundational problems of modern historical thought.

V. Preview

The short outline and the analysis of the five volumes *Historical Discourse* showed a clear shift of the original emphasis, which Hübinger indicated in his *afterword*: it proved to be the case that „the gain of historical knowledge ... can not be organized as linearly as the promise of the success story from the history of the Enlightenment to Historicism, to the Historical Social Science and finally to Cultural Anthropology.“[230] Dichotomies that

228 SCHLEIER (1994, no. 155); ERNST (1994, no. 156); HU (1994, no. 157).

229 LUTZ NIETHAMMER: „Die postmoderne Herausforderung. Geschichte als Gedächtnis im Zeitalter der Wissenschaft“, in: *GD* I, pp. 31-49, here p. 37. Cf. *ibid.*: *Posthistoire. Ist die Geschichte zu Ende?*, Reinbek bei Hamburg (Rowohlt) 1989.

230 GANGOLF HÜBINGER: „Nachwort zu *Geschichtsdiskurs* Bände 1-5“, in: *GD* V, pp. 395-401, cit. p. 395.

still determined the character of the theory discussion of the 1970s and 1980s were not taken up again in this form[231]; rather, during the course of the conferences „a constant expansion of subject matter towards more comprehensive questions of historical culture and its functions within the process of cultural orientation and social communication took place“[232], a fact that Hübinger interpreted as a symptom „of a considerable increase in thoughtfulness and self criticism“: „In the end we therefore have disillusionment and a new modesty with which history presents the past as an indispensable realm of experience for our present actions and for the expectations to the future. Nevertheless, this also makes high demands on methodological achievements, standards and levels of self-reflection, an understanding of the range and limits of scientific thought in the wider area of historical culture, together with demands on orientation through enlightenment, with which historical thought has to prove itself for the future.“[233]

Hübinger is right: Many of the former front positions no longer play a role; what matters is no longer the establishment and legitimization of the scientific paradigm 'Historical Social Science'; and the question of the relationship between history during the Enlightenment and Historicism is obviously no longer as important as it was ten years ago. The formulation of the questions have changed decisively.

The history of historiography is more than a mere collection of examples for history, but nonetheless, properly understood, it is always connected to it. *Historical Discourse* has circumscribed and to a certain extent outlined the direction that further research into the history of historiography can take. That this can only be realized to a certain extent is obvious. We can look forward to new works that take up these current challenges.

231 *Ibid.*, p. 396.
232 *Ibid.*, p. 397.
233 *Ibid.*, p. 401.

Chapter 14

Philosophy of History After the Philosophy of History: Toward a Cultural History with Historical-Philosophical Background

HEINZ DIETER KITTSTEINER

I. A Contested Experience
II. Mourning Hegel
III. Orientation Through "Signs of History"
IV. Philosophy of History and Cultural History

I. A Contested Experience

I do not mean to address primarily the philosophical interrogation of history after the demise of classical German philosophy of history from Kant to Hegel, nor the turn to thinking about history during the period which Herbert Schnädelbach labelled as "Philosophy of History after Hegel" in his 1974 volume. I rather mean to save the insights gained by classical philosophy of history at the turn from the 18th to the 19th century. For this philosophy of history, allegedly passed away, cannot be criticised with reference to its teleology. Hidden behind this teleology we can find a problem which has not yet been solved, the problem of the unavailability of history. Taking a look at Immanuel Kant's "Idea for a general history with a cosmopolitan intent" from 1784 sheds light on the starting point. Kant begins with the philosophical unease when looking at history that people do not act in their history "according to a commonly devised plan" like cosmopolitan citizens. Ideas such as "natural purpose" or "providence", which he introduced relying on a "teleology in practical intention", only show that we are concerned with an attempt at bringing order into the unpredictable. The specific figures of thought which were created by the philosophy of history from approximately 1780 onward are a first academic reaction to the experience that humankind, the growing master of nature, is trapped in a dynamic process of history he cannot consciously "make". Their solutions show how they underlay the objective process with "providence" or "reason", partly even in the application of physicotheology which was already declining at the end of the century. A "God" based on moral philosophy is supposed to achieve what man cannot achieve on his own: to guarantee to his history a morally beneficial end.

It is, then, fairly easy to show how Kant teleologically superforms supposed "means" in the Fourth Paragraph of the "Idea" and how he subordinates the societal "antagonism", which, of its own, could also lead to quite different consequences, to a benevolent "natural purpose". But we ought not to concern ourselves here with Kant's *answer* to this form of history, but with this form itself. For it shows that man is not the master of his own historical development. For *homo faber*, this insight must be an offence which should not be underestimated.[1]

This hurting insight is also often suppressed. Scholars who conceptualise the Enlightenment simply as a continuation of the tradition of human self-assertion dating back to the 17th century will remain blind to this genuine late 18th century insight. "In modern history, better, in the history of modern humankind, man tries everywhere and every time to bring himself as the centre and the means into a position of dominance out of himself, and this means to promote his security."[2] He who argues this way intercepts, following Nietzsche's underestimation of the 18th century, the innovations brought about in historical thought in that period. It is not man who is "centre and means" in the history of modern "humankind", but, quite to the contrary, he must be content with becoming an object of a subject of "history itself" processing above him. However, he has libidinously filled this subject; it is sup-

1 IMMANUEL KANT: *Idee zu einer allgemeinen Geschichte in weltbürgerlicher Absicht*, Akademie-Ausgabe, Berlin (Walter de Gruyter) 1902ff., in the following cited as AA vol. VIII, pp. 16-31. – Cf. for the whole problem: H. D. KITTSTEINER: *Listen der Vernunft. Motive geschichtsphilosophischen Denkens*, Frankfurt a.M. (Fischer) 1998.

2 MARTIN HEIDEGGER: *Nietzsche: Der europäische Nihilismus*, Gesamtausgabe Abt. II, Bd. 48, Frankfurt a.M. (Vittorio Klastermann) 1986, p. 185.

posed to help humankind to realise what they cannot create by their own conscious actions. With Hegel the history of philosophy loses its rather hypothetical character with a pragmatic intent and seems to be able to become a real knowledge which makes sensible this subjection under a "ruse of reason"; Hegel offers to his listeners nothing less than a dynamic theodicy.[3] Kant makes no such high demands; in fact, *his* philosophy of history is nothing but an auxiliary for morality – to not let it despair at the world.

Thus teleology only overlies the experience of a process which moves beyond human intentions, even if it results from human actions. Kant has nicely captured this basic constellation – the projection of human aims onto history combined at the same time with the inability to directly "make" it:

> Since from her, or rather (as highest wisdom is required to attain this goal) from *providence* alone can we expect a success which aims at the whole and from there at the parts, because men, on the contrary, base their *concepts* only on the parts and remain with them and can only extend their ideas but not their influence onto the whole as such which is too great for them; mainly because they would, as their concepts contradict one another, probably not unite voluntarily to achieve such a success.[4]

From experience we know that ever since he thus wrote nothing has changed this basic constellation.

II. Mourning Hegel

There is a tendency in the recently re-awakened interest in the philosophy of history to go back behind Hegel, to Kant.[5] In *Time and Narrative*, Paul Ricœur has outlined this tendency as follows: It is precisely the grief over the

3 G.W.F. HEGEL: *Die Vernunft in der Geschichte*, ed. by J. Hoffmeister, Hamburg (Meiner Verlag) 1955, p. 48.

4 IMMANUEL KANT: *Über den Gemeinspruch: Das mag in der Theorie richtig sein, taugt aber nicht für die Praxis*, AA vol. VIII, p. 310.

5 HERTA NAGL-DOCEKAL: "Ist Geschichtsphilosophie heute noch möglich?", in: HERTA NAGL-DOCEKAL (Ed.): *Der Sinn des Historischen. Geschichtsphilosophische Debatten*, Frankfurt a.M. (Fischer)1996, pp. 7-63.

loss of absolute knowledge which leads us back to Kant. And we had to have first followed Hegel to be able to go this way back. "For which student of Hegel who has not himself be seduced once, like ourselves, by the power of his thinking does not feel the renunciation of Hegel as a wound which, different from those of the absolute spirit, does not heal? We wish this student, if he does not want to fall into weak yearning, the courage to mourn."[6] What is meant by mourning? Mourning in this respect is an "intrapsychological process following the loss of a reference object which enables the subject to let go of it progressively." Freud specifies this process as follows: "Every single one of these memories and expectations by which libido was linked to the object is cancelled, overvalued and used for untying libido."[7] In our case this means nothing but a critique of the different categories of the philosophy of history. They must be interrogated for the hopes they aroused, for the disappointments they caused, and finally for how to "let go of them progressively" – thus to gain a critical relation to them.[8] A partial reading of chapter 6 of the third volume of *Time and Narrative* will lead us toward addressing this exercise.

Ricœur lets the "Hegelian temptation" begin with Hegel's replacement of the former "universal history" by "world history" and his philosophical imposition with which he confronts his students. After browsing through the "forms of historiography" with a rather pedagogical attitude, he goes on to the "concept of the philosophy of world history": The only thought it brings with it is the simple thought of *reason*, that reason rules the world, that thus the course of world history has happened.[9] For the historian, writes Ricœur, the

---

6 PAUL RICŒUR: *Zeit und Erzählung*, München (Wilhelm Fink Verlag) 1991, vol. III, p. 332 and p. 411.

7 J. LAPLANCHE, J.-B. PONTALIS: *Das Vokabular der Psychoanalyse*, Frankfurt a.M. (Suhkamp) 1975, 2 vols, vol. II, p. 512. – SIGMUND FREUD: "Trauer und Melancholie", in: *Gesammelte Werke*, Frankfurt a.M. (Fischer) 1963, vol. X, p. 430.

8 Cf. H. D. KITTSTEINER: "Kants Theorie des Geschichtszeichens. Vorläufer und Nachfahren", in: H. D. KITTSTEINER (Ed.): *Geschichtszeichen*, Weimar (Böhlau) 1999, p. 114.

9 RICŒUR, l c., vol. III, p. 314. – G. W. F. HEGEL: *Die Vernunft in der Geschichte*, l c., p. 28. – However, Hegel practically anticipates in his "reflective historiography" the later neo-Kantian procedure of "value relations" and expresses his unease about a historiography based in the last resort on contemporary political/cultural problems. Cf. H. D. KITTSTEINER: *Listen der Vernunft. Motive geschichtsphilosophischen Denkens*, l. c., p. 8.

sudden introduction of reason remains but a hypothesis – for Hegel, the philosopher, it carries out a thesis from the *Philosophy of Law*: "What is, is *reasonable* – and what is reasonable, *is*." Ricœur explores the route to the problem of theodicy in a footnote comment: Thus only he can speak who claims to have understood the role of evil in history: "As long as evil has not found its place in the grand plan of the world, the belief in Nous, in providence or the divine plan must remain in the balance." Indeed, the section on the general idea of world history ends with a historical theodicy.

> Our examination is insofar a theodicy, a justification of God, which Leibniz has still attempted metaphysically, with abstract, indefinite categories: evil in the world as such, including malice, ought to be comprehended, the thinking spirit ought to be reconciled with the Negative; and it is in world history that the whole mass of concrete evil is brought before our eyes.[10]

The thoughtful contemplation of history shall not remain with abstract final purpose, *purpose* shall be realised through its *means*. "And here we encounter the famous thesis of the *ruse of reason*." Ricœur embeds it in a more general "theory of action". The acting subject shall and must come to his justice, but:

> Everyone who does somethings achieves unwanted consequences so that his actions slip his intentions. As a rule we can record 'that in direct deed there may be rooted something greater than the deed's will and consciousness'.[11]

If we consider that this was the experience of the eyewitness generation to the French Revolution, we have gained a fixed position from which this question was first posed by Kant and Schelling.[12] History develops "unconsciously" in a literal sense: Humans are subject to a historical condition "because of which [they] have to become the cause of something they never wanted, through their own actions but against their will."[13] Even today, this relation to history has not yet stopped existing – and thus the scope of Hegel's

10 HEGEL: *id.*, p. 48.

11 RICŒUR: *Zeit und Erzählung*, Bd. III, l c., p. 318.

12 FRANK R. ANKERSMIT: "Die postmoderne 'Privatisierung' der Vergangenheit", in: NAGL-DOCEKAL (l c., p. 201).

13 J. W. SCHELLING: *System des transcendentalen Idealismus, Werke*, ed. by M. Schröter, Munich (C. H. Beck) 1927, vol. II, p. 594.

promise becomes truly visible. Ricœur summarises it regarding the stages of original and reflective history:

> For 'original' or 'reflective' history would this unintended be the last word, of course. But not for the 'ruse' of reason, which lets the unintended become precisely the intention of the world spirit.[14]

Therefore, there is not only an "unconscious" in Sigmund Freud's sense – there is also an "unconsciousness" in history – and Hegel's world spirit informs us about its purpose. The claim is outrageous. Its immediate consequence is the critique of Hegel. On the other hand, if we go back to the unintended side effects of action which no light is allegedly shed upon by a 'ruse of reason', we end up in the bright darkness of incomprehended historical "background metaphors". We will return to this problem.

"One must admit that a critique of Hegel is impossible if it is supposed to express more than the sheer disbelief in face of the decisive phrase: 'The only thought which it (philosophy) carries is but the simple thought of *reason*, that reason rules the world, that thus world history was sensible, too.' This is the philosophical creed which just enhances the ruse of reason apologetically and which the *concept of stages* projects into time." One could only leave Hegel. Ricœur sees the foundation for our contemporary thinking laid in the end of Hegelianism – be it with Kierkegaard, Feuerbach or Marx, with the German school of historiography or with Nietzsche. What is it that is impossible for us to maintain? "Things that Hegel still thought went together have in our eyes parted company: spirit in itself, development, difference which together make up for the idea of a *stage process* of *development*." According to Ricœur, Hegel wrote in moment favourable to "eurocentrism", at a time which for us has disappeared behind the experience of the 20th century: "The political suicide of Europe in the First World War, the ideological split following the Russian Revolution, and the new peripheral position of Europe after the abolition of colonial rule, as well as the unequal – and possibly as antagonistic – development the industrialised nations set against the rest of the world, all this led to death" – not only of eurocentrism, but also of Hegelian philosophy. *Difference* revolts against the *stage process*; the world spirit dismembers into purpose and means back to the *membra disjecta* of an impossible totalisation.

14 RICŒUR (*ibid.*, p. 319).

"The expression 'ruse of reason' does not even make us curious any more: it rather repels us, like the triumphant magician's trick turned out badly."[15]

The "fable of fables" cannot be written. "The end of Hegelianism means to renounce trying to decipher the highest fable." This renunciation – we cannot think *like* Hegel any more, we can only think *after* Hegel – is indeed painful. The "courage to mourn" shall now steer us back from Hegel to Kant. "Furthermore, a return to Kant is only possible after a necessary detour via Hegel. (...) Hegel (...) has taught us the patience of the idea. (...) And if we do not believe anymore that these great mediations culminate in an absolute knowledge resting in the eternal present of contemplation – it is nonetheless particularly the grief for absolute knowledge which leads us back to Kant's *idea* now forming the horizon of historical reason."[16] To be sure, an "idea" that only "extends" over the "whole" of history (cf. n.4) is something completely different from the claim of a conscious mediation between purpose and means; the renovation of theodicy is more massive than a "teleology in practical intent" which in the end makes the philosophy of history a mere auxiliary for moral action. We can – all criticism notwithstanding – speak of the "epistemic modesty" of Kantian philosophy of history and emphasise that to him teleological principles are only regulatory, not consecutive, for systemising cognition.[17] And nevertheless: the prefigurations of the 'ruse of reason' in the subordination of "means" under a "purpose" can already be found in the fourth section of the "Idea for a general history with a cosmopolitan intent" – and even the fall from grace of the philosophy of history, the overlapping of speculation and empiricism, is already indicated here:

> We see: philosophy could have its *chiliasm*; but one of whose advent its idea itself can be supportive, even if only from very far away, which is thus nothing less than effusive. It only depends on whether experience discovered something *similar to such a development of natural purpose.*[18]

---

15 RICŒUR (*id.*, pp. 329f.).

16 RICŒUR, (*id.*, p. 332 and p. 412).

17 PAULINE KLEINGELD: „Zwischen kopernikanischer Wende und großer Erzählung. Die Relevanz von Kants Geschichtsphilosophie", in: NAGL-DOCEKAL (l c., p. 185 and p. 190).

18 KANT: *Idee zu einer allgemeinen Geschichte in weltbürgerlicher Absicht*, l c., vol. VIII, p. 27.

It is this demand to experience, to discover something similar to the development of natural wit, which leads Kant to the late theory of "signs of history". The sign of history is not yet a mediation in Hegel's sense; it simply overlays a historical event – the French Revolution – with a floating, sublime *enthusiasm* of the uninvolved spectator from Königsberg.

III. Orientation Through "Signs of History"

Before we continue with all due caution on this track, we have to return to Ricœur 's narrative about the breakdown of Hegelian philosophy of history. The thinkers he mentions: Kierkegaard, Feuerbach, Marx and Nietzsche, all begin with the individual's revolt against the dominance of the general – even Nietzsche writes sometimes like a Young Hegelian who has come too late. Only Marx leaves this phalanx and later on returns, after beginning similarly, to a renewed idea of a dominant general. The foundation is already laid in the "German Ideology" – in the transformation of the dominance of the *world spirit* into the tyranny of the *world market*. It is precisely at this point that Marx, while passing through the forms of capital flow, lets himself be caught again by Hegel; of all chapters, the one on the "tendential fall of the profit rate" comes back to teleological thinking of purpose and means.[19] If we ignore this teleological overlap in Marx, what remains at first is the idea of a non-teleologically pre-secured general, of a historical process which designs itself *blindly but dynamically* into the future. Insofar even these huge ruins left by Marx with their strict sense of form – that of value form – stand crosswise to all ideas of a "post-modern" conception of history, to which history has become a huge, shapeless mass through which every historian can, so to speak, dig himself privately.[20] In other words: We cannot get rid of the world market and its power allegorising the specific by simply taking offence and turning away from it. Against this background we must ask for a critical

19 H.D. KITTSTEINER: „Zur Konstruktion der historischen Zeit bei Karl Marx", in: *Listen der Vernunft* (l c., p. 121).

20 ANKERSMIT (l c., p. 204).

treatment of all – as Lukacs once called it – historical-philosophical interpretation of signs.[21]

We gain something else from the renunciation of teleology in Marx than we gain from the renunciation of teleology in Hegel. Here, we have distorted the idea of an "absolute mediation of history and truth";[22] in Marx, what remains behind overlaying of the capitalist process by a socialist goal is precisely this process without truth. Thus the idea is destroyed to ever become the master of this process – a master's dream which both Nietzsche and Heidegger dreamt in their respective ways. After 200 years of bad experience with attempts at making history as whole more human, humanity had slowly better get used to living with an un-makeable history, without being imposted as homo faber. What is left is a need for "orientation" in this history; but to do this, we can do with more flexible horizons than it could have seemed so far.

For an attempt at rethinking Kant's theory of the "sign of history", I deem it necessary to come back to the two categories of "space of experience" (*Erfahrungsraum*) and "horizon of expectation" (*Erwartungshorizont*), which were first developed by Reinhart Koselleck and are also discussed by Paul Ricœur. In Ricœur 's reading we find a little more emphasis on the problem of the unmakeability of history, introduced via Marx, than we do in Koselleck. He expresses this himself: "The topic of dominance over history rests thus on the fundamental ignorance of this other side of thinking history (...), namely the fact that we are affected by history and *affect* ourselves by the history we make."[23] If we consider, in this context, self-orientation in history as possible nevertheless only if we can read its "signs", and if we introduce Ernst Cassirer's concept of the symbol as mediator between space of experience and horizon of expectation, we can see that a perceptive experience (*Wahrnehmungs-erlebnis*) as sensitive experience always carries a surplus of meaning which transposes the single phenomenon of perception (*Wahrnehmungsphänomen*) to a "whole of meaning (*Sinn-Ganzes*)". Space of experience and horizon of expectation create symbolic forms of world interpretation which, in turn, can be considered as transcendental preconditions of new perception. As Cassirer's treatment of Simmel shows, we would then have to deal with symbolic forms or signs which do not close off a historical horizon

21 GEORG LUKÁCS: *Die Theorie des Romans. Ein geschichtsphilosophischer Versuch über die Formen der großen Epik*, Darmstadt, Neuwied 1981, p. 137.

22 RICŒUR (l c., p. 333).

23 RICŒUR (*id*., p. 345).

once and for all but which may also be used to break up crusts again. Unilinear-teleological historical thought becomes impossible in the context of this kind of thinking. The anticipated horizons of expectation and the "signs of history" gained from them by re-projection to events or historical forms are experimentally constructed; they can criticise themselves pluralistically.

The problem with Cassirer is that he seems to have no sufficient idea about the "unconscious production" of history. The position the furthest advanced to decipher worlds of things, which are at the same time worlds of capitalist commodity production, has so far been put forward by Walter Benjamin; thus we have no reason to turn away from his thinking or to trade it for some instruments from post-modern *quincailleries.* If things wear their "surrealist" face, there is a moment of possible recognition. Now not a meaningful horizon of expectation is the precondition for a re-projection onto the contemporary space of experience, nor does perception combine to a round "symbolic form", but inside of a senseless whole, configurations appear which can be read as expressions of unconscious fears or forebodings in the face of the unmakeable. The use value in its certain form – the commodities' *design* – is somewhat censored by value character; the result is a misshapen use value which can, however, become a "sign of its time" in this misshape. Benjamin uses the word "phantasmagoria". Deciphering commodities as phantasmagorias of dreaming humans, unconsciously making their history, would be Benjamin's equivalent to Kant's "sign of history".[24] We can understand the birth of classical German philosophy of history as an emergence from the question of the sign of history; if its original sin was linked to this, undoing this original sin can only begin with the question of orientation in history.

24 Cf. for the argument which can only be abbreviated here: H. D. KITTSTEINER: *Kants Theorie des Geschichtszeichens*, l c., pp. 107-114.

IV. Philosophy of History and Cultural History

Now I am not a philosopher of history; I reconstruct its insights not as an end in itself. I strive for a new *cultural history* informed by problems posed by philosophy of history. "Cultural history" must sound not too good in the eyes of institutionalised historiography; this because it first came into being as field for outsiders, this also because – Jacob Burckhardt is the best example – it never lost contact with the philosophy of history altogether, all criticisms of Hegel notwithstanding. Institutionalised historiography, on the other hand, severed the link between itself and the philosophy of history in the course of its professionalisation during the 19th century. What appeared at first sight to be a liberation from the dialectical stretch-bed of the world spirit had to be dearly paid for, since as consequence historiography exposed itself to a merely *political spectrum* its questions' final embodiment. It descended, so to speak, from the level of the world spirit down to the level of people's spirits, and it did so eagerly. Questions for the process character of history as a whole were excluded as unscientific and thus also the insights into the subjection under an unmakeable process. Quite to the contrary: the supposed historical being-able-to-make on the political field dominated German thought in the era of the emerging nation-state – and the historians joined in enthusiastically.

Since then, a majority of historians – exceptions prove the rule – have been would-be politicians whose picture of the world changes within the value paradigms of political camps. Hayden White has aptly outlined this process:

> The 'theory' on which its scientization was ultimately based was nothing other than the ideology of the middle sectors of the social spectrum, represented by Conservatives on the one hand and Liberals on the other.[25]

This embodiment in value paradigms has been promoted to historical method in the frame of Rickert's and Weber's "value relation" (*Wertbeziehung*). No matter if they explicitly put this foundation before their work or if the reader may derive it from the tone of narration – historiography never overcame this cultural/political last embodiment of its questioning. "What becomes the object of inquiry, and how far this inquiry extends into the infini-

---

25 HAYDEN WHITE: *Metahistory. The Historical Imagination in Nineteenth-Century Europa*, Baltimore/London 1973, p. 138.

tude of causal relations is defined by the scholars and the value paradigms dominating their times."[26]

There is nothing to be brought forward against this method *prima facie*; it is seen as the foundation of solid historiography. "Objectivity" can be reached only in quotation marks, and the plurality of value relations guarantees a control of the results in academic debate. However, there is a little problem – also and especially with Max Weber. From time to time concepts appear, for example the concept of fate, which we would not expect of such a rational thinker, concepts I would like to call *background metaphors*. For something else prevails above the values. In *Science as a Vocation*, Weber rather contemporaneously, in 1919, comments on the value foundations of the opponents of the Great War:

> I do not know how to 'scientifically' decide between the value of French and Germany culture. Here, different gods dispute with each other, and for all times. It is like in the old world not yet demystified of its gods and demons. (...) And above these gods and their battle fate, but certainly not 'science', prevails.

Maybe this world was not as demystified as Weber had thought, so that he now had to search for a divine or demonic equivalent for concepts he had before, following Heinrich Rickert and Emil Lask, proudly expelled from the temple of science.[27] And what do we gain if we repulse an *emanatistic reason* to the front door but let *fate* come in again through the back door? At first sight we can see what is intended by this "fate": It is the de-teleologised, now irrational expression of the superiority of the historical process, of the unmakeability of the whole paralleling the rational typologisation of the single event.

Apparently, it is impossible not to have concepts for the "whole" of history. The reduction to the value relation cannot consequently be maintained because the form of history does not fit to it. Criticising the philosophy of history does not go unpunished. What is justly criticised as "teleology" reappears unreflected as "fate" in our backs. Max Weber is not as precise as some

26 MAX WEBER: „Die 'Objektivität' sozialwissenschaftlicher und sozialpolitischer Erkenntnis", in: *Gesammelte Aufsätze zur Wissenschaftslehre*, ed. by J. Winckelmann, Tübingen (J. C. B. Mohr) 1968, p. 184.

27 MAX WEBER: „Wissenschaft als Beruf"; and: „Roscher und Knies und die logischen Probleme der historischen Nationalökonomie", in: *Wissenschaftslehre*, l c., p. 604 and p. 15.

would want him to be. But it is disturbing that his method has been fortified as an alleged knowledge which mainly knows that philosophy of history is dogmatic and outdated. All prejudices which can be gathered against the "old German philosophy of history" are spread out, especially when contributions to these issues are only taken notice of if they appear in the domestic publications.[28] In the end, the defence against the philosophy of history is only a minor battlefield in a war which is essentially about something completely different: about the power to define what can be called "historiography" and what cannot.

To dispel at least one misunderstanding: The "philosophy of history" cannot claim a privileged knowledge; nor must we reconnect to its old answers, but it is important to rescue the problem that was – and still is – the basis for these answers. Of course, the answers must be different today. The way back from Hegel to Kant, the inclusion of Cassirer and Ricœur clearly show that a teleologically closed horizon is neither possible nor desirable for a thinking extending to the "whole" of history.[29] But if this is the case, if the horizons of expectation projected onto the whole of history (as Kant said: We can project our ideas but not our actions onto the whole; cf. n. 4); if they criticise one another, we will come to a new pluralism of value relations which is different from the pluralism of value relations of Rickert and Weber because of the scope of its concepts. Weber wanted to bring "order" into "chaos"; he concentrated on action, but he left aside the unintended side effects of action. The proposal derived from a renewed philosophy of history here aims as well at the "unintended side effects" of action as of the movement of things as Marx had envisaged – but it does not claim to be able to bring them *together into a conception* as if it were the world spirit (cf. n. 14).

These renewed historical-philosophical drafts must face rational evaluation, of course. Already Max Weber did not rule out the possibility that concepts based on different value perspectives may partially overlap in their empirical findings. That he focuses on the battle of cultural significances and argues against a "middle line" has nothing to do with this but is due to his dispute with Schmoller.[30] If we do not address this problem with Weber

28 Cf. HANS-ULRICH WEHLER: „Die Hybris einer Geschichtsphilosophie", in: *Rechtshistorisches Journal,* 18 (1999). Dieter Simon, ed., Frankfurt a.M., pp. 540-547.

29 Cf. KITTSTEINER: *Geschichtszeichen,* l c., p. 107.

30 WEBER: *Wissenschaftslehre,* l c., p. 154.

anymore but with Paul Feyerabend, it will sound as follows: If falsification of theories understood as hypotheses is not optimal according to Popper's model but if a maximum of criticism can only be reached with the help of alternative theories, we should propose a pluralistic collection of theories which "consists *of a whole lot of partially overlapping theories which are compatible with the facts but incompatible with one another*."[31] The renewed concepts of a philosophy of history must find their place in this collection of theories. What they can achieve will be determined when they explore new perspective compatible with the facts.

A piece of written cultural history, which is guided by a question from the philosophy of history, this much we can conclude, will derive none of its questions from the scope of the political/cultural spectrum. It will not be conservative, liberal, socialist, ecological, feminist or body-centred. It will not be based on the post-modern affinity to difference, but again on a powerful, not-available whole which still prevails above all these differences and which calls for a new narrative. A *grand narrative* in the sense of Lyotard's critique is not necessary for this, as it can no longer be concerned with the "fable of fables". We should not speak of *totality* anymore, suggests Paul Ricœur, but of *totalisation*, not of a complete, but only of an incomplete mediation with the whole. However, we must also renew the idea of "humanity" as the subject of this narrative for his proposed "post-Hegelian Kantian style". He agrees with Kant "that every expectation must be a hope for all humanity; that humanity is a 'human-kind' (*Gattung*) only by virtue of its history; that on the other hand history exists only insofar as humanity as a whole, as a collective singular, is its subject."[32] If we let go of this subject we are confronted with the battle of differences. But as this "subject" is still subjected to a strange subject of an unavailable history, this narrative must tell us about the *condition humaine* in history. It is a history of men "who attempt to make their history and who endure the evil that derives from these attempts.[33]

---

31 HELMUT F. SPINNER: „Gegen Ohne Für Vernunft, Wissenschaft, Demokratie, etc*. Ein Versuch, Feyerabends Philosophie aus dem Geist der modernen Kunst zu verstehen", in: HANS PETER DUERR, (Ed.): *Versuchungen. Aufsätze zur Philosophie Paul Feyerabends*, vol. I, Frankfurt a.M. (Sührkamp) 1980, pp. 35-109; at p. 48.

32 RICŒUR: *Zeit und Erzählung*, l c., vol. III, p. 401 and p. 438.

33 RICŒUR (*id.*, p. 409).

List of Authors

HANS MICHAEL BAUMGARTNER was Professor of Philosophy, University of Bonn, Bonn, Germany, until his death in the year of 2000.

HELMUT BERDING is Professor of History, University of Giessen, Giessen, Germany.

HORST-WALTER BLANKE is Professor of History, University of Bielefeld, Bielefeld, Germany.

EGON FLAIG is Professor of History, Department of Classics, Ernst-Moritz-Arndt-University Greifswald, Greifswald, Germany.

DANIEL FULDA is Assistant Professor at the Institute of German Language and Literature, University of Cologne, Cologne, Germany.

HEINZ DIETER KITTSTEINER is Professor of History, Department of Cultural Studies, European University Viadrina, Frankfurt an der Oder, Germany.

PETER KOSLOWSKI is Professor of Philosophy, Vrije Universiteit Amsterdam, Amsterdam, the Netherlands.

MATTHIAS LUTZ-BACHMANN is Professor of Philosophy, University of Frankfurt am Main, Frankfurt am Main, Germany.

KARL H. METZ is Professor of History, University of Erlangen-Nuremberg, Erlangen, Germany.

HERTA NAGL-DOCEKAL is Professor of Philosophy, University of Vienna, Vienna, Austria.

PETER L. OESTERREICH is Professor of Philosophy, Augustana University, Neuendettelsau, Germany.

JOHANNES ROHBECK is Professor of Philosophy, University of Dresden, Dresden, Germany.

MARIO SIGNORE is Professor and Director of the Department of Philosophy and Social Science, University of Lecce, Lecce, Italy.

ANNETTE WITTKAU-HORGBY is Assistant Professor for the History of Science, University of Hannover, Hannover, Germany

Index of Names

Page numbers in italics refer to quotations in footnotes or references

Acham, K. *5*, *236, 248, 261*
Adorno, T. W. 176, *191*
Altvater, E. *200*
Angehrn, E. *173*
Angeli, F. *137*
Ankersmit, F. R. *114, 121, 128*, 212-216, 219, 221f., *261, 272, 275*
Apel, K.-O. *202*
Appadurai, A. *202*
Arendt, H. *207*
Aristotle *19*, 117, 119, 163, 207
Asendorf, M. *235*
Augustine *19*, 117, 159

Baader, F. v. 31-38
Bachelard, G. 216
Bacon 70
Bancroft, G. 47
Barker, E. *110*
Baudrillard, J. 204
Bauer, W. *233*
Baumgardt, D. *31*
Baumgart, F. *230*
Baumgartner, H. M. 117, *128, 151, 157, 162, 168*, 188, *192*, 220, 222
Bayertz, K. *195*
Becher, U. A. J. *240*
Beck, U. *198-202, 205, 207*, 208
Bell, D. *205*
Below, G. v. 225, 227, 233, 245
Belting, H. *239f.*
Benjamin, W. 175f., 277
Berg, D. *263*
Berg, G. *49*
Bergson, H. 215
Berkhofer, R. F. *114, 128*
Bernheim, E. 228
Bernstorff, Chr. G. v. 54
Berthold, W. 234f.
Bialas, W. *75f., 255, 263*
Bianco, F. *137*
Bismarck, 54, 108
Blanke, H. W. *120f., 128, 223ff., 229, 232, 237, 240, 242, 246, 249, 251, 253f., 261, 264f.*
Bloch, E. 185
Blumenberg, H. *115, 128, 173*
Bödeker, H. E. *120, 128, 254*
Bodin, J. 239
Boeckh, A. 61, 96
Boeder, H. *137*
Boehlich, W. *107, 110*
Bollmann, S. *191*
Bonald, L. G. A. 81
Boockmann, H. *229*
Braudel 240, *241*
Breisach, E. 226
Bresslau, H. 229
Breysig, K. 225, 227
Brocke, B. v. 227

Brockmann, J. *223*
Bruch, R. v. 231, *251, 260, 265*
Bubner, R. *142*
Burckhardt, J. 51, 59, *60*, 62, 67, *72, 75*, 77-97, 105, 150, 251, 278
Bußmann, W. *101, 110*
Byron, Lord G. 14

Calabro, G. *137*
Carr, D. *118*, 128
Cassirer, E. 276f., 280
Ceram, C. W. *232*
Christ, K. *230*
Cicero *19*, 159
Comte, A. 169
Condorcet *189*
Constant, B. 81ff.
Cortés, D. 81, 89
Coulanges, F. de 84-91
Creuzer G. F. 225
Cusa, N. de *19*

Daheim, H. *205*
Dahrendorf, R. *204*
Danto, A. C. *128, 192*
DeMaistre, J. 81
Demant, A. *113, 128*
Democritus 70
Derrida, J. 215
Descartes, R. 70, 137, 215
Dickerhof, H. 227
Diderot, D. *196*
Dierkes, H. *9*
Dierse, U. *173*
Dilthey, W. 4, *5, 9*, 45f., 50, 64, 116, *128*, 134-140, 154, 169
Disraeli, B. 109
Döbert, R. *203*
Dorpalen, A. *98, 110*
Dotterweich, V. 231
Droysen, J. G. 3, 38, 46, 59-76, 115, *116*, 122, 126f., *128f.*, 154, 156, 158, 169
Duerr, H. P. *281*
Dülmen, R. v. *246*
Dux, G. 159

Eckert, A. *265*
Eggert, H. *114, 129*
Elias, N. 239
Erdmann, J. E. 34
Erdmann, K. D. 228
Ernst, W. *266*

Faber, K.-G. *236*, 238, 241, *248*
Falkenhausen, S. v. *262f.*
Ferguson, A. *189*
Feuerbach, L. 273, 275
Feyerabend, P. 281
Fichte 12f., 43, *153*, 159, 168
Flaig, E. *79, 261, 263*
Fleischer, D. *120f., 128, 224f., 240*
Fleischer, H. *240*
Flusser, V. *191, 196*
Fontenelle 239
Foucault, M. 117, 216-219, 221, 240, 253
Frank, M. *21*
Frank, W. 228
Freeman, E. A. 47
Freitag, U. *264*
Freud, S. *271*, 273
Freyer, H. *50*
Friedländer, S. *260*
Friedrich Wilhelm IV 54
Fuchs, E. *264*

Fueter, E. 226f.
Fulda, D. *113f., 120-124, 127, 129*
Fustel 86

Gadamer, H.-G. 4, *46*, *137,* 156
Ganz, P. *67, 75*
Gardiner, P. *174*
Gatterer, J. C. 121, *129*, 224, *225*
Gehlen, A. *191*
Geiss, I. 235
Gerhard, D. *41*
Gervinus, G. G. 57, 102, 227, 233, 236ff., 240f.
Gibbon, E. 254
Goertz, H.-J. *246*
Goethe, H. W. 31, 43, 112, 123ff.
Goldfriedrich, J. 229
Gooch, G. P. 109f., *110*
Gortz, A. *204*
Gottlob, M. *120, 129*, 259, *265*
Graf, F. W. *263*
Grau, W. *233*
Grever, M. *262*
Grün-Oesterreich, A. *18*

Haarmann, U. *253, 264*
Habermas, J. 135, *136*, 159, *160, 199*, 204, *207*
Halbwachs, M. 215
Haller, J. 225
Hamann, J.G. *16*, 35, *36*, 115
Hamilton, A. 106
Hammerstein, N. *75, 242*
Harth, D. *124, 129f.*
Hardtwig, W. *59, 66, 75, 124, 127, 129*
Hasler, L. *151*

Herder, J. G. 42, 115f., 122f., *130, 161*, 174, 235
Hegel, G. W. F. 1-3, *9*, 14, 23, 26, 29-38, 44ff., 61, 66-69, 137, 153, 159, 175ff., *178*, 214, 218, 220f., 268, 270-276, 228, 280
Heiber, H. 228
Heidegger, M. 156, 216f., 221, *269*, 276
Heraclitus 70
Herodotus 224, 238, 244
Hesiodus 92
Hinrichs, C. 43, *46*
Hintze, O. 234, 236
Hippokrates 251
Hobbes 90, 98f.
Holmes, S. *82*
Homer 92
Horawitz, A. H. 233
Horkheimer, M. 176, *191*
Hörnig, K. H. *206*
Hu, Chang-Tze *264, 266*
Hübinger, G. 227, *229, 249, 257, 263*, 266f.
Humboldt, W. v. *113*, 123
Hume, D. 120, 173f.
Husserl, E. 141f.

Iggers, G. G. *47, 75, 123, 125, 130, 223,* 235, 245f., *252*, 257, *258*
Izzo, A. *137*

Jacobi, F. H. 12ff.
Jacobs, W. G. *151*
Jaeger, F. *255*, 258, *263*
Jarausch, K. H. *223, 261*
Jaspers, K. *140*

Joach, H. *136*

Kallweit, H. *240f., 253, 262*
Kant, I. 3, 12ff., *16*, 66, 123, 152, 154, 159, 163, 172-186, 215, 220, 268-272, 274-277, 280f.
Kehr, E. 236
Kellner, H. *114, 128, 213*
Kessler, E. *239*
Kierkegaard 168, 273, 275
Kittsteiner, H. D. *240, 269, 271, 275, 277, 280*
Kleingeld, P. *274*
Knodt, E. *122, 130*
Knopf, J. *223*
Kocka, J. 225, 234, *236, 242*
Kohlberg, L. 159, *160*
Koselleck, R. 112, 117ff., *130*, 158, 165, *173, 188, 197, 236, 238, 240*, 243f., *248*, 276
Koslowski, P. *5, 38*
Kreibich, R. *205*
Krohn, W. *251*
Krumeich, G. 231
Küttler, W. *223*, 249, *252, 257f., 262*

La Popelinière, S. de 224
Lamprecht, K. 57, 225, 227, 242, 245
Langewiesche, D. *228*
Laplanche, J. *271*
Lask, E. 279
Latour, B. *196*
Lau, V. *123, 131*
Lederbogen, F. *10*
Leibniz, G. W. 272
Leipprand, E. *108, 110*
Lenz, M. 57
Lessing, L. 43
Leyh, P. *61, 64f.*
Lichtblau, K. *75*
Lieber, F. 106
Lorenz, O. 48
Löwith, K. 168, 173
Lübbe, H. 188, *193*
Luhmann, N. *197*, 201
Lukăcs, G. 276
Lüsenbrink, H.-J. *254, 256, 263ff.*
Luther, M. 18, 43, 107
Lütterfelds, W. *203*
Lutz, H. *240*
Lutz-Bachmann, M. *222*
Lyotard, J.-F. 176f., 281

Mably, G. B. De 81
Macaulay 108
MacCabe, J. *108, 111*
Machiavelli 98f., 104f.
Magill, A. 212, *213*
Mahnkopf, B. *200*
Mainberger, G. K. *19*
Mann, G. *238*
Marcks, E. 57
Marek, K. W. *232*
Marheineke, Ph. 36, *37*
Marini, A. *137*
Marini, G. *137*
Marquard, O. 151, *164*, 165, 172, 187f.
Marx, Chr. *257, 265*
Marx, K. 3, *35*, 104, 135, 153, 168, 176, 207, 209, 214, 222, *236*, 240f., 244, 273, 275f., 280
Masur, G. *44f.*
Meek, R. L. *197*
Meier, Chr. *236*, 238f., *240, 261*

Meinecke, F. *43*, 46, *49*, 57, 125, *131*, 134, 225, 230, *235*, 245
Meissner, J. *265*
Melville, G. *239*
Menger, C. 73
Meran, J. *246*
Metz, K. H. *98f., 106, 108, 111, 124, 131*
Michailow, M. *206*
Michelet, J. 107, 256
Millar *189*
Mink, L. 117
Mitchell, W. J. *197*
Mittag, A. *258f.*, 264
Mohrs, T. *203*
Mommsen, W. J. *54, 238*, 241
Muhlack, U. 125, *131, 242, 262f.*
Müller, H. *254, 256, 263, 265*

Nagl-Docekal, H. *177, 188, 212, 252, 262, 270, 272, 274*
Napoleon 51
Nau, H. H. *5*
Negt, O. *204f.*
Nida-Rümelin, J. *203*
Niebuhr, B. 43, 45ff., 61, 244
Niehaus, J. *76*
Niethammer, L. *266*
Nietzsche, F. 51, 59-76, 105, 168, 175, 216f., 221, 269, 273, 275f.
Nippel, W. *230, 240f., 252*, 253, *254ff., 262ff.*
Nipperdey, T. 59, *76, 236*
Nowak, K. *263*

Oberkrome, W. *243*
Obermann, W. *76*
Oesterreich, P. L. *9, 18*
Oexle, O. G. *60, 64, 75f., 246, 255*
Offe, C. *205ff.*
Orth, M. W. *137*
Osterhammel, J. *249*, 250, *251, 253, 257, 263f.*
Overbeck, F. 105

Pandel, H.-J. *261*
Pelt, R.-J. v. *256, 264*
Perniola, M. *137*
Philo 70
Piaget, J. 159
Pieterse, J. N. *198, 200*
Plato, A. v. *261*
Plato 163, 217
Pöggeler, O. *137*
Polanyi, K. 240
Polibius 244
Pontalis, J.-B. *271*
Popper, K. 174f., 183, 281
Powell, J. M. *123, 130*
Prinz, W. *240*
Profitlich, U. *114, 129*
Prüfer, T. *113, 123, 131*

Quintilianus, M. F. *19*

Ranke, L. v. 4, 31, 38, 41-58, 61, 100, 102, 108, *115*, 123ff., *131f.*, 169, 212, 233, 236, 241, 244
Raphael, L. *249f.*, 259, *264*
Raulet, G. *59, 75f., 255*
Raynal, G. *196*
Reill, P. H. *121, 132, 240, 243, 253, 262*
Reinhardt, V. *265*

Rickert, H. 134-140, 155, 158, 278f.
Ricœur, P. 117f., *132*, *144*, 145, *146*, *270*, 271ff., *274*, 275f., 280f.
Riedel, M. *204*
Ringer, F. *256, 264*
Ritter, M. 225, 227, *228*, 229, 235, 245
Robertson, R. 120, *198f.,* 200
Rochau, L. A. v. *102, 111*
Rohbeck, J. *173, 189, 194, 207*
Ropohl, G. *204, 206*
Rorty, R. 215
Roscher 61
Rothacker, E. *42*
Rousseau, J. J. 81, 190, *191*
Rückert, J. *257, 263*
Rüsen, J. *56, 75f., 78*, 117f., *124*, 126, *128, 132*, 156, *157, 162, 229,* 236, *237f.,* 241-246, 249, *254f.*, 261-264
Ryle, G. 215

Saul, N. *132*
Savigny, F. C. 61
Schäfer, W. *196*
Schatz, O. *191*
Schelling, F. W. J. 1ff., 23-38, 43, 135, 151f., 159, 162, 168, 220, 272
Scherpe, K. R. *114, 129*
Scherrer, J. *260, 264*
Schestow, L. *32*
Schieder, T. *42, 52*, 229, 237
Schiller, F. 32, 123, 126
Schlegel, F. 9-22, 123
Schleier, H. *236, 250, 253, 255, 257, 266*
Schlobach, J. *239f.*
Schlosser, F. C. 102
Schlözer, A. L. 120f., *132*
Schmidt, G. *137*
Schmidt-Biggemann, W. *18*
Schmidt-Glintzer, H. *253, 264*
Schmoller, G. 57, 107, 280
Schnabel, F. *229*
Schnädelbach, H. 268
Scholtz, G. *173, 255*
Schönbauer, G. *205*
Schorn-Schütte, L. 227
Schulin, E. *51, 119, 132*, 249, *250, 252, 254*, 256, *261*
Schulze, W. *230, 236, 240, 243, 246*
Schütz, A. 140-143, 145
Schwabe, K. 231
Schwarz, I. 227
Schwentker, W. 259, *265*
Seeba, H. C. *122, 132*
Sennet, R. *205*
Shakespeare *115, 123*
Shimada, S. *260*
Sieburg, H.-O. *231*
Sieyès, E. J. Abbe 81
Signore, M. *141*
Simmel, G. 134, *140*, 155, 276
Simon, Chr. *120, 132, 265*
Simon, E. 44
Simon, J. *16*
Simonetti, Chr. E. 224
Sloane, Th. O. *18*
Smith, A. *189*
Snow, C. P. *193*
Sorlin, P. 258
Spranger, E. *140*
Spengler, O. 153, 159
Spinner, H. F. *281*

Spinoza, B. 1, 12, 137
Srbik, H. R. v. 225, 227, 230, 245
Stammen, T. *265*
Stammler, R. 73
Steinbüchel, T. *44, 46*
Straub, J. *132*
Süßmann, J. *120, 133*
Sybel, H. v. *47*, 231, 241

Taubes J. 173
Tenbruck, F. H. 143
Tessitore, F. *137*
Thadden, R. v. 239, *240*
Thukydides 84, 238, 244
Tocqueville, A. de 84-91, 106, 239
Treitschke, H. v. 98-111, 233, 241
Tschopp, S. S. *114, 129*
Turgot, A. R. J. 120, *189, 197*

Vasari, G. 239
Veeser, H. A. *114, 133*
Vetter, H. *177*
Vierhaus, R. *42, 53*, 56
Virilio, P. *191, 196*
Voisin, H. L. *224*
Voltaire 120, 165, 168, 173f.
Voss, H. W. *224*
Vossius, G. J. 224f.

Wach, J. 229
Wachler, L. 224f.
Wachsmuth, C. 228
Waechter, M. *264*
Wagner, I. *251, 263*
Wallerstein, I. 200
Wartenburg, P. Y. v. 50
Weber, M. 73ff., *76*, 134, 140-143, 234, 236, 242, 244, 278ff.
Weber, W. 231, *253*
Wegele, F. X. v. 225ff.
Wehler, H.-U. *78*, 234, 236, *238, 280*
Weingart, P. *240*
Weizsäcker, F. *234*
Wellenreuther, H. *229*
Wendt, A. *201*
White, H. *21*, *114*, 115, *133*, 228, 247, 278
Windelband, W. 135-140
Wingens, M. *205*
Wittkau, A. *67, 73, 76*
Wittkau-Horgby, A. *76*
Wittram, R. 237
Wolf, G. 228, 234
Wrede, H. *253, 263*
Wülfing, W. *256, 263*
Wunder, H. *254*

Zagorin, P. *114, 133*

The Historical School

Publications of the Research Project in the
Series Studies in Economic Ethics and Philosophy

P. Koslowski (Ed.)
The Theory of Ethical Economy in the Historical School.
Wilhelm Roscher, Lorenz von Stein, Gustav Schmoller, Wilhelm Dilthey and Contemporary Theory
XI, 343 pages. 1995, reprint 1997
ISBN 3-540-59070-6

P. Koslowski (Ed.)
Methodology of the Social Sciences, Ethics, and Economics in the Newer Historical School. From Max Weber and Rickert to Sombart and Rothacker
XII, 564 pages. 1997
ISBN 3-540-63458-4

P. Koslowski (Ed.)
The Theory of Capitalism in the German Economic Tradition:
Historism, Ordo-Liberalism, Critical Theory, Solidarism
XII, 577 pages. 2000
ISBN 3-540-66674-5

P. Koslowski (Ed.)
The Discovery of Historicity in German Idealism and Historism
VIII, 293 pages. 2005
ISBN 3-540-24393-3

Studies in Economic Ethics and Philosophy

P. Koslowski (Ed.)
Ethics in Economics, Business, and Economic Policy
X, 178 pages. 1992
ISBN 3-540-55359-2 (out of print)

P. Koslowski and Y. Shionoya (Eds.)
The Good and the Economical: Ethical Choices in Economics and Management
X, 202 pages. 1993.
ISBN 3-540-57339-9 (out of print)

H. De Geer (Ed.)
Business Ethics in Progress?
IX, 124 pages. 1994
ISBN 3-540-57758-0

P. Koslowski (Ed.)
The Theory of Ethical Economy in the Historical School
XI, 343 pages. 1995, reprint 1997
ISBN 3-540-59070-6

A. Argandoña (Ed.)
The Ethical Dimension of Financial Institutions and Markets
XI, 263 pages. 1995
ISBN 3-540-59209-1 (out of print)

G. K. Becker (Ed.)
Ethics in Business and Society
Chinese and Western Perspectives
VIII, 233 pages. 1996
ISBN 3-540-60773-0

P. Koslowski (Ed.)
Ethics of Capitalism and Critique of Sociobiology. Two Essays with a Comment by James M. Buchanan
IX, 142 pages. 1996
ISBN 3-540-61035-0

F. Neil Brady (Ed.)
Ethical Universals in International Business
X, 246 pages. 1996
ISBN 3-540-61588-1

P. Koslowski and A. Føllesdal (Eds.)
Restructuring the Welfare State. Theory and Reform of Social Policy
VII, 402 pages. 1997
ISBN 3-540-62035-4 (out of print)

G. Erreygers and T. Vandevelde (Eds.)
Is Inheritance Legitimate?
Ethical and Economic Aspects of Wealth Transfer
X, 236 pages. 1997
ISBN 3-540-62725-1

P. Koslowski (Ed.)
Business Ethics in East Central Europe
XII, 151 pages. 1997
ISBN 3-540-63367-7

P. Koslowski (Ed.)
Methodology of the Social Sciences, Ethics, and Economics in the Newer Historical School. From Max Weber and Rickert to Sombart and Rothacker
XII, 565 pages. 1997
ISBN 3-540-63458-4

A. Føllesdal and P. Koslowski (Eds.)
Democracy and the European Union
X, 309 pages. 1998
ISBN 3-540-63457-6

P. Koslowski (Ed.)
The Social Market Economy.
Theory and Ethics of the Economic Order
XII, 360 pages. 1998
ISBN 3-540-64043-6

Amitai Etzioni
Essays in Socio-Economics
XII, 182 pages. 1999
ISBN 3-540-64466-0

P. Koslowski (Ed.)
Sociobiology and Bioeconomics.
The Theory of Evolution in Biological and Economic Theory
X, 341 pages. 1999
ISBN 3-540-65380-5

Studies in Economic Ethics and Philosophy

J. Kuçuradi (Ed.)
The Ethics of the Professions:
Medicine, Business, Media, Law
X, 172 pages. 1999
ISBN 3-540-65726-6

S. K. Chakraborty and S. R. Chatterjee (Eds.)
Applied Ethics in Management.
Towards New Perspectives
X, 298 pages. 1999
ISBN 3-540-65724-X

P. Koslowski (Ed.)
The Theory of Capitalism
in the German Economic Tradition.
Historism, Ordo-Liberalism, Critical Theory, Solidarism
XII, 577 pages. 2000.
ISBN 3-540-66674-5

P. Koslowski (Ed.)
Contemporary Economic Ethics
and Business Ethics
IX, 265pages. 2000
ISBN 3-540-66665-6

L. Sacconi
The Social Contract of the Firm.
Economics, Ethics and Organisation
XV, 229 pages. 2000
ISBN 3-540-67219-2

M. Casson and A. Godley (Eds.)
Cultural Factors in Economic Growth
VIII, 244 pages. 2001
ISBN 3-540-66293-6

Y. Shionoya and K. Yagi (Eds.)
Competition, Trust, and Cooperation
IX, 252 pages. 2001
ISBN 3-540-67870-0

B. Hodgson
Economics as Moral Science
XIV, 380 pages. 2001
ISBN 3-540-41062-7

A. Labrousse and J.-D. Weisz (Eds.)
Institutional Economics in France and Germany.
German Ordoliberalsm versus
the French Regulation School
IX, 384 pages. 2001
ISBN 3-540-67855-7

F. Vandenbroucke
Social Justice and Individual Ethics
in an Open Society.
Equality, Responsibility, and Incentives
XIII, 305 pages. 2001
ISBN 3-540-41636-6

G. Brennan, H. Kliemt and R. D. Tollison (Eds.)
Method and Morals
in Constitutional Economics.
Essays in Honor of James M. Buchanan
XVI, 571 pages. 2002
ISBN 3-540-41970-5

H. H. Nau and B. Schefold (Eds.)
The Historicity of Economics.
Continuities and Discontinuities
of Histrical Thought
in 19th and 20th Century Economics
X, 245 pages. 2002
ISBN 3-540-42765-1

J. Wieland (Ed.)
Standards and Audits
for Ethics Management Systems
VIII, 253 pages. 2003
ISBN 3-540-40206-3

P. Koslowski, C. Hubig and P. Fischer (Eds.)
Business Ethics and the Electronic Economy
IX, 248 pages. 2004
ISBN 3-540-22150-6

B. Hodgson (Ed.)
The Invisible Hand and the Common Good
XVI, 463 pages. 2004
ISBN 3-540-22353-3

Printing and Binding: Strauss GmbH, Mörlenbach